Roots of Wisdom,
Branches of Devotion

Companion Volumes

Charming Beauties and Frightful Beasts: Non-Human Animals in South Asian Myth, Ritual and Folklore
Edited by Fabrizio M. Ferrari and Thomas W.P. Dähnhardt

Soulless Matter, Seats of Energy: Metals, Gems and Minerals in South Asian Traditions
Edited by Fabrizio M. Ferrari and Thomas W.P. Dähnhardt

Roots of Wisdom, Branches of Devotion

Plant Life in South Asian Traditions

Edited by
Fabrizio M. Ferrari and Thomas W.P. Dähnhardt

equinox

SHEFFIELD UK BRISTOL CT

Published by Equinox Publishing Ltd.
UK: Office 415, The Workstation, 15 Paternoster Row, Sheffield, South Yorkshire S1 2BX
USA: ISD, 70 Enterprise Drive, Bristol, CT 06010

www.equinoxpub.com

First published 2016

British Library Cataloguing-in-Publication Data
A catalogue record for this book is available from the British Library.

ISBN-13 978 1 78179 119 6 (hardback)
978 1 78179 120 2 (paperback)

Library of Congress Cataloging-in-Publication Data

Names: Ferrari, Fabrizio M., editor. | Dähnhardt, Thomas W.P., 1964- editor.
Title: Roots of wisdom, branches of devotion : plant life in South Asian traditions / Edited by Fabrizio M. Ferrari and Thomas W.P. Dähnhardt.
Description: Bristol, CT : Equinox Publishing Ltd, 2016. |
Includes bibliographical references and index.
Identifiers: LCCN 2016005258 (print) | LCCN 2016006633 (ebook) |
ISBN 9781781791196 (hb) | ISBN 9781781791202 (pb) |
ISBN 9781781794494 (e-PDF) | ISBN 9781781794500 (e-epub)

Subjects: LCSH: South Asia–Religion. | South Asia–Religious life and customs. | Plants–Religious aspects. | Plants–Folklore. |
Plants–Mythology–South Asia.
Classification: LCC BL1055 .R66 2016 (print) | LCC BL1055 (ebook) | DDC 202/.12–dc23
LC record available at http://lccn.loc.gov/2016005258

Typeset by S.J.I. Services, New Delhi
Printed and bound by Lightning Source Inc. (La Vergne, TN), Lightning Source UK Ltd. (Milton Keynes), Lightning Source AU Pty. (Scoresby, Victoria).

Contents

Section Three: Ritual, Power, Myth

Section Four: Myth, Food, Nature

Figures

Tables

Introduction

FABRIZIO M. FERRARI AND
THOMAS W.P. DÄHNHARDT[1]

The idea of this volume arose in the aftermath of the publication of *Charming Beauties, Frightful Beasts: Non-Human Animals in South Asian Myth, Ritual and Folklore* (Ferrari and Dähnhardt 2013). The growing number of publications on nature in the context of Indian religions led us to consider the possibility of extending our initial study to include plant life and the mineral world. This and the following volume (Ferrari and Dähnhardt 2016) are the result.

Plant life figures prominently in the traditions of South Asia. Recent advances in archaeobotany and studies on the early development of agriculture in the Indian subcontinent (Fuller 2006; Fuller et al. 2011) have made it possible to evaluate the place of plants and trees in a number of aspects of Indian culture. As Southworth noted:

> in South Asia we are fortunate to have three language families which provide reliable data for the period of early agriculture: Indo-Aryan, with texts dating back to the late 2nd millennium B.C. (as well as reconstructed forms of Proto-Indo-Iranian, going back perhaps another 500 years); Dravidian, for which comparative evidence provides reconstructions dating back to probably the third millennium B.C.; and Munda, a branch of the Austro-Asiatic family, which provides reconstructions dateable to about the second millennium B.C. (Southworth 1988: 649–50)

1 Fabrizio M. Ferrari is Professor of Indology and South Asian Religions, Department of Theology and Religious Studies, University of Chester (UK).
Thomas W.P. Dähnhardt is Lecturer in Hindi and Urdu Languages and Literatures, Department of Asian and North African Studies, Ca' Foscari University of Venice (Italy).

The domestication of plants and animals and organized food production are attested in the west of the subcontinent, in the lower Gangetic basin (from c. 3000 BCE) and in upper South India, with agriculture spreading southward around 1800 BCE. Additional indigenous centers of food production in Odisha/Jharkhand and in western Gujarat/southern Rajasthan are likely to have existed, although there is no conclusive evidence in this regard (Witzel 2009: 1–2).[2]

In northern India, Ārya clans – though pastoralists and nomadic – were familiar with some form of agriculture which they practiced during periods of settlement. A hymn of the *R̥gveda* (IV.57)[3] – a text dated between c. 1200 and 1000 BCE – bears witness to the existence of agricultural deities who are invoked alongside agricultural tools (*sī́ra*, plough) and cereals (*yáva*, a variety of barley).[4] Witzel informs us that around 1000–500 BCE, Middle Vedic texts mention seven or ten important domestic plants.

> The 7 plants are: rice, barley, sesame, mung beans, millets, wheat, lentil, other beans, and the pulse *Dolichos biflor*, and the 10 are: *vrīhí* rice, *Oryza sativa*; *yáva* barley, *Hordeum vulgare*; *tíla sesame*, *Sesamum indicum*; *mā́ṣa* mung beans, *Phaseolus mungo*; *áṇu* millet, *Panicum miliaceum*; *priyáṅgu* millet, *Setaria italica* (L.), *Panicum italicum*; *godhū́ma* wheat, *Triticum aestivum/sativum*; *masū́ra* lentil, *Lens culinaris*; *khálva* beans, *Phaseolus radiatus*, a variety of *Phaseolus mungo* = *māṣa*(?); *khalá-kula Dolichos biflorus L.* These Vedic lists begin with the food most favorable to the gods (and humans), rice and barley. (Witzel 2009: 4)

Evidence of reverence for plants and trees, and their use in various sacrificial contexts, is attested in a number of Vedic sources (particularly in the *Yajurveda*, the *Brāhmaṇas* and the later ritual *sūtras*). Trees are celebrated along with the chief Vedic gods:

> In (the airy realm) without a base, King Varuṇa of purified skill firmly
> holds the crest of the (nyāgrodha) tree on high.

2 See also Southworth (1988), Wojtilla (2003) and Witzel (2006). On Dravidian and Munda terminology, with special reference to agriculture, see Masica (1979). For a survey of Proto-Indo-European flora, see Chapter 10 in Mallory and Adams (2006) and Friedrich (1970). On prehistoric sites, see the chapters collected in 'Section One. Origins and Beginnings of Agriculture' in the richly informative volume edited by Gopal and Srivastava (HAI).

3 Cf. AV^{Ś} III.17, particularly vv. 4–5.

4 The hymn makes reference to a Lord of Fields (*kṣétrasya páti*, vv. 1–3), Pūṣan (v. 7), Cloud (*parjánya*, v. 8), Furrow (*sī́tā*, vv. 6 and 7) and the dual invocation to Prosperity and Plough (*śúnāsīrā*; vv. 5 and 7). Indra, though not an agricultural god, is summoned so he may "lay down Furrow" (*índraḥ sī́tāṃ ní gr̥hṇātu*, v. 7).

They [=its trunks] reach downward, their base above. They should be set down as beacons within us.
(RV I.24.7; tr. Jamison and Brereton)

Grasses like *dūrvā*, *darbha* and *kuśa* are prescribed in a number of Vedic sacrifices (Gonda 1985; Mahdihassan 1987; Dore and Pontillo 2013).[5] In AiB VII.31–32 the fruits of the *nyāgrodha* (*Ficus benghalensis* L.), the *udumbara* (*Ficus racemosa* L.), the *aśvattha* (*Ficus religiosa* L.) and the *plakṣa* (*Ficus lacor* Buch.-Ham.) trees provide the sacrificial drink – alternative to *soma* – which the king has to sip in order to be confirmed as such. In RV X.97, plants are invoked as mothers (*ambā*) and are praised for their healing proprieties.

You mother is the 'Restorer' by name, and you all are the 'Expellers.'
You are strembeds [=stalks] with wings [=leaves]. You expel what causes affliction.
(RV X.97.9; tr. Jamison and Brereton)

In the *Atharvaveda* too, plants are of utmost importance for the preparation of drugs ($AV^{Ś}$ VIII.7.18–19) and amulets ($AV^{Ś}$ II.9), and even for surgical procedures ($AV^{Ś}$ IV.12 and its parallel AV^{P} IV.15).[6] The (unidentified) *soma* plant is celebrated as the king of plants (RV X.97.18–19)[7] as well as a god (Soma). Its centrality in Vedic sacrificial culture is undisputed.[8] A whole book of the *R̥gveda* is devoted to its self-purification (*pavamāna*). The 114 hymns of the Soma Maṇḍala (RV IX) inform us about 'the pressing of the plant, the straining of the juice by pouring it over a sheep's fleece to trap the impurities (twigs and the like), the mixing of the juice first with water and then with milk, and the pouring into containers prior to offering it to the gods, especially Indra.' (Jamison and Brereton 2014: 42)

Although poetic similes can be found,[9] Vedic literature reflects a sacrificial culture where plants and trees, though endowed with life, tend

5 The identification of these grasses is still disputed (see Meulenbeld 1974, s.v.). On cereals, see Gonda (1987). On *soma* see Staal (2001) and Spess (2000). The literature on trees is vast. For a summary see Smith's (2012) notes on *yajña*.

6 On AV^{P} IV.15 see Griffiths and Lubotsky (2000–2001). On herbalism, healing and magic in AV, see Bahulkar (1994).

7 Zysk notes that in the Vedas there are only four hymns where Soma is praised as a healing plant: RV VIII.72: 17; VIII.79: 2; X.25: 11; and X.97: 18 (Zysk 2010: 139).

8 For a summary and review of various theories on *soma*, see Houben's guest editorial in *EJVS*, May 2003. See also Falk (1989), Spess (2000), and Stuhrmann (2006).

9 See, for instance, sporadic mention in RV of the lotus, a flower ubiquitously present in later Indian culture. As detailed by Garzilli (2003), the flower and its

to be seen as ritual objects.[10] With the emergence of the belief in rebirth and karmic retribution, two elements extraneous to early Vedic literature, non-human life begins to be discussed from rather different positions.[11] The early *śramaṇas*[12] (from c. mid-first millennium BCE) and their teachers – notably Vardhamāna Jñātṛputra (Pkt. Vaddhamāṇa/Vaḍḍhamāṇa Nāyaputta/Ṇāttiya), celebrated as Mahāvīra (the last Jina), Makkhali Gosāla (Skt. Gośāla Maṅkhaliputra), a prominent Ājīvika teacher, and Siddhārtha Gautama (the Buddha Śākyamuni) – have informed philosophical debates with ground-breaking doctrinal interpretations. The shift from *karma* as Vedic sacrifice (*yajña*) to the idea of karmic retribution and liberation from rebirth (Skt. *mukti*, *mokṣa*, *nirvāṇa*) permits critical reflection about various manifestations of life, and their hierarchy in nature. If the soul (*jīva*) transmigrates, then it may well be embodied not only in human and non-human animals but also in trees, flowers, grass, plants, et cetera.[13] And if so, how should human beings deal with the surrounding flora? Indian traditions have acknowledged this problem since the late Vedic period (700–500 BCE).

Early (i.e. pre-Buddhist) Upaniṣads show a concern with death and the afterlife. In KauṣU I.2, we learn that after death human beings ascend to the moon where they are interrogated. If the newly deceased demonstrate sound knowledge and answer the questions of the moon, they pass through it (waxing phase). If not, they return to life (waning phase) on earth in a variety of forms, depending on their actions. While KauṣU provides a list of animal rebirths (worm, insect, fish, bird, lion, boar, rhinoceros, tiger,

parts are associated with fertility (RV V.78.7) and with the goddess Sarasvatī (VI.61.2). The lotus embellishes natural landscapes (X.107.10; 142.8) and gods (i.e. the heads of the Aśvins) (X.184.2). Further, in VI.16.13, the *atharvan* priest is described churning Agni from the lotus whereas in VII.33.11 the *ṛṣi* Vasiṣṭha is installed on it by the gods.

10 See the study of Sani on sesame (*tila*) in ancient India and particularly AV (Sani 2003).

11 It should be noted that in ancient India the belief in rebirth and karmic retribution is often discussed as a law of nature and 'the model was agriculture. One sows a seed, there is a time lag during which some mysterious invisible process takes place, and then the plant pops up and can be harvested. The result of an intentional act is in fact normally referred to as its "fruit". The time between the act and its fruit is unpredictable.' (Gombrich 2009: 19)

12 The label *śramaṇa* (Skt. 'one who strives') is an umbrella term for communities of ascetics from the most disparate backgrounds.

13 For a discussion on souls and the mineral world in Indian traditions, see Ferrari and Dähnhardt (2016).

man, or some other creature), ChU provides a different etiology. Ordinary people – i.e. non-ascetics:

> [...] remain there [in the moon] as long as there is a residue, and then they return by the same path they went – first to space, and from space to the wind. After the wind has formed, it turns into smoke; after the smoke has formed, it turns into a thundercloud; after the thundercloud has formed, it turns into a rain-cloud; and after a rain-cloud has formed, it rains down. On earth they spring up as rice and barley, plants and trees, sesame and beans, from which it is extremely difficult to get out. When someone eats that food and deposits the semen, from him one comes into being again. (ChU v.10: 5–6; tr. Olivelle)[14]

In another passage of ChU (vi.1–16), sage Uddālaka Āruṇi uses the pronouncement *tat tvam asi* ('in that way you are', 'that is how you are') to explain to Śvetaketu that his self (*ātman*), and therefore his true essence, is of the same nature as the rest of the world.[15] To exemplify his teaching, Uddālaka points to the *nyagrodha* tree (*Ficus benghalensis* L.) and observes that just as the tree is pervaded by an invisible force that permits it to grow and expand, so is Śvetaketu, who 'like the tree and the whole world, is pervaded by this essence, which is his final reality and true self.' (Brereton 1986: 109)

Though the Upaniṣads, and Vedic texts in general, acknowledge plants and trees as living beings, they seem not particularly concerned with their sentience. Very different is the position held by Jainism. In a passage of the *Ācārāṅgasūtra* (Pkt. *Āyāraṁgasutta*), 'probably the earliest surviving detailed description of the road leading to liberation in the Jaina texts' (Bronkhorst 2007: 16), release from this world is described as a practice entailing death by immobilization (i.e. restraint from action, *karma*) in the utmost effort to avoid karmic consequences and further rebirth (Āyār i.7.7.2–8). Towards the very end of his path, the Jain ascetic should not even lie on living plants, and fast to death (Bronkhorst 2007: 16–17). This monastic choice implies absolute restraint from hurting (*ahiṃsā*) what is

14 A similar account is given in TaitU ii.1. A somehow different explanation is found in BĀU iii.2.13, where the constituents of human beings (speech, breath, sight, mind, hearing, physical body, self, hair, blood and semen) after death are absorbed by the universe. We so learn that 'the hair of his body [disappears] into plants, the hair of his head into trees.'

15 Vedic texts confirm that the self (*ātman*) may take different forms. In plants (*auṣadhi*) and trees (*vanaspati*) this is 'sap' (*iṣ*, *rasa*), while in animals (*prāṇabhṛt*) it is 'thought' (*citta*) (AiĀ ii.3.2; ChU i.1.2–3). On *rasa*, see below.

infused with life.[16] Vardhamāna himself uses plants as similes for human life and argues so:

> He who injures these (plants) does not comprehend and renounce the sinful acts; he who does not injure these, comprehends and renounces the sinful acts. Knowing them, a wise man should not act sinfully towards plants, nor cause others to act so, nor allow others to act so. He who knows these causes of sin relating to plants, is called a reward-knowing sage. Thus I say. (Āyār I.1.5.7; tr. Jacobi)

This teaching echoes early, possibly Pārśva's (Vardhamāna's predecessor), formulations on matters of self-restraint[17] which were later elaborated by Mahāvīra as the five great vows.[18] Amongst the latter, the first pronunciation is particularly revealing:

> I renounce all killing of living beings, whether subtle or gross, whether movable or *immovable*. (Āyār II.15.1; tr. Jacobi; emphasis added)

According to the non-anthropocentric worldview of Jainsim, plants – like animals, stones and also the elements – host a *jīva* and are characterized by forms of consciousness and awareness of their surroundings. In texts like *Viyāhapaṇṇattī* (= *Bhagavatīsūtra*) plants are described as being even capable of progress to human rebirth and hence to achieve liberation (XIV.8, cited in Deleu 1970: 211).

The position of Ājīvikas on the sentience of plants is not fully clear due to a lack of direct sources. A useful yet isolated reference is found in an episode of Viy (xv.46–47, 55–56). During their peregrinations, Vardhamāna and Makkhali Gosāla passed a fully blooming sesamum (*tila*) shrub. Gosāla – wishing to ascertain Mahāvīra's miraculous capacity to predict events – asked whether the shrub was to bear fruit and what was to happen to its flowers. Vardhamāna's response was extremely detailed: 'These seven sesamum flower living beings (*satta tilapuppajīvā*), after they gradually

16 On categories of living beings in Jainism, see the contribution of Ana Bajželj (Chapter 11) in Ferrari and Dähnhardt (2016).

17 Pkt. *cātuyāmasaṁvara* (Skt. *cāturyāmasaṁvara*), or fourfold control of forbearance, which Balcerowicz (2015: 113) indicates as '(1) abstention from killing, (2) sincerity, (3) honesty, [and] (4) indifference to wealth' [...].

18 Pkt. *paṁcamahavvaya* (Skt. *pañcamahāvrata*): (1) strict nonviolence in thought, word, and deed (*ahiṃsā*), (2) absolute truthfulness (*satya*), (3) non-stealing (*asteya*), (4) absolute celibacy (*brahmacarya*) and (5) non-attachment (*aparigraha*).

develop, will bear seven sesamum seeds [pods] in one seed cluster of this very sesamum shrub.'[19] To prove him wrong, an envious Gosāla uprooted the plant.[20] A sudden shower, however, made it possible for the shrub to take root again, and on their way back the two ascetics found confirmation of Mahāvīra's prediction. Vardhamāna, fully aware of Gosāla's behavior, informs us that plants are capable of 'reanimation without transmigration' (Pkt. *pauṭṭaparihāra*). The episode, which marks the parting of the two ascetics, is significant in that it convinces Gosāla of what appears to be a prominent aspect of Ājīvikism.[21] According to the doctrine of determinism (*niyātivāda*) typical of this śramaṇic order, the seven sentient births (Pkt. *satta sannigabbha*) and seven reanimations (Pkt. *satta pauṭṭaparihāra*) are part of a larger process by which every being is destined to pass through to achieve cessation (Pkt. *nivvāṇa*) of all sorrow (Pkt. *savvadukkhāṇam*). A similar theory is attributed to Gosāla in the *Samaññaphalasutta* (53–54) of the Buddhist DN. Here the Ājīvika teacher explains that, amongst the others, there are 'seven sentient births and seven insentient births' (P. *satta saññigabbhā satta asaññigabbhā*). The use of paired technical terms such as *pauṭṭaparihāra* (reanimation) and *sannigabbhā* (birth) in Viy and that of *saññigabbhā* (sentient birth) and *asaññigabbhā* (insentient birth) in *Samaññaphalasutta* suggest that Ājīvikas too regarded plants as not only infused with a soul (*jīva*)[22] but also sentient.

Buddhism, unlike Jainism and Ājīvikism, remains ambiguous concerning the status of plants. Early canonical texts neither accept nor reject the notion that the vegetable world is sentient (P. *viññaṇa*). Though verses that include plants in the category of animate beings can be found, these are very few and rather oblique (Schmithausen 1991: 64). Furthermore, whereas in Jain texts like *Bhagavatīsūtra* plants and trees can achieve higher rebirths

19 Tr. Balcerowicz (2015: 24). The whole passage is translated in Balcerowicz (2015: 23–26).

20 Buddhist and Jain sources portray Makkhali Gosāla as a charlatan – a feature reflecting acrimonious sentiments between the three traditions as well as philosophical divergence.

21 Whether this idea was passed to Ājīvikism or vice versa cannot be confirmed. What appears certain is that Ājīvikas applied the theory of reanimation or 'discontinuance/stoppage [of a subsequent birth in a new body] through/due to a continuation [in the same reanimated body] (*pauṭṭa-parihāra*)' (tr. Balcerowicz 2015: 23; see ibid. 79–84) to all living beings, whereas Jains restricted it to plants.

22 *sabbe sattā sabbe pāṇā sabbe bhūtā sabbe jīvā avasā abalā aviriyā niyati-saṅgati-bhāva-pariṇatā chass' evābhijātisu sukha-dukkhaṃ paṭisaṃvedenti* (*Samaññaphalasutta* 53).

(a fact unambiguously announcing they are a lower form of existence), in early Buddhism plants, and particularly trees, serve primarily as metaphors. As Freschi observes in her critique to Findly (2008: 500 *et passim*): 'Buddhist texts that refer to trees as "saints" do indeed see trees as models for saintly *human* behavior insofar as they are models for deep meditation.' (Freschi 2011: 381, emphasis in the original) We so learn that monks are advised to refrain from harming seeds and plants (DN *Sāmaññaphalasutta*, I.64; MN II.196) and that by failing to do so, they commit an atonable offence (*bhūtagāmapātavyatāya pācittiyam*) (*Pātimokkhasutta*, *Pācittiya* 11). This radically changes '[i]n doctrinally consolidated Buddhism, [where] there is even a tendency to disregard the peculiar features of vegetal life and put plants on a par with the mineral world.' (Schmithausen 2009: 22; cf. Gombrich 2009: 51–52) In his study on philosophical botany, Hall summarizes Schmithausen's conclusions and highlights eight principal reasons for (late) Buddhist scholars to deny plants the status of sentient beings:

1. Plants lack autonomous motion or locomotion.
2. Plants lack body heat.
3. Plants do not perceptibly breathe as do men and animals.
4. Plants do not get perceptibly tired.
5. Plants do not open or close their eyes, i.e., referring to the opening and closing of eyelids showing sleeping and waking and the changes of consciousness that these relate to.
6. Plants can regrow branches and stems which are cut, but animals cannot regrow limbs.
7. Plants do not answer when spoken to.
8. Plants do not perceptibly move when violently injured, from which it is deduced that they do not feel pain or pleasure. (Hall 2011: 91)

In general it can be argued that Buddhism extends respect to plant life on the basis of a general principle of *ahiṃsā*. Whether or not seeds and plants were considered sentient remains unclear (Sahni 2008: 127).

Though radically divergent positions are attested,[23] the discourse on the sentience of plant life has continued to inform Indian ontology, soteriology, and ethics, and developed alongside proper tree/plant cults. It is

23 The materialist school known as Cārvāka or Lokāyata categorically rejects the existence of rebirth and 'other worlds' after death for the plain reason that there is no transmigrating self. A famous Cārvāka aphorism (*sūtra*) attributed to Bṛhaspati confirms this (*paralokino 'bhāvāt paralokābhāvaḥ*) (cited in Bronkhorst 2007: 151; cf. Bhattacharya 2008: 82).

thus not surprising that the domestication of plant life, and more generally agriculture, is even discussed in soteriological terms. In the famous gambler's hymn of RV (x.34), the addicted dice player is invited to redeem himself by giving up vice and cultivating his land (vv. 13ab).[24] In post-Vedic times, with the crystallization of *varṇāśramadharma*, issues of violence (*ahiṃsā*) towards sentient beings are variously debated.

Ascetics are expected to live away from villages and 'plowed land' (*phālakr̥ṣṭa*)[25] and to eat 'uncultivated roots and fruits' (*akr̥ṣṭaṃ mūlaphalaṃ*) (VasDhS ix.2–4; cf. SuS.Sū 36: 10). Conversely, agriculture – a profession inevitably entailing the possibility to harm living and sentient beings (Manu x.83–84) – is assigned to a specific caste, i.e. *vaiśya* (ĀpDhS ii.10.7; GauDhS x.49; BauDhS i.18.4; VasDhS ii.19; KauAŚ i.3.7). On this, however, there is no agreement.[26] Gautama indicates that agriculture may be a respectable source of livelihood for brahmins (GauDhS x.5) whereas Baudhāyana is categorical:

> Vedic study impedes agriculture, and agriculture impedes vedic study. A man who is able may pursue both, but if he is unable, he should give up agriculture. (BauDhS i.10.30)

Manu (iv.5) confirms this view and presents agriculture as a 'fatal' (*pramr̥ta*) occupation for the righteous brahmin in view of the likelihood that it may harm sentient/living beings. Though philosophical schools such as Nyāya-Vaiśeṣika and Mīmāṃsa seem to deny the sentience of plants and their ability to experience (*bhogānupalambha*) (e.g. NS i.1.11; TR ii, pp. 17–18),[27] Manu, in an effort to explain hierarchical structure on the basis of *karma*, accepts that plants are worthy of respect for they are indeed sentient, and represent a particular stage (i.e. the lowest) in the cycle of rebirth:[28]

24 *akṣaír mā́ dīvyaḥ kr̥ṣím ít kr̥ṣasva*
vitté ramasva bahú mányamānaḥ ||

25 This echoes the *vrātyas*, sodality of young secluded sacrificers described in details in AV^{Ś} xv, who '... neither practice the study of Veda nor do they plough or trade.' (PB xvii.1.2)

26 The confusion in professions is generally ascribed to the present Kali Yuga. See Chakravarti (2008: 232–33).

27 Rāmānujācārya glosses that the body (*śarīra*) is the abode of experience (*bhogāyātana*) and since plants cannot experience there is no such thing as a 'plant body' (ibid.).

28 See Medhāthiti's *bhāṣya* to Manu i.49, where the fixity (*sthāvara*) of plants is explained in relation to *sāṃkhya* categories. In particular, *adharmic* actions are

Various kinds of shrubs and thickets and different types of grasses, as also creepers and vines – all these also grow from either seeds or cuttings. [48] Wrapped in a manifold darkness caused by their past deeds, these come into being with *inner awareness* (*antaḥsaṃjñā*), able to feel pleasure and pain (*sukhaduḥkhasamanvitāḥ*). [49] In this dreadful transmigratory cycle of beings,[29] a cycle that rolls on inexorably for ever, these are said to represent the lowest condition, and Brahmā the highest. [50] (Manu I.48–50; tr. Olivelle; emphasis added)

Philosophical arguments notwithstanding, a whole set of rules for the cultivation and protection (but also commerce) of plants, trees and crops finds a special place in the *Arthaśāstra*, a treatise on statecraft traditionally ascribed to the brahmin Cāṇakya (nicknamed Kauṭilya, the 'Crooked One'), the chief minister of Emperor Candragupta Maurya (320–293 BCE). From this text we learn that the king should always protect agriculture from excess labor and taxes (KauAŚ II.1.37) as farming – unlike other economic activities (e.g. mining) – provides wealth and food (VII.11.10–12). The list of seeds, plants and crops given in the text is impressive (II.24, IV.5). It includes various species of cereals, beans and pulses, stalks, root crops, fruit trees, fibrous plants (e.g. cotton, linen and hemp), spices, medicinal and poisonous herbs,[30] perfumery plants, flowers,[31] et cetera. The text, moreover, informs us of injunctions for the protection of plant life:

For cutting sprigs from trees in city parks that produce flowers and fruits and give shade, the fine is six Paṇas [coins]; for cutting small branches, 12 Paṇas; for cutting stout branches, 24 Paṇas; for cutting the trunk, the lowest seizure fine; for uprooting, the middle. [28] In the case of bushes and creepers that produce flowers and fruits and provide shade, the fines are cut in half, as also in the case of trees growing in a holy place, ascetic grove, or cemetery. [29] In the case of trees marking boundaries, sanctuary trees,

---

the reason why beings like plants are pervaded by *tamas* (obscurity; ignorance; immobility) and therefore experience pains of all sort (*vicitraduḥkhānubhava*). However, it is conceded, since every existing thing is constituted by all the three *guṇas*, then plants – due to small percentages of *sattva* (light; knowledge) and *rajas* (action; power) – might experience limited degrees of pleasure.

29 Olivelle points us at Manu XII, where the fruits of action are discussed. In particular, Manu XII.9 says that: 'On account of faults resulting from bodily actions, a man becomes an immobile creature (*sthāvaratā*).'

30 On references to poisonous plants in KauAŚ see Meulenbeld (2007–2008).

31 Cf. KS IV.1.6–9, where among the duties of the only wife are listed gardening activities and the kind of flowers and plants to be cultivated.

distinguished trees, and those in royal forests, double the same fines should be imposed. [30] (KauAŚ III.19.28–30; tr. Olivelle)[32]

Forestry is another important aspect of the economy. Forests should be maintained for the cultivation of useful plants (e.g. timber, hardwoods, varieties of bamboo and reeds, leaves for writing, medicinal herbs, poisonous plants, creepers and fruit plants) but also as a refuge for ascetics (KauAŚ II.2.2), for the leisure of the king and his court, and as animal sanctuaries (ibid. II.2.3–4).[33]

At the beginning of the Common Era, with the institutionalization of monasticism and the establishment of fixed communities of monks (particularly Buddhists; see Zysk 2010: 38–49), a systematic study of the medical properties of the indigenous flora began. The knowledge of traders, herders, wandering ascetics, forest-dwellers and members of tribal communities too (CaS.Sū I.120–23) would contribute to a rich *materia medica*, systematized and gathered in compendia (*saṃhitā*). It was the beginning of Indian medicine, or the science of longevity (*āyurveda*) as opposed to the healing magic of the *Atharvaveda* and other early Indian texts. The use of all sorts of plants and trees in Indian medicine would develop across the centuries and benefit from exchanges with both Indian and non-Indian medical and healing traditions: Siddha, Tantra and Yoga, Chinese, Tibetan, Unani medicine, and more recently, Western biomedicine. This rich culture continues today at an institutional level with the Indian National Medicinal Plants Board (Ministry of AYUSH, i.e. Ayurveda, Yoga & Naturopathy, Unani, Siddha and Homoeopathy) as well as in a range of research institutes and cultural organizations in South Asia and elsewhere that promote herbal medicine.

Going back to pre-modern times, from c. the tenth century, a number of texts (legal, didactic, lexicographic, et cetera) flank Āyurvedic compendia in an effort to study and classify trees and plants. Among these it is worth mentioning Vṛkṣāyurveda, the knowledge of the life of trees, Kṛṣiśāstra, treatises on agriculture, and Nighaṇṭus, dictionaries.

Vṛkṣāyurveda – a term first appearing in KauAŚ II.24.1 (*vṛkṣāyurveda-jñana*, lit. 'the one who knows the science of trees') (Roy 2008: 550) – is a heterogeneous tradition specifically dealing with the health and wellbeing

32 The edicts of Aśoka (reigned 265–232 BCE) confirm this preoccupation and demonstrate governmental policies in matter of green management. See: seventh pillar edict, Delhi-Toprā pillar (R) or Second Rock Edict, Girnār (D) (AL_1 and AL_2).

33 See Olivelle's note on 'guest animals' in KauAŚ, p. 496.

of plants and trees. Although there exist specific texts on arboriculture,[34] most information is derived from a variety of works including medical compendia, ritual digests, Purāṇas (AgP CCLXXXI), Śāstras (*gulmavṛkṣāyurveda* in KauAŚ II.24) and astrological treatises (*vṛkṣāyurvedādhyāya* in BS LIV).[35] Unlike agricultural texts (see below), Vṛkṣāyurveda is the science that studies how to grow trees and plants, how to rid them of diseases and pests, and how to obtain desired flowers, fruits, roots, et cetera.[36] Branches of Indian arboriculture and botany include plant embryology, anatomy and morphology, physiology, planting, fertilizing, feeding, reproduction, breeding, heredity, ecology, taxonomy, disease, treatment and protection.[37] Flora are usually divided and classified as trees (*vṛksa*), shrubs (*gulma*), creepers (*latā*), vegetables (*śāka*), grasses (*tṛṇa*) and grains (*dhānya*). Plants are de facto discussed as living beings endowed with senses of perception and feelings as well as with naturally assigned genders and sexual desires (Das 1986: 9).[38] Further, the care of trees and plants permits the fulfillment of the four *arthas* (SuVĀ I.7–8).[39]

Along with botanical works, trees and plants are studied in technical texts dealing with agriculture and known as Kṛṣiśāstra or Kṛṣitantra. This literary genre primarily reflects concerns with food production. Ethical issues are also debated, especially with respect to caste. One of the most popular themes is represented by the issue of whether agriculture is an occupation suitable for *vaiśyas* only. Unlike early Dharmaśāstras (see below), later legal texts indicate that in this dark age brahmins too can take to the cultivation of the land (PS II.1–2) provided they perform appropriate sacrifices on the threshing floor (10) and pay a reparation fee[40]

34 See for instance the *Vṛkṣāyurveda* (c. twelfth century) of the Bengali scholar Surapāla (SuVĀ) and the *Vṛkṣāyurveda* of Parāśara (Kanjilal 1999; Prasad et al. 2006).

35 Other sources are listed in Majumdar (1927: 1–10), Kanjilal (1999: 129) and Roy (2008: 551–52).

36 Further sections may include details on harvesting and storage of fruits, flowers and crops.

37 Magical incantations and rituals are also included, especially to ward off droughts, heavy rains and pests (Das 1986: 8–9).

38 On tree marriages, see Biardeau (1989: 94–95), Nugteren (2005: 324–26) and Haberman (2013: 151–59).

39 Arboriculture (*vṛkṣāyurvedayogāḥ*) is listed as the forty-first out of sixty-four fine arts (*catuḥ-ṣaṣṭir aṅga-vidyā*) to be known in KS I.3.15.

40 The fee consists of: 'one-sixth of the crop to the king, one-twentieth to the gods and one-thirtieth to brāhmaṇas learned in the Vedas.' (Ritschl cited in Wojtilla 2006: 16).

(12; Furui 2005: 157). A more relaxed approach features in the Kṛṣiśāstras proper, where agriculture, besides bringing wealth, frees the cultivator from all sins, including those resulting from causing injury (KP I.5.2). Some plants – because of their privileged position in the local economy – assume a special place in Indian culture:

> Rice is vitality, rice is vigour too, and rice (indeed) is the fulfilment of all ends (of life). Gods, demons and human beings all subsist on rice. (KP I.6)[41]

Authors of Kṛṣiśāstras provide us with precious information concerning not only the cultivation of the soil and botany, but also animal husbandry, veterinary, human labor, astrology, meteorology, economy, technology and farming implements, trade and storage. Kṛṣiśāstra literature, like Vṛkṣāyurveda, is disseminated in a number of texts such as Purāṇas (AgP CXXI), Śāstras (KauAŚ II.24, PS II), dictionaries (Amara II.9.6–77), astrological works (BS XL),[42] and celebrations of gods such as, for instance, Rāmkṛṣṇa Kabicandra's *Śibāẏan* and Rāmeśvar Bhaṭṭācārya's *Śib'saṁkīrtan* both in Bengali.[43] The largest extant Sanskrit text is the *Kāśyapiyākṛṣisūkti* (c. tenth century CE). Other important works include the mid-eleventh century *Kṛṣīparāśara*,[44] the *Viśvavallabha* of Cakrapāṇi (sixteenth century) and the early twentieth century *Kṛṣiśāsana* by Daśarathaśāstrī. Vernacular works too abound. They include poems, myths, and folk proverbs, such as the sayings of Ḍāk and Khanā in Bengali.

Nighaṇṭus, which began to be composed from c. the twelfth century, are lexicons and therefore distance themselves from previous literature in style, content and rationale.[45] Among the most important texts dealing with botanical species, worth mentioning is the *Nighaṇṭuśeṣa*, an extensive vocabulary authored by Hemacandra (1088–1172). Of the same author is the *Abhidhānacintāmaṇi*, where animals, elements, and plants are arranged by the increasing number of their sense-organs (from one to five) and by

41 *yanna prāṇā balaṃ cānnamannaṃ sarvārthasādhanam* |
devāsuramanuṣyāśca sarve cānnopajīvinaḥ || (KP I.6.1–2, tr. Wojtilla 2006: 16).

42 More passages are listed in Wojtilla (2006: 69–70).

43 See Chapter 11 in this volume, p. 255.

44 For a summary of alternative dates of KP, see Wojtilla (2006: 34).

45 For a list of Nighaṇṭus, see Vogel (1979: 374–78). The earliest Nighaṇṭu is unanimously believed to be the *Dhanvantarinighaṇṭu*, which traditionally assigned to the fourth century CE. Recent studies, however, have demonstrated the text is likely to have been composed at around the beginning of the twelfth century, or shortly before (Vogel 1979: 374; Zimmerman 2011: 99).

their natural habitat (land, air, water) (Vogel 1979: 337). The listing criteria, however, are not always clear. In a recent article, Hellwig has investigated such aspect in texts as diverse as Manu I.46–48, CaS.Sū. I.71–72, Amara II.55–58 (c. sixth century)[46] and, particularly, Narahari's *Rājanighaṇṭu* (c. early fifteenth century). Most Nighaṇṭus conform to the listing criteria found in Manu, i.e. non-blossoming fruit-trees (*vanaspati*), blossoming fruit-trees (*vānaspatya*), bushes and shrubs (*guccha*, *gulma*), creepers (*vallī*, *vīrudh*), annual plants (*oṣadhi*) and grasses (*tṛṇa*) (Hellwig 2010: 207; see also Sivarajan 1991: 64–79). A close reading of (the first part of) a section known as *Guḍūcyādivarga*[47] of *Rājanighaṇṭu*, however, reveals four more criteria: (1) synonymy, (2) previous arrangements from influential works, (3) pharmacological proprieties and (4) botanical similarity,[48] which Hellwig discusses as in between a '"general system" resembling the Linnean taxonomy or [...] "folk taxonomy"' (Hellwig 2010: 222).

Plants and trees, it so appears from a conspicuous body of literature, have been cultivated, studied, and catalogued since Vedic times as the core ingredients of food, beverages, medicine, luxury products (e.g. cosmetics and perfumes)[49] and psychostimulants (wine, opium, cannabis but also coffee, tea and pān).[50] They have served as raw material in the most disparate sectors (engineering, architecture, jewelry, landscaping and gardening, textile arts, music and handicrafts) but also as similes (*upamā*) in the Sanskrit grammatical tradition (Vyākaraṇa)[51] and in Sanskrit poetics (Alaṃkāraśāstra) and its literature (Kāvya).[52] In the latter case, it is

46 The second section of Amara deals specifically with everything that inhabits the earth (*bhūmi*), including trees and plants (*vanauṣadhi*). A description of the Bodhi tree in relation to the Buddha's awakening as well as other plants is given there (Amara II.4.20ff.).

47 Sections are named after the first plant of a certain class (*varga*), in this case *guḍūcī* (*Tinospora glabra* [Burm.f.] Merr.).

48 Cf. the way in which plants are listed in the *Āyurvedasaukhya* of *Ṭoḍarānanda*, an encyclopaedic text in Sanskrit commissioned between the sixteenth and seventeenth centuries by Ṭoḍaramalla – Emperor Akbar's finance minister – to a board of scholars of Varanasi.

49 On essences, see McHugh (2012) and Chapter 4 in this volume.

50 On cannabis, see Wujastyk (2003).

51 See the analysis of Candotti and Pontillo (2007) on Patañjali's formula *vṛkṣaḥ pracalan sahāvayavaiḥ pracalati* ('A tree when it shakes, shakes with its parts') in *Mahābhaṣya* (on Pāṇini's *Aṣṭādhyāyī* VI.1.1.1) to illustrate the linguistic relationship of units with the whole.

52 See the studies of Boccali (2007 and 2011–2012) on nature and plant similes in *kāvya* and Pontillo (2006) in relation to Kālidāsa. Flowers, plants and trees have

germane to point out that the pervasive concept of *rasa* ('taste'), which is profusely used in fields as diverse as philosophy, mysticism and theology, is a term originally indicating the 'sap' or 'essence' of plants (e.g. the *rása* of *soma*; see ŚB^{K} v.1.1.7–11; ŚB^{M} iv.4.5.15 and vi.7.1.13; TS ii.4.9.2).

In the context of medieval Indo-Islamic culture, the subcontinent's ruling Muslim élite, most prominently the Mughal emperors Jahāngīr (r. 1605–27) and Shāh Jahān (r. 1628–48), cultivated the art of garden architecture already well-developed in the Persianate environment, leading to the construction of Mughal gardens all over the Indo-Gangetic plain and, most notably, in the Kashmir Valley. With its elaborate and rich variety of trees, shrubs and flowers watered by a sophisticated irrigation system relying on canals and springs, the Mughal garden was projected both aesthetically and symbolically as a tangible image of paradise (A. *jannat*; F. *firdaus*) on earth. Elsewhere, the regional Muslim rulers in the Deccan achieved a unique blend of Sultanate and pre-Mughal traditions of garden building. Taking into account the specific characteristics of the soil and terrain as well as the cultural environment of the Deccan plateau, they resorted to elaborate techniques of irrigation and the use and knowledge of innumerable indigenous plant species for the development of a distinctive Deccani-Muslim garden architecture.[53]

Plants and trees have been employed across the millennia for the preparation of all sorts of ritual paraphernalia and have arisen as aesthetic models and status symbols. They figure prominently in ritual and devotional culture[54] of greater India as manifestations of the divine, abodes/symbols of gods and spirits,[55] and protectors of sages, ascetics, mystics, et

been also studied in relation to modern and contemporary vernacular Indian poetry. See, for instance, Hříbek (2007) on Tagore.

53 For diversified approaches to this topic, see Wescoat and Wolschke-Bulmahn (1996) and Husain (2000).

54 The *tulasī* plant (*Ocimum tenuiflorum* L.), or holy basil, enjoys special reverence across India, as does the neem tree, which is associated to the worship of popular goddesses such as Śītalā in the North (Ferrari 2015: 13–14 and 57–59) and Māriyammaṉ in the South. The *rudrākṣa* (*Elaeocarpus serratus* L.) is a known Śaiva symbol whose beads are used for rosaries (*māla*) worn by *sādhus*. The goddess Caṇḍī is invoked as residing in the *bilva* or *bel* tree (*Aegle marmelos* (L.) Corrêa), which is also a manifestation of Durgā and associated with Śiva.

55 Of significant importance is the cult of *yakṣas* and *yakṣiṇīs* in ancient India. See Coomaraswamy (1928–1931) and Sutherland (1991). Indra's pleasure garden (*nandanavana*), with its lush trees, fragrant flowers and rich variety of plants, is mentioned in a number of Purāṇas (e.g. BhP iii.23.40; v.16.24; VP ii.2.25;

cetera,[56] as well as powerful signifiers for devotees of all South Asian religious traditions.[57]

Finally, it is worth mentioning the place of Indian flora in South Asian sacred geography. From the Purāṇic tradition we learn that the known world is Jambudvīpa, a denomination found in Jain and Buddhist literature too and usually rendered in English as the 'Island of the Rose-Apple Tree'.[58] The universe is envisioned as a concentric series of islands (MP cxxii.79; VāmP i.88) floating in the middle of the Salt Sea (VāyP xi.31; VP ii.3.28; BhP v.20). Jambudvīpa is the innermost island and, like other lands, is divided into different regions (*varṣa*) and is distinctively featured by seven mountains and seven rivers, each with its peculiar flora. A similar image reverberates also in more recent renderings, such as the *Vande Mataram* anthem found in Bankim Chandra Chatterji's 1882 novel *Ānandamaṭh*:

> I revere the Mother! The Mother
> Rich in waters, rich in fruit,
> Cooled by the southern airs,
> Verdant with the harvest fair.
> The Mother – with nights that thrill
> in the light of the moon,
> Radiant with foliage and flowers in bloom,
> Smiling sweetly, speaking gently,
> Giving joy and gifts in plenty.[59]
> (Chatterji 2005: 145; tr. Lipner)

---

v.7.66). As for South Asian Islam, of particular interest is the figure of (A.) K̲h̲wād̲j̲a K̲h̲iḍr (F. and U. al-K̲h̲iẓr; K̲h̲ẉāja K̲h̲iẓr), the Green One, a pre-Islamic fertility spirit appearing in Qur xviii.60–82 as Moses' guide. He is worshiped as a *pīr* across the subcontinent and is associated with plants and the waters (Dähnhardt 2004).

56 See Chapters 1 and 5 in this volume.

57 Among recent studies, see Findly (2008); Haberman (2013) and Kent (2013).

58 The *jambū* tree is correctly identified with *Eugenia jambolana* Lam., which is a scientific synonym of *Syzygium cumini* (L.) Skeels, the current accepted name. This tree however, as persuasively argued by Wujastyk, is black plum, or jambul, and not rose apple (2004: 293 *et passim*). For a list of scientific synonyms of *jambu*, see Meulenbeld (1974: 555–56).

59 *vande mātaram*
sujalāṃ suphalāṃ malayajaśītalāṃ
śasyaśyāmalāṃ mātaram.
śūbhrajyotsnāpulkitayāminīm
phullakusumitadrumadalaśobhinīm
suhāsinīṃ sumadhurabhāṣiṇīṃ
sukhadāṃ varadāṃ mātaram

The aim of the contributions gathered in this volume is to respond to some of the many questions arising from a survey of the literature on plant life in South Asian traditions, with particular reference to religious culture.

The first section revolves specifically around themes such as nature, landscape and devotion. In Chapter 1, Antonio Rigopoulos explores the significance of divine trees in the construction of the charismatic persona of Sathya Sāī Bābā (1926–2011), the famous god-man of Puttaparthi in southern Andhra Pradesh. Particular attention is paid to the *pārijāta*, the tamarind tree as *kalpavṛkṣa* and the *vaṭa/bodhi* tree, which in the saint's hagiography are related to his advent, his miraculous powers and the meditative practice conducive to final liberation (*mokṣa*), respectively. In the following chapter, Shailendra Bhandare examines the way in which the rich symbolism of trees and foliate motives appear on Indian coinage pertaining to two historical periods: ancient India (from c. the fifth century BCE to the fifth century CE) and the Islamic period. This, the author argues, demonstrates an interesting continuity in the tradition of representation of Indian flora. The last chapter of the first section investigates the wondrous and sensuous beauty of plants, trees, fruits and flowers in the Rāsa Līlā as described in the *Bhāgavata Purāṇa*. Graham Schweig explores the role of flora within the experience of devotion (*bhakti*) as expressed in the Vaiṣṇava narrative celebrating Kṛṣṇa, and the interdependent dialectical relationship between natural phenomena and the movements of the *bhakta*'s or devotee's heart.

In the second section, we move from devotion in order to discuss how ritual practice is informed by ecological reflections. Mikko Viitamäki opens up this section with his study of *ʿitr*, volatile essential oils extracted from different plant material and widely used within the religious culture of Indian Sufis. From as early as the medical work of Ibn Sīnā (Avicenna, d. 1037), Sufis have contributed to create a culture of scent through which essential oils enable them to engage the olfactory sense in boosting their personal religious practice. Through his ethnographic fieldwork conducted at the Sufi shrine of Nizamuddin Auliyaʾ in Delhi, Viitamäki assesses an enduring tradition vis-à-vis the impact on the contemporary market where more affordable and long-lasting synthetic oils are available. In the following chapter, Antonella Comba discusses the place of plants in the Pali *Tipiṭaka*. Although Indian Buddhists came to regard plants and seeds as insentient beings, the respect and love the Buddha felt for living plants was so deep that he did not allow monks to destroy plants, to pick fruits from trees, or to eat living seeds as these could generate new plants. Trees are ubiquitous in Buddhist narratives, and the forest is praised as the most suitable place for an ascetic to let go of any distraction and obtain awakening. Preaching the *dhamma*, the Buddha used many similes from the vegetable kingdom, because he was speaking to ascetics who like him were living in the forest and had direct experience of the inspiring power of that milieu. Albertina Nugteren's chapter, which brings the second section to conclusion, maintains a focus on ecology but privileges an analysis of tradition and ritual praxis, namely the burning of bodies as part of the final sacrifice (*antyeṣṭi*). By relating prescriptive Sanskrit texts to fieldwork conducted in Nepal, the author explores the centrality of fire in Hindu funerary rites, the ongoing insistence on open pyres, and the religious symbolism investing in trees. The staggering quantity of dry wood required for such practices – preferably even enriched with rare woods such as sandalwood – is being challenged by today's environmental realities, yet emerging alternatives such as electric crematoria are largely seen as clashing with a consolidated tradition.

The third section of the volume investigates the power derived from ritual performance and the narratives in which such rituals are encapsulated. This section is opened by Michael Slouber, who discusses early medieval Bhūta and Bāla Tantras. On the basis of unedited manuscript sources, this chapter describes the role played by plants in religion and life as seen through the lens of exorcism rituals. Datura, red oleander, mustard seeds, rice, sesame, garlic, fig, Flame of the forest, wood-apple: these and many more formed the basis of tantric exorcisms. Plants were used to attract, feed and repel demons. They were made into incense, oil, and weapons, as well as cakes, mannequins and medicines. Auspicious and noxious qualities of sacred plants and trees were infused into water, milk and cooling ointments, or made into sweet fragrances or foul-smelling fires. In short, the universe of early tantric exorcism ritual was suffused with plants whose powers resonate in contemporary exorcist practice across South Asia. Next, Finnian Gerety analyses the early use of the *udumbara* tree (*Ficus racemosa* L.) and its milky, sap-filled wood as a ritual object as well as offering. One rite centered on the *udumbara* that has received scant attention is the erection of the post of *udumbara* (*audumbaryutthāpana*) as described in the *Sāmaveda*. As his first act in the Soma sacrifice, the *udgātar* (lead singer) of the *Sāmaveda* raises the *audumbarī*, addresses it with *mantra*s and offerings, wraps it with cloth and embraces it. Gerety analyses this rite of tree hugging with special reference to Jaiminīya texts. By advancing the *audumbarī* rite as the inauguration of the *udgātar*'s office, the SV texts present an arboreal embodiment of the musical qualities they most prize: swelling, sweetness, nourishment, and vigor. When the singer hugs the trunk, he actualizes this potency in his own performance.

The fourth and final section investigates South Asian mythical narratives on edible plants and the celebration of nature in its various divine embodiments. All three chapters in this section report from research conducted in eastern India. Stefano Beggiora presents his extensive fieldwork among the Lanjia Saoras in the Rayagada district of southern Odisha. In particular, he discusses the ritual use of local palm wine (toddy) extracted primarily from the jaggery palm (*Caryota urens* L.). The custom of drinking this fermented beverage is a characteristic feature of the tribal culture of this region. Besides its social aspect, toddy is of central importance in a wide range of shamanic rituals and in the worship of ancestors. The following chapter too investigates traditions of Odisha. Uwe Skoda discusses rice culture amongst the Aghrias, a local peasant community. The chapter introduces various categories of rice and cultivation techniques, thus demonstrating the extensive agricultural knowledge of Aghria peasants. Furthermore it is shown how rice unites and synchronizes various human and earth cycles in its manifestations as plant, as food, and finally as the goddess Lakṣmī. The last chapter offers an overview of the botanical lore in *Śūnyapurāṇ*, a heterogeneous Bengali Śaiva text attributed to Rāmāi Paṇḍit and celebrating the god Dharmarāj, a figure overlapping with local forms of Śiva. In this work, Fabrizio Ferrari analyses the place of flowers in the worship of Dharmarāj, the birth of paddy (*dhānyer janma*) in the popular tale of the farming (*kṛṣak*) Śiva, and the auspicious song of the husking pedal (*ḍheṅkīmaṅgalā*), the vehicle of sage Nārada. The chapter naturally links with the preceding study and, by means of its focus on nature and devotion, also brings us full circle to connect with Chapter 1.

One of the major problems emerging from this study is the way to deal with cross-cultural taxonomic approaches, and particularly the identification of plants mentioned in Indian texts. While the general tendency has been to equate Indian names to Latin/Linnean names, the editors concur this is still a major and to date unresolved Indological problem. Indian nomenclature pre-dates current classification by several centuries, if not millennia, as in the case of plants listed in Vedic texts (e.g. the *Sāmaveda* in Chapter 8), early Āyurvedic compendia,[60] and the Pali canon (see

60 *Carakasaṃhitā* (circa first-second centuries CE), *Suśrutasaṃhitā* (circa third-fourth centuries CE), *Aṣṭāṅgahṛdayasaṃhitā* (attributed to Vāgbhaṭa, circa sixth-seventh centuries CE) and *Mādhavanidāna* (attributed to Mādhavakara, eighth century CE).

Chapter 5). An equation between Latin and Indian names remains inaccurate for two main reasons. First, plants may have mutated from their earliest recording in Indian texts. Second, any serious historical study of cross-cultural botanical taxonomy should include a systematic study of Sanskrit and vernacular names of plants, including their etymologies, vis-à-vis their morphological features and use as recorded in Indian sources. Unfortunately, tree and plant names are often given without any description or details about their usage. Especially in mythological or devotional texts, but also in poetry and song, plants are invoked without providing details for their identification, as the rationale of such works transcend botany and the names of plants and trees have culturally embedded features which are obvious to the intended audience. Conversely, in ritual and scientific texts (e.g. Brāhmaṇas, medical compendia, Tantras), lengthy and detailed descriptions of the features and properties of a plant facilitate identification. Yet even when the identification seems a consolidated one, Western botanical archives list multiple Accepted Scientific Names on which even trained botanists often disagree.

In this collection, the botanical names of the species encountered have been checked across a number of resources such as Monier-Williams' *Sanskrit-English Dictionary*, Turner's *A Comparative Dictionary of Indo-Aryan Languages*, Burrow and Emeneau's *A Dravidian Etymological Dictionary* (1984) and the Online *Sino-Tibetan Etymological Dictionary and Thesaurus* (STEDT). Indian lexicographic sources have been consulted too, primarily the already mentioned *Amarakośa* and the more recent *Śabdakalpadruma* (ŚKD) of Rādhākānta Deva (1784–1867).

Botanical and medical works consulted include Bose's *A Manual of Indian Botany* (1920), Kirtikar and Basu's four-volume *Indian Medicinal Plants* (1918), Quattrocchi's *World Dictionary of Medicinal and Poisonous Plants* (2012); Khare's *Indian Medicinal Plants* (2007), Meulenbeld's 'Sanskrit Names of Plants and Their Botanical Equivalents' in his critical edition of *Mādhavanidāna* (1974: 520–611) and Wujastyk's 'Vocabulary Index: Flora, Fauna, and Medical Terms' at the end of his *The Roots of Ayurveda* (2003: 300–61). Along with such resources, the editors have counter-checked every botanical entry through the *Index Kewensis* and its digital version (the Medicinal Plant Names Service provided by Royal Botanic Gardens, Kew), the Taxonomic Name Server (TNS) of uBio, the Pandanus Database of Plants, the online archive offered by Tropicos, the Foundation for the Revitalisation of Local Health Traditions in Bangalore, and the multiple database of The Plant List. Unless indicated otherwise by an author, we have decided to always attempt identification of plants. The Latin names provided, however, should not be regarded as conclusive, but are the most recurrent Accepted Scientific Names, or the names on which botanists' opinions seem to converge. All Latin names are thus followed by the author's name(s). In so doing, we have followed Meulenbeld's warning against the unsound yet widespread practice of omitting author's names after scientific names of plants (1974: 520). Since a scientifically valid identification of Indian plants is beyond the scope of this volume, the editors hope that this study will contribute to the debate on current problems in classifications of plant life in India, and the dilemma of cross-cultural taxonomic approaches in general.

ABBREVIATIONS AND BIBLIOGRAPHY

A. = Arabic; F. = Farsi (Persian); P. = Pali; Pkt. = Prakrit; Skt. = Sanskrit; U. = Urdu

AgP — *Agnipurāṇa*. Mitra, R. (ed.) (1870–1879). *Agni Púrana. A Collection of Hindu Mythology and Traditions*. Calcutta: Asiatic Society of Bengal.

AiĀ — *Aitareya Āraṇyaka*. Keith, A.B. (tr.) (1909). *Aitareya-Āraṇyaka*. London: Oxford University Press.

AiB — *Aitareya Brahmanam*. Haug, M. (ed. and tr.) (1922). *Atareya Brahmanam of the Rigveda Containing the Early Speculations of the Brahmans on the Meaning of the Sacrificial Prayers and on the Origin, Performance and Sense of the Rites of the Vedic Religion*. Allahabad: Panini Office.

AL$_1$ — Ashoka Library. (2015). 'Delhi-Toprā, Delhi-Mīraṭh, Lauṛiyā-Ararāj, Lauṛiyā-Nandagaṛh, Rāmpūrva, Allahabad-Kosam Pillar Edicts (Synoptic, Māgadhī and English).' *Bibliotheca Polyglotta*, <http://www2.hf.uio.no/polyglotta/index.php?page=fulltext&view=fulltext&vid=370&cid=381790&mid=635603&level=2> (accessed 6 August 2015).

AL$_2$ — Ashoka Library. (2015). 'Girnār, Kālsī, Shāhbāzgaṛhī Rock Edicts (Māgadhī and English).' *Bibliotheca Polyglotta*, <http://www2.hf.uio.no/polyglotta/index.php?page=fulltext&vid=362&view=fulltext> (accessed 6 August 2015).

Amara — Amarasiṁha: *Amarakośa* (=*Nāmaliṅgānuśāsana*). Oka, K.G. (ed.) (1913). *The Nāmaliṅgānuśānaṁ. Amarakośa of Amarasiṁha. With the Commentary (Amarakośodghāṭana) of Kṣīrasvāmin*. Poona: Law Printing Press.

ĀpDhS — Āpastamba: *Dharmasūtra*. In Olivielle (1999: 20–115).

ĀSau — Ṭoḍarānanda: *Āyurveda Saukhyaṃ*. Dash, B. and L. Kashyap. (eds. and trs.) (1980). *Materia Medica of Āyurveda, Based on Āyurveda Saukhyam of Ṭoḍarānanda*. New Delhi: Concept.

AV^{P} — *Atharvavedasaṃhitā, Paippalāda* recension. Vira, R. (ed.) (1936). *Atharva Veda of the Paippalādas*. Books 1–13. Lahore: Arya Bharati Press.

AV$^{\acute{S}}$ — *Atharvavedasaṃhitā, Śaunaka* recension. (1) GRETIL e-text based on Orlandi, C. (tr. and ed.), *Gli inni dell' Atharvaveda (Saunaka)*, trasliterazione a cura di Chatia Orlandi, Pisa 1991, collated with Roth, R. and W.D. Whitney (trs. and eds.), *Atharva Veda Sanhita*, Berlin 1856, <http://gretil.sub.uni-goettingen.de/gretil/1_sanskr/1_veda/1_sam/avs_acu.htm> (accessed 15 October 2015). Input by: Vladimir Petr and Petr Vavrousek. (2) Whitney, W.D. (tr.) (1905). *Atharva-Veda Saṃhitā*. Harvard Oriental Series, vol. VII. Cambridge, Mass.: Harvard University Press.

Āyār — *Āyāraṁgasutta* (Pkt.) = *Ācārāṅgasūtra* (Skt.). Jacobi, H. (tr.) (1884). *Gaina Sûtras, Part I. Âcârâṅga Sûtra and Kalpa Sûtra*, pp. 1–213. Oxford: Clarendon Press.

Bahulkar 1994 — Bahulkar, S.S. (1994). *Medical Ritual in the Atharvaveda Tradition*. Pune: Tilak Maharasthra Vidyapeeth.

Balcerowicz 2015 — Balcerowicz, P. (2015). *Early Asceticism in India. Ājīvikism and Jainism*. London: Routledge.

Basham 2009 — Basham, A.L. (2009). *History and Doctrines of the Ājīvikas. A Vanished Indian Religion*. Reprint of 1951 edition. Delhi: Motilal Banarsidass.

BĀU — *Bṛhadāraṇyaka Upaniṣad*. In Olivielle (1998: 29–165).

BauDhS — Baudhāyana: *Dharmasūtra*. In Olivielle (1999: 569–630).

Bhattacharya 2008 — Bhattacharya, R. (2008). *Studies on the Cārvāka-Lokāyata*. Delhi: Manohar.

BhP — *Bhāgavatapurāṇa*. Śāstrī, K. (ed.) (1965). *Śrīmad Bhāgavata Mahāpurāṇam*. Ahmedabad: Śrībhāgavatavidyāpīṭha.

Biardeau 1989 — Biardeau, M. (1989). *Histoires de poteaux: Variations védiques autour de la déesse Hindoue*. Paris: Ecole Française d'Extrême-Orient.

Boccali 2007 — Boccali, G. (2007). 'Descriptions of nature in Kāvya and Greek lyric poetry.' *Pandanus* 7: 9–22.

Boccali 2011–2012 — Boccali, G. (2011–2012). 'Kālidāsa, *Kumārasambhava*, "L'origine di Kumāra": lettura di I, 19–61.' *Incontri di Filologia Classica*, 11: 171–90.

Bose 1920 — Bose, G.C. (1920). *A Manual of Indian Botany*. Bombay: Blackie and Son Limited.

Brereton 1986 — Brereton, J. (1986). '"Tat Tvam Asi" in Context.' *Zeitschrift der Deutschen Morgenlandischen Gesellschaft*, 136(1): 98–109.

Bronkhorst 2007 — Bronkhorst, J. (2007). *Greater Magadha. Studies in the Culture of Early India*. Leiden: E.J. Brill.

BS — Vārahamihira: *Bṛhatsaṃhitā* (Version 4.3, May 8, 1998). GRETIL e-text based on the edition of A.V. Tripathi (Sarasvati Bhavan Granthamala Edition) with reference to H. Kern's text and his translation, <http://gretil.sub.uni-goettingen.de/gretil/1_sanskr/6_sastra/8_jyot/brhats_u.htm> (accessed 10 October 2015). Input by: Michio Yano and Mizue Sugita.

Burrow and Emeneau 1984	Burrow, T., and M.B. Emeneau. (1984). *A Dravidian Etymological Dictionary*. Second edition. Oxford: Clarendon Press.
Candotti and Pontillo 2007	Candotti, M.P. and T. Pontillo. (2007). 'The (In)separable Parts of a Plant in the *Mahābhaṣya* Imagery, i.e. how nature may inspire a grammarian.' *Pandanus* 7: 43–63.
CaS	*Carakasaṃhitā*. Sharma, R.K. and B. Dash (tr.) (2011). *Carakasaṃhitā. Text with English Translation and Critical Exposition Based on Cakrapāṇi Datta's Āyurveda Dīpikā*. 7 vols. Reprint 1977 edition. Varanasi: Chowkhamba Sanskrit Series Office.
Chakravarti 2008	Chakravarti, R. (2008). 'Agricultural Technology in Early Medieval India (c. A.D. 500–1300).' *The Medieval History Journal*, 11(2): 229–58.
Chatterji 2005	Chatterji, B. (2005). *Ānandamaṭh, or the Sacred Brotherhood*. Translated with an Introduction and Critical Apparatus by J. Lipner. Oxford: Oxford University Press.
ChU	*Chāndogya Upaniṣad*. In: Olivelle (1998: 166–287).
Coomaraswamy 1928–1931	Coomaraswamy, A.K. (1928–1931). *Yakṣas*. 2 vols. Washington: Smithsonian Institution.
Dähnhardt 2004	Dähnhardt, T.W.P. (2004). 'Encounters with al-Khiḍr: Saint-Immortal, Protector from the Waters and Guide of the Elected Ones beyond the Confluence of the Two Oceans.' In Rigopoulos, A. (ed.), *Guru: the Spiritual Master in Eastern and Western Traditions. Authority and Charisma*, pp. 105–20. New Delhi: D.K. Printworld.
Das 1986	Das, R.P. (1986). 'Some Notes on Vrksayurveda.' *Ancient Science of Life*, 6(1): 6–9.
Deleu 1970	Deleu, J. (1970). *Viyāhapaṇṇatti (Bhagavaī): the Fifth Aṅga of the Jaina Canon*. Brugge: Rijksuniversiteit te Gent.
DN	*Digha-Nikaya of the Sutta-Pitaka*, Vol. I; *Silakkhandavagga*, *Suttantas* 1–13. GRETIL e-text based on the edition by T.W. Rhys Davids and J.E. Carpenter, London: Pali Text Society 1890. <http://gretil.sub.uni-goettingen.de/gretil/2_pali/1_tipit/2_sut/1_digh/dighn1ou.htm> (accessed 25 August 2015). Input by: The Dhammakaya Foundation, Thailand (1989–1996).
Dore and Pontillo 2013	Dore, M. and T. Pontillo. (2013). 'What Do Vrātyas Have to Do with Long-Stalked Plants *Darbha*, *Kuśa*, *Śara* and *Iṣīkā* in Vedic and Classical Sources.' *Pandanus* 13(1): 35–61.
Falk 1989	Falk, H. (1989). 'Soma I and II', *Bulletin of the School of Oriental and African Studies* , 52(1): 77–90.
Ferrari 2015	Ferrari, F.M. (2015). *Religion, Devotion and Medicine in North India. The Healing Power of Śītalā*. London and New York: Bloomsbury.
Ferrari and Dähnhardt 2013	Ferrari, F.M. and T. Dähnhardt (eds.) (2013). *Charming Beauties, Frightful Beasts. Non-Human Animals in South Asian Myth, Ritual and Folklore*. London: Equinox.
Ferrari and Dähnhardt 2016	Ferrari, F.M. and T. Dähnhardt (eds.) (2016). *Soulless Matter, Seats of Energy. Metals, Gems and Minerals in South Asian Traditions*. London: Equinox.

Findly 2008 — Findly, E.B. (2008). *Plant Lives. Borderline Beings in Indian Traditions*. Delhi: Motilal Banarsidass.

Freschi 2011 — Freschi, E. (2011). Review Article: 'Plant Lives: Borderline Beings in Indian Traditions by Allison Banks Findly.' *Philosophy East and West*, 61(2): 380–85.

Friedrich 1970 — Friedrich, P. (1970). *Proto-Indo-European Trees. The Arboreal System of a Prehistoric People*. Chicago: The University of Chicago Press.

Fuller 2006 — Fuller, D.Q. (2006). 'Agricultural Origins and Frontiers in South Asia: A Working Synthesis.' *Journal of World Prehistory*, 20(1): 1–86.

Fuller et al. 2011 — Fuller, D.Q., N. Boivin, T. Hoogervorst and R. Allaby. (2011). 'Across the Indian Ocean: The Prehistoric Movement of Plants and Animals.' *Antiquity*, 85(328): 544–58.

Furui 2005 — Furui, R. (2005). 'The Rural World of an Agricultural Text: A Study on the *Kṛṣiparāśara*', *Studies in History, New Series*, 21(2): 149–71.

Garzilli 2003 — Garzilli, E. (2003). 'The Flowers of *Ṛgveda* Hymns: Lotus in V.78.7, X.184.2, X.107.10, VI.16.13, and VII.33.11, VI.61.2, VIII.1.33, X.142.8.' *Indo-Iranian Journal*, 46(4), 293–314.

GauDhS — Gautama: *Dharmasūtra*. In Olivelle (1999: 116–90).

Gombrich 2009 — Gombrich, R. (2009). *What the Buddha Thought*. London: Equinox.

Gonda 1985 — Gonda, J. (1985). *The Ritual Function and Significance of Grasses in the Religion of the Veda*. Amsterdam: North-Holland Publishing Co.

Gonda 1987 — Gonda, J. (1987). *Rice and Barley Offerings in the Veda*. Leiden: E.J. Brill.

Griffiths and Lubotsky 2000–2001 — Griffiths, A. and A. Lubotsky (2000–2001). 'Paippalādasaṃhitā 4.15. To heal an open fracture: with a plant.' *Die Sprache*, XLII/1–2 [appeared 2003]: 196–210.

Haberman 2013 — Haberman, D. (2013). *People Trees: Worship of Trees in Northern India*. New York: Oxford University Press.

HAI — Gopal, L. and V.C. Srivastava (eds.) (2008). *History of Agriculture in India (up to c. 1200 AD)*. New Delhi: Concept Publishing Company.

Hall 2011 — Hall, M. (2011). *Plants as Persons: A Philosophical Botany*. Albany: State University of New York Press.

Hellwig 2010 — Hellwig, O. (2010). 'The Arrangement of Plant Names in Sanskrit Dictionaries.' *Pandanus*, 4(10): 205–26.

Houben 2003 — Houben, J.E.M. (2003). 'The Soma-Haoma Problem: Introductory Overview and Observations on the Discussion.' *Electronic Journal of Vedic Studies*, 9(1), <http://www.ejvs.laurasianacademy.com/ejvs0901/ejvs0901a.txt> (accessed 5 June 2015).

Hříbek 2007 — Hříbek, M. (2007). 'Flowers and Trees in Tagore's Songs Relating to Summer, Autumn and Winter.' *Pandanus* 7: 141–54.

Husain 2000 — Husain, A.A. (2000). *Scent in the Islamic Garden: A Study of Deccani Urdu Literary Sources*. Karachi: Oxford University Press.

Kanjilal 1999	Kanjilal, D.K. (1999). 'A note on the *Vṛkṣāyurveda* of Parāśara.' *Indian Journal of History of Science*, 34(2): 127–31.
KauAŚ	Kauṭilya: *Arthaśāstra.* Olivelle, P. (tr.) (2013). *King, Governance, and Law in Ancient India. Kauṭilya's Arthaśāstra.* New York: Oxford University Press.
KauṣU	*Kauṣītaki Upaniṣad.* In Olivelle (1998: 324–62).
Kent 2013	Kent, E. (2013). *Sacred Groves and Local Gods: Religion and Environmentalism in South India.* New York: Oxford University Press.
Kew	*Index Kewensis*, Royal Botanic Gardens: Medicinal Plant Names Service: <http://www.kew.org/science-conservation/research-data/resources/medicinal-plant-names-services> (accessed 10 April 2015).
Khare 2007	Khare, C.P. (2007). *Indian Medicinal Plants. An Illustrated Dictionary.* New York: Springer.
Kirtikar and Basu 1918	Kirtikar, K.K. and B.D. Basu. (1918). *Indian Medicinal Plants.* 4 vols. Allahabad: Lalit Mohan Basu.
KP	Parāśara: *Kr̥ṣiparāśara.* Śāstrī, D.P. (ed.) (2003). *Parāśaramuniviracitaḥ Kr̥ṣiparāśaraḥ.* With Hindī translation. Vārāṇasī: Caukhambā Saṃskr̥t Sīrīj Ākhis.
KS	Vātsyāyana Mallanāga: *Kāmasūtra.* Doniger, W. and S. Kakar. (trs.) (2002). *Kamasutra.* New York: Oxford University Press.
Mahdihassan 1987	Mahdihassan, S. (1987). 'Three Important Vedic Grasses.' *Indian Journal of History of Science*, 22(4), 286–91.
Majumdar 1927	Majumdar, G.P. (1927). *Vanaspati. Plants and Plant Life as in Indian Treatises and Traditions.* Calcutta: The University of Calcutta.
Mallory and Adams 2006	Mallory, J.P. and D.Q. Adams (2006). *The Oxford Introduction to Proto-Indo-European and the Proto-Indo-European World.* Oxford: Oxford University Press.
Manu	*Manusmr̥ti* or *Mānavadharmaśāstra.* Olivelle, P. (ed. and tr.) (2005). *Manu's Code of Law. A Critical Edition and Translation of the Mānava-Dharmaśāstra.* New York: Oxford University Press.
Masica 1979	Masica, C.P. (1979). 'Aryan and Non-Aryan Elements in North Indian Agriculture.' In: Deshpande, M.M. and P.E. Hook (eds.), *Aryan and Non-Aryan in India*, pp. 55–151. Ann Arbor: Center for South and Southeast Asian Studies.
McHugh 2012	McHugh, J. (2012). *Sandalwood and Carrion: Smell in Indian Religion and Culture.* New York: Oxford University Press.
Medh	Medhātithi: *Manubhāṣya.* Jha, G. (tr.) (1999). *Manusmṛti with the Manubhāṣya of Medhātithi.* Volume 1. Delhi: Motilal Banarsidass.
Meulenbeld 1974	Meulenbeld, G.J. (ed.) (1974). 'Appendix Four. Sanskrit Names of Plants and Their Botanical Equivalents.' In: *The Mādhavanidāna and its Chief Commentary. Chapters 1–10*, pp. 520–611. Leiden: E.J. Brill. <http://www.sanskrit-lexicon.uni-koeln.de/scans/SNPScan/2014/web/index.php> (accessed 10 September 2015).

Meulenbeld 2007–2008	Meulenbeld, G.J. (2007–2008). 'A Quest for Poison Trees in Indian Literature, Along with Notes on Some Plants and Animals of the Kauṭilīya Arthaśāstra.' *Wiener Zeitschrift für die Kunde Südasiens*, 51: 5–75.
Ministry of AYUSH	Ministry of AYUSH, Government of India (2015). *National Medicinal Plants Board*, <http://www.nmpb.nic.in/index.php> (accessed 5 June 2015).
MN	Mādhava: *Nidāna*. Meulenbeld, G.J. (1974). *The Mādhavanidāna and Its Chief Commentaries. Chapters 1–10. Introduction, Translation and Notes*. Leiden: E.J. Brill.
MP	*Matsyapurāṇa*. = *Śrīmaddvaipāyanamunipraṇītaṃ Matsyapurāṇam*. (1981). Puṇyākhyapattane: Ānandāśramasaṃskr̥tagranthāvaliḥ, Granthāṅkaḥ 54.
MWSED	Monier-Williams, Sir M. (1995). *A Sanskrit-English Dictionary: Etymologically and Philologically Arranged with Special Reference to Cognate Indo-European Languages*. Reprint, 1899. Delhi: Motilal Banarsidass.
NS	Gotama: *Nyāyasūtra*. Vidyâbhuṣana, S.C. (tr.) (1913). *The Nyâya Sutras of Gotama*. Allahabad: The Pâṇini Office.
Nugteren 2005	Nugteren, A. (2005). *Belief, Bounty, and Beauty. Rituals around Sacred Trees in India*. Leiden: E.J. Brill.
Olivelle 1998	Olivelle, P. (ed. and tr.). (1998). *The Early Upaniṣads. Annotated Text and Translation*. New York: Oxford University Press.
Olivelle 1999	Olivelle, P. (tr.) (1999). *Dharmasūtras. The Law Codes of Āpastambha, Gautama, Baudhāyana and Vasiṣṭha*. Oxford: Oxford University Press.
Pandanus	*Pandanus Database of Plants*: Seminar of Indian Studies, Institute of South and Central Asia, Faculty of Arts, Charles University, Prague (1998–2009): <http://iu.ff.cuni.cz/pandanus/database/> (accessed 20 April 2015).
PB	*Pañcaviṃśabrāhmaṇa*. Caland, W. (tr.) (1931). *Pañcaviṃśa Brāhmaṇa. The Brahmana of Twenty Five Chapters*. Calcutta: Asiatic Society of Bengal.
Pontillo 2006	Pontillo, T. (2006). 'The Names of Fruits, Roots and Flowers Included in Kālidāsa's Works and the *Aṣṭādhyāyī* Rules IV,3, 163–167 with their commentaries.' *Pandanus* 6: 161–75.
Prasad et al. 2006	Prasad, G.P., G. Neelima, G.P. Pratap and G.K. Swamy. (2006). 'Vṛkşăyurvĕda of Parăśara: An Ancient Treatise on Plant Science.' *Bulletin of the Indian Institute of History of Medicine (Hyderabad)*, 36(1): 63–74.
PS	Parāśara: *Dharmasaṃhitā*. Islāmapurkar, Pdt. V.Ś. (ed.) (1893–1919). *The Parāšara Dharma Saṃhitā or Parāśara Smṛti with the Commentary of Sāyaṇa Mādhavāchārya*. Edited with various readings, critical notes, an index, appendices etc. Bombay: Government Central Book Depot.

Quattrocchi 2012	Quattrocchi, U. (2012). *CRC World Dictionary of Medicinal and Poisonous Plants. Common Names, Scientific Names, Eponyms, Synonyms, and Etymologies*. London: CRC Press.
Qur	*Qur'ān*. Abdel Haleem, M.A.S. (tr.) (2008). *The Qur'ān. A New Translation*. Oxford: Oxford University Press.
Roy 2008	Roy, B.P. (2008). '*Vṛkṣāyurveda* in Ancient India.' In: HAI: 550–96.
RV	*Ṛgvedasaṃhitā*. Jamison, S.W. and J.P. Brereton (trs.) (2014). *The Rigveda. The Earliest Religious Poetry of India*. 3 vols. New York: Oxford University Press.
Sahni 2008	Sahni, R. (2008). *Environmental Ethics in Buddhism. A Virtues Approach*. London: Routledge.
Sani 2003	Sani, S. (2003). 'Il sesamo nell'India antica.' *Studi Linguistici e Filologici Online* 1, 383–402, http://www.humnet.unipi.it/slifo/ (accessed 25 August 2015).
ŚB^{M}	*Śatapathabrāhmaṇa, Mādhyandina* recension. Eggeling, J. (tr.) (1882–1900). *The Satapatha Brâhmana According to the Text of the Mâdhyandina School*. Parts I–V. Sacred Books of the East, vols. XII, XXVI, XLI, XLIII, XLIV. Oxford: Clarendon Press.
ŚB^{K}	*Śatapathabrāhmaṇa, Kāṇvīya* recension. Swaminathan, C.R. (ed., tr.). *Kāṇvaśatapathabrāhmaṇam*. 5 vols. Delhi: Indira Gandhi National Centre for the Arts.
Schmithausen 1991	Schmithausen, L. (1991). *The Problem of the Sentience of Plants in Earliest Buddhism*. Tokyo: International Institute for Buddhist Studies.
Schmithausen 2009	Schmithausen, L. (2009). *Plants in Early Buddhism and the Far Eastern Idea of the Buddha-Nature of Grasses and Trees*. Lumbini: Lumbini International Research Institute.
Sivarajan 1991	Sivarajan, V.V. (1991). *Introduction to the Principles of Plant Taxonomy*. Second edition. Cambridge: Cambridge University Press.
ŚKD	Deva, R. (1886–1991). *Śabdakalpadrumaḥ*. 5 vols. Re-edited by V. Vasu and H. Vasu. Calcutta: The Baptist Mission Press.
Smith 2012	Smith, F. (2012). 'Trees and Plants.' In Jacobsent, K.A. et al. (eds.), *Brill's Encyclopedia of Hinduism*. Leiden: Brill Online.
Southworth 1988	Southworth, F.C. (1988). 'Ancient Economic Plants of South Asia: Linguistic Archaeology and Early Agriculture.' In Jazayery, M.A. and W. Winter (eds.), *Languages and Cultures. Studies in Honor of Edgar C. Polomé*, pp. 659–68. Berlin/New York: Mouton de Gruyter.
Spess 2000	Spess, D.L. (2000). *Soma. The Divine Hallucinogen*. Rochester, Vermont: Park Street Press.
Staal 2001	Staal, F. (2001). 'How a Psychoactive Substance Becomes a Ritual. The Case of Soma.' *Social Research*, 68(3), 745–78.
STEDT	University of California, Department of Linguistics. (2010–2013). *Sino-Tibetan Etymological Dictionary and Thesaurus*, http://stedt.berkeley.edu/~stedt-cgi/rootcanal.pl (accessed 5 June 2015).

Stuhrmann 2006	Stuhrmann, R. (2006). 'Ṛgvedische Lichtaufnahmen. Soma botanisch, pharmakologisch, in den Augen der Kavis.' *Electronic Journal of Vedic Studies*, 13(1): 1–93.
Sū	*Sūtrasthāna*
SuS	*Suśrutasaṃhitā*. Bhishagratna, K. (tr.) (2011). *Suśruta Saṃhitā*. 3 vols. Reprint. Varanasi: Chowkhambha Sanskrit Series Office.
Sutherland 1991	Sutherland, G.H. (1991). *The Disguises of the Demon: The Development of the Yakṣa in Hinduism and Buddhism*. Albany: State University of New York Press.
SuVĀ	Surapāla: *Vṛkṣāyurveda*. (1) Das, R.P. (1988). *Das Wissen von der Lebensspanne der Bäume. Surapālas Vṛkṣāyurveda kritisch ediert, übers und kommentiert von Rahul Peter Das; mit einem Nachtrag von G. Jan Meulenbeld zu seinem Verzeichnis 'Sanskrit names of plants and their botanical equivalents.'* Stuttgart: Steiner-Verlag-Wiesbaden-GmbH. (2) Śrīkṛṣṇa 'Jugnū' (ed.). *Vaidhyavidhyāvareṇyasurapālamuniviracitaḥ Vṛkṣāyurveda (upavana-dakārgalavijñāna-taruropaṇa va cikitsā vidhi)*. Sanskrit text with Hindī translations. Vārāṇasī: Caukhambā Saṃskṛt Sīrīj Āphis.
TaitU	*Taittirīya Upaniṣad*. In Olivelle (1998: 288–314).
The Plant List	*The Plant List* (2013). Version 1.1. Published on the internet; <http://www.theplantlist.org/> (accessed 10 October 2015).
TR	Rāmānuja: *Tantrarahasya*. Rāmaswami Śāstri, K.S. (ed.) (1956). *Tantrarahasya. A Primer of Prābhākara Mīmāṃsā*. Critically edited with Introduction and Appendices. Baroda: Oriental Institute.
Tropicos	*Tropicos.org*: Missouri Botanical Garden: <http://www.tropicos.org> (accessed 10 April 2015).
TS	*Taittirīyasaṃhitā*. Weber, A. (ed.) (1871–1872). *Die Taittirīya Saṃhitā. Indische Studien* XI and XII. Leipzig: F.A. Brockhaus.
Turner 1962–1966	Turner, R.L., Sir. (1962–1966). *A Comparative Dictionary of Indo-Aryan Languages*. London: Oxford University Press.
uBio	*uBio Project*: The Marine Biological Laboratory, Woods Hole Oceanographic Institution: <http://www.ubio.org/> (accessed 10 April 2015).
VāmP	*Vāmanapurāṇa*. Gupta, A. (ed.) (1967). *Śrī Vāmanapurāṇam: paṭhasamīkṣatmakasaṃskaraṇam*. Vārānasī: Sarvabhāratiya-kāśirājanyāsa.
VasDhS	Vasiṣṭha: *Dharmasūtra*. In: Olivelle (1999: 631–704).
VāyP	*Vāyupurāṇa*. Mitra, R.L. (ed.) (1880–1888). *Vāyupurāṇam*. Calcutta: Asiatic Society, Bibliotheca Indica no. 85.
Viy	*Viyāhapaṇṇattisuttaṁ* (Pkt.) = *Vyākhyāprajñaptisūtra* (Skt.). Doshi, B.J. and A.M. Bhojak (eds.) (1974–1982). *Viyāhapaṇṇattisuttaṁ*. 3 parts. Bombay: Śrī Mahāvīra Jaina Vidyālaya.
Vogel 1979	Vogel, K. (1979). *Indian Lexicography*. A History of Indian Literature, edited by Jan Gonda, Volume V, Fasc. 4. Wiesbaden: Otto Harrassowitz.

VP	*Viṣṇupurāṇa*. GRETIL e-text based on: Pathak, M.M. (ed.) (1997–1999). *The Critical Edition of the Viṣṇupurāṇam*. Vadodara: Oriental Institute, <http://gretil.sub.uni-goettingen.de/gretil/1_sanskr/3_purana/vipce_pu.htm> (accessed 10 October 2015). Input by: Peter Schreiner.
Wescoat and Wolschke-Bulmahn 1996	Wescoat, J.L. and J. Wolschke-Bulmahn (eds.) (1996). *Mughal Gardens: Sources, Places, Representations, and Prospects*. Harvard: Harvard University Press.
Witzel 2006	Witzel, M. (2006). 'South Asian Agricultural Vocabulary.' In Osada, T. (ed.). *Proceedings of the Pre-Symposium of RHIN and 7th ESCA Harvard-Kyoto Round Table*, pp. 96–120. Kyoto: Research Institute for Humanity and Nature (RHIN).
Witzel 2009	Witzel, M. (2009). 'The Linguistic History of Some Indian Domestic Plants.' *Journal of BioSciences*, 34(6): 829–33, <http://dash.harvard.edu/handle/1/8954814> (accessed 16 April 2015).
Wojtilla 2003	Wojtilla, G. (2003). 'What Can the Ṛgveda Tell Us on Agriculture.' *Acta Orientalia Academiae Scientiarum Hungaricae*, 56(1): 35–48.
Wojtilla 2006	Wojtilla, G. (2006). *History of Kṛṣiśāstra*. Wiesbaden: Otto Harrassowitz.
Wujastyk 2003	Wujastyk, Dominik. (2003). *The Roots of Ayurveda*. Second edition. New Delhi: Penguin.
Wujastyk 2004	Wujastyk, Dominik. (2004). '*Jambudvīpa*: Apples or Plums?' In Burnett, C., J.P. Hogendijk, K. Plofker and M. Yano (eds.), *Studies in the History of the Exact Sciences in Honour of David Pingree*, pp. 287–301. Leiden: E.J. Brill.
Wujastyk 2012	Wujastyk, Dagmar. (2012). *Well-Mannered Medicine. Medical Ethics and Etiquette in Classical Ayurveda*. Oxford and New York: Oxford University Press.
Zimmerman 2011	Zimmermann, F. (2011). *The Jungle and the Aroma of Meats. An Ecological Theme in Hindu Medicine*. Delhi: Motilal Banarsidass.
Zysk 2010	Zysk, K.G. (2010). *Asceticism and Healing in Ancient India. Medicine in the Buddhist Monastery*. Delhi: Motilal Banarsidass.

Section One

Nature, Landscape, Devotion

Chapter 1

A Modern *Kalpavṛkṣa*: Sathya Sāī Bābā and the Wish-Fulfilling Tree

ANTONIO RIGOPOULOS[1]

kā kalpalatā loke
sacchiṣyāyārpitā vidyā |
ko 'kṣayavaṭavṛkṣaḥ syād
vidhivatsatpātradattadānaṃ yat ||

What is in this world the fabulous creeper granting all desires?
Liberating knowledge, that is offered to worthy disciples.
What is the immortal banyan tree?
That gift which is granted to a worthy person, according to the rules.
(Śaṅkara, *Praśnottararatnamālikā* 39)

Ratnākaram Sathyanārāyaṇa Rāju alias Sathya Sāī Bābā (1926–2011), the charismatic saint of the village of Puttaparthi in the Anantapur district of Andhra Pradesh, was undoubtedly one of the most famous gurus of our times. His followers, both in India and throughout the world, count in the millions, predominantly from the urban upper-middle classes.[2] Revered by his Hindu devotees as a *pūrṇāvatāra*, a 'full manifestation of the divine,' over the years Sathya Sāī Bābā (Tel. Satya Sāyibābā) was successful in transforming what was originally a local cult into a transnational phenomenon,

1 Antonio Rigopoulos is Professor of Sanskrit and Indology, Department of Asian and North African Studies, Ca' Foscari University of Venice (Italy).

2 For an up-to-date introduction to Sathya Sāī Bābā, see Srinivas (2013: 625–33). See also Srinivas (2008, 2010).

making the ashram of Prasanthi Nilayam[3] the headquarters of a global, cosmopolitan movement.

The saint's teaching, steeped in devotion (*bhakti*), was Vedāntic through and through. His organization, as is typical of neo-Hinduism, is based on a universalistic or, better, inclusivistic ideology.[4] In both theory and practice, the saint of Puttaparthi placed special emphasis on ethics (through his education in human values program) and social service (through the creation of schools, hospitals and a variety of charitable works). Sathya Sāī Bābā's towering fame, however, is not due to his teachings or social works but rather to his charisma and alleged miraculous powers, which are inextricably woven into his life and message.[5]

This chapter explores the peculiar function of trees in the construction of his cult. In particular, attention is paid to Sathya Sāī Bābā's appropriation of the myths of the *pārijāta*, *kalpavṛkṣa* and *vaṭa/bodhi* trees, which in the saint's hagiography are linked to his advent, his miraculous deeds and the meditative praxis conducive to final liberation (*mukti*), respectively (figure 1.1). My purpose is to show the ways in which these trees have been effectively 'transplanted' in Puttaparthi and highlight the role they have played – and continue to play – in substantiating Sathya Sāī Bābā's claim to being a divine 'incarnation.' Their symbolism is at the center of a remarkable network of sacred narratives which tie together memory and history, binding the village's destiny to the holy man's avatāric career.[6]

3 Lit. 'abode of highest peace.'

4 On the notion of inclusivism, see Halbfass (1988: 403–18).

5 Over the years the guru of Puttaparthi has had to face various accusations. Starting from the mid-1970s, he was charged with sleight of hand and, especially from the 1990s, he was accused of sexual abuses as well as financial mishandlings. Despite all this, he succeeded in expanding his fame and fabulously rich 'kingdom.' Indeed, he has become a national figure, a trademark of India's spirituality.

6 This essay is based on fieldwork I carried out in Puttaparthi in November 1985, December 1991 and August–September 2001.

Figure 1.1. The meditation tree in Puttaparthi, 1980.

THE *PĀRIJĀTA* AND SATHYA SĀĪ BĀBĀ'S ADVENT

The first tree to which Sathya Sāī Bābā is linked to is the *pārijāta*, that is, the night-flowering jasmine (*Nyctanthes arbor-tristis* L.).[7] This tree is related to the holy man's birth and plays a relevant function in the founding hagiography celebrating Sathya Sāī Bābā's divinity. The *pārijāta* makes its appearance in a premonitory dream that Ratnākaram Kondama Rāju (1840–1952), Sathya Sāī Bābā's paternal grandfather, is said to have had prior to his grandson's birth. In order to appreciate the significance of this dream I must first recall the popular Hindu myth centered upon this tree.

According to Hindu mythology, the fabulous *pārijāta* was produced when at the beginning of time the gods and demons churned the ocean of milk (*kṣīrasāgara*) in order to obtain the nectar of immortality (*amṛta*). The tree was then claimed by Indra, the king of the gods, and taken to his paradise where his wife Indrāṇī took care of it. Subsequently, it so happened

7 Its flowers open at night and their sweet perfume pervades the surrounding area. In the early morning following the night bloom, the flowers drop to the ground, carpeting it with their fragile beauty. On this tree, supposed to have fecundating powers, see Gupta (1991: 63–65); Nugteren (2005: 35).

that Kṛṣṇa offered the *pārijāta*'s beautiful flowers – characterized by snow-white petals and an orange-red center – to Rukmiṇī, his senior wife. Jealous of her, the proud Satyabhāmā, the third of Kṛṣṇa's eight wives, asked her beloved spouse to bring home to her the whole tree. In order to please her, Kṛṣṇa, who was especially fond of Satyabhāmā despite her capricious temper, did not hesitate to steal the *pārijāta* from Indra's paradise. Kṛṣṇa's theft led to a war with the king of gods in which the latter was ultimately defeated. The tree was taken to Dvārakā, Kṛṣṇa's capital, and planted there; at Kṛṣṇa's death, however, it returned to Indra's heaven.[8]

Ratnākaram Kondama Rāju was a simple peasant and a pious Vaiṣṇava. He belonged to the Bhatrāju caste, a Kṣatriya sub-caste whose occupation is to popularize sacred literature through songs and poetry.[9] Apparently, Ratnākaram Kondama Rāju had musical and dramatic talent and knew by heart many epic and Purāṇic myths culled from Sanskrit and Telugu sources. The story goes that one night he had a dream in which Satyabhāmā asked him to provide shelter for her. Here is how N. Kasturi, Sathya Sāī Bābā's main biographer, reports the episode:

> Sri Kondama Raju lived to be a centenarian and I remember how tears of joy ran down those wrinkled cheeks whenever he recollected that enthralling experience. In the dream, Kondama Raju saw Sathyabhama, alone, expectant and forlorn, waiting anxiously for her Lord, who had gone on an errand to bring her from Heaven the much-coveted Parijatha flowers. The minutes increased to hours and the hours accumulated into days but still there was no sign of Krishna! Sathyabhama broke into tears. There ensued a huge storm accompanied by thunder, lightning and a heavy shower of rain. Luckily, Her eyes fell on Kondama Raju who was passing across the place where she stood and she asked him to provide some shelter. (Kasturi 1980: 4)

8 On the *pārijāta* legend in Sanskrit sources, see HV II.64 ff. and VP V.30 ff. For a review of the main Purāṇic loci, see Dikshitar (1995: vol. 2, 317). In Telugu literature, popular is the *Pārijātapaharanamu* poem written by Timmana under the patronage of the Vijayanagar king Kṛṣṇadevarāya (r. 1509–1529), which is a staple of Kūcipuḍi performers; see Rao (2007: vol. IV, 3099–100). On Satyabhāmā in epic and Purāṇic lore, see Mani (1975: 704–05); Dikshitar (1995: vol. 3, 513). On Satyabhāmā in Telugu literature and dance, see Soneji (2004). In Andhra Pradesh, Satyabhāmā is the model of the jealous woman.

9 See Rao (1985: 4); Padmanaban (2000: 11, 24 n. 6). On the Bhatrāju caste, see Thurston and Rangachari (1909: vol. I, 223–30); Nanjundayya and Ananthakrishna Iyer (1930–1936: vol. II, 259–76).

Ratnākaram Kondama Rāju thought that in order to offer protection to the goddess (Devī) he must erect a temple for her. Therefore, presumably sometime in the late 19th century, a Satyabhāmā temple was built that came to incorporate the shrine of the village deity (*grāmadevatā*) Satyamma.[10] The co-identification of the two goddesses was favored by the similarity in their names and by the fact that both, Satyamma and Satyabhāmā, are understood to be manifestations of Bhūdevī, i.e. Mother Earth.[11]

The guru of Ratnākaram Kondama Rāju was one Veṅkāvadhūta.[12] Ratnākaram Kondama Rāju and his wife Lakshmamma (1852–1931) named their two sons 'Veṅka' after him: Pedda Veṅkama Rāju (1885–1963) – destined to become Sathya Sāī Bābā's father – and Chinna Veṅkama Rāju (1898–1978). Veṅkāvadhūta was well-known in the area; his name implies that he was an *avadhūta*, an ascetic of a radical type, possibly consecrated to god Veṅkaṭeśvara[13] whose abode is in Tirupati, the major pilgrimage center of Andhra Pradesh.

Ratnākaram Kondama Rāju is reported to have had a memorable encounter with his guru one afternoon in Puttaparthi, underneath a banyan tree.[14] After he had devoutly offered him some food, Veṅkāvadhūta, much to his amazement, solemnly announced that Viṣṇu Nārāyaṇa would soon manifest himself in the village in order to rescue Bhūdevī, who was in deep distress (Padmanaban 2000: 12, 25 n. 9).

In both Ratnākaram Kondama Rāju's dream and Veṅkāvadhūta's prophecy, Bhūdevī's alias Satyabhāmā/Satyamma's anguish mirrors the desolate condition of the village. Indeed, the Satyabhāmā/*pārijāta* tale is set within the wider context of a termite mound myth, which is the founding myth of Puttaparthi (Rigopoulos 2014). According to this legend – a variant of a typical folk motif – the village was once a prosperous locale. Its original name was Gollapalle/Gollapalli, the 'village of cowherds' (Gollas) who

10 See Kasturi (1980: 3–4); Padmanaban (2000: 11–12).

11 On Bhūdevī, see Venkatesan (2009: 491–98).

12 For a description of this holy man, see Kasturi (1984: 12–13). Apparently, he hailed from Maharashtra and died at Hussainpur in today's Karnataka, Pavagada Taluk. His tomb in Hussainpur is located in the so-called Veṅkāvadhūta temple; see Padmanaban (2000: 25 n. 11).

13 Lit. 'lord of the Veṅkaṭa hill.' On this originally folk god who came to be revered as a manifestation of Viṣṇu, see Narayanan (2009: 781–85).

14 In many hagiographies this tree is the site of glorious epiphanies. The name banyan appears to have been first bestowed on a famous tree of this species growing in the vicinity of the Persian Gulf, under which Banias or Hindu merchants used to camp.

tended beautiful cows. The story goes that once a *nāga*, a divine cobra, issued out from a termite mound (*puṭṭa*) and, applying its mouth on a cow's teat, started sucking the milk that she willingly offered. This incredible scene caused one cowherd to react, hitting the snake with a stone. This sin brought the *nāga*'s curse upon the village, triggering its decline. To harm or kill a *nāga* is an act of sacrilege which is thought to cause a blemish (*nāgadoṣa*) and hence entail the malediction of infertility. Thus the hamlet was turned into arid land and renamed Valmikipura and subsequently Puttaparthi (Tel. Puṭṭaparti), 'the land where termite mounds multiply.'

Various narratives emphasize the power of the *nāga*'s curse and the incapacity of Satyamma/Satyabhāmā – who *is* the village – in restoring the pristine prosperity of the place through her own forces. In order to atone for their sin, the first response devised by locals was to worship the stone that hit the *nāga*, which came to be identified as Veṇugopālasvāmin or Kr̥ṣṇa Gopāla playing the flute. However, the inauguration of this cult, which is a typical reaction to *nāgadoṣa*, was not effective in countering the curse. The subsequent exile of all cowherds from Puttaparthi – on the orders of Satyamma as conveyed through a local woman whom she possessed – though believed to ease the curse, was still deemed insufficient to wash it away.

Local hagiography interprets Sathya Sāī Bābā's birth as the fulfillment of Veṅkāvadhūta's words. Satyabhāmā's grief is thought to have come to an end thanks to Sathya Sāī Bābā's advent, that is, thanks to Kr̥ṣṇa Gopāla's (= Viṣṇu Nārāyaṇa's) return to his beloved wife and village.[15] What we witness here is the tying together of three distinct narratives: the village's founding myth of the termite mound – itself open to a variety of interpretations – with its nefarious consequences; the startling prophecy of Veṅkāvadhūta, the guru of the Ratnākaram family; and Ratnākaram Kondama Rāju's own premonitory dream. These tales are construed as sequences in a plot, being understood as the unfolding of a divine saga. In the end, Satyabhāmā's anguish due to the separation (*viraha*) from her lord is Puttaparthi's anguish, which is eventually overcome only through Sathya Sāī Bābā's descent on earth.

The appropriation of the Kr̥ṣṇaite myth of the *pārijāta* as a prelude to the holy man's appearance on the scene appears most fitting. It constitutes a theatrical climax by highlighting powerful, intertwined emotions: the utter desperation of Satyabhāmā/Puttaparthi at the god's absence and,

15 The cowherd Kr̥ṣṇa and Viṣṇu Nārāyaṇa are typically identified with each other. Indeed, Kr̥ṣṇa is regarded as a *pūrṇāvatāra* of Viṣṇu.

at the same time, her/its ardent longing for his glorious return. Sathya Sāī Bābā's birth is interpreted as the fulfillment of a renovated communion, ushering in a new era of plenty.[16] By descending from his heavenly abode he offers himself to his spouse/village, and the scented flowers that he, as Kṛṣṇa, carries with him, are symbolic of his seductive appeal, of the fragrance of his pure love (*preman*).[17] Moreover, the *pārijāta* flowers are symbolic of asceticism and renunciation (*saṃnyāsa*), given that the saffron robe of renunciants – which Sathya Sāī Bābā started wearing from the 1940s (Padmanaban 2000: 432) – is traditionally prepared with the orange-red pistils of the *pārijāta*.[18] An early hagiographic source reports a telling episode of young Sathya Sāī Bābā's identification with Kṛṣṇa and the *pārijāta* flowers:

> On another day, while climbing down the stairs, He halted midway like a wooden doll. Men stood around Him in a circle. After a few minutes, Swami[19]

16 Here is the testimony of Venkamma, Sathya Sāī Bābā's elder sister:

> Milk was always scarce in Puttaparthi then ... After the advent of Sathya conditions improved and the place overflowed with milk, curds and butter ... There is nothing surprising in this since Sathya is also thought to be Lord Krishna, the divine cowherd. (Balu 1981: 41)

The idea is that thanks to the coming of Sathya Sāī Bābā – the vanquisher of the *nāga*'s curse – the village regained its pristine welfare and cowherds and cows once again thrived. In the late 1970s, Sh. Balu reported:

> The Sathya Sai *Gokulam* (cow stabling) is on the outskirts of Puttaparthi village. It houses over a hundred cows and it is administered under the strict supervision of Sri Sathya Sai Baba. A graceful figure of Krishna with a cow stands at the entrance. The whole area has fresh green patches of lawn and lovely flowering trees. There are clean and bright sheds for the cows and water buffaloes; indeed, the whole place is spic and span. It also has neatly laid out living quarters for the cowherds who tend the cattle. (Balu 1981: 118)

17 As Vijayakumari observed:

> The great boon, the priceless diamond, God gives to His devotee is devotion. Swami is verily a Parijatha flower to His humble devotees. (Vijayakumari 1999: 175)

18 Hindu ascetics dye their robes a rich fiery colour. When the *pārijāta* flowers fall to the ground, people collect them and separate the orange tubes from the white petals and dry them. Once they are dried they can be used for making this saffron-coloured dye; see Pellegrini (forthcoming). Already in 1948, Ratnākaram Kondama Rāju emphasized that his grandson was an *avadhūta*, a great ascetic: not an otherworldly ascetic, however, but an ascetic *in* the world and *for* the world; see Kasturi (1982: 85).

19 Honorific term meaning 'master.'

> said with a smile, 'Today is Gokulashtami,[20] you see. That is why I went to visit Brindavan.' He went on standing on the stairs and, when we asked Him, 'Swami, shall we go down?' he showed us His feet. Heaps of *parijatha* flowers exuding divine fragrance were covering His Lotus Feet. We collected handfuls of those flowers, and kept them safely like we would some treasure.[21] (Vijayakumari 1999: 132)

THE *KALPAVṚKṢA* AND SATHYA SĀĪ BĀBĀ'S WONDERS

When the saint of Puttaparthi was fifteen or sixteen years old, he used to take his friends and devotees (*bhaktas*) up the crest of the Obuladevara Gutta hill on the left bank of the Chitravathi river, to a huge boulder under a solitary tamarind tree which soon came to be known as the *kalpavṛkṣa* or wish-fulfilling tree.[22] It is noteworthy that as early as 1949 Sathya Sāī Bābā himself narrated that when he was just thirteen he spent six months under this particular tree:

20 The festival celebrating Kṛṣṇa's birthday. It falls on the eighth day of the dark fortnight of the month of Śrāvaṇa (July–August).

21 The scent of *pārijāta* flowers is similar to a combination of jasmine and orange blossom. The saint's materialization of flowers and leaves was not frequent; see Rao (1985: 187–88); Padmanaban (2000: 288, 307, 315). Among the plays written by Sathya Sāī Bābā in his youth there was even a *Pārijātapaharaṇa* ('The Offering of the *Pārijāta*') in which he interpreted the role of Satyabhāmā instead of Kṛṣṇa, probably because he didn't want to embarrass his partner Narasimha Dass. Here is the latter's testimony:

> Rāju observed propriety even in selecting the roles. I always thank Swami for having given me the role of Sri Krishna and taking up the role of Sathyabhama Himself, instead of doing the converse, which would have saddled me with the sin of touching [the person of an *avatar*] ... with my foot. (Padmanabhan 2000: 137)

According to the traditional plot, when Kṛṣṇa tries to appease Satyabhāmā she kicks his head with her left foot.

22 The *kalpavṛkṣa*, also known as *kalpataru* and *kalpadruma*, is said to have first emerged when the gods and demons churned the ocean of milk (VP I.9.95; BhP VIII.8.6; MP CCL.5). Together with the *pārijāta*, the *kalpavṛkṣa* is among the five fabulous trees of Indra's paradise: it is famed for its golden fruits of exquisite flavor, nourishment of the gods. On the wish-fulfilling tree, see Crooke (1978: vol. 2, 87–88); Bhattacharyya (1990: 78); Dubois (1990: 633–34); Malla (2000: 104–08); Nugteren (2005: 43, 327–30). For an overview on sacred trees and plants, see Smith (2013: 161–67).

> In my thirteenth year, coming to know that I had become a 'Baba' and had left home, one of my friends became mad ... Another friend jumped into a well and died ... One friend became an ascetic. For the next six months, keeping out of sight of everyone, I remained hidden in an underground tunnel, under a tree that has since come to be known as Kalpa Vriksha ... That tunnel still exists. But most of it is closed with rocks and pebbles. Inside it are still to be found a kamandalam (the vessel with a handle in which sages carry drinking water), dandam (a staff carried by ascetics), a writing desk, a pen, an ink bottle, a copy of the *Bhagavad Gita* and a few letters. Devotees who had gone there with true devotion have seen them and come back ... People with doubting minds cannot even find the opening of the tunnel, and they come back disappointed.[23] (Vijayakumari 1999: 218–19)

In those early days, young Sathya – as he used to be called – climbed up the hillock innumerable times with his pals. He often challenged them in a race to reach the top of the Obuladevara Gutta from the river bed, the finish line being invariably the tamarind tree. The hagiographies report that even though Sathya allowed his companions to have a lead start, he would always win the race: his bewildered pals, though running as fast as they could, would find him placidly seated on the tamarind's branches smiling at them.[24]

He would then prove his astounding powers by telling his friends to ask for any fruit, in or out of season, and the same would appear hanging off the branches of the tree. Apparently, the tamarind bore not only fruits but also sweets such as *laḍḍūs*, sugar candies, et cetera.[25] These *mirabilia*

23 Vijayakumari and her brother Murthy visited the tunnel and said that they could find all the objects mentioned by the saint as well as a lion who roared at them: terribly frightened, they managed to escape and were later scolded by Sathya Sāī Bābā for going there without permission; see Vijayakumari (1999: 219–21). The *kamaṇḍalu* and the *daṇḍa* are the symbols of young Sathya's new ascetic identity, whereas the desk, the pen and the ink bottle are reminiscent of his schooldays. He attended school up to 1943, when he was admitted to Form Three (Standard VIII) in the High School at Uravakonda; see Padmanaban (2000: 128–29). The presence of a copy of the BhG is in keeping with his identification with Kṛṣṇa and his Vedāntic teaching centered upon *bhakti* and *karmayoga*.

24 On these and other marvels taking place at the tamarind tree, see Murphet (1981: 69–72); Padmanaban (2000: 426). On occasion people could see a huge halo surrounding Sathya Sāī Bābā, a vibrant circle of light like a *cakra* (wheel): they felt as if lord Viṣṇu himself stood before them; see Balu (1981: 151). For a rare photo of the *kalpavṛkṣa* in 1946, see Vijayakumari (1999: between pages 124–25).

25 On the constitutive link of magic trees with food, see Narayan (1989: 200–03).

are part of a large repertory of astonishing deeds (*camatkāras*) associated with Sathya Sāī Bābā's youth, analogous to Kṛṣṇa Gopāla, the charming cowherd boy of Vṛndāvana, paradigm of the juvenile god performing all sorts of marvels (Kasturi 1980: 64; Vijayakumari 1999: 52–58; Steel 1997: 133, 1999: 40). To be sure, the biographies of the saint of Puttaparthi are replete with the miraculous, first and foremost a bewildering variety of materializations (ashes, food, rings, pictures, idols, et cetera).[26] He used to say that the first sixteen years of his life would be marked mainly by *līlās*, that is, playful actions,[27] the next sixteen by *māhimās* or miracles, and the subsequent years by *upadeśas* or teachings (Kasturi 1980: 62).

The Kṛṣṇaite flavor of Sathya Sāī Bābā's early days is corroborated by his habit of swinging.[28] Devotees would hang two ropes from the sturdy branches of a tree on the banks of the Chitravathi and, with a wooden plank, improvise a swing (*jhūlā*) on which the boy would merrily ride. The sources report that, while swinging, he would throw sweets at people from his empty hands (Vijayakumari 1999: 127–28; Padmanaban 2000: 300–01).[29]

Numerous are the testimonies centered upon the *kalpavṛkṣa*. For instance, Kamalamma, one of the two wives of the village *karnam*,[30] recalled:

26 One of the earliest documented materializations is a photo of Shirdi Sāī Bābā with Kṛṣṇa, Rāma, Śiva and Hanuman in the background; see Padmanaban (2000: 136). N. Kasturi, presenting the extraordinary features of Sathya Sāī Bābā as a young boy, narrates:

> His playmates called Him, 'Guru' (Preceptor). For He was always correcting them and consoling them; He comforted them in distress and never seemed to get cross or tired. He was a liberal giver, even at that age; for, He pulled out of empty bags, delectable sweets, pencils, pieces of rubber, toys, flowers and fruits for them. When asked how He got them, He answered: 'O, the village Goddess gives me what I want.' That was only to slake their thirst; that was the only answer which would quiet their doubts. But the wonder remained! (Kasturi 1981a: 2)

For a review of Sathya Sāī Bābā's alleged miracles, see Steel (1997: 129–71).

27 Identifying himself with Kṛṣṇa, young Sathya Sāī Bābā even danced with his female devotees, plunging them in bliss. He explained the experience as the reenactment of the *rāsalīlā*, Kṛṣṇa's dance with the *gopīs* or female cowherds (BhP X.29–33); see Vijayakumari (1999: 122–25). On the concept of *līlā*, see Schweig (2010: 793–97).

28 While on the *jhūlā*, he even gave visions of himself as Kṛṣṇa; see Kasturi (1980: 64).

29 On swinging, see Nugteren (2005: 107–17, 336–39).

30 The hereditary chieftain and revenue official in charge of land records and tax collection.

And, His *leelas*! How wonderful they were! He would take Subbamma[31] and myself to the *Kalpa Vriksha* ... and ask us to hold its leaves. Each day the tree would give different fruits according to our requests. (Padmanaban 2000: xv)

The *rāja* of Veṅkaṭagiri, who used to visit Puttaparthi in the early years, observed:

Once or twice I was with Swami when He went to the *Kalpa Vriksha* tree ... He used to ask the devotee to request any kind of fruit, including the ones out of season. I am a serious type and so I did not ever ask Him for fruit out of season, but I was present when other people did. Many people would ask for something and whatever they wanted, they would get. They did not get it from Swami's hand, but from the tree itself. Swami would be sitting far away from the tree. 'What fruit do you want?' He would say. 'Then go and get it,' He would tell them. (Padmanaban 2000: 482)

The implicit assumption in all testimonies is that the veritable *kalpavṛkṣa* is none other than Sathya Sāī Bābā: he himself used to openly say so,[32] echoed by the words sung daily during the closing *āratī* ceremony in Prasanthi Nilayam, which praise him as *āśritakalpalatikā*, 'the wish-fulfilling creeper to those who seek refuge in him.'[33] The two-hundredth of his 1008 names extols him as the wish-fulfilling tree (*Oṃ Śrī Sāī Kalpataruve Namaḥ*)[34] and the sixty-ninth of his 108 names states that he is like heaven for his devotees (*Oṃ Śrī Bhakta Mandarāya Namaḥ*). Here is how Kasturi interprets this latter name:

Mandara[35] means Heaven; Baba is as Heaven to the Bhaktas. He is their Heavenly wish-fulfilling Tree ... Even when Baba was fifteen or sixteen years old He used to take Bhaktas up the hill on the bank of the Chitravathi, to the Tamarind Tree that is still there and pluck from its branches whatever fruit

31 First wife of the brahmin Lakṣmīnārāyaṇa Rao, the village *karnam*. Subbamma was much devoted to Sathya Sāī Bābā from the time he was a little boy.

32 He even sang: 'When you have before you the wish-fulfilling tree, why do you desire to foster inferior trees?' (Kasturi 1981b: 104). See also Kasturi (1980: 63).

33 A famous saint who identified himself with the wish-fulfilling tree was Ramakrishna (1836–1886). On 1 January 1886, he played out the role of the *kalpataru* showering his blessings on the devotees, revealing himself as an *avatāra*. It is worthwhile noticing that in Tantric Yoga the *kalpataru* is equated with the *anāhatacakra*, the esoteric center located at the heart; see the *Ṣaṭcakranirūpana* of Pūrṇānanda (16th century).

34 See Narasappa et al. (1985: 27).

35 The mountain that the gods and demons used as a stick to churn the primeval ocean.

each one asked for; of course no one asked for the Tamarind fruit! So Baba had to transcend the laws of nature that He has framed, in order to make apples, mangoes, figs and plantains grow upon that tree. That tree is called Kalpavriksha ... but really it is only a Sankalpavriksha (a tree that behaves as He wills). Take shelter under Him! ... He is Kalpavriksha, indeed! In fact, He is even more magnificent. He moves among Bhaktas of all places instead of being like the Tree in one place only. He gives, without asking, whatever is good for us. (Kasturi 1979: 69)

The saint of Puttaparthi was deemed capable of making any tree at any time a wish-fulfilling tree (Steel 1997: 133–35; Padmanaban 2000: 357).[36] Among Hindus, nonetheless, the tamarind tree (*Tamarindus indica* L.; Skt. *tintiḍīka*; Tel. *cintaceṭṭu*) is generally considered inauspicious. Its fruit, which flourishes during the dry season, is extremely sour and the traditional belief is that the offering of it causes the fruitlessness of any ceremony (Gupta 1991: 91). It has been suggested that Sathya Sāī Bābā's choice of this tree as his *kalpavṛkṣa* is one of the few Islamic links to Shirdi Sāī Bābā[37] (Aitken 2004: 84) – his purported prior 'incarnation' – given that the tamarind is revered by Indian Muslims and specimens of it are found surrounding their settlements and cemeteries (Ali 1974: 312; Crooke 1978, vol. 2: 109). On the other hand, it might be argued that the saint of Puttaparthi selected this tree precisely because it is ill-omened. He could thus demonstrate his omnipotent will (*saṃkalpa*), capable of transmuting what is deemed unfavorable into a treasure trove of plenty, in this case the sourness of the tamarind fruit[38] into pure nectar.

More to the point, I think that Sathya Sāī Bābā's choice of the tamarind was related to the village's founding tale of the termite mound. Indeed,

36 He is even reported materializing fruits out of thin air; see Rao (1985: 187); Padmanaban (2000: 370).

37 Shirdi Sāī Bābā (d. 15 October 1918), one of the most popular saints of India, was an unconventional *faqīr* who lived the greater part of his life up to his death in a dilapidated mosque of the village of Shirdi in the Ahmednagar district of Maharashtra. For an introduction to this figure, see Rigopoulos (2013a: 641–50).

38 In his discourses the saint of Puttaparthi would sometimes establish an analogy between the tamarind fruit and man. Once he noticed that striking an unripe tamarind fruit (= man) wounds it, while striking a ripe one doesn't. He also pointed out that just as it is impossible to separate the rind, pulp and seed when the tamarind fruit is green, in the same way it is impossible to discard identification with body, senses and mind until one is ripe in experience; see Gries and Gries (1993: 253).

termite mounds and tamarind trees are closely associated.[39] In particular, it should be noted that the origin of the cult in Tirupati was a termite mound raised beside a tamarind tree, in which Veṅkaṭeśvara was believed to reside.[40] Given the sacredness of the tamarind in Tirupati's cult, it seems plausible to suggest that Sathya Sāī Bābā chose a tamarind as the wish-fulfilling tree of Puttaparthi – the village of termite mounds – in order to establish a correspondence between his abode and Tirupati, thus stressing the special sanctity of his birthplace.[41]

The delicious fruits offered by the *avatāra* symbolize the bliss (*ānanda*) he has come to shower upon his fellow villagers and devotees, especially as a giver of worldly enjoyments. The bountiful tree[42] has been universally perceived as a potent instrument of Sathya Sāī Bābā's grace, and for more than 75 years people have thronged to the *kalpavr̥kṣa* in search of solace and answer to their supplications.

Paying one's respects to the tamarind tree has always been a must for all his *bhaktas*. The popularity of this site is proven by the small shops that one finds along the steep path leading towards it. The tree and its surroundings are a place of intense worship and prayer. The people that come to take the tree's *darśana*[43] – climbing the 190 odd steps of the hill – tie pieces of string with countless messages containing their wishes to its branches (figures 1.2 and 1.3). They then walk away comforted that their concerns will be taken care of. When Sathya Sāī Bābā was alive, this practice used to be regarded as a good substitute in case he didn't take one's letters during the morning and afternoon *darśana* rounds at the ashram. At many pilgrimage sites in India, expressing wishes and prayers in front of sacred trees is a common ritual practice, as well as leaving messages and votive gifts on their branches and near their trunk. The custom of tying pieces of cloth and threads on trees in the hope of relieving diseases and other troubles is also well-known (Abbott 1974: 326–34; Nugteren 2005: 329).

39 Termite mounds help mitigate the effects of drought on tamarind trees under increasing drought conditions, while tamarind trees offer food to termites; see Fandohan et al. (2012: 345–55).

40 On the tamarind tree/forest at the origin of Veṅkaṭeśvara's cult as well as of the holy sites of Paṇḍharpūr and Cidambaram, see Dhere (2011: 43–55). On Veṅkaṭeśvara as a god of trees, see Neelima (2013: 89–90). On the link between the termite mound and the tamarind tree in South Indian folk religion, see König (1984: 180–81, 188, 258).

41 On Puttaparthi as another Tirupati, see Rigopoulos (2014).

42 On the generosity of sacred trees, see Nugteren (2005: 59–61, 328).

43 Lit. 'vision,' the experience of seeing the divine and being seen by it; see Valpey (2010: 380–94).

Figure 1.2. The path leading to the wish-fulfilling tree in Puttaparthi, 1980.

It should be noted that the saint of Puttaparthi taught his devotees to place a ceiling on desires, i.e. to keep one's wishes under control and practice detachment (*vairāgya*). He warned his *bhaktas* by reminding them that desires are a prison and that man can be freed only by limiting his wants. Already in one of his early discourses dated 24 October 1963, he cautioned his followers by saying:

> Desire leads to ultimate ruin. It can never be destroyed by fulfillment. It grows upon each satisfaction and becomes a monster that devours the victim himself; so, try to reduce your desires; go on reducing them. There was once a pilgrim who accidentally sat under the *Kalpatharu* (a wish-granting tree)! He was terribly thirsty and said to himself, 'How I wish someone gave me a cup of sweet cool water!' And, immediately, there was placed before him a cup of deliciously cool water. He was surprised, but, drank it nevertheless. Then, he wished for a meal of tasty dishes, and he got it in a trice. This led to a wish for a cot and a bed and when he wished his wife was there to see all this wonder, she appeared in an instant. The poor pilgrim mistook her for an apparition and when he exclaimed, 'O she is an ogress!' she became

Figure 1.3. The wish-fulfilling tree in Puttaparthi, 1980.

> one, and the husband shook in terror, crying, 'She will now eat me up,' which she promptly did! The chain of desire binds one to the point of suffocation. Control, curb your tendency to wish for this and that. Tell the Lord, 'You are enough for me. I do not wish for anything else.' Why pine after golden jewels? Pine for gold. The *Gita* teaches the lesson of *Saranagati* (unconditional surrender to the Lord); wish for His Will to prevail, not your wish to succeed. This is what Krishna meant when He said, 'Be a *Sarvarambha parityagi*' (one who renounces all self-centered actions).[44] (Sathya Sai Baba 2008: 233–34)

If in the old days the tamarind stood solitary on top of the hillock that overlooks the Chitravathi river, in later years the area was transformed into a green paradise of sorts with many trees, shrubs, bushes and grass covering it. Amidst the vegetation, the *kalpavṛkṣa* stood tall as its crest-jewel, revered by all as an immortal tree, until a terrible thunderstorm hit the place on the night of 19 May 2011, causing the tree to collapse.[45]

44 BhG XII.16c, XIV.25c.

45 On the association of sacred trees with immortality, see Nugteren (2005: 51–54).

This was an additional shock to villagers and devotees who less than a month before had to cope with the death of their master and lord: on 24 April 2011, Sathya Sāī Bābā had died of cardio-respiratory failure at Puttaparthi's super-specialty hospital. The afflicted *bhakta*s interpreted the tree's collapse as an ominous sign, a catastrophe adding salt to their emotional wounds.

Quite soon, however, people realized that the tree's roots and main trunk had remained intact and that the stump protruding from the ground was not dead since a fresh, lively shoot had sprouted and was growing rapidly towards the sky. Everybody was greatly relieved: the *kalpavṛkṣa* was not gone, it had rather changed its outer shape and rejuvenated itself. Devotees have extended the analogy to their beloved guru, maintaining that he has not died; he has simply worn out his 'old clothes.' The 'resurrection' of the *kalpavṛkṣa* is thus interpreted as a confirmation of the ongoing divine presence.

THE MEDITATION TREE AND SATHYA SĀĪ BĀBĀ'S POST-SECTARIAN CHARISMA

A third tree that is especially significant in Sathya Sāī Bābā's cult is a banyan or *vaṭa*[46] (*Ficus benghalensis* L.; Skt. *nyagrodha*; Tel. *marri ceṭṭu, vaṭamu*) which the guru himself planted within the premises of the ashram on 29 June 1959. Devotees flock to it to practice meditation (*dhyāna*) as the tree is thought to be charged with great spiritual energy given that the saint of Puttaparthi installed at its root a *yantra*, a thick copper plate – 15 inches long and 10 inches wide – upon which special *mantra*s and mystic markings are etched. In the list of Sathya Sāī Bābā's 108 names, the 97th extols him precisely as *Oṃ Śrī Sādhakānugraha Vaṭavṛkṣa Pratiṣṭhāpakāya Namaḥ*. Here is Kasturi's explanation of it:

> One Vaisakha Purnima day,[47] years ago, Baba was on the sands of the River Chitravathi in the evening, with about a hundred Bhaktas.[48] The talk inevitably moved towards Buddha whose birth, illumination, and release happened on that day of the year. While speaking on the Bodhi Tree at Gaya to which Buddha proceeded for Tapas,[49] someone asked, 'why did he go so far

46 The name *vaṭa* is derived from the Sanskrit verbal root *vaṭ*, 'to surround.'
47 The full moon day in the month of Vaiśākha (April–May).
48 This episode took place in April 1959.
49 Lit. 'heat;' ascetic practices.

and select that tree?' And Baba replied giving an account of mystic *yantras* over which such trees grow, *yantras* which keep out evil forces and stimulate spiritual impulses and help concentration. Even while He was describing these *yantras*, He created from the sands a shining copper plate on which was drawn in squares the mystic symbols and numbers of which He spoke. He said that He would be depositing it in the Tapovana (on the hills behind the Prasanthi Nilayam) and plant a Vatavriksha (*Ficus benghalensis*) thereon. 'It will act as the *yantra* which I am describing. Yogis wherever they are, when they reach a certain stage of sadhana,[50] will know of this congenial spot and hurry hither, to be benefited by this mystic potency,' He said. Baba is therefore indicated by this Name: He who is the Pratishtapaka (person who planted firmly) the Vatavriksha (the Banyan tree of Dakshinamurthi – Shiva as the teacher) as an Anugraha (boon) to the Sadhakas.[51] (Kasturi 1979: 99–100)

This meditation tree cum *yantra* – a diagram supposed to carry occult powers (Bühnemann 2010) – is presented as a spiritual magnet attracting *yogins* and *sādhakas* from all over the world (Steel 1997: 40). It is thought of as the center of a penance grove (*tapovana*) that is conducive to liberation, an analogy with the Buddha's enlightenment (*bodhi*) tree. The practice of installing *yantras* at the root of trees so as to charge them with spiritual power is not uncommon, especially among Tantric adepts.[52] Sathya Sāī Bābā's assumption is that the Buddha himself was drawn to the Bodhgayā tree precisely because it was charged by a potent *yantra*.

It must be pointed out that the Buddha's *bodhi* tree was not a banyan but an *aśvattha* or *Ficus religiosa*, also known as *pīpal* (Nugteren 2005: 143–241).[53] The banyan and the *aśvattha*, though very different, are nonetheless frequently confused. A reason for this confusion might be that banyan

50 A generic term for spiritual practice.

51 The *sādhakas* are spiritual practitioners. On this episode, see Kasturi (1980: 96); Rao (1985: 198–99); Steel (1997: 29); Vijayakumari (1999: 265–66).

52 These *yantras* function as underlying supports. On the analogy with architectural *yantras* laid into the foundation of temples, see Khanna (1994: 143–52). Magic *yantras* are often inserted into a deity's image (*mūrti*), which then undergoes burial.

53 Interestingly, Sathya Sāī Bābā – appearing in his Shirdi form – would have told a lady devotee that he had his ashram near the holy Vidura *aśvattha*, an ancient *Ficus religiosa* supposedly planted by sage Vidura. This fig tree, which is still an object of worship, is located about thirty miles away from Puttaparthi; see Kasturi (1982: 118); Rice (1887: 130). In BhG xv.1–3, which echoes KU vi.1, the *aśvattha* – with roots aloft and branches below – is symbolic of *saṃsāra*; see Coomaraswamy (1984).

trees figure prominently in the Buddha's legendary biography, both before and after his enlightenment (Nugteren 2005: 153–54). The huge banyan, also believed to be a wish-fulfilling tree, is a powerful symbol of immortality (*akṣaya*).[54] It is even known as *bahupāda*, 'many-footed,' since it supports itself through the development of adventitious prop roots from its branches, roots that grow downwards to the ground into thick woody trunks which, over time, become indistinguishable from the main trunk.[55]

It is noteworthy that Sathya Sāī Bābā narrated that in his previous incarnation as Shirdi Sāī Bābā he was born under a banyan tree (Rigopoulos 1993: 23). In Hindu tradition, the banyan or *vaṭa* is linked to Viṣṇu – who is said to sleep in its large leaf during *pralaya*s, the periods of cosmic dissolution – and especially to Śiva, with whom it is identified. As recalled by Kasturi, the archetypal *yogin* and guru Śiva Dakṣiṇāmūrti[56] is described as manifesting himself at the foot of a *vaṭa* while teaching his disciples the knowledge of the Self (*ātmajñāna*) through silence (*mauna*). The idea is that just like the aerial roots of the *vaṭa* suffocate all other plants, in the same way the thought of the Absolute (*Brahman*) must suffocate all other human aspirations.[57] The association of the *vaṭa* with asceticism is highlighted in both literary and ethnographic accounts (Nugteren 2005: 54–55 n. 128, 281, 340–41).

54 On the banyan tree, see Upadhyaya (1965: 5–6); Crooke (1978, vol. 2, 98–99); Gupta (1991: 47–49); Malla (2000: 33–35); Nugteren (2005: 54).

55 On the *nyagrodha* that develops from a tiny seed and symbolizes the all-pervading *Brahman*, see ChU VI.12.1–2.

56 Lit. 'having one's face turned to the South.' This form of Śiva faces death which is thought to come from the South.

57 Here are two significant verses (11–12) taken from the *Dakṣiṇāmūrtistotra*, a hymn attributed to the great Vedāntin master Śaṅkara (c. 700 CE):

I bow to Śrī Dakṣiṇāmūrti in the form of my guru
Seated upon the earth by yonder banyan tree;
I bow to Him who bestows on the sages direct knowledge of Ultimate Truth;
I bow to the Teacher of the three worlds,
The Lord Himself, who dispels the misery of birth and death.
Behold, under the banyan are seated the aged disciples about their youthful teacher,
It is strange indeed: the teacher instructs them only through silence,
Which, in itself, is sufficient to scatter all his disciples' doubts.
(Nikhilananda 1947: 239–40)

In accordance with his master's neo-Vedāntic universalism (Srinivas 2010), Kasturi interpreted the tree as a symbol of the eternal religion (*sanātanadharma*):[58]

> The tree may be said to symbolize Sanathana Dharma, for its branches reach out in all directions and draw sustenance from every type of faith and every spiritual striving. (Kasturi 1980: 95)

In his *sarvadharma* emblem Sathya Sāī Bābā incorporated all world religions, acknowledging them as different paths leading towards the same ultimate goal, though reserving for Hinduism, the 'mother' of all religions, the highest place in the hierarchy of faiths. His appropriation of the *bodhi* tree via the *vaṭa* tree shows his willingness to assimilate the Buddha and Buddhism in his post-sectarian teaching and charisma, while at the same time stressing his identity as Śiva.[59] When on 6 July 1963, the day of *gurupūrṇimā*,[60] he announced his future 'incarnation' as Prema Sāī – to be born in the State of Karnataka (Steel 1997: 204–05) – he linked the Sāī Bābā avatāric lineage to Śiva's mythology, that is, to a boon Śiva and Śakti would have granted to the seer Bharadvāja due to the latter's piousness in the preparation of a sacrifice taught to him by Indra. [61] On

58 On the crucial notion of *sanātanadharma*, see Halbfass (1988: 343–46).

59 Sathya Sāī Bābā spoke symbolically of the *aśvattha* as the tree of life. Kasturi reports:

> He says that the tree of life, the Aswattha, has its roots in the *ātman*. If that faith is absent, we dry up and are wafted hither and thither by every wind of fortune – wayward whiffs of transience. The trunk and the branches, the leaves and twigs of the tree of life are the ramifications of our contacts and commitments with the outer world, the kith and kin, the I and mine, the plus and minus into which life proliferates. The flowers of the tree are words, thoughts, and deeds of love; and the *ānanda* derived is the fruit. But, Baba says, the sweetness in the fruit is virtue, *seela*, good godly character. Without *seela*, which makes the fruit worthwhile, and the ātmic root which sustains the tree, life is a mere plowing of sands, the body is but fuel, fodder for vermin. (Kasturi 1974: 36–37)

The saint of Puttaparthi also said that *karmayoga* is the trunk of the tree of life, *bhaktiyoga* its branches, leaves and flowers, and *jñānayoga* its ripe fruit; see Gries and Gries (1993: 255).

60 This festival honoring the guru falls on the full moon day in the month of Āṣāḍha (June–July).

61 For an analysis of this claim and of the Bharadvāja myth, see Swallow (1982: 136–45).

this solemn occasion, Sathya Sāī Bābā presented himself as the *avatāra* of Śiva-Śakti.[62]

If through his wish-fulfilling tree the saint of Puttaparthi stressed his willingness to grant *bhukti*, i.e. to fulfill the needs and aims of his devotees in the realms of *kāma* (pleasure in all its forms) and *artha* (material wealth and worldly success), through his meditation tree he stressed his eagerness to grant *mukti* or liberation from the painful cycle of transmigration (*saṃsāra*), that is the highest of all legitimate goals of human life (*puruṣārtha*). The mission of the *avatāra* is to restore righteousness (*dharma*) and protect the good (*sādhu*), leading them to take refuge in him and realize their true nature through the 'austerity of knowledge' (*jñānatapas*).[63] As Sathya Sāī Bābā himself declared on various occasions:

> In my present *Avatar*, I have come armed with the fullness of the power of formless God to correct mankind, raise human consciousness and put people back on the right path of truth, righteousness, peace and love to divinity. (Sandweiss 1985: 236)

Through the implementation of the meditation tree, Sathya Sāī Bābā established himself as the guru of gurus, as none other than Śiva as 'lord of Yoga' (*yogeśvara*). Within an overall *bhakti*-oriented perspective, he highlighted the need to practice contemplation in order to discipline and silence once and for all what he used to call the 'monkey mind.'[64]

CONCLUSION

All in all, the three trees I have examined played a considerable role in setting the stage of Sathya Sāī Bābā's life and mission, being as it were the signposts of his advent (the *pārijāta*), of the disclosure of his divine

62 On 29 June 1963, Sathya Sāī Bābā had a stroke that caused the paralysis of the left side of his body. His severe illness lasted eight days. For a detailed report of the saint's sickness, miraculous recovery and momentous disclosure, see Kasturi (2012). On Sathya Sāī Bābā being both Śiva and Śakti, see Babb (1986: 159–201; 1987: 168–86). He stressed his Śiva-hood through the daily production of ashes (*vibhūti*) and through the emission of Śiva *liṅgas* from his mouth during Mahāśivarātri festivals; see Steel (1997: 113–19); Bhatnagar (2011); Rigopoulos (2013b: 181–83). Mahāśivarātri, 'the great night of Śiva,' is held on the fourteenth day of the dark fortnight of the month of Māgha (January–February).

63 See BhG IV.8–10.

64 On Sathya Sāī Bābā's *bhaktiyoga*, see Srinivas (2014: 261–79).

status (the tamarind as *kalpavṛkṣa*), and of his consecration as dispenser of the summum bonum of liberation (the *vaṭa*). If the *pārijāta* is a 'dream tree,' in the sense that it was appropriated by local hagiography through a 'revelation' that Sathya Sāī Bābā's paternal grandfather had in his sleep, the *kalpavṛkṣa* and *vaṭa* are real, physical trees that the saint of Puttaparthi deliberately consecrated. And yet the *pārijāta* is no less real than the other two, given that in the context of shared memory the distinction between fact and fiction is ultimately irrelevant.

To this day, these trees are at the center of a complex interplay of sacred narratives, combining the oral and literary dimensions in a shared idiom of recollection that crosses temporal boundaries. In particular, the *kalpavṛkṣa* and the *vaṭa* are powerful memorials celebrating the spiritual presence of the saint of Puttaparthi. Part and parcel of Sathya Sāī Bābā's transnational cult – whose center is nowadays constituted by the tomb (*samādhi*) housing his body[65] – these sites bring together memory and history, texts and practices, past and present. Devotees come to these trees both in order to share/retell the memories of the old days, as well as to experience here and now the living (*jāgṛta*) fragrance of the divine through the performance of an array of ritual observances and meditative techniques.[66]

As *sarvadevātmasvarūpa*, the embodiment of all gods, Sathya Sāī Bābā claimed to incorporate all deities in his post-sectarian persona. There is no doubt that his appropriation of the myths of the *pārijāta*, *kalpavṛkṣa* and *vaṭa/bodhi* trees proved remarkably efficacious in supporting his claim to divinity. In time, he grew into a veritable *viśvavṛkṣa*, a world-tree providing shade and shelter to the ever-expanding international gathering of his devotees.[67] He consistently presented himself as the quintessential godhead, beyond the boundaries of institutionalized religion, be it Hinduism, Buddhism, Christianity or Islam:

> I have come to repair the ancient highway to God.... I have not come on behalf of any sect or creed or religion. I have come to light the lamp of love in the hearts of all humanity. (Mason and Laing 1982: 225)

Along these universalistic lines, the *kalpavṛkṣa* as well as the *vaṭa* have come to be regarded as symbolic of a divine sap which enlivens all beings.

65 On Sathya Sāī Bābā's perfect body and the conceptualization of the body among his devotees, see Srinivas (2012: 185–205).

66 On the interplay of history, memory and a tree in the cult of the 13th-century Marathi poet-saint Jñāneśvar, see Novetzke (2009: 212–32).

67 See Kasturi (1974: 43).

This sap or essence is love, and it is not accidental that one of the saint's most frequent terms of address used to be *premasvarūpa*, 'embodiment of love.' Finally, the true nature of the *kalpavṛkṣa* – identified as Sathya Sāī Bābā *sub specie arboris* – is said to be none other than pure love:

> This *Prema* is My distinctive mark, not the creation of material objects or of health and happiness, by sheer exercise of Will. You might consider what you call 'miracles' as the most direct sign of Divinity, but the *Prema* that welcomes you all, blesses all, that makes Me rush to the presence of the seekers, the suffering and the distressed in distant lands or wherever they are, that is the real sign! It is that which declares that I am Sai Baba.[68] (Sathya Sai Baba 1967: 169–70)

ABBREVIATIONS AND REFERENCES

Tel. = Telugu Skt. = Sanskrit

Abbot 1974 — Abbott, J. (1974). *The Keys of Power. A Study of Indian Ritual and Belief*. Seacaucus, NJ: University Books.

Aitken 2004 — Aitken, B. (2004). *Sri Sathya Sai Baba. A Life*. New Delhi: Viking.

Ali 1974 — Ali, M.H. (1974). *Observations on the Mussulmauns of India*. Reprint 1832. Karachi: Oxford University Press.

Babb 1986 — Babb, L.A. (1986). *Redemptive Encounters. Three Modern Styles in the Hindu Tradition*. Berkeley: University of California Press.

Babb 1987 — Babb, L.A. (1987). 'Sathya Sai Baba's Saintly Play.' In Hawley, J.S. (ed.), *Saints and Virtues*, pp. 168–86. Berkeley: University of California Press.

Balu 1981 — Balu, Sh. (1981). *Living Divinity*. London: Sawbridge Enterprises.

BEH — Jacobsen, K.A., H. Basu, A. Malinar and V. Narayanan (eds.) (2009–2014). *Brill's Encyclopedia of Hinduism*. 6 vols. Leiden: E.J. Brill.

Bhatnagar 2011 — Bhatnagar, S.C. (2011). *Sai Vibhuti Prasadam and Its Significance (Based on Sai's Teachings). A Humble Offering to Bhagavan Sri Sathya Sai Baba*. Prasanthi Nilayam: Sri Sathya Sai Sadhana Trust Publications Division.

Bhattacharyya 1990 — Bhattacharyya, N.N. (1990). *A Glossary of Indian Religious Terms and Concepts*. New Delhi: Manohar.

BhG — *Bhagavadgītā*. Van Buitenen, J.A.B. (ed., tr.) (1981). *The Bhagavadgītā in the Mahābhārata*. Chicago: The University of Chicago Press.

BhP — *Bhāgavatapurāṇa*. Goswami, C.L. (tr.) (1952–1960). *Śrīmad Bhāgavata Mahāpurāṇa*. With Sanskrit text and English translation. 2 vols. Gorakhpur: Gītā Press.

68 On the centrality of love in Sathya Sāī Bābā's teachings, see Gries and Gries (1993: 109–13).

Bühnemann 2010 Bühnemann, G. (2010). 'Mandalas and Yantras.' BEH (vol. II): 560–73.

ChU *Chāndogya Upaniṣad*. In Olivelle 1998: 166–287.

Coomaraswamy 1984 Coomaraswamy, A.K. (1984). *L'Arbre Inversé*. Milano: Archè.

Crooke 1978 Crooke, W. (1978). *The Popular Religion and Folk-lore of Northern India*. 2 vols. Reprint 1896. New Delhi: Munshiram Manoharlal.

Dhere 2011 Dhere, R.C. (2011). *The Rise of a Folk God. Vitthal of Pandharpur*. New York: Oxford University Press.

Dikshitar 1995 Dikshitar, V.R.R. (1995). *The Purāṇa Index*. 3 vols. Reprint 1952. Delhi: Motilal Banarsidass.

Dubois 1990 Dubois, J.A. (1990). *Hindu Manners, Customs and Ceremonies*. Reprint 1906. New Delhi; Madras: Asian Educational Services.

Fandohan et al. 2012 Fandohan, B. et al. (2012). 'Which One Comes First, the Tamarind or the *Macrotermes termitarium*?' *Acta Botanica Gallica: Botany Letters*, 159(3): 345–55.

Gries and Gries 1993 Gries, D. and E. Gries. (1993). *An Index of Sathya Sai Speaks, Volumes I–XI. Covering Discourses by Bhagavan Sri Sathya Sai Baba 1953–1982*. Tustin, Ca.: Sathya Sai Book Center of America.

Gupta 1991 Gupta, S.M. (1991). *Plant Myths and Traditions in India*. Reprint 1971. New Delhi: Munshiram Manoharlal.

Halbfass 1988 Halbfass, W. (1988). *India and Europe. An Essay in Understanding*. Albany: State University of New York Press.

HV *Harivaṃśa*. P.L. Vaidya (ed.). (1969). *The Harivaṃśa, being the Khila or Supplement to the Mahābhārata*. 2 vols. Critical edition. Poona: Bhandarkar Oriental Research Institute.

Kasturi 1974 Kasturi, N. (1974). *Sathyam-Sivam-Sundaram. Part III*. Prasanthi Nilayam: Sri Sathya Sai Books and Publications.

Kasturi 1979 Kasturi, N. (1979). *Garland of 108 Precious Gems. Ashtothara Sathanama Rathnamala*. Bangalore: Sri Sathya Sai Education and Publication Foundation.

Kasturi 1980 Kasturi, N. (1980). *Sathyam-Sivam-Sundaram. Part I (1926–1960)*. Prasanthi Nilayam: Sri Sathya Sai Books and Publications.

Kasturi 1981a Kasturi, N. (1981). *Sathyam-Sivam-Sundaram. Part II*. Prasanthi Nilayam: Sri Sathya Sai Books and Publications.

Kasturi 1981b Kasturi, N. (1981). *Sathyam-Sivam-Sundaram. Part IV*. Prasanthi Nilayam: Sri Sathya Sai Books and Publications.

Kasturi 1982 Kasturi, N. (1982). *Loving God. Eighty-five Years under the Watchful Eye of the Lord*. Prasanthi Nilayam: Sri Sathya Sai Books and Publications.

Kasturi 1984 Kasturi, N. (1984). *Easwaramma. The Chosen Mother*. Prasanthi Nilayam: Sri Sathya Sai Books and Publications.

Kasturi 2012 Kasturi, N. (2012). *Siva Sakthi Swarupa*. Reprint 1963. Prasanthi Nilayam: Sri Sathya Sai Sadhana Trust Publications Division.

Khanna 1994 Khanna, M. (1994). *Yantra. The Tantric Symbol of Cosmic Unity*. Reprint 1979. London: Thames and Hudson.

König 1984 König, D. (1984). *Das Tor zur Unterwelt. Mythologie und Kult des Termitenhügels in der Schriftlichen und Mündlichen Tradition Indiens*. Wiesbaden: Franz Steiner.

KU *Kaṭha Upaniṣad*. In Olivelle 1998: 372–403.

Malla 2000 Malla, B.L. (2000). *Trees in Indian Art Mythology and Folklore*. New Delhi: Aryan Books International.

Mani 1975 Mani, V. (1975). *Purāṇic Encyclopaedia. A Comprehensive Dictionary with Special Reference to the Epic and Purāṇic Literature*. Delhi: Motilal Banarsidass.

Mason and Laing 1982 Mason, P. and R. Laing. (1982). *Sathya Sai Baba. Embodiment of Love*. London: Sawbridge.

MP *Matsyapurāṇa = Śrīmaddvaipāyanamunipraṇītaṃ Matsyapurāṇam* (1981). Puṇyākhyapattane: Ānandāśramasaṃskṛtagranthāvaliḥ, granthāṅkaḥ 54.

Murphet 1981 Murphet, H. (1981). *Sai Baba. Man of Miracles*. New Delhi: Macmillan.

Nanjundayya and Ananthakrishna Iyer 1930–1936 Nanjundayya, H.V. and R.B.L.K. Ananthakrishna Iyer. (1930–1936). *The Mysore Tribes and Castes*. 5 vols. Mysore: The Mysore University.

Narasappa et al. 1985 Narasappa, A.P., R. Narasappa, and R. Seethalakshmi (trs.). (1985). *Sahasradalakamala (1008 Names of Bhagavan Sri Sathya Sai Baba)*. Talkad: T.A. Appaji Gowda.

Narayan 1989 Narayan, K. (1989). *Storytellers, Saints, and Scoundrels. Folk Narrative in Hindu Religious Teaching*. Philadelphia: University of Pennsylvania Press.

Narayanan 2009 Narayanan, V. (2009). 'Veṅkaṭeśvara.' BEH (vol. I): 781–85.

Neelima 2013 Neelima, K. (2013). *Tirupati, a Guide to Life*. Noida, UP: Random House India.

Nikhilananda 1947 Nikhilananda, S. (1947). *Self-Knowledge. An English Translation of Śaṅkarāchārya's Ātmabodha with Notes, Comments, and Introduction*. Mylapore, Madras: Sri Ramakrishna Math.

Novetzke 2009 Novetzke, C.L. (2009). 'History, Memory, and Other Matters of Life and Death.' In: Pemberton, K. and M. Nijhawan (eds.), *Shared Idioms, Sacred Symbols, and the Articulation of Identities in South Asia*, pp. 212–32. New York: Routledge.

Nugteren 2005 Nugteren, A. (2005). *Belief, Bounty, and Beauty. Rituals around Sacred Trees in India*. Leiden: E.J. Brill.

Olivelle 1998 Olivelle, P. (ed. and tr.). (1998). *The Early Upaniṣads. Annotated Text and Translation*. New York: Oxford University Press.

Padmanaban 2000 Padmanaban, R. (2000). *Love is My Form. A Biographical Series on Sri Sathya Sai Baba*. Vol. 1: *The Advent (1926–1950)*. Bangalore: Sai Towers Publishing.

Pellegrini (forthcoming) Pellegrini, G. (forthcoming). 'Pistillo di rinuncia, fuoco senza fiamma! Riflessioni intorno alla simbologia del gelsomino notturno nel mondo indiano.' *Kervan. International Journal of Afro-Asiatic Studies*, 20.

Rao 1985 Rao, M.N. (1985). *Sathya Sai Baba. God as Man.* Tustin, Calif.: Sathya Sai Baba Society and Sathya Sai Book Center of America.

Rao 2007 Rao, S.S.P. (2007). 'Parijatapaharanamu.' In Lal, M. (ed.), *Encyclopaedia of Indian Literature.* Vol. IV, 3099–100. New Delhi: Sahitya Akademi.

Rice 1887 Rice, B.L. (1887). *Mysore: A Gazetteer Compiled for Government.* London: A. Constable & Co.

Rigopoulos 1993 Rigopoulos, A. (1993). *The Life and Teachings of Sai Baba of Shirdi.* Albany: State University of New York Press.

Rigopoulos 2013a Rigopoulos, A. (2013). 'Shirdi Sai Baba.' BEH (vol. V): 641–50.

Rigopoulos 2013b Rigopoulos, A. (2013). 'Vibhūti.' BEH (vol. V): 181–83.

Rigopoulos 2014 Rigopoulos, A. (2014). 'The Construction of a Cultic Center through Narrative: The Founding Myth of the Village of Puttaparthi and Sathya Sāī Bābā.' *History of Religions*, 54(2): 117–50.

Sandweiss 1985 Sandweiss, S.H. (1985). *Spirit and the Mind.* San Diego: Birth Day.

Sathya Sai Baba 1967 Sathya Sai Baba. (1967). *Sathya Sai Speaks.* Vol. 7. Prasanthi Nilayam: Sri Sathya Sai Books and Publications Trust.

Sathya Sai Baba 2008 Sathya Sai Baba. (2008). *Sathya Sai Speaks.* Vol. 3. Prasanthi Nilayam: Sri Sathya Sai Books and Publications Trust.

Schweig 2010 Schweig, G. (2010). 'Līlā.' BEH (vol. II): 793–97.

Smith 2013 Smith, F. (2013). 'Trees and Plants.' BEH (vol. V): 161–67.

Soneji 2004 Soneji, D. (2004). *Performing Satyābhāma. Text, Context, Memory and Mimesis in Telugu-Speaking South India.* Unpublished PhD dissertation, McGill University.

Srinivas 2008 Srinivas, S. (2008). *In the Presence of Sai Baba. Body, City, and Memory in a Global Religious Movement.* Leiden: E.J. Brill.

Srinivas 2010 Srinivas, T. (2010). *Winged Faith. Rethinking Globalization and Religious Pluralism through the Sathya Sai Movement.* New York: Columbia University Press.

Srinivas 2012 Srinivas, T. (2012). 'Relics of Faith: Fleshly Desires, Ascetic Disciplines and Devotional Affect in the Transnational Sathya Sai Movement.' In: Turner, B.S. (ed.), *Routledge Handbook of Body Studies*, pp. 185–205. London and New York: Routledge.

Srinivas 2013 Srinivas, T. (2013). 'Sathya Sai Baba.' BEH (vol. V): 625–33.

Srinivas 2014 Srinivas, S. (2014). 'Sathya Sai Baba and the Repertoire of Yoga.' In: Singleton, M. and E. Goldberg (eds.), *Gurus of Modern Yoga*, pp. 261–79. New York: Oxford University Press.

Steel 1997 Steel, B. (1997). *The Sathya Sai Baba Compendium. A Guide to the First Seventy Years.* York Beach, Maine: Samuel Weiser.

Steel 1999 Steel, B. (1999). *The Powers of Sathya Sai Baba.* Delhi: B.R. Publishing Corporation.

Swallow 1982 Swallow, D.A. (1982). 'Ashes and Powers: Myth, Rite and Miracle in an Indian God-man's Cult.' *Modern Asian Studies*, 16(1): 136–45.

Thurston and Rangachari 1909 Thurston, E. and K. Rangachari. (1909). *Castes and Tribes of Southern India.* VII vols. Madras: Government Press.

Upadhyaya 1965	Upadhyaya, K.D. (1965). 'Indian Botanical Folklore.' In: Sen Gupta, S. (ed.), *Tree Symbol Worship in India. A New Survey of a Pattern of Folk-Religion*, pp. 1–18. Calcutta: India Publications.
Valpey 2010	Valpey, K. (2010). 'Pūjā and Darśana.' BEH (vol. II): 380–94.
Venkatesan 2009	Venkatesan, A. (2009). 'Bhūdevī.' BEH (vol. I): 491–98.
Vijayakumari 1999	Vijayakumari. (1999). *Anyathā Saranam Nasthi. Other Than You Refuge there is None*. Ekrattuthangal, Chennai: Sai Shri Ram Printers.
VP	*Viṣṇupurāṇa*. Pathak, M.M. (ed.). (1997–1999). *Viṣṇupurāṇam*. Vadodara: Oriental Institute. GRETIL e-text available at: <http://gretil.sub.unigoettingen.de/gretil/1_sanskr/3_purana/vipce_pu.htm> (accessed 10 October 2015). Input by: Peter Schreiner.

Chapter 2

'Pagoda Tree': Plants and other Foliate Motifs on Indian Coins through History

SHAILENDRA BHANDARE[1]

'Shaking the Pagoda Tree' entered the English language as a metaphor for sudden enrichment through the association of South Indian gold coins, which the Westerners named 'Pagodas' (HJ 657). Enterprising British men would go to India and return rich in a relatively short time, having made their fortunes in the Asiatic trade, the monetary component of which comprised these gold 'Pagodas'. The entry in *Hobson-Jobson* also mentions that "... the idea of a coin tree may have arisen from the practice... of making cash in moulds, the design of which is based on the plan of a tree" (ibid.). But it also finds an echo in a similar metaphor in many Indian languages such as Marathi, Hindi and Gujarati, where money gained easily is envisaged as 'growing on trees.' Many young Indians would have heard this familiar retort from their seniors if they made a demand that was beyond the usual purchasing power of the household – 'Do you think money grows on trees?' Bringing the themes of money and trees together, this serves as an excellent starting point for our journey into how trees have been shown on Indian money through its history of over two millennia. In this exposition, we will see how the depictions worked in a visual sense, what particular cultural and historical connections they might have invoked and what, at least in some instances, were the specific roles these depictions played.

It will be appropriate to provide an outline of Indian monetary history to situate this paper in time and space. The date of inception of coinage in India is a hotly debated topic, but it cannot date much later than the

1 Shailendra Bhandare is Assistant Keeper (South Asian Numismatics), Heberden Coin Room, Ashmolean Museum, University of Oxford (UK).

fifth century BCE.[2] The history of coinage then follows a discursive trajectory which reflects the traditional periodization of Indian history, into 'Ancient,' 'Medieval' subdivided into 'Hindu' and 'Islamic,' followed by the 'Colonial' or 'Modern.' In the 'Ancient' period, distinguishing categories of 'Indian' versus the 'Foreign' are used; the latter trope accommodating coins struck by non-indigenous ruling entities like the 'Indo-Greeks,' the 'Indo-Scythians,' the 'Indo-Parthians' (c. 250 BCE–100 CE), the Kushans (c. 50–350 CE) and the Hunnic tribes (c. 450–650 CE). The 'Indian' trope is represented by the 'Empires,' namely the Mauryas (c. 340–297 BCE), the 'Sungas' (c. 320–100 BCE), the kingdoms of the Sangam Age in the Deep South (c. 150 BCE–200 CE), the Satavahanas (c. 150 BCE–250 CE) and the Guptas (c. 320–550 CE). Interspersed among these are coinages issued by a host of local monarchies, city-states and 'tribal' republics. The coinage of the Gupta Empire is often seen as a paradigm for the 'Golden Age' of Ancient India. Between the Guptas and the advent of Islam from c. the tenth or eleventh centuries, Indian coinage is widely believed to have been in a state of 'limbo,' with demonetization and de-urbanization dominating the economic milieu, but lately this view has been coming under persistent criticism.

With the advent of Islam, the look of Indian coinage changed drastically. As depictions of motifs and icons are not encouraged in the Islamic coinage tradition, inscriptions and calligraphy came to dominate the expressive genius of the Indian coin-engraver. For first few centuries (c. 1200–1500) under the rule of various Sultanates, Islamic coinage in India maintained a puritan and plain design, showing not much more than the name, the (often lofty) titles of the sovereign and the date/place where the coin was struck.

This austere look changed with the advent of the Mughals, particularly under the aegis of a syncretic Indo-Persianate culture fostered under the 'Great' Mughals, beginning with Akbar (1556–1605). *Nastaʿlīq*, the 'heavy-hanging' calligraphy of Farsi script became the norm and coinage once again reflected the aesthetic sense and inclination of the rulers with verse inscriptions in Farsi emerging as the most favored form of coin legends. The period also saw the rise and popularity of the silver 'rupee' as a national and international denomination, bolstered by strict minting practices under the heavily centralized apparatus of the Mughal Empire, which led to a uniform and trustworthy production of the coinage.

The influx of silver for Mughal coinage was largely facilitated by the trading activities of Europeans sailing to the Indian coasts. Although

2 For a detailed discussion, see Cribb (1985).

European presence in India had been established in the early sixteenth century through the Portuguese, they followed the model of political conquest to undertake commerce and their coinage reflects this attitude. But other European entities, like the British, the Dutch and the French, rested their activities on joint-stock companies founded in Europe. Their main objective was to trade and not to gain political control – at least to begin with. They all struck coinage largely in the name of the reigning Mughal emperor, by obtaining a permit to undertake it, usually through one of his appointees.

The British East India Company emerged supreme in this situation and by the mid-eighteenth century their approach was increasingly towards trading benefits accrued as a result of political intervention and flexing of a superior technological 'muscle' in terms of warfare equipment and tactics. Coinage however, continued to be struck in the name of the Mughal emperor because he was seen as the font of sovereign legitimacy by the general population, who would not accept circulatory coins struck with any other name. This situation changed only in the mid-nineteenth century when the 'Uniform Coinage Act' was passed in 1835, enabling the monetary integration of the constituent provinces of British India, and the effigies of the British monarch appeared on Indian coins for the first time. After the Revolt of 1857–1859, the government of the Company was supplanted by the British Crown and the change was witnessed in coinage, where a new, more 'regal' portrait of Queen Victoria was employed. The tradition was continued till Indian independence in 1947.

The political expansion of the British in India resulted in the creation of another India – the one characterized by its *mahārājas* and a host of other chieftains. Some of these traced their ancestries well back to the medieval times. They represented the 'Indian Princely States,' subservient to the British in matters of inter-state and international relations and most fiscal and financial issues, but wielding considerable civil and judicial powers. As vestiges of the older ruling order they became 'bastions' of feudal and traditional kingship and orthodoxy, steeping their conduct in a myriad of social, religious and traditional hierarchies. As notionally 'independent' princes they often sought to assume the right to mint coinage, which was contested by their colonial overlords who were more interested in streamlining circulatory currency in order to achieve fiscal stability and superiority. These dynamics initially resulted in a period of chaos, which was slowly remedied by legislation and a steady supply of machine-made coins which alleviated the demand for circulatory coins. The silver crisis of the late-nineteenth century finally made the manufacture of coins a loss-making proposition for most princely states and very few of them continued to strike their own coins into the twentieth century.

PLANTS AND TREES ON INDIAN COINS: THE RELIGIOUS CONNECTIONS

Plants have been a part of Indic religious systems for over two millennia and tree-worship has been a focus of attention of many scholars of religion and culture. In the nineteenth century, James Fergusson's study about depictions of tree-worship from the Buddhist monuments of Sanchi and Amaravati (Fergusson and Waterhouse 1868) provides a starting point of an interdisciplinary inquiry into the practice, glossing the textual evidence and comparing it with what visual and material culture had to offer. Philpot's study (1897) spans a great geographical and cultural sweep, in which she elaborates on the practice of tree-worship from the Mediterranean to the East, and discusses various European cultural practices in which the cult of the tree survived from the pre-Christian past. Most recently, Haberman (2013) has provided an anthropological study of such practices, with a view to restore the subject of tree worship to the broader discipline of religious studies.

The trope of tree worship appears to have carried into Vedic religions as can be seen through references to trees which belong to 'beings which are divinely animated,' called the 'Lords of the Forest,' as described by Oldenberg (1993: 128–29). This concept perhaps is deep-rooted in the 'popular' element of Indic religions and is further developed in Buddhism, where a range of 'spirits' of 'deities' are associated with trees. Usually these were of the *yakṣa* (male) or *yakṣī/yakṣiṇī* (female) categories. They were guardians of the locale and could be of the benevolent or malevolent kind – and either or both of these needed to be propitiated to bring forth desired results. The basis of propitiation considered transgression into their realm as an 'affront' to these guardians. They therefore needed to be pacified with offerings to keep them happy.

While most trees associated with such guardians were very much part of the quotidian existence, there are other trees which are 'heavenly' or mythical, which have qualities associated with plenitude. *Kalpavṛkṣa*, or the 'wish-fulfilling tree' is one such heavenly tree which grants earthly and heavenly pleasures to those who have enough merit to make demands from it. However, 'heavenly trees' are not confined to the category of fantasy. There exist myths about earthly trees which often posit them in the heavens as part of lore or myths. Some of these stories make some trees, flowers and leaves particular 'favorites' of certain gods and goddesses, and elaborate ritual complexes are often created around them. The 'thousand-leaves-offering' (*sahasrabilvapatra arcana*) practiced in Śaivite worship, or a similar offering of the 'holy basil' leaves performed by Viṣṇu-worshipers, are good examples of such ritual practice. Both practices involve a steady offering of one leaf at a time accompanied by hymns or *mantras*, and can last for hours.

Alongside religious beliefs and ritual practices, trees or plants with their parts such as leaves, fruit or flowers are also associated in a 'totemic' fashion with a large number of Indian clans, particularly of the 'warrior' castes. The plant or plant objects associated in such a fashion are often worshiped in their own totemic right by the clans or groups of people to whom they belong. They can be included in a variety of cultural and ritual practices. But some can also have 'taboos' associated with them, which often results in their total exclusion from social customs and traditions.

PLANTS ON ANCIENT INDIAN COINS

It is in this context that we need to understand and appreciate the representation of trees on the earliest Indian coins. By far the earliest 'tree' depictions are not of entire trees but of branches or individual leaves, and they occur on the so-called 'pre-Imperial,' or 'archaic' silver punch-marked coins, dateable to an epoch before the expansion of Magadha, circa 400–300 BCE (figure 2.1). The representation is symbolic and schematic – shown

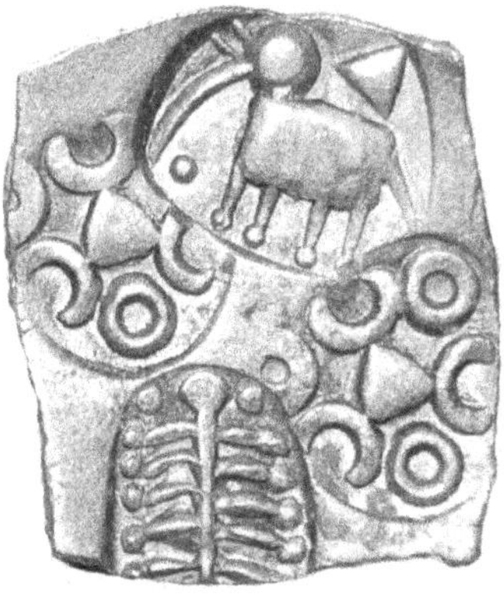

Figure 2.1. Silver punch-marked coin, Godavari Valley, Maharashtra, c. 350–300 BCE, with 'palm frond' as one of the punches.

as a single branch with many leaves. Much like other symbols we find on this class of uninscribed and entirely symbolic coins, the exact meaning of the 'tree'/'branch' symbols cannot be ascertained. However, it is certain that they are all drawn from a 'cultural collective' or 'pool' of symbolism and as such they must have been familiar to those who used the coins. In a purely numismatic sense, there is room to believe that the symbols served a mint-related function, to indicate where a coin was struck, when and perhaps by whom.

The religious context of the tree is further augmented in coins attributed to the Magadhan Empire, which are found all over India and were the first 'universalized' currency of the subcontinent. Here, alongside 'stand-alone' trees or foliate parts thereof, we also find trees enclosed in a railing, associated with a cow-like animal, or emanating from the top of an arched hill. Some of these depictions perhaps had a Buddhist connotation. It is not possible to discern what particular trees these symbols represent but it is certain from the articulation of their leaves and their general arboreal structure that they are intended to be shown as belonging to specific sorts. A few, such as a palm-like tree with typical fan-shaped leaves with fruit hanging underneath, could be discerned. Like the symbols on the predecessor coins, the exact meaning of these symbols still eludes us, but we can be certain that their context is drawn from a common cultural pool.

The symbols that we see on the Magadhan coins develop further on the coins of the successor issuing authorities, attributed to the so-called 'Sunga' period (c. 185–50 BCE). Here for the first time, we see trees that can be identified and associated with various religious and cultic movements which popularized their worship. The 'sacred tree-in-railing' symbol becomes ubiquitous in this period and appears on a host of inscribed and uninscribed series of Indian coins. On copper punch-marked coins, bearing the name of local dynasts, from the urban center of Vidisha, dated to c. 150 BCE, we find a tree with an umbrella placed at the top of its stem, thereby indicating it was a venerated tree (figure 2.2). On some coins, additional objects indicating veneration, such as parasols, are shown attached to the cardinal points of the railing that surrounds the tree. Of course, the depiction is highly stylized and schematic owing to the fact that a coin never offers space large enough for the artist to show a realistic perspective. But there are some rare instances, in which the tree in railing symbol is shown in a three-dimensional perspective, rather than the more usual, and flat, two-dimensional one. This can be seen on coins of the ancient city-state of Vārānā (present-day Bulandshahr in Uttar Pradesh), struck in the name of a local ruler named Gomitra (figure 2.3).

Figure 2.2. Copper punch-marked coin of Bhumidatta, a king in Eastern Malwa, c. 150 BCE, having a tree topped with a parasol as the central punch.

Figure 2.3. Coin of Gomitra, a king in the Western Gangetic Valley, Bulandshahr district, Uttar Pradesh, c. 100 BCE, showing venerated trees in 3-D perspective on both sides. The obverse has a palm tree within a railing.

That the tree was an object of veneration is also shown by contextual alignment of the tree motif in association with other religious symbols. Some of these coins are found in very specific locations and therefore a regional style can be made out in these depictions. Thus, a particular sort of tree, with leaves emanating upwards from horizontal branches is seen on coins from Mathura and another very specific form of tree, where each horizontal branch has three further branches, is seen on coins encountered at the ancient city of Kaushambi, near Allahabad (figure 2.4) Surrounding the tree-in-railing motif is a host of other symbols – some of which (such as the elephant) allude to kingship, some others (like a banner) allude to cultic or ritual practice, and yet others (like a river with aquatic creatures in it) locate the position of the tree in a 'sacred landscape.' Situating the tree in amidst what are purely religious symbols is best evident on silver coins of King Amoghabhūti of the Kuṇinda people, whose kingdom nestled in the Himalayan foothills during the first century BCE (figure 2.5). Here the

Figure 2.4. Uninscribed copper cast coin of Kaushambi region, Allahabad, Uttar Pradesh, c. 100 BCE, with a parallel-branched stylized tree within railing depicted on the reverse.

Figure 2.5. Silver drachm of Amoghabhūti, the king of the Kuṇinda people, Himachal Pradesh, early decades of the first century BCE, showing a tree within railing with a host of other religious symbols.

tree is depicted amongst the *svastika*, the *triratna*, the *nandipada* and the *śrīvatsa*.

An example of a tree motif associated with a particular religious cult is the palm tree that is evident predominantly on coins of the city-state of Erikachha, or modern day Erach,[3] located on the banks of the river Betwa (Skt. *Vetravatī*). It is depicted in various fashions; some depictions are more realistic and some others very much schematic (figure 2.6). This has direct reference to a hero-cult named *Pāñcarātra*, involving the worship of five heroes, which was later assimilated into the Vaiṣṇava fold of Hinduism. In lore associated with this cult there is a story that involves the palm tree. In this story, Balarama, who is one of the *Pāñcarātra* heroes, has a fight with a demon in form of an ass as part of his heroics. He flings the ass on the top of a tall palm tree and the demon is killed by the pointed branches of the palm running through his flesh. On some coins, the palm is depicted on the top of a hill. In this representation it is possible that a reference to a cultic shrine situated atop a hill is being made. It is also plausible that the symbol, particularly in its schematic form, is referring to a cultic monument rather than a natural tree. Indeed we know of a massive palm-tree capital sculpted in stone which once stood atop a stone pillar which was found at Pawaya, in the same region as Erach (presently in the Gujari Mahal Museum, Gwalior).

Figure 2.6. Copper punch-marked coin of the city state of Erikachha (modern Erach in Eastern Uttar Pradesh), c. 150 BCE, with two punches showing sacred trees, one clearly being a palm.

3 The name 'Erikachha' is derived from Skt. *ekakakṣa* (var. *erakakṣa*), which indicates a sort of reed-grass.

TREES ON GANDHARAN COINS: 'EAST MEETS WEST'

The region of Gandhara, located in the Northwest part of the Indian subcontinent, witnessed a most amazing syncretism of Eastern and Western cultures during c. 200 BCE–300 CE. The region was ruled in succession by the Indo-Greeks, the Indo-Scythians and the Indo-Parthians. Greek culture, brought into the region by Alexander the Great's armies and perpetuated under his successors the Seleucids and the Greco-Bactrians, fused with local Indian culture, religion and belief systems. Greek cults like that of Dionysus flourished, adopting Indian 'visual language'. These developments are reflected in visual and material culture of the region, to which coins are no exception.

On coins of Indo-Greek rulers Agathocles and Pantaleon, dated to c. 195–185 BCE, we come across a depiction of a grapevine, symbolizing the cultic association of the god with wine-making. A panther stands in its front, which is a direct reference to mythical account of Dionysus's journey and conquest of the East (figure 2.7). The portrait of Bacchus on the obverse completes the Dionysian context. The Indo-Greek coinage is particularly rich in divine depictions, and trees and plants often feature on coins as divine associates. Palm fronds, associated with Greek divinities like Dioskuroides and Nike, are shown either in association with anthropomorphic depictions of such deities, or as 'stand-alone' symbols, showing the presence of these gods by proxy. The motif of vines with bunches of

Figure 2.7. Cupro-nickel coin of Agathocles, Indo-Greek ruler in Greater Gandhara, c. 195–185 BCE, showing a panther in front of a grapevine in reference to the myth of Dionysus.

grapes is also evident on some near-contemporary coins associated with the region of Taxila, which bear no inscriptions (figure 2.8). The Indic belief that trees were associated with guardian spirits such as *yakṣas* and *yakṣiṇīs* is well-encapsulated in a depiction of a female figure emanating out of a *Ficus* tree with characteristic leaves that we see on coins of Indo-Scythian kings Maues and Azes (c. mid-first century BCE). True to the popular artistic idiom, she is shown in a 'Greek' garb, with her body draped in a dress with 'Greek' folds articulated by lines around her torso (figure 2.9).

Figure 2.8. Uninscribed die-struck copper coin, commonly attributed to Taxila, c. 100–50 BCE, with representation of vine and bunches of grape.

Figure 2.9. Copper coin of Indo-Scythian ruler Azes, c. 58–35 BCE, with depiction of a 'tree spirit' or *yakṣī* emanating out of the branches of a Pipal tree on the reverse.

If there is one Indic icon that is exemplary in its association with plants, it is Śrī Lakṣmī, the goddess of fertility and plenitude – and by implication, money. The plant she is closely associated with is the lotus (*Nelumbo* spp.), the symbol of 'primordial creation.' She is lauded as 'lotus-seated,' 'lotus-born,' 'lotus-eyed,' 'lotus-colored,' et cetera in the *Śrīsūktam*, one of the *Ṛgveda khila* hymns. One of her earliest dateable representations is found on the silver coins of Indo-Scythian ruler Azilises (c. 70–55 BCE). Here she is shown standing in the center of a lotus-bloom, making a gesture of reassurance. Two elephants lustrate her with waters sprinkled from their trunks; they too stand on long-stemmed lotuses (figure 2.10). The symbolism this icon invokes is of Lakṣmī as the Earth Principle, being rendered fertile with waters brought along by dark rain-bearing clouds which are the metaphoric elephants. The icon of Gajalakṣmī', or elephant-lustrated Lakṣmī, is also witnessed on numerous coins from a wide area of India, covering the Gangetic Valley, Central India and the Deccan.

By far the most attractive representation of the goddess Lakṣmī is found on gold coins of the Gupta emperors Chandra Gupta II, Kumara Gupta and Skanda Gupta (figure 2.11). Here she is not shown with elephants, but sits in the center of a majestic lotus bloom, using its inverted cone-shaped gynoecium as her pedestal. She also carries a long-stemmed lotus bloom in one of her hands. Her depictions became a standard feature on most Gupta coins and her lotus-mount may or may not be always shown, but she is invariably shown holding the long-stemmed lotus flower.

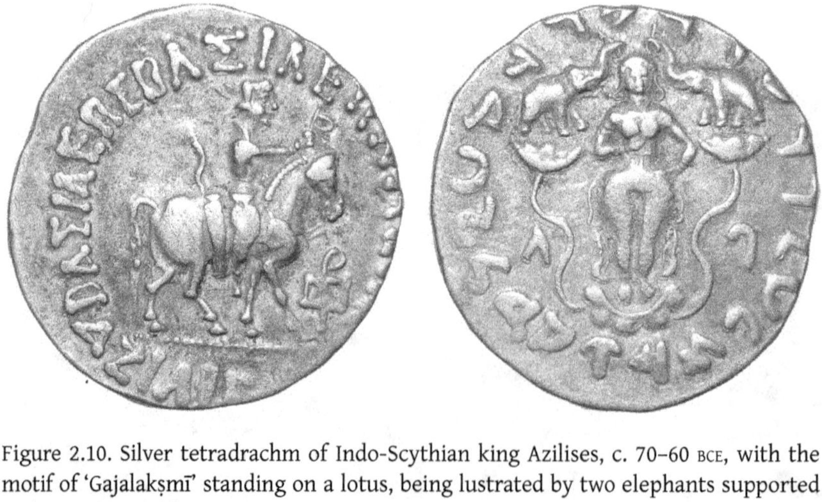

Figure 2.10. Silver tetradrachm of Indo-Scythian king Azilises, c. 70–60 BCE, with the motif of 'Gajalakṣmī' standing on a lotus, being lustrated by two elephants supported on long-stemmed lotuses.

Figure 2.11. Gold dinar of Chandra Gupta II (c. 375–415 CE), with the depiction of Lakṣmī seated cross-legged on a large lotus bloom and holding a long-stemmed lotus in her hand.

PLANTS AS DECORATIVE MOTIFS

With the advent of Islamic-style coinages in India, anthropomorphic or figurative depictions became very rare on coins. Images of deities or rulers and their attributes no longer found a place in coin design. But the situation rapidly changed with Mughal coins, particularly from Akbar's reign onwards, where plant-life assumed an entirely different role. Mughal coins were viewed as 'calligraphic panels' by their Mughal designers. Calligraphy in itself had been perfected as an art form in Islamicate cultures from Morocco to the East Indies. Mughal calligraphic art was heavily influenced by the Persian schools, in accordance with the general 'Persianization' of the Mughal court culture in the late sixteenth century, which was a result of a very active movement of 'peoples of skills' across the wider Islamic world. As skillful artisans, calligraphers and scribes were patronized by a number of Muslim courts in India. Coinage, being a 'reflection of the sovereign's divine duty' was initially out of bounds for figurative depictions, but under the Mughals, this attitude changed considerably.

A vast number of Mughal coins show a variety of foliate motifs which act as a 'backdrop' for the calligraphic inscriptions they bear. In this role they are comparable to the borders and decorations often seen in contemporary calligraphic panels and/or miniature paintings, and in their execution show a very close similarity in the choice of floral motifs with these manifestations. Tulips, narcissi, irises, lilies, roses, peonies – all with their leaves, buds and shoots – feature prominently as decorations on coins (figure 2.12).

Figure 2.12. Gold mohur of Akbar (1556–1605 CE), minted at Asirgarh, with deployment of delicate floral and foliate motifs as a backdrop for the depictions on obverse and reverse.

As a backdrop for calligraphy, they work in two fashions – firstly, to provide a contrast of small and delicate lines for the bold and thick letter-forms which are usually employed in the *Nastaʿlīq* style and secondly, to offer a visual 'counterpoise' to the heaviness of the flow of this script, the letter forms of which are usually 'base-heavy.' The arrangement of the floral backdrops many times takes some of the essential features of the letter-forms, such as bold dots or *nuqtas*, as a starting or emanating point; in some instances the *nuqtas* themselves blend into a floral form such as a bud (figure 2.13). The choice, arrangement and disposition of

Figure 2.13. Silver rupee of Shahjahan (1627–1658), minted at Daulatabad, with intricate floral designs that act as a 'bed' for the letters of the Persian calligraphy to lie on.

the floral motifs thus presents a very carefully thought artistic dynamic. As coin-making was a heavily technical process, it is conceivable that the choice of such features must have involved interactions between different artisans such as the 'pen-and-ink' calligrapher or painter/illustrator, and the metal-engraver who would ultimately transfer these motifs onto the implements or 'dies' used to strike coins, usually made of steel.

Floral decorations often appear as 'borders' to calligraphic cartouches on coins, too – much like they do in case of Mughal and Persian miniature paintings, helping them to be visually 'framed' in an aesthetically pleasing way and acting as a technical feature for the coin dies to establish their margins (figure 2.14). These aspects draw very close parallels with the Mughal 'Art of the Book,' conforming to a Mughal 'style' or artistic idiom which pervades other expressions of artistic form and content, such as architectural decoration. The floral decorative motifs on Mughal coins therefore suggest a close connection and a 'dialogue' between numismatic art and the other, more familiar and extensively studied visual art forms of the period. They also shed important light on how the coins were viewed as a 'text' in miniature by the political authorities. Noteworthy in this context is the choice of using Persian verse forms for coin inscriptions. Along with decorations, these poetic legends make the coins almost like compact and succinct metallic 'manuscripts' with texts which circulate, much like an illuminated manuscript would change hands from patron to patron, but on a much larger scale, through their audience who used the coins primarily as a medium of exchange.

Figure 2.14. Gold mohur of Jahangir (1605–1627), struck at Agra with floral borders decorating elegant Persian inscriptions.

PLANTS AS FUNCTIONAL ASPECTS OF COIN DESIGN

With the advent and preponderance of a coinage that was entirely inscriptional, a need to 'recognize' the coin mattered a lot for people who could not read what was written on it. Together with this rather subjective and simple need, other complicated aspects such as how coins were issued, exchanged and circulated, resulted in a phenomenon which saw the employment of plants, flowers and other foliate motifs being put to a very practical use – that of attribution and identification. This was largely an eighteenth century phenomenon, when the edifice of the Mughal Empire began to crumble. The emperors became progressively weaker, the courtiers stronger, and political machinations with various factions in the court rife with confusion, assertions and skullduggery. There were also several 'regional nationalists,' like the Marathas from the Deccan, or the Rajputs and Jats from Western India, and the Sikhs in the Punjab, who came out in defiance of the Mughal authority. Added to this, there were ambitious Western mercantile interests like the British and French 'East India Companies' which embroiled themselves in various local disputes in order to stake a claim to a slice of the political 'cake.'

All these aspects contributed to the rapid decentralization of Mughal political authority. Coinage suffered considerably as a result. To replenish the ever-depleting coffers and to finance campaigns, the emperors after Aurangzeb (1658–1707) delegated or 'farmed out' the right to operate mints to various aspirants and contenders. Some resurgent authorities even assumed the right on their own accord. Over the course of half a century, the centrally controlled and trustworthy Mughal monetary apparatus had almost vanished. Mints proliferated throughout the subcontinent and the Rupee, which had been the bedrock of financial stability under the Mughal rule, fragmented into several regional and political varieties.

But in spite of these developments and the lack of power on the part of later Mughal emperors, the coinage remained, at least nominally, in their name. This was partly due to the popular reverence towards the dynasty, which was seen as the font of sovereign legitimacy, and partly due to political and economic realities. This led to a curious situation where nominally, all coins would be recognized as 'Mughal' but in reality they were issued by a host of different authorities. This coinage thus qualified to be classed as 'quasi-Mughal.' To recognize who was the real issuer, it became necessary to add a visually identifiable aspect into the coin design. This is where plants, trees and foliate motifs came in handy.

The system of employing such motifs as identity markers is already evident in the case of some Mughal mints. Originally intended to be pure decorations, some leafy designs became mint-specific. For example on coins of the Multan mint, a sprig-like ornament adorned the coin inscription at a particular place in the context of its design (figure 2.15), which probably acted as a 'mint-mark.' But now such marks began to carry a variety of meanings which were rooted in the political, religious or social leanings of the authority that issued the coin. In this context, they became 'identity markers' in more than one sense – they identified the coin and they also identified who the issuers were and what were their political or socio-religious proclivities. Some political entities emergent in the eighteenth century, like the Sikhs, did not issue coins in the name of the Mughals but the principle language of inscriptions on their coins remained Farsi. Therefore in terms of coin design the deployment of marks served a purpose very similar to that on the 'quasi-Mughal' coins.

Three examples illustrate plant motifs employed in these ways amidst an inscriptional Farsi coin design. The first is the symbol of a branch, popularly called a *jhāṛ* (tree) which appears on the mid-eighteenth century coins of Jaipur. Typically it occupies a significant 'space' on the face of the coin – above the mint-indicator word of the inscription and beside the details of the regnal year of the Mughal emperor, in whose name the coin is nominally struck (figure 2.16). The coin is appropriately referred to as *jhāṛ-śāhī* (tree-styled). The symbol consistently appeared on coins of Jaipur through the nineteenth and twentieth centuries and served as an 'identity marker' for its coins – so much so, that in the twentieth century,

Figure 2.15. Silver rupee of Farrukhsiyar (1712–1719), minted at Multan, with a floral sprig appearing on the reverse as a decoration that doubles as a 'mint identifier.'

Figure 2.16. Gold mohur of Jaipur state, struck in the name of Bahadur Shah II, the last Mughal emperor, with the 'tree' or *jhāṛ* symbol which became a specific identifier for the state.

even after the launch of 'modern' machine-struck coins with the name of the state and its mahārāja clearly spelled out, it continued to prominently feature as a 'symbol' of Jaipur state money. In this way, it is comparable to a 'brand' symbol. It is worth noting that the *jhāṛ* symbol appears to have no particular socio-religious context behind its employment. Its journey in functionality in terms of coin design appears to be an entirely natural evolution, from being a 'mint mark' to becoming a 'visual marker' for the sovereign authority of the state.

The second example where a foliate motif serves as an 'identity marker' is that of a 'leaf' mark on coins of the Sikhs. Unlike the Jaipur example just described, this is more than just a functional mark which evolves into a 'visual marker.' The leaf here can actually be identified as that of a *ber* tree (*Ziziphus jujuba* Mill.) – its shape and characteristic palmately convergent reticulate venation are the identifying markers (figure 2.17). This tree is particularly sacred to Sikhs and there are no less than three *ber* trees, each associated with its own myths, within the sacred precinct of the Golden Temple at Amritsar. They form a part of the sacred complex of the pre-eminent Sikh shrine, with the *Dukh-bhañjanī* ('Sorrow-remover') *ber* tree even having its own temple. It is noteworthy that Sikh coins, although they employ Farsi script, do not bear the name of the Mughal emperor; instead, their legends invoke the last Sikh Guru Gobind Singh, who is accredited with sovereign legitimacy from Guru Nanak the first Guru. Sikh coin legends are therefore connected with the hagiocentric basis of Sikh

Figure 2.17. Silver rupee of Ranjit Singh, Mahārāja of the Punjab (1799–1839), with the symbol of the *ber* leaf on reverse, Amritsar mint.

sovereignty. The symbol of the *ber* leaf, as an object intimately associated with the most sacred Sikh shrine which was the seat of the continuation of this tradition, fits in well with this context. It was first employed on the coins of the Amritsar mint, but as the Sikh realms spread, it appeared on coins of many other mints, including Multan, Peshawar and Kashmir. On some coins of Amritsar mint, we find other aspects of the *ber* tree – like its flowers, or a bunch of fruit – also employed as marks of Sikh sovereignty.

The use of the *ber* leaf was not confined to Sikh coins alone. As numismatic motifs often are, it was carried over to issues of other states which were feudatory to the Sikhs. In this way, it also featured on the coins of the Dogra rulers of Jammu. After the Dogra ruler Gulab Singh purchased Kashmir from the British in the mid-nineteenth century, this motif was carried on the coins of Jammu and Kashmir state and employed as a mark on coins struck in the mints of Jammu and Srinagar. However, it later lost its 'Sikh' character on these coins and appeared in the form of a turban ornament, shaped more ornately in a 'paisley' fashion.

Two instances where a foliate symbol served as an identity/mint mark illustrate how numismatic symbols link up with the religious leanings of a particular issuer or head of state (in contrast with the Sikh coins described above, where a numismatic symbol represented a religion and sovereignty rested within it). This is best illustrated on the coins of Indore state, initiated under the dowager Queen Ahilya Bai Holkar (1767–1795). The Holkar family was ardently Śaivite and as such its coins employ marks with a

Figure 2.18. Silver ½-rupee of Indore state, struck during the reign of Ahilya Bai Holkar (1767–1795), with the emblem of the *bel* leaf and *liṅga*, as a sign of her devotion to Śiva.

particular Śaiva affinity. The symbol of the *liṅga* occurs on them but so does the characteristically trifoliate *bel* leaf (*Aegle marmelos* (L.) Corrêa), which is associated with Śiva as being his 'favorite' (figure 2.18). On some copper coins of her time, a branch of the *bel* tree is shown hanging on top of a *liṅga* in profile, in front of which is shown a seated bull, identified as Nandi, the sacred bull associated with Śiva. Together the design conjures up a neat Śaivite context.

The other example where a flower served to distinguish a mint was at the Maratha mint of Phulgaon, near Pune, in the early nineteenth century. The principle currency of the region consisted of silver rupees bearing the mark of an elephant goad, popularly known as *ankuśi* in Marathi. *Ankuśi* rupees were struck under license issued by the Maratha government from a number of places, but the chief mint was located at Pune, the Maratha center of power. When Bajirao II, the Maratha Peshwa (1796–1818) took a fancy to the picturesque village of Phulgaon, located on the banks of the river Bheema in 1814, he decided to 'urbanize' it as an estuarine retreat. Together with the creation of several mansions and embankments, a mint was also established here. The design of the coins produced here was in principle similar to the *ankuśi* currency of Pune, but a small Hibiscus flower was added to the design (figure 2.19). Both the elephant goad and the Hibiscus flower are associated with Gaṇeśa, the patron deity of the brahmin Peshwas. The Peshwas were known to be ardent worshipers of the elephant-headed god and followed a particular sect named Gānapatya

Figure 2.19. Silver rupee of Phulgaon mint, struck during the reign of Maratha Peshwa Baji Rao II (1796–1818), with the symbol of a Hibiscus flower added to the reverse design.

which centred on Gaṇeśa worship. The addition of a flower was also a pun on the location of the mint, because the word *phul* in the name 'Phulgaon' means 'flower' in the Marathi language.

TREES AS ALLEGORIES

Pictorial coinage reappeared in India when the East India Company's government passed the 'Uniform Coinage Act' in 1835 and introduced a new coinage in all its constituent presidencies. These coins were machine-made in newly equipped mints in Bombay, Calcutta and Madras. They had the bust of William IV, the ruling British monarch, and their design was 'Western,' largely employing the English language, the Roman script and features such as a vertical milling on the edges. It was a tri-metallic coinage – comprising gold 'mohurs' or 'ashrafis', silver 'rupees' and fractions, and copper fractions of the 'anna'.

It is in the gold regime of this new coinage that a tree features prominently – this time as a part of an allegorical representation of Britain's supremacy in the 'Orient.' This was embodied in a design known as 'Flaxman's Lion and Palm Tree' and as the name suggests it was the creation of John Flaxman, a prominent British sculptor of the early nineteenth century (figure 2.20). Romanticism and neo-Classicism were the dominant artistic trends in Flaxman's time. The study of Classical art and

Figure 2.20. Gold two-mohur coin of the East India Company showing the allegory of 'British Empire in the East' through the 'lion and palm tree' design of John Flaxman, 1835.

its re-employment in contemporary design was a major feature of these trends, and numismatic portraiture and motifs were no exception. The motif of the 'palm tree' to allegorically symbolize the 'Orient' was first evident in the art of French medals of the Napoleonic period. It was most likely rooted in Napoleon's encounter with Egypt and also in the fact that the palm featured as a motif on some Roman 'conquest coinage' struck to celebrate the conquest of Eastern regions such as Judaea.

Flaxman artistically made the palm tree a backdrop for a majestic British lion which had already been a familiar emblem in English and Scottish heraldry and had served as an emblem of the 'Empire.' Its association with the palm tree thus became an allegoric reference to the Empire's presence in the East. The 'lion-and-palm' design featured on the East India Company's gold coinage till its eventual replacement with 'crown' coinage in 1862, after the abolition of Company's rule in India following the Indian revolt of 1857–1859. It was also suggested to be employed for an early postage stamp issue of 1854 and, in a curious way, continues even now as the emblem of the Reserve Bank of India – the only change made is to replace the British lion with a more Indian striped tiger!

The palm tree thus becomes a generic and specific marker in its numismatic employment. Adapted from Classical traditions, it first serves as an allegory for the 'Orient' and is subsequently utilized more to denote 'India' in particular in a 'stereotyping' manner. The Orientalist notions of the 'colonized Other' as well as 'exoticism' are seen to be at play here.

Figure 2.21. Reverse of the rupee of King Edward VII's reign, 1910, with 'Jugendstil'-style lotuses flanking the central denomination inscription.

On the 'crown' coinage of British India, foliate motifs dominate more in a decorative than allegorical sense. The coins of all rulers from Victoria to George VI have floral and foliated borders for the denomination panel. They represent artistic conventions of their times – the border used on Queen Victoria's coins is reminiscent of the 'Arts-and-Crafts' design; it is entirely decorative with no semblance to a real plant, but some of its curvy and pointed aspects are reminiscent of the older, rather decadent 'Mughal' style. After all, the coinage was visually designed to substitute the Queen, who was later proclaimed as an 'Empress' in 1877, as the figurative head of state replacing the Mughal emperor. Coins of Edward VII have panels of lotus leaves and blooms on either side of the denominative text. These are represented in a sparse 'Jugendstil' realism (figure 2.21). Allegory makes a brief return on silver coins of George V and VI. Here we see the flowers of Britain – rose, thistle and shamrock – entwined at cardinal ends with lotus blooms shown from a lateral and an apical view.

TREES ON MODERN INDIAN COINAGE

After independence, India emerged as a republic which based its economic principles and activities on a particular socialist ideology. Articulated and envisaged by the first Prime Minister, Jawaharlal Nehru, it is often dubbed as 'Nehruvian Socialism.' The emphasis then was on heavy industrialization and governmental engagement with projects of civil engineering,

Figure 2.22. Obverse of one-rupee coin of independent India, 1950, with wheat stalks flanking the denomination.

mining and agriculture. Exploitation and harnessing of natural resources for the greater good of the population was a dominant theme in these developments. But in the early years the main problem for the nascent republic was to feed its millions. Agricultural motifs therefore dominated on coinage – the design of the very first coinage for independent India, launched in 1950 with the adoption of the constitution and the declaration of the republic, showed stalks of wheat as a dominant design for coins of ¼, ½ and one rupee denominations (figure 2.22). The 'ears of wheat'

Figure 2.23. Reverse of a 25-paise coin, 1985, issued under the FAO coinage scheme with slogan 'forestry for development,' showing a stylized tree in context with forest produce and fauna.

thereafter became a constant design feature on one-rupee coins well into the twenty-first century.

The dominance of agrarian themes on post-independence Indian coinage meant that plant life of some sort featured on many coins from time to time. Some of these were issued to commemorate world-wide initiatives like 'Grow More Food' or 'Food For All' led by apex organizations such as the FAO. Some were specifically the Indian Government's initiative – such as 'Forestry for Development.' In a curious way, we find the deployment of trees on these modern coins come full circle to their most ancient counterparts – the trees remain anonymous and can rarely be identified, but they perform the same schematic role their numismatic ancestor-depictions did. On the 1970 'Food for All' coins, the lotus emerges once again as a symbol of fertility and plenitude. On the 'Forestry for Development' coinage we see the depiction of a Banyan-like tree with many leaves which not only represents a 'forest' but also the developmental 'greater good' that it brings forth (figure 2.23). In this manner it harks back to the tradition of the *kalpavṛkṣa*, or the 'wish-fulfilling tree' of Indian yore.

EPILOGUE

As we have seen in the preceding pages, trees, plants and other foliate motifs have been an integral part of the Indian coin design for over two millennia. Originating in obscure symbolic traditions, which have all but lost their precise meaning, the depictions track a trajectory which is mainly religious in the ancient period. Cultic movements, their popularity and associations of divinities with plants guide the choice in terms of numismatic portrayal. Myth and lore play an important part in this choice too.

During the Islamic period, the depictions move on to a very different role – from a cultural or visual to a more decorative and subsequently a functional one. Here 'recognition' and 'identity' emerge as the key components that facilitate the inclusion of plant motifs in numismatic art and design. But apart from serving such a functional role, the motifs also bring the 'art of the coin' into context with other more famous and well-studied aspects of the art of the period, such as illuminated manuscript art or painting as it developed in India. Religious affiliations also feature in the choice of these functional depictions, but only after the Islamic (Mughal) authority that stands behind the coinage begins to falter, giving way to many other players in eighteenth century politics.

With the advent of the European-style coinage, artistic concepts and traditions dominating the European cultural milieu see plants and trees depicted on coins in a yet another way. Allegoric depictions lead to colonial 'stereotypes', such as that of the palm tree and the lotus representing the exotic 'Orient' particularly India. More modern artistic conventions and styles such as 'Jugendstil' are often seen married to these stereotypes, bringing forth an 'Orientalization' of the coin design.

The metaphoric role played by plants, flowers and trees continues on post-independence coinage in India where agrarian anxieties dominate and India forges the identity of a developing 'nation-state.' In an interesting way, the numismatic depiction of plants and flowers come full circle here because they draw from the same cultural notions that had made their appearance possible two thousand years ago – those of plenitude and fertility. The choice here is once again dominated by symbols like the lotus, but not in an exoticizing 'colonial' sense. The 'Pagoda Tree' thus continues to flourish through the ebb and flow of continuity and change.

ABBREVIATIONS AND REFERENCES

Skt. = Sanskrit

Cribb 1985 — Cribb, J. (1985). 'Dating India's Earliest Coins.' In Schotsmans, J. and M. Taddei (eds.), *South Asian Archaeology 1983*, vol. 1, pp. 535–54. Naples: Istituto Universitario Orientale.

Fergusson and Waterhouse 1868 — Fergusson, J. and J. Waterhouse (1868). *Tree and Serpent Worship, or, Illustrations of Mythology and Art in India in the First and Fourth centuries after Christ. From the Sculptures of the Buddhist Topes at Sanchi and Amravati*. London: W.H. Allen & Co.

Haberman 2013 — Haberman, D. (2013). *People Trees. Worship of Trees in Northern India*. New York: Oxford University Press.

HJ — Yule, H. and A.C. Burnell (1903). *Hobson-Jobson. A Glossary of Colloquial Anglo-Indian Words and Phrases, and of Kindred Terms, Etymological, Historical, Geographical and Discursive*. New ed. edited by William Crooke. London: J. Murray.

Oldenberg 1993 — Oldenberg, H. (1993). *The Religion of the Veda*. Reprint. Delhi: Motilal Banarsidass.

Philpot 1897 — Philpot, J.H. (1897). *The Sacred Tree, or, The Tree in Religion and Myth*. London; New York: MacMillan.

Chapter 3

Divine Flora, Divine Love: The Place of Natural Scenery in the Ultimate Vision of Kṛṣṇa *Bhakti*

GRAHAM M. SCHWEIG[1]

The wondrous, sensuous beauty of nature in general, and in particular, flora such as plants, trees, fruits, flowers, and so on, are engaged in Hindu sacred narratives and poetry, as well as Indian *kāvya* and *nāṭya* artistic expression. In this chapter, I explore the role of flora within one of the most celebrated and honored narratives of *bhakti*, or divine love, in Hindu traditions: the five-chapter divine drama that culminates in the performance of the great circle dance known as the Rāsa Līlā, located in the *Bhāgavatapurāṇa*. Among the numerous sacred stories of extraordinary persons and divine epiphanies within the twelve books of BhP, the Rāsa Līlā stands out as the most elevated and exalted expression of *bhakti*. It is the ultimate literary and theological focal point for the whole of the Bhāgavata text.

The hero of the divine drama of the Rāsa Līlā is Kṛṣṇa, the divinity known for sending out a love-call to all souls with the music of his flute. The heroines of the story are the cowherd maidens of Vraja, the Vraja *gopikās*, or simply 'the *gopīs*,' known for their most passionate love for Kṛṣṇa. The location of the Rāsa Līlā in the voluminous Bhāgavata text is chapters 29 through 33 of its tenth book, the book that is already famous for containing the most adored and celebrated stories of Kṛṣṇa's divine birth and childhood.[2] The culminating event of the great circle dance of

1 Graham M. Schweig is Professor of Philosophy and Religious Studies and Director of the Asian Studies Program, Christopher Newport University (USA).

2 Although the episode is found in less theologically rich and poetically elaborate forms within the *Harivaṃśa* and *Viṣṇupurāṇa*, the Bhāgavata version has

the *rāsa* is one of the ultimate symbols of boundless love in *bhakti*. Thus it is here among the various scenes of this special *līlā*, or divine drama, that we can expect to find a most exemplary and significant employment of flora in the experience of *bhakti*.[3]

Natural phenomena are not merely dramatic devices or decorative ornaments in the drama of the Rāsa Līlā (RL), nor are they merely a convenient palette of conventional metaphors on which the poet can rely. Rather, as I will show, they themselves constitute special autonomous manifestations of the divine that function independently of the devotee and even the divinity. These manifestations of flora not only frame, embrace, support and intensify the passion in the purest love *for* and *from* the divine, but they perform the essential function of extending the presence of a beloved whose very being is experienced as absent by the lover. Furthermore, the powerful and significant role that flora plays in the RL for divinity as well as devotee points to a more complete and thoroughgoing understanding and definition of the term *bhakti* – we learn that *bhakti* not only entails the soul's love for the divine beloved, but this is so in response to the beloved's divine embrace of all souls.

THE DRAMA OF THE RĀSA LĪLĀ

This classic sacred love story is narrated in eloquently rich and flowing Sanskrit poetry. It constitutes a powerful religious vision, one that has been an endless source of meditative inspiration for the devout worshiper, and it has been celebrated in Indian art, poetry and drama throughout the centuries.[4] Indeed, this passage has been cherished as the greatest vision of supreme love in India, and has been recognized as one of the most beautiful love poems in world literature. Vaiṣṇava traditions within the Hindu

---

been the most celebrated and honored source of the Rāsa Līlā. Especially for the Caitanya School of Vaiṣṇavism for whom this episode is held as the most sacred and ultimate culmination of all other *līlās* of Kṛṣṇa, the Bhāgavata is the authoritative text.

3 In Schweig (2005a) I present how the Bhāgavata text itself indicates or expresses the elevated status of the Rāsa Līlā above all others, and how it is the ultimate focal point of the text (section entitled 'Bhāgavata as the Ultimate Scripture,' pp. 11–16). Additionally, important commentators from the Caitanya School refer to the Rāsa Līlā passage as the *līlā-sāra*, 'the essence of *līlās*,' and the *sarva-līlā-cūda-maṇi*, 'the crown-jewel of all *līlās*.'

4 For some samples of works that extend the voice of the Vraja *gopikās* into poetry and drama, see Schweig (2005b).

complex of religion have extolled the Rāsa Līlā as the 'crown jewel of all *līlās*' and the 'essence of all *līlās*,' and venerate the dance itself as the great and central symbolic focal point of their worship. Moreover, it is specifically the *rāsa* dance itself within the Rāsa Līlā chapters that becomes the great vision, the great icon and the symbol of boundless love between divinity and devotee. As many Christians embrace the image of the cross as their great symbol of divine love, similarly certain major Vaiṣṇava Hindu traditions embrace the image of the Rāsa Līlā as the highest and most sacred revelation of boundless love in divine union.

The concept of the Rāsa Līlā originates in a certain ancient South Asian dance form that was performed during the harvest season. This dance consists of a circular formation, known as the *rāsa-maṇḍala,* of many female dancers, whose hands or arms are interlocked with one another in a chain-like manner, and around whose necks the arms of their male dance partners are placed. In the *līlā* or play of Kṛṣṇa's *rāsa* dance with the *gopīs*, however, it is Kṛṣṇa who becomes the sole male partner for each and every one of the *gopīs*. He does so by manifesting himself multiple times by virtue of his divine power (*yoga-māyā*), while remaining at the center of the *rāsa-maṇḍala* or 'circle of the *rāsa* dance.' In artistic depictions of the *rāsa* dance, it is very common to have Kṛṣṇa standing at the center with his most favored *gopī*, understood to be his supreme consort, the goddess Rādhā.[5] As the *gopīs* move in circular formation, each experiences the exclusive attention of Kṛṣṇa while all sing songs of love in harmony with Kṛṣṇa. These songs are accompanied by the percussive sounds of the bells on their ankles and belts, while their bracelets clang to the rhythmic movements of their forms, and celestial beings shower flowers down, joining in with their voices and drumming from the heavens.

This harvest dance, however, takes on special significance in the Rāsa Līlā of BhP. It is a dance that harvests the fruits of divine love, loveliness and playfulness. The dance is performed in the paradisiac forest of Vraja in which the lotus flowers, full fruit trees and honey bees come alive, the place to which the cowherd maidens blossom from their homes into the forest during one enchanting autumn night, when this divine dance is

5 The Rāsa Līlā story makes no explicit mention of Rādhā by name. However, there is a special *gopī* with whom Kṛṣṇa runs off in the second of the five Rāsa Līlā chapters, and it is assumed by various traditions that this favored *gopī* is Rādhā herself. And although there is no mention of any *gopī* whatsoever in the middle of the *rāsa* dance itself, Rādhā is typically placed in the center dancing with Kṛṣṇa. To many Vaiṣṇava worshipers, it is unthinkable to not have the great goddess at the center with Kṛṣṇa.

performed with Kṛṣṇa under the full moon of the harvest season. It takes place in the paradisiac countryside of Vraja in India, a region about 80 miles south of the modern capital city of Delhi. The enactment of the *rāsa* dance itself within the Rāsa Līlā chapters of BhP becomes the climactic event that occurs in the final fifth chapter of its story.[6]

The five-chapter story possesses the distinct structure of a drama. It is necessary, however, to provide a summary of the Rāsa Līlā story here before we analyze its dramatic and theological dimensions. The following summary of the story is also intended to give a sense of its poetic tone:

The Rāsa Līlā is set in a sacred realm of enchantment in the land known as Vraja, far beyond the universe, within the highest domain of the heavenly world. This sacred realm also imprints itself onto part of our world as the earthly Vraja Maṇḍala ('the circular area of Vraja') in northern India. Vraja is described as a land of idyllic natural beauty, filled with abundant vegetation heavy with fruit and bloom, roaming cows, and brightly colored birds singing melodiously. The Rāsa Līlā takes place in the earthly Vraja during the bountiful autumn season, when the evenings are pleasant with soothing scents and gentle river breezes.

One special evening, the rising moon reached its fullness with a resplendent glow. Its reddish rays lit up the forest as night-blooming lotus flowers began to unfold. The forest during that night was decorated profusely with delicate star-like jasmine flowers, resembling the flowing dark hair of goddesses adorned with blossoms. So rapturous was this setting that the supreme lord himself, as Kṛṣṇa, the eternally youthful cowherd, was compelled to play captivating music on his flute. Moved by this beauteous scene, Kṛṣṇa was inspired toward love. The opening four verses of exquisite poetry paint the scene and set the tone for the whole drama (BhP x.29.1–4).

Upon hearing the alluring flute music, the cowherd maidens, known as the *gopīs*, who were already in love with Kṛṣṇa, abruptly left their homes,

6 In modern times, dramatic performances of reenactments of Kṛṣṇa's various *līlās* are performed in two areas of India, and are called *rās līlā*. (The spelling of *rāsa* as *rās* is the Hindi form of the word.) That these performances open with the *rāsa* dance underscores that the *rāsa* is regarded as the ultimate *līlā* of Kṛṣṇa. In the village of Vṛndāvana, sacred to the devotees of Kṛṣṇa as Kṛṣṇa's spiritual center on this earthly plane, the *rās līlā* dramatic and musical performances are choreographed with young boys playing the parts of the *gopīs* and Kṛṣṇa. However, in the northeastern state of Manipur, young female dancers play the various parts. And in recent years, members of the Hare Kṛṣṇa movement, who themselves have popularized Kṛṣṇa *līlā* throughout the modern world since the late 1960s, have sponsored world-wide tours of Manipuri dancers presenting their performances of the *līlās of* Kṛṣṇa.

families and domestic duties. They ran off to join him in the moonlit forest. Kṛṣṇa and the *gopīs* met and played on the banks of the Yamunā river. When the maidens became proud of his loving attention, however, their beloved lord suddenly vanished from their sight. The *gopīs* searched everywhere for Kṛṣṇa. Discovering that he had run off with one special maiden, they soon found that she too had been deserted by him.[7] As darkness engulfed the forest, the cowherd maidens gave up their search, singing sweet songs of hope and despair, longing for his return. Then Kṛṣṇa cleverly reappeared and spoke to them on the nature of love (x.32.16–22).

In the final verse of this passage, we witness the power of love and how this power melts the heart of god. Here Kṛṣṇa explains to the *gopīs* that the purity of their love is its own reward, beyond anything that even he as the supreme being can reciprocate. The tradition then expresses how love is ultimately boundless, in that it is more powerful than even god. It is to love that god submits, and further, it is love by which god himself is intimately known and conquered. The great message here is that it is in the very act of love itself, or the purity of love that constitutes an offering of one's whole heart to the divine, that we find the greatest reward. The reward is not that our love is reciprocated – the reward is found simply in the endlessness or boundlessness of the love itself.

The story culminates in the great celebration of this pure love in the performance of the *rāsa* dance. The *gopīs* link arms together, forming a great circle:

> The festival of the Rāsa dance blossomed
> as a circular formation of *gopīs*.
> The supreme Lord of yoga, Kṛṣṇa,
> entered among them between each pair –
> Each thought she alone was at his side
> as he placed his arms around
> the necks of those young women.
> (BhP x.33.3)[8]

7 This special *gopī* with whom Kṛṣṇa ran off is most commonly understood by Hindu traditions as the most favored of all cowherd maidens, identified as Rādhā, though the name for this special *gopī* is not specifically mentioned. For more information on how persons of the Vaiṣṇava faith have perceived this special *gopī* within the Rāsa Līlā passage, and how she is related intimately with the other cowherd maidens, see Schweig (2005a: 147–51).

8 All translations in this chapter are by the author. The translated verses from the five chapters of the Rāsa Līlā are taken from Schweig (2005a).

By divine arrangement, Kṛṣṇa dances with every cowherd maiden at once, yet each one thinks she is dancing with him alone. Supreme love has now reached its perfect fulfillment and expression through joyous dancing and singing long into the night, in the divine circle of the Rāsa. Retiring from the vigorous dancing, Kṛṣṇa and the *gopīs* refresh themselves by bathing in the river. Then, reluctantly, the cowherd maidens return to their homes.

The five chapters of the Rāsa Līlā fall neatly into the structure of a five-act drama, and within them, thirteen subdivisions of scenes are discernible. Let us briefly review here the dramatic elements and structure of the passage. As we have noted, the hero of the drama is Kṛṣṇa, the supreme divinity, and the heroines are 'the *gopīs*.' The story is narrated by the sage Śuka to the king Parīkṣit. While the reader hears the narrator's voice throughout the acts, two short catechismal dialogues between the sage and king, once toward the beginning and the other instance toward the end of the story, ensue, offering theological discourse on the proper way to understand the *līlā*. But it is the voices of the hero and the heroines that dominate the text, not only within their dialogue scenes and a middle act consisting completely of the heroines' nineteen verses of monologue, but also within narrative verses which quote words and phrases spoken by the hero or heroines. Each of the five chapters constitutes an 'act' of the total drama or play, within which there are observable subdivisions that function as distinctive 'scenes,' totaling thirteen. These scenes are discernible by natural shifts both in the text's voice and in the distinct events within the story line. Furthermore, a study of the poetic meter of the verses seen in conjunction with these naturally observed shifts in the story line finds that they provide further support of such chapter subdivisions or scenes within the acts.

In order to understand the place and function of flora and the role of the natural in the RL, we must first appreciate the progression in the emotions experienced by the *gopīs* in the course of the whole *līlā*. I have attempted to outline the nine phases of love through which the cowherd maidens move in this *līlā*:[9] (1) awakening, (2) anticipation, (3) meeting, (4) conflict, (5) separation, (6) loss, (7) reunion, (8) rejoicing and (9) returning.

9 I present 'Eight Phases' of Supreme Love within the Rāsa Līlā in Schweig (2005a: 173). In this chapter, however, I present a ninth phase of 'returning,' a phase which originally eluded me. Indeed, the *gopīs* do return home to the original place of 'awakening' at the end of the story, indicated in a short line within the penultimate verse of the passage (see BhP x.33.39). The *gopīs* must return home

First, comes the lover's awakening to love: this is illustrated by the scene of the *gopīs* hearing Kṛṣṇa's alluring love call in the form of his flute music coming from the forest into their homes – below, I will discuss the powerful initial scene that describes how flora precipitates this love call of Kṛṣṇa. Second, the lover anticipates the meeting with the beloved: the *gopīs* drop all household duties and run to the forest to be with Kṛṣṇa. Third, the meeting of the lovers takes place: the *gopīs* come before Kṛṣṇa – they converse with Kṛṣṇa and then they become playful. Fourth, there is conflict between the lovers: Kṛṣṇa observes each *gopī* momentarily considering herself the most fortunate woman in the whole world, and he then disappears to punish them for their pride. These first four phases of emotion are found in the first chapter. The fifth phase is the one of separation from the beloved: it is here, at the beginning of the second chapter, when the *gopīs* experience Kṛṣṇa's absence and attempt to search for him, that we find them talking to plants of the forest. This phase moves into the third chapter, to the sixth phase of loss and devastation in love: here the *gopīs* simply sing songs of prayer and calling after they have given up their search for Kṛṣṇa. The seventh phase is found in the fourth chapter, which is the reuniting of lover with the beloved: Kṛṣṇa reappears to the *gopīs* and they converse about the nature of love. The eighth phase occurs in the final chapter, with the rejoicing of lovers in the triumph of love: Kṛṣṇa and the Vraja *gopikās* enact the love dance of the Rāsa, which is the climactic event. And the ninth phase is one in which the lover returns to the place in which the initial awakening took place: the *gopīs* return to their homes, the place where it all started.

VRAJA AS PASTORAL PARADISE

'Glorious is Vraja, surpassing all,' the *gopīs* extol the place. So wondrous is Vraja that the author of the Bhāgavata has devoted a full chapter to an elaborate description of its rainy and autumn seasons, often cleverly drawing parallels between characteristics of nature and the behavior of the spiritual aspirant (BhP x.20.1–49). The sacredness and pastoral beauty of Vraja are engaged in essential ways throughout the Rāsa Līlā, and therefore deserve treatment as one of the constituent principals of the drama.

---

so that they can move through the phases of divine love yet again the next evening! This ninth phase of divine love is very important because of the way it completes the other eight phases so as to make a cycle that the *gopīs* endlessly experience repeatedly.

The natural Vraja of this world is the geographic region of central northern India, in which the pilgrimage town of Vṛndāvana – depicted in the Rāsa Līlā as a small agricultural village – is situated. The name Vṛndāvana means 'the forest of Vṛndā or *tulasī*' (Kṛṣṇa's favorite plant and the goddess who embodies it). The setting of the Rāsa Līlā is in this world, but not exactly of this world. The divine realm of Vraja, manifest in this world and known as Gokula, is identical with its divine counterpart, the 'heavenly Vraja,' known as Goloka, though the practitioner must develop the proper vision to appreciate this phenomenon. Vraja is a world in which every being, including all plants, trees and animals, participates in and fully experiences the love between Kṛṣṇa and the cowherd maidens. The world of Vraja is devotionally alive as every object and soul exists only for the sake of the beloved lord. Every being and everything in this spiritual setting is full of knowledge and bliss, and gives off a splendor like the various luminaries of the sky.

The spiritual realm of Vraja is described as a place that clearly contrasts with the world as we know it. It is a mystical world of beauty; the ground is covered with devotional jewels named *cintāmaṇi*, each 'a fabulous gem supposed to yield to its possessor all desires.' Even the trees are not ordinary, and are called *kalpataru* ('wishing trees').[10] Vraja is a land of extraordinary abundance: the trees produce fruit during every season, cows give milk unlimitedly, and the water is nectar. Here, all walking is dancing and all talking is singing, and time is only an eternal present within which unlimited varieties of divine events occur.[11]

The reader becomes acquainted with the landscape of the Rāsa Līlā in the first three verses, and it continues to play an indispensable role in various phases of the story. In the second verse, the moon casts a reddish light above the horizon, contributing to the beauteous scene that inspires Kṛṣṇa toward love. The light of the decorative stars and glowing full moon illuminate the sky and forest at night. Indeed, the narrator compares the beauty of Kṛṣṇa among the *gopīs* to that of the moon among the many stars. Images of the bountiful forest and plant life are described by both the narrator and the hero or heroines. Flowers in general are mentioned, with special attention given to night-blooming varieties. The *gopīs*, when separated from Kṛṣṇa, talk to an array of forest plant life – from trees of all kinds to plants, vines and other botanicals. Kṛṣṇa also runs through the

10 See in this volume, Chapter 1, p. 10, n. 22.

11 These images of Vraja are taken from *Brahmasaṃhitā* and *Caitanyacaritāmṛta*.

forest with the *gopīs*. Enticed by its beauty early in the story, he shares his appreciation with the maidens:

> You have seen the forest
> filled with flowers,
> glowing with the rays
> of the full moon;
> Made beautiful by leaves of trees,
> playfully shimmering
> from the gentle breeze
> off the river Yamunā.
> (BhP x.29.21)

The Yamuna river, with its shores of cooling sands, is the place where Kṛṣṇa and the *gopīs* retreat in the first and final acts, in order to either play or refresh themselves after dancing. Gentle autumn breezes carve ripples in the waters of the Yamuna. In the second act, the wind becomes a messenger carrying news of which direction Kṛṣṇa has gone, by sending scents from his garland to the *gopīs*.

Essential to the story is the emphasis on flowers that bloom at night, since it is these flowers that inaugurate the Rāsa Līlā drama. Kṛṣṇa, in the first act, suggests to the *gopīs* that their coming to the forest is due to the alluring beauty of the flower-filled scene. He also gathers flowers for the special *gopī* with whom he disappears, and the other *gopīs* observe that 'here, flowers were gathered by the lover for his beloved' (x.30.32). At the conclusion of the drama, Kṛṣṇa roams the banks of the Yamuna river 'in the direction of the gentle breeze that was carrying the fragrances of flowers over the land and the water' (x.33.25).

Jasmine flowers assume a diverse role throughout the drama, and appear in the very first verse in which the beloved lord is inspired toward love. Note that it is not merely one night that is strikingly beautiful, but many 'nights.' These autumn nights are curiously filled with 'blooming jasmine flowers.' This is surprising, since the plant typically does not produce blossoms in the harvest season, but only during the spring and summer – an indication of the exceptional nature of these nights.

Jasmine is a delicate flower with a star-like form, most often white, though sometimes light pink or yellow, and is particularly known for its intoxicating fragrance capable of arousing amorous and erotic feelings.[12] The scent of jasmine pervades the air of the Vraja forest. Kṛṣṇa's teeth are

12 The powerful scent of jasmine is conveyed in RL IV.11.

compared to jasmine flowers, and some of the *gopīs* wear the flower during the *rāsa* dance. The cowherd maidens speak to varieties of jasmine when they are madly searching for Kṛṣṇa (x.30.8), and they are moved by the fragrance of the flowers coming from his garland (x.30.11). The beloved lord is also delighted by both the sight and alluring fragrance of these pervasive jasmine flowers in full night bloom (x.29.1).

The reader is informed that certain lotus flowers are night-blooming as well, and the narrator often refers to lotuses. The lotus flower is a frequently occurring symbol among Indian religious traditions.[13] In fact, the heavenly Vraja is in the shape of a lotus-flower blossom.[14] Within the Rāsa Līlā in particular, the image of the flower is used to convey beauty and passion a total of thirty times. The narrator begins the first scene by describing the autumn night that comes alive with the opening of lotus flowers, along with the rising moon. Kṛṣṇa is pleased by their appearance (x.29.3), and later by their scent: 'He delighted in breezes that carried the fragrance of white lotuses, joyfully dancing in the waves of the river' (x.29.45cd). While searching for Kṛṣṇa, the *gopīs* identify their beloved as the one who holds a lotus flower. Upon discovering his footprints, they are able to identify them easily because of the lotus emblem, along with other symbols, embellishing his prints. Kṛṣṇa's arm is said to possess the fragrance of a lotus flower. The *gopīs* themselves wear the flowers in their hair and behind their ears. Even the celestial beings shower lotuses upon Kṛṣṇa and the cowherd maidens as they perform the *rāsa* dance.

Earlier in the tenth book of the Bhāgavata, the reader is informed that night-blooming lotuses are born from the water, and are not the same as varieties found in the forest. The special power of such night-blooming flowers is indicated in the following verse:

> When the sun rises
> water-born flowers blossom,
> except for night-blooming lotus flowers,
> As subjects in the presence of their ruler
> are without fear, O king,
> except for the thieves.
> (BhP x.20.47)

13 See verse illumination to RL i.3.

14 The lotus can represent cosmic evolution, since the creator god, Brahmā, is born from the lotus. Forms of the powerful Vishnu are found standing on lotus flowers, and the lotus is one of several possible items that a Vishnu form may be holding in one of his four hands.

This thief-like trait of the night-blooming lotus is also a characteristic of the hero of the story, since Kṛṣṇa, in his boyhood, is known for stealing butter from the women of Vraja in order to feed the monkeys. He is called Hari ('one who steals') because he 'steals' the hearts of his devotees. And in the RL, he steals the hearts of the *gopīs* (x.29.8). Yet these night-blooming flowers are able to steal even the mind and heart of Kṛṣṇa!

The *tulasī* plant also plays a prominent role in the drama, as it does in the lives of Vaiṣṇava practitioners. This plant is considered to be a great female devotee of Kṛṣṇa, even a consort of Vishnu, who has taken the bodily form of a plant that is worshiped on a daily basis in Vaiṣṇava temples and homes. Her minty leaves are used to garnish food preparations for sacred offerings, and are found decorating the feet of sacred images of Kṛṣṇa. The wood of expired *tulasī* plants is carved into beads that are worn around the neck by Vaiṣṇavas and also strung into rosaries for the recitation of god's names. The special significance of the *tulasī* plant is recognized by the *gopīs* when they speak of Tulasī and Śrī (Lakṣmī): 'The Goddess Śrī desires, along with the sacred *tulasī* plant, the dust of your lotus feet' (x.29.37). Kṛṣṇa's garland is made up of the delicate and fragrant flowerets produced from the sacred plant and, in the second act, the *gopīs* inquire from the *tulasī* plant concerning Kṛṣṇa's whereabouts.

The natural surroundings of Vraja clearly assist in awakening the love between Kṛṣṇa and the *gopīs* when they are apart from each other. In the absence of his beloved consorts, Kṛṣṇa becomes inspired by the enchanting landscape and is compelled to produce melodious flute music, drawing the cowherd maidens to his side (x.29.3). Following Kṛṣṇa's sudden disappearance at the end of act 1 (x.29), the *gopīs* remain apart from him in acts 2 and 3 (x.30 and 31). They sing like madwomen as they frantically question the trees in the forest for any indication of Kṛṣṇa's whereabouts (x.30.4). Commentators point out that the *gopīs* first speak to the larger plant life in the Vraja forest, specifically the trees, but get no response. As they become more and more desperate they approach plants of all kinds and sizes, including the sacred *tulasī* and varieties of jasmine.

The maidens perceive these various plants and trees, in their selfless position, as beings 'whose very existence is for the sake of others,' thereby indirectly expressing how they feel – that their own existence is for the sake of Kṛṣṇa (x.30.9). Convinced that the vines on the trees must have had contact with their beloved lord, the *gopīs* feel that their textured bodily surfaces are actually 'ecstatic eruptions' (*utpulakāni*) caused by his divine touch (x.30.13). They envision the trees and plants, the branches of which are heavy with fruits and flowers during the harvest season, to be bowing before Kṛṣṇa, whom they have just seen pass by (x.30.12).

We have shown that both Kṛṣṇa and the *gopīs* relate intimately to or communicate personally with the beauteous Vraja setting, especially during periods of separation, as it serves to enhance their love play. In other words, the landscape is very much in the foreground when the hero and heroines are apart from one another. Conversely, when Kṛṣṇa and the *gopīs* come together in the first and final acts, the landscape assumes a background role. During these times, they roam the forest and use the shores of the Yamunā for play, then bathe in the river to cool off. Thus the forest provides an enchanting arena for the *rāsa* dance itself, and becomes a place of recreation following the dance. Clearly, both hero and heroines are closely connected in various ways to the exquisite landscape of Vraja, when they are separated as well as when they unite. It is the power known as Yogamāyā that arranges for the divine cowherd and his maidens to come together in this paradisiac landscape of love.

EVEN GOD IS MOVED BY NATURE'S BEAUTY

Let us look more closely at the opening verses of the Rāsa Līlā passage, for there could be no greater example of how flora takes on a most powerful and dramatic literary and theological function. In the very first verse we immediately encounter the power of flora:

> Even the Beloved Lord,
> seeing those nights
> in autumn filled with
> blooming jasmine flowers,
> Turned his mind toward
> love's delights,
> fully taking refuge in
> Yogamāyā's creative powers.
> (BhP x.29.1)

I have written extensively about this first verse, but let me just point out some of the literary and theological ways these flowers function. First it must be pointed out immediately that it is on these very jasmine flowers that the whole *līlā* turns. By just *seeing* jasmine flowers blooming that autumn night, Kṛṣṇa Bhagavān is inspired toward love. Moreover, it is precisely these flowers that allow for the emergence of Kṛṣṇa's love call and the divine love that is so celebrated in this ultimate *līlā.* This feature alone delivers a sudden and dramatic opening. But there is more.

The narrator's voice informs the reader that this jasmine amazingly blossoms here during the autumn, when it is well known that jasmine blossoms in India only during the spring and at the latest during the summer. This unusual season for jasmine signals that something extraordinary is occurring. This exceptional season for jasmine is further reinforced by the picture created in this first verse: that of the beautiful blossoms of jasmine opening up against a background of the deep darkness of night, an unusual time of the day for its blossoming. I have pointed out elsewhere that the word employed in this verse for night, *rātrī,* the name of the Vedic goddess of night, triggers a complex metaphor in which the reader anticipates this *extraordinary* event in which the cowherd maidens of Vraja emerge from their homes, *blossoming* forth, as it were, into the night to be with Kṛṣṇa.[15] Thus the dark night was adorned with jasmine to attract Bhagavān Śrī Kṛṣṇa, just as young Indian women decorate their hair with aromatic jasmine to attract a suitable husband. The beauty of jasmine flowers set in the darkness of night during the harvest season within the paradisial realm of Vraja turns the mind of the divinity, who is Kṛṣṇa, toward harvesting 'love's delights,' and therefore he is moved to make sweet music with the flute to attract those very maidens of Vraja for whom he has a divine passion:

> Seeing lotus flowers bloom
> and the perfect circle of the moon
> Beaming like the face of Ramā,
> reddish as fresh *kuṁkuma;*
> Seeing the forest colored
> by the moon's gentle rays,
> He began to make sweet music,
> melting the hearts of
> fair maidens with beautiful eyes.
> (BhP x.29.3)

Note that here, in addition to jasmine, Kṛṣṇa is also further inspired by the night-blooming lotus flowers. Put simply, it is the exquisite beauty of the Vraja flora that singularly gives rise to Kṛṣṇa's divine love call, the music of the flute for which Kṛṣṇa is so well known, a love call that is to attract the 'fair maidens with beautiful eyes,' the Vraja *gopikās.*

15 See Schweig (2005a: 139–40 and 193–94).

THE VRAJA *GOPIKĀS* SPEAK TO PLANTS

Let me emphasize here that it is flora that immediately becomes prominent when Kṛṣṇa experiences a longing for the Vraja *gopikās*. Flora takes the foreground at the very start of the *līlā*, causing Kṛṣṇa to remember the Vraja *gopikās*, to long for and desire their presence, and to become moved to call for them with the sounds of his flute. When the lover feels alone and far away from the beloved, flora moves into the foreground and manifests qualities of the beloved, intensifying the remembrance, the longing, and the calling for the beloved.

Yet flora also takes on a vital role in the background of this *līlā*. Flora at the very least always frames and embraces the *līlā* in the background during any of the interchanges between Kṛṣṇa and the *gopīs* – it is the forest of Vraja in which both Kṛṣṇa and the cowherd maidens meet, play and dance, and which is the setting for the climactic event of the *rāsa* dance itself. But flora is most prominently engaged in the foreground, as significant players in the *līlā* as we've seen in the beginning scene, and also in the second chapter of the *līlā*. After the *gopīs* find themselves suddenly without Kṛṣṇa, when he disappears from them due to their pride, they begin talking to various plants of the forest. They speak to trees, bushes and plants, including Tulasī herself, and even to insignificant ground-covering vines, desperately needing to know Kṛṣṇa's whereabouts. I will now turn to this series of verses from chapter 30 of the tenth book, weaving select traditional interpretations of them. Here is the first verse that introduces this key passage:

> Singing out loud about him
> like deranged persons,
> Together they searched
> from forest to forest.
> They inquired from trees,
> the lords of the forest,
> about the supreme Person
> Who is present internally and
> externally for all living beings,
> as heavenly air pervades all beings,
> within and without.
> (BhP x.30.4)

The divine appears to the maidens within their own hearts, and he appears to them in the forms of the trees, vines and flowers of the

Vṛndāvana forest. In support of his commentary, Jīva Gosvāmin quotes another verse of the Bhāgavata that states: 'just as the vines and trees of the forest were revealing an abundance of flowers, they (the *gopīs*) were revealing Vishnu in their own hearts.'[16] Jīva states in his commentary that Kṛṣṇa, even while he is alone with the presiding goddess of Vṛndāvana, is aware of the questions that the *gopīs* ask in their state of love intoxication and madness of separation, since he is all-pervading.[17]

The Caitanya School takes this passage of the *gopīs* talking to plants as an example of how one should inquire about the supreme being in *bhakti*. Their example demonstrates how the *bhakta* looks everywhere and sees only Kṛṣṇa (CC II.25.127). The Vraja *gopikās* pursue all varieties of flora here:

O Aśvattha fig tree,
Plakṣa and Nyagrodha trees,
have you seen the son of Nanda?
He has stolen our minds
with his loving smiles
and glances.

O Kurabaka tree,
Aśoka and Nāga trees,
O Punnāga and Campaka plants,
Has the younger brother of Rāma
passed this way?
His smile steals the conceit
of all proud women.

O most fortunate Tulasī
to whom the feet
of Govinda are so dear,
Have you seen Acyuta, our beloved,
wandering about in this forest
followed by a swarm of bees?
(BhP X.30.5–7)

In this last verse, the *gopīs* talk to the *tulasī* plants because they know that the delicate blossoms of *tulasī* are always included among the other flowers in Kṛṣṇa's garlands. Their understanding is made more explicit in verse 12 below.

16 *vana-latās tarava ātmani viṣṇuṃ vyañjayantya iva puṣpa-latāḍhyāḥ* (BhP X.35.9).

17 See Jīva Gosvāmin's KrSa commentary to BhP X.35.9 in BPSa.

O Mālati, Mallikā, Jāti, and
Yūthikā jasmine flowers,
have you seen him?
When Mādhava was passing by,
did he cause you great delight
with the gentle touch of his hand?
(BhP x.30.8)

The *gopīs* know how attracted Kṛṣṇa is to jasmine flowers, evidenced by their talking to varieties of aromatic jasmine, 'Mālati, Mallikā, Jāti, and Yūthikā,' in the Vraja forest, when they search for him in their madness. And as we've already seen, it was jasmine that initiated the Rāsa Līlā in the first place. So the *gopīs* reason, why can't he be enticed by these varieties of jasmine in the forest again?

O Cūta mango and Priyāla trees,
Panasa jackfruit tree,
Āsana and Kovidāra trees;
O Jambū tree, small Arka plant,
Bilva wood-apple tree, Bakula tree,
Āmra mango and Nīpa palms;
O all other plants and trees
growing by the banks
of the Yamunā
Whose lives are devoted
to the service of others –
please show us the path to Kṛṣṇa,
for we are losing our minds!
(BhP x.30.9)

The Arka plant is a very insignificant vine, which expresses how desperate the *gopīs* are to find Kṛṣṇa, and how they are moved to address such little plants due to the lack of any response from the more prominent plants and trees of the forest. In this verse, they express the madness they experience in their loving search, 'we are losing our minds!' Commentators explain that they are actually losing their very selves in remembrance of their beloved while experiencing the intense absence of their beloved ... this is the goal of *viraha bhakti*.

Kṛṣṇadāsa explains the reason why the trees and plants do not respond when they are questioned by the cowherd maidens – they may be male, and as Kṛṣṇa's friends, will not reveal his whereabouts. Kṛṣṇadāsa further describes how the *gopīs* then inquire from the female plants. Upon still receiving no response, they think that these plants must be maidservants of Kṛṣṇa, and out of fear, cannot speak (CC II.15.32–42).

O Earth,
what severe austerity
have you performed?
Ah, you appear resplendent
with the grass hairs of your body
blissfully standing erect, elated
from the touch of Keśava's feet.
Is this perhaps
the result of footsteps coming
from his earlier descent
as Urukrama?
Or, even before that, is it
coming from the embrace
of his divine form of Varāha?
(BhP X.30.10)

Jīva Gosvāmin makes a distinction between *premā*, or intimate and pure love for god, and *aiśvarya-jñāna*, or love mixed with knowledge of god's greatness and power. This verse illustrates both types of love: the first two *padas* express the intimacy of *mādhurya-bhāva*, and the second two express love combined with *aiśvarya-jñāna*.[18] Jīva suggests that both the third and fourth *padas* regarding the *aiśvarya* forms of Kṛṣṇa are actually rhetorical questions. In other words, the ecstatic signs of bristling hair-like grasses of the earth rise not due to the 'wide strides' of Urukrama over the earth, or because of the divine boar, Varāha, who lifts the earth with his tusks to protect it. Rather the bristling grasses are certainly due to the touch of Kṛṣṇa's feet.[19]

The *gopīs* appear to be projecting their own emotions onto the earth when they interpret the earth's erect grasses to be signs of ecstasy, due to having been in the presence of Kṛṣṇa. Rather the hairs of the earth that the maidens observe are the grasses and sprouts growing from its surface that stand on end because Kṛṣṇa walks the earth.[20]

O wife of the deer,
have you encountered Acyuta

18 From Jīva Gosvāmin's KrSa commentary to BhP X.30.10 in BPSa.

19 BPSa 310–12.

20 From Viśvanātha Cakravartin's commentary BhP X.30.10 in SāD.

in this place with his beloved?
O friend, have your widened eyes
received great pleasure from
the sight of his beautiful limbs?
The garland of jasmine
worn by the Lord of this group
is tinged with *kuṁkuma* powder
Coming from the breasts of his lover
whom he has embraced;
its scent is blowing in our direction.
(BhP x.30.11)

Here the *gopīs* treat a deer as a 'friend,' inquiring as to whether Kṛṣṇa is with another *gopī*, who is identified by the tradition as Kṛṣṇa's dearest consort, Rādhā.[21] Here, again, jasmine is prominent. But this time it becomes evidence of another lover.

Perhaps the younger brother of Rāma,
holding a lotus flower in one hand
and resting his other arm
on the shoulder of his beloved,
Was followed here by a swarm of bees
hovering around his garland of *tulasī*,
all of them blinded by madness.
O trees,
when walking by,
Did he graciously accept
your respectful bowing
with his affectionate glances?
(BhP x.30.12)

The *gopīs* perceive the trees and plants, whose branches are heavy with fruits and flowers during the harvest season, to be bowing before Kṛṣṇa, due to having just seen him pass by. The reason the trees do not answer the maidens is that they have apparently become unconscious, as a result of the unhappiness they experience in separation from Kṛṣṇa (CC ii.15.52–54).

Let us inquire from these vines,
even though they are embracing
the branch-like arms
of their tree-husband.

21 BPSa 108.

Certainly they must have been
touched by his fingernails –
just see how they are elated
with bodily ripplings of bliss!
(BhP x.30.13)

Here the *gopīs* wish to inquire from the vines, which are embracing their husbands' arms (the branches of the trees). As both Viśvanātha and Śrīdhara suggest, the cowherd maidens are sure that the vines have had contact with Kṛṣṇa, since they could not be experiencing such eruptions of ecstasy (*utpulakāni*) merely because of contact with their husband-trees.[22] These could only be caused by contact with Kṛṣṇa.

CONCLUDING REFLECTIONS

The act of speaking to plants appears to be unprecedented in Indian tradition, even within Vaiṣṇava tradition. The instance of the Vraja *gopikās* talking to plants is unique, elevating the role and status of plants to a level that we do not find elsewhere. These plants to which the *gopīs* speak are certainly no longer merely in the background, establishing a setting or functioning metaphorically, nor are they only in the foreground as mere dramatic props. As one finds in the worship of sacred plants, there is an elevated level of interaction with plants in the RL chapters, an interaction that is also observable in the Vaiṣṇava appreciation and practice of worshiping *tulasī.*

But it must be underscored how divine flora directly enhances divine love. Vraja flora is an intimate partner in *śṛṅgāra rasa*, further intensifying the expression of devotional passion of separation or *viraha* within *prema-bhakti.* The flora of Vraja constitutes a special autonomous manifestation of the divine that functions independently of the devotee and even the divinity for purposes of bringing them together most intimately. Both devotee and divinity depend upon the natural beauty and presence of flora in order to experience intimate connection, comfort and a powerful sense of nearness with the beloved when feeling alone while the beloved is far away. The roles that flora takes in the RL, as it comes into the foreground as an intimate partner with a lover who is feeling the loss and hopelessness in the absence of the beloved, and as it moves more into the

22 From Śrīdhara Svāmi's *Bhāvārthabodhinī* and Viśvanātha Cakravartin's commentary to BhP x.30.13 in SāD.

background decorating and enveloping the joy and celebration of united lovers, bespeak the universal human need for nature and its flora.

Undoubtedly the greatest and the most celebrated sacred text on *bhakti* and its teachings along with the *Bhagavadgītā* is the *Bhāgavatapurāṇa*. Given that the RL is the very heart of the great BhP text, its theological and literary focal point, it becomes the ultimate vision of supreme love and the highest achievement in *bhakti*. And so it is significant that the RL drama commences with the way Bhagavān Śrī Kṛṣṇa is moved toward love by the paradisiac natural beauty in front of him. Indeed, the first words in the first half of the first verse are devoted to and establish the relationship between *bhagavān* and the natural beauty of a jasmine decorated forest. Indeed, at the start of the RL, we immediately come to know of Kṛṣṇa's *viraha*, that is, the lover's experience of separation from the beloved, or more specifically, the experience of 'feeling alone (*-raha*) and far away (*vi-*)' from the beloved. It is in this state of *viraha* that the natural world moves into the foreground of *līlā* and, further, takes center stage in the drama of divine love in order to nourish and intensify god's love for souls.

It is thus Kṛṣṇa's state of *viraha* in chapter 1 that makes the whole RL drama possible. Following this, at the very start of the following chapter, is the *viraha* experienced by the *gopīs*. The various stages of their *viraha* unfold throughout this second chapter and reach a certain pitch of intensity in and throughout the third chapter, titled the *Gopī Gīta*, or 'The Song of the *Gopīs*.' In each case, whether it be divinity's longing for souls or souls longing for the divine, the natural beauty of flora moves to the foreground as the beloved recedes into the darkness, and the experience of separation, loss and unbearable absence now becomes most powerfully felt.

So, flora and natural scenery have a powerful role in the RL – first in awakening love and bringing lovers together, then in comforting lovers as they find themselves apart from one another, again in their celebration of love, and finally in the parting of lovers following their time together. The natural world accompanies the *bhakta* in all the phases of ever-increasing love for the *bhagavat*, or divine beloved. Nature's role may shift at different times, may have greater or lesser prominence according to the phase of love. But in one role or another nature always supports the further intensification of love directly when it comes into the foreground during the various experiences of lovers as they move apart, as well as indirectly during periods when lovers move closer together. Indeed, its role is the sine qua non of the RL, and thus in my study I have deemed it one of the four essential elements within this great passage.

Finally, the role of flora in the RL invites further reflection on the nature and character of *bhakti* itself. It is significant that the RL, the most important *līlā* in the Bhāgavata and the most celebrated by sixteenth century Vaiṣṇava traditions, commences its sacred narrative with the way that the beauty of Vraja flora and natural scenery inspire amorous love in *bhagavān* Śrī Kṛṣṇa for his most beloved among all *bhaktas*, namely the Vraja *gopikās*, which in turn precipitates their intense, passionate *bhakti* for him. *Bhakti* is normally understood as the devotee's love for the divine, and thus it is most often translated simply as 'devotional love,' or 'loving devotion,' or just 'devotion.' And while scholars have pointed out that *bhakti* never means the *bhagavat*'s love for the *bhakta*, it can be deduced from the opening several verses of the RL that the *bhagavat*'s love nevertheless is the necessary precondition for *bhakti* itself.

The essential role of flora in the RL broadens and expands what is normally meant by the word *bhakti*. But we can even take this further. The morphology of the word implies both the soul's intimate connection with the divine and at the same time the soul's longing for an even closer connection with the divine. Thus *bhakti* is the practice of the *bhakta*, which itself means 'one who is loved' as well as 'one who offers all one's heart to the divine.' The former meaning indicates an intimate connection to the divine, on the one hand, and the latter meaning indicates a desire to be closer to the divine, on the other. These two meanings of the word *bhakta* constitute the mutuality of the embrace between humanity and divinity within *bhakti*. First, the *bhakta* shares in the very being of the divine, the *bhagavat*. The *bhakta* is a part of the divine. The *bhakta* owes its very existence to the divine. And yet the *bhakta* is simultaneously always apart from the divine. These two meanings together express the kind of sustained tension between the experience of god's ubiquitous and translucent presence in all reality and yet at the same time god's transcendent aloofness as a discrete divine being in his highest heaven.

Thus while it is the love transacted between god and his most beloved souls that conquers them both, that nourishes yet overtakes them both in their embrace within the *rasa* of divine passion, it is the flora and natural scenery that yet support and embrace the very conquest of divine love itself, bringing yet a greater union between the divine and the human. No matter how infinitely close to the divine they may have been previously, such closeness can never satisfy *bhaktas*, for it inevitably and eventually is experienced by them as still too great a distance, an unbearable distance that must be overcome. It is flora and natural scenery that beckon them to strive indefinitely, eternally, for ever greater closeness and intimacy with the divine and forever plunge into the depths of infinite love.

REFERENCES AND ABBREVIATIONS

Skt. = Sanskrit

BhP — *Bhāgavatapurāṇa*. Śāstrī, K. (ed.). *Śrīmad Bhāgavata Mahāpurāṇam*. Ahmedabad: Śrībhāgavatavidyāpīṭha.

BPSa — Jīva Gosvāmin: *Bhaktiprītisandarbha*. Jīva Gosvāmin. (1951). *Bhāgavata-sandarbha: Bhakti-Prīti Sandarbha*. Sanskrit text in Bengali script. Critical notes by Haridās Śarman. Vrindaban: Purīdās.

CC — *Caitanya Caritāmṛta*. Kṛṣṇadāsa Kavirāja Gosvāmī. (1957). *Śrī Śrī Caitanya Caritāmṛta. Amṛta Pravāha-bhāṣya by Bhaktivinoda Ṭhākura*. Calcutta: Gaudiya Mission.

KrSa — Jīva Gosvāmin: *Krama Sandarbha*. Sanskrit text in Bengali script. Critical notes by Haridās Śarma (1952). Vṛndāvana: Puridās.

SāD — Viśvanāthan Cakravartin: *Sārātha Darśinī*. In Śāstrī, K. (ed.) (1965). *Śrīmad Bhāgavata Mahāpurāṇam*. Sanskrit text; multi-commentary edition. Ahmedabad: Śrībhāgavatavidyāpīṭha.

Schweig 2005a — Schweig, G.M. (2005). *Dance of Divine Love. India's Classic Sacred Love Story: The* Rāsa Līlā *of Krishna from the Bhāgavata Purāṇa*. Princeton: Princeton University Press.

Schweig 2005b — Schweig, G.M. (2005). 'The Divine Feminine in the Theology of Krishna.' In Bryant, E.F. (ed.), *Sources of the Krishna Tradition*, pp. 441–74. New York: Oxford University Press.

Section Two

Devotion, Ecology, Ritual

Chapter 4

Perfumed Islam: The Culture of Scent at the Nizamuddin Basti

MIKKO VIITAMÄKI[1]

'To tell you the truth, Sufism cannot be perfected without attar,' I was told a few years ago by Kamal Nizami, a perfume trader belonging to the hereditary custodians of the Nizamuddin shrine in Delhi. I had been aware of the Sufis' profuse use of attars,[2] perfume oils prepared from various plant materials and a few substances of animal origin, but I had always attributed this to the general emphasis Muslims laid on purity and pleasant fragrance. When I started to investigate this aspect more in depth, it became clear that the Sufis' interest in attars goes beyond mere self-grooming. This chapter intends to map some aspects of the culture of scent, and its relation to selected plants, in the religious dimension of a Delhi neighborhood that clusters around the shrine of the city's patron-saint, Niẓām al-Dīn Auliyā'.

Despite the widespread use of perfumes, both the material culture of the scent – raw materials, manufacturing processes, marketing organization, vessels used for storage, et cetera – and the variegated meanings attributed to the olfactory sensation are still largely neglected in the field of Asian studies. A special issue of the *Journal of the Royal Asiatic Society* published in 2013 was a pioneering attempt to extensively map the connections between scents on one hand, and ritual, self-grooming, trade and

1 Mikko Viitamäki is Lecturer of South Asian Studies, Department of World Cultures, University of Helsinki.

2 The correct spelling of the word is *'iṭr*, but the pronunciations *'iṭar* and *'aṭar* have in the South Asian context led to attributing the word attar, denoting specifically rose oil in English, to the entire range of perfumes.

therapeutics on the other. The issue comprised the proceedings of a conference organized in Heidelberg in 2010. The approaches of the contributions ranged from medieval archeology mapping the history of amber in China (Fo 2013) and a wider cultural biography of agarwood in the region (Jung 2013) to discussing fragrance as a ritual offering in Tibetan Buddhist paintings (Bazin 2013) and to describing perfume culture in twentieth century Taiwan (Yunjun 2013). In the fields of Islamic and Indian studies, the historians Amar Zohar and Efraim Lev (2013) have traced the changes in the culture of scent that followed the Arab conquest in the centuries subsequent to the death of the Prophet Muhammad in 632 CE. Bahram Grami (2013) has listed instances where aromatic plant and animal materials feature in early Persian poetry while James McHugh (2013) discusses the use of 'sweet hoof,' the opercula of certain marine snails, as described in Sanskrit texts. The diversity of the approaches indicates the vastness of the topic and the variety of perspectives (Michaels 2013: 3).

The significance of scent in Indo-Muslim culture has been discussed by Ali Akbar Husain in a compelling study entitled *Scent in the Islamic Garden. A Study of Literary Sources in Persian and Urdu* (2002; second edition 2012). Husain combines his background in architecture and landscape architecture with a textual study of Persian and Urdu sources analyzing garden-laying in the Deccan between the sixteenth and eighteenth centuries. In discussing the use of scents, Husain notes that Ibn Sīnā (Avicenna; d. 1037) prescribes aromatic substances for the treatment of the heart in his *al-Adwiyat al-Qalbiyya* ('Cardiac Drugs'), a key medical treatise discussing cardiac treatment in Graeco-Arabic medicine – called Unani Tibb in South Asia.[3] Pleasant things like music, good company and scents are believed to fortify the spirit (*rūḥ*), keeping it in balance and free from worries. The gardens laid by Muslim nobility served the same purpose by providing an environment for carefree pleasure that was boosted by the scent of the plantings. Significantly, many of the aromatic substances doubled as aphrodisiacs, and their use in private pleasure gardens and royal bedchambers also served the purpose of increasing sexual enjoyment (Husain 2012: 73–77).

Most coveted aromatic substances were highly prized and it is not surprising that in India the rulers and the nobility became patrons of merchants and perfume-makers as well as consumers of scents. Abū'l-Faẓl, who chronicled the reign of the Mughal emperor Akbar (r. 1556–1605), devotes

3 *Yunānī ṭibb*, lit. 'Ionian medicine.' For an in-depth discussion on Unani medicine and its transformation in colonial India, see Alavi (2007) and Attewell (2007).

an entire chapter of his *Āʾīn-i Akbarī* to listing significant perfumes with their prices, reserving a more elaborate treatment to the most important ones (ĀA: 78–93). Slightly later in Bijapur, a text called *ʿIṭr-i Nauras Shāhī* was written for the ruling monarch Ibrāhīm ʿAdīl Shāh II (r. 1580–1627). The text is dedicated to various uses of aromatic substances in scenting the environment, body and breath. In addition, it describes nine different methods for perfuming the royal bedroom by, for example, arranging particular flower bouquets at certain heights (Husain 2012: 81).

While sensual pleasure is of key importance when scents are discussed in royal courts, the enthusiasm of Sufis for attars follows a different rationale. Drawing their inspiration from the medical theories laid out by Ibn Sīnā, they capitalize on the scents' power to strengthen heart and spirit while engaged in religious practice. At the same time, Sufis – fully conscious of the association of scents with a luxurious lifestyle – present them as valued offerings in their shrines.

This study is based on fieldwork conducted at the Nizamuddin Basti in 2014, where I interviewed professionals and connoisseurs of attar. In selecting informants, I focused specifically on people with a long-standing expertise in trading attars. Not only are these informants familiar with most aspects of scent culture beginning with the harvesting of raw materials and ending with selling the final product, they are also knowledgable about the properties of their merchandise and readily share advice concerning the use of attars with their customers. Furthermore, most of them link attars with religion in one way or another.

My key informant concerning both the attar industry and the religious significance of scents was Kamal Nizami, a gentleman who belongs to the family who are hereditary custodians of the shrine. Unlike his younger brother, he has chosen not to earn his living by guiding pilgrims. Instead, he trades in perfumes. Before opening his shop in the Basti almost four decades ago, he was involved in supplying skins used in luxury items such as shoes and handbags. When he discovered that dealing with the most expensive snakeskins was forbidden by the standards of Sharia, Islamic law, he moved to the attar business, a trade sanctified by religion.

In addition to self-grooming, scents play a significant role in the rituals of the Nizamuddin shrine. Arthur Saniotis (2008: 22–23) has noted the pervasiveness of the olfactory stimuli in his article exploring the sensual landscapes at the shrine. In order to find out about the importance of scent in the shrine, I interviewed one of its hereditary custodians, Afsar Ali Nizami. He belongs to the younger generation, but unlike many of his peers, he has chosen to dedicate his life to the activities of the shrine and not to pursue academic or vocational training. Like other custodians of the shrine, Afsar Ali has a particular clientele among the pilgrims, which includes a number of successful businessmen as well as people involved with the film industry. In addition to a taste for designer clothing, he shares a passion for attars with many of his pilgrim guests. The most luxurious attars used in the shrine are usually provided by them.

In the following sections, I introduce the religious institutions present in the Nizamuddin Basti and then map the different kinds of perfume in use, their production and the patterns of consumption. Though these data apply more generally to a specifically Indian culture, the exploration of religious significance attached to scents reveals how differing perceptions of Islam shape the material culture and commerce in the case of attars. The conceptualization of the religious significance of attars is intimately connected with the question of whether synthetic perfumes can replace the natural varieties. This question leads to the concluding remarks on the changing values affecting the culture of scent in the contemporary South Asian Islamic milieus.

THE NIZAMUDDIN BASTI

The Nizamuddin Basti is built around the tomb of the illustrious Chishti Sufi master Niẓām al-Dīn Auliyāʾ (d. 1325). The shrine is one of the most important Sufi sanctuaries in India.[4] Although the literature produced by Niẓām al-Dīn's followers was essential for the immortalization of his fame, a shrine in the capital city has helped to diffuse it among people who may have had neither the chance nor the inclination to submerge themselves in studying Sufi writings.

The shrine is situated in the heart of the Nizamuddin Basti (or Basti Hazrat Nizamuddin) named after the saint. Over the past fifty years or so, well-to-do residential areas like Nizamuddin East, Sundar Nagar and Lodi Estate, where free-standing houses fill the plots shaded by thick foliage, have risen around the medieval neighbourhood. Although the entire Basti bustles with intense life, it is also a virtual necropolis where Sufis, poets, nobles and royals have been buried in the course of the past seven centuries. Most devotional activities revolve around the two tombs belonging to Niẓām al-Dīn and his renowned poet-disciple Amīr Khusrau (1253–1325 CE).

4 For a general discussion on Indian Sufi shrines, see, e.g. Currim and Michell (2004) and Troll (2004).

The Nizamuddin shrine is situated, both ideologically and geographically, in between two contrasting versions of Sufism. East of the shrine lies the Delhi centre (*markaz*) of the Tablighi Jamaat (Missionary Society), a grassroots organization founded in 1927 by Muhammad Ilyas Kandhlawi (d. 1944) to spread Deobandi ideals and reform the practices of Indian Muslims, particularly those living in villages (Metcalf 1993, 2003). The Markaz is an imposing concrete building housing a mosque and residential quarters for members who are trained in Delhi before they move on to more remote locations where they engage in the organization's typical missionary work (*tablīgh*). Members are frequently seen inside the Nizamuddin shrine, watching what they perceive as corrupt Islamic practices. The main access road to the shrine passes by the Markaz and the Tablighi Jamaat members sometimes attempt to convince pilgrims to renounce their intention of visiting the shrine. However, their activities do not seem to have significantly affected the number of pilgrims. According to the observations of Peter Manuel (2008: 381), this applies to Sufi shrines in general. Similarly, Hindu attendance at these shrines has remained stable notwithstanding the exclusivist Hindutva rhetoric.

Although adverse to shrines and shrine worship, Tablighi Jamaat does not reject Sufism altogether. However, it reduces the process of inner growth to the minute observation of pietistic Islamic practice. In contrast to this approach, the followers of Inayat Khan (d. 1927), whose centre is located south of the Nizamuddin shrine, eschew the connection with Islam altogether and contest the relevance of common Muslim rituals to their Sufi tradition. They advocate 'universal Sufism' as a manifestation of perennial spirituality that can be found in every religion. Inayat Khan was a classical Hindustani musician and a Sufi master who gave recitals and preached in the USA and Europe in the early twentieth century. He returned to India shortly before passing away in 1927, and was buried in the Basti.[5] The members of various movements that have drawn their inspiration from his legacy over the past century hail primarily from the USA, Europe and New Zealand. They arrive at the Basti during periodical retreats and on the occasion of the death anniversary (*'urs*) of Inayat Khan, but rarely visit the main shrine complex.

In contrast to Tablighi Jamaat, the custodians of the Nizamuddin shrine advocate visiting shrines and engaging in a variety of Sufi rituals and practices. However, unlike the followers of Inayat Khan, they insist on the Islamic character of Sufism even if they simultaneously acknowledge that

5 On Inayat Khan, see Hermansen (2001) and Ernst and Lawrence (2002: 140–43).

the saint's blessings are meant for all human beings irrespective of their religious background.

ATTARS AND THE CULTURE OF SCENT

Attar is a term that denotes a liquid, oil-based perfume that does not include alcohol. At present, the term has come to include also synthetic varieties, but traditionally, the majority of attars have been essential oils obtained by distillation. The manufacturing is localized and attars are usually produced where the plant material is grown. This applies especially to floral attars whose raw material does not bear transportation over long distances without compromising the quality of the end product. Thus, the production of saffron oil (*za'farān*) is centred in Kashmir whereas the best quality jasmine oil (*yāsmīn*) is produced in Sikandarpur (district Ballia, eastern Uttar Pradesh), where the flowers reputedly have a particularly high oil content.

Most attars are used as single perfumes without mixing them with others. In Nizamuddin Basti, the commonly used single attars include vetiver (U. *khas*; *Chrysopogon zizanioides* (L.) Roberty), varieties of jasmine and narcissus (*nargis*) and screwpine (U. *kevṛā*; *Pandanus tectorius* Parkinson ex Du Roi). Sandalwood (U. *ṣandal*; *Santalum album* L.) is available as well, but it is more commonly used as a fixative in mixed perfumes.[6] Sandalwood is also employed to capture the scent of materials with a low oil content, such as *campā* (flower of a magnolia species), or no oil at all. Among the latter is one of the most peculiar attars, the earth (*miṭṭī* or *gil*). This attar is produced by conducting the vapours of pieces of earthenware boiling in water through sandalwood oil to the base oil. The resulting perfume recreates the fragrance of earth moistened by a rain shower.

Rose (U. *gulāb*; *Rosa centifolia* L.) and agarwood (U. *'ūd*; *Aquilaria sinensis* [Lour.] Spreng.) are the most valued and most expensive single attar varieties. The former is commonly believed to have been invented by the Mughal emperor Jahāngīr's wife Nūr Jahān (d. 1645) when flowers soaking in the water courses of the royal palace released a thin film of superbly fragrant oil in the scorching midday sun. Since rose oil had been distilled long before the seventeenth century, Annemarie Schimmel is probably right in pointing out that merely a new method of distilling was invented at the Mughal court.

6 For more information on correspondences between accepted scientific names and Indic names, see Husain (2012: 126–37).

Moreover, she avers that the lady behind the innovation was Nūr Jahān's mother, not the legendary queen herself (Schimmel 2005: 210).

Rose is the most expensive of the floral attars and the production process of the highest quality oil requires great care. The manufacturer of the oil provides farmers with the seedlings of the shrubs and pays them in advance for growing them. The process is made cost-deficient by the fact that the shrubs last only one year and yield a crop of around two hundred flowers each. When the flowers are harvested in February–March, the distilling apparatus is set up next to the fields. The flowers for the highest quality oil are plucked before sunrise and immediately sealed inside the distillation pots to be boiled over a low flame. The harvest of the first few hours after sunrise yields the second best oil whereas the flowers that have been exposed to sunlight for a longer time are normally sold to flower vendors working outside Sufi shrines and temples. Armed guards are not an exceptional sight where the best quality oil is distilled. This is no wonder, since in winter 2014 a *tola*[7] of the best quality rose-oil sold at ₹8000 (€118) on the Indian market. The rose flowers yielding the second-class oil are often distilled together with sandalwood. The resulting attar is more affordable and although the fragrance is not as intensive, it lingers longer on the skin or cloth.

Unlike most attars, rose oil is extremely volatile and exposing it to sunlight or air quickly affects its quality. It is a common practice in India to refresh attars every now and then by exposing them in open containers to the sunlight. The attar traders follow this practice when a season is about to change and the demand for attars shifts from warming to cooling varieties, or vice versa. Formerly, a constant breathing of attars was ensured by storing them in purpose-made leather bottles (*kuppī*). These were manufactured by pasting wet strips of camel or goat skin on the surface of a clay model and removing the clay after the skin had dried in the sun. At present, most merchants use leather bottles for purely decorative purposes, since the material absorbs a certain amount of its valuable content.

Yet another legendary attar is produced from agarwood. Agarwood is obtained from *Aquilaria* tree species native to the Indo-Malayan region.[8] The wood of these trees is normally odourless, of low density and yellow

7 Attars are traditionally measured in *tolās*. The *tolā* is an Indian unit of mass equalling 11.7 g. The attar merchants use custom-made glass phials of a quarter *tolā*, half *tolā* and one *tolā* for selling their wares. In addition to attars, the *tolā* is commonly used in weighing gold bullion and hashish (*caras*).

8 *Aquilaria malaccensis* Lam. and *Aquilaria sinensis* (Lour.) Spreng.

or whitish in colour. However, when the tree is wounded or infected, an immune reaction causes it to produce aromatic oleoresin that turns the affected wood dark brown and increases its density. The fragrance of this wood presents, according to Dinah Jung, 'one of the most complex olfactory accords known in perfumery today.' Agarwood had been in high demand in China before its use was introduced into Arabo-Islamic culture during the seventh and eighth centuries, possibly through contacts with Chinese merchants in Southeast Asia (Jung 2013: 105–106, 114). During the period from the eleventh to the thirteenth centuries, when Arab merchants dominated the Mediterranean commerce, Indian agarwood was together with ambergris the most widely traded aromatic substance (Zohar and Lev 2013: 10). Because of its complex scent, the global demand is growing exponentially and the wild trees are becoming increasingly endangered. Agarwood features in the IUCN Red List of Threatened Species (2015) and its export from India has been prohibited.

In India, agarwood grows in Assam and producing attar from it is a trade secret preserved by the local Muslim community. Larger pieces are used as incense burned on embers and at present the best quality agarwood with the highest content of oleoresin fetches around ₹100,000 (€1340.21) per kilo. Since about one kilo of agarwood is required for producing one to two *tola*s of attar, using the best quality pieces for distilling the oil would make the price exorbitantly high. For this reason, small chips, semi dust and dust are used for the oil. Even so, agarwood remains the most precious attar, the best quality selling at around ₹15,000 (€221) per *tolā*.

Although single attars are common, a mixture called *shamāmat al-ʿambar* has a pride of place among traditional scents. *Shamāmat al-ʿambar* literally means 'the scent of ambergris,' but the word *shamāma* specifically denotes a mixture or melange of scents in contrast to single attars. *Shamāmat al-ʿambar* contains aromatic materials of both plant and animal origin. Its main ingredient is ambergris, which is produced as a biliary secretion in the intestines of the sperm whale. It is found floating on the sea or lying on seashores in regions where sperm whales move, that is, practically everywhere in the world. Ambergris is extremely rare and coveted by the perfume industry because of its fixative abilities.[9] However, its fragrance alone is not particularly pleasant. This is perhaps the reason why it is often combined with other aromatic substances.

The first step in the preparation of *shamāmat al-ʿambar* consists of roasting the ambergris that is then distilled. The product of the first distillation

9 For the most comprehensive study of ambergris to date, see Kemp (2012).

is combined with a paste obtained from different plant materials and distilled anew. The second distillation turns the dirty brown viscous liquid into beautifully flowing red-brown perfume oil with a complex note. This resembles the process of turning the opercula of certain marine snails into a fragrant perfume, as described in two Sanskrit texts studied by James McHugh, Niścalakara's *Ratnaprabhā* ('Shine of Jewels', early second millennium CE, a commentary on Cakrapāṇidatta's medical text *Cakradatta*), and Gaṅgādhara's treatise on perfume entitled *Gandhasāra* ('Essence of Perfume', mid-second millennium).[10] The formula and ratio of the plant material added during the second distillation process is a carefully guarded secret. However, the attar merchants are able to tell that it includes at least sandalwood, cloves (U. *lauṅg*; *Syzygium aromaticum* L.), Indian bay leaves (U. *tezpatta*; *Cinnamomum tamala* [Buch.-Ham.] T.Nees & C.H.Eberm.), saffron and bergamot (U. *turunj*; *Citrus × limon* [L.] Osbeck), in addition to the leaves of the henna plant (U. *ḥinā*; *Lawsonia inermis* L) that give the attar its characteristic reddish hue.

The finest Indian-made absolutes are bought by international perfume labels and in the domestic market for use in different industries; only a fraction is sold as attar. A number of aromatics are used in both Ayurvedic and Unani medicine whereas attars are mixed with chewing tobacco and *pān masālā* (jasmine and rose) or used to flavour the syrup for mixing cold drinks (rose and vetiver).

TRADING ATTARS IN NIZAMUDDIN BASTI

In addition to religious institutions, commercial areas that specialize in wares connected to religion dot Nizamuddin Basti. The selection varies according to the clientele. Books, skull-caps and prayer-beads are ubiquitous. Religious ephemera from music and calligraphic Quranic verses to gemstones and rings tend to be found around the shrine, whereas the equipment for the demanding conditions of preaching in the field, such as sleeping bags and foldaway mosquito nets, are available closer to the Markaz. Here, the shops eschew recorded music and concentrate on sermons instead. Attar shops that, by a quick count, number as many as thirty are spread throughout the Basti. In addition, many shops selling religious paraphernalia include a limited range of bestselling fragrances in their selection.

10 See McHugh (2013: 61–64).

Kamal Nizami has been running a small shop in one of the alleys inside the Basti since 1978. Outwardly, the shop is very modest, but many of its old glass bottles include some of the finest and most expensive Indian attars. In addition, he sells several grades of agarwood, sandalwood and different types of frankincense (U. *lobān*; *Boswellia serrata* Roxb.). Over the years, he has created an extensive network with producers across India in order to ensure that he is delivered the best products. These include agarwood harvested in Assam, rose oil distilled near Aligarh and *shamāmat al-ʿambar* made in Kannauj, the traditional centre of the attar industry. The best wares are so expensive that a trusted man delivers these by hand to his shop.

Nizami insists on providing only natural attars to his customers and is adamant in his avoidance of synthetics. To justify his choice, he recounted an incident where the ear of a man had swollen because he had applied a synthetic perfume on a cotton wad kept in the curve of the right ear. However, Nizami was instantly able to cure him by applying pure sandalwood oil to the affected area. The perfumer and biochemist Luca Turin (2006: 25–26) points out that the synthetic ingredients are not automatically worse than natural ones, and their advantage is their even quality that does not depend on climatic conditions or the harvesting and handling of the raw material. But in India the surveillance of chemicals is not as strict as, for instance, in the European Union, and there remain some doubts as to whether the safety of the synthetic perfumes has been thoroughly tested. However, limiting oneself to naturals means a restricted local market. The majority of inhabitants of the Basti belong to the lower-income classes and natural vetiver or sandalwood oils costing more than thousand rupees per *tola* are beyond their means, not to speak of rose or agarwood. For this reason, Nizami's customers include foreign diplomats from embassies of countries such as Saudi Arabia and the Gulf states. They appreciate the fine quality of Indian attars and are prepared to pay for them. Many Western followers of Inayat Khan professing an interest in aromatherapy have also found their way to Nizami's shop that can be trusted to sell pure essential oils.

Since the shop is situated in the back alleys of the Basti, most customers are regulars. A more attractive location is found near the Markaz. The shopping area does not bear an official name, but it is locally referred to as Markaz Bazar. Many of its customers are foreign Muslims staying at the Markaz and the merchandise on display reflects their needs. The shops sell religious literature in English and Arabic, Arabian-style clothing as well as the field equipment mentioned above. There are also several moneychangers and internet cafes. This is also the area where attar shops cluster. Some of them are small rooms, merely enough to accommodate the counter, attars and a chair for the salesman, whereas others are big showrooms with large windows and sliding doors. What is common to all the shops, however, is the elaborate décor. The windows and shelves are filled with cut-glass bottles that include a selection of liquids ranging in colour from light blue to deep purple and pink. As the colour scale of natural attars is rather limited, ranging from pale yellow to different shades of dark brown, it is immediately obvious that the majority of the merchandise on display is synthetic.

Zia Siddiqui, a graduate of Dār al-'Ulūm Deoband, runs a small shop here. He speaks fluent Arabic and is thus able to communicate with a number of foreign customers. The walls of his shop are beautifully lined with mirrored shelves filled with delicate perfume bottles. Most of the perfumes are synthetic mixtures of Indian manufacture and bear religious-sounding names like *Jannat al-Firdaus* (The Garden of Paradise), *'Iṭr al-Ka'ba* (Scent of the Kaaba) and *Mubakhkhar al-Raḥīm* (Perfumed by the Merciful). Average prices range from fifty to two-hundred rupees per *tola*. The only natural attar sold by Siddiqui is vetiver. At a thousand rupees per *tola* it is also the most expensive item in his selection. In contrast to Kamal Nizami, Zia Siddiqui's customers are either members of the Tablighi Jamaat or local residents. His affordable prices cater for their needs. It is important to note that most shopkeepers trading in synthetics do not claim that their products are naturals. For most customers, this simply is not an issue.

Attars are also part of the consumerism of middle-class Muslims, and the opening of new stores in Nizamuddin West, a posh residential area located next to the Basti, over the past few years indicates a growing interest. These are airy showrooms with air-conditioning and long counters made of glass and dark wood. The shelves feature cut-glass bottles of fanciful shapes and their contents are again closer to the more natural colour scale. Raqibuddin Ahmed works in one of the newly opened shops. According to him, the owner of the shop is a great aficionado of attars who, sensing the growing market, decided to open a shop in Nizamuddin West. The shop concentrates on natural oils, produced both in India and West Asia. Raqibuddin acknowledges that the naturals are expensive and their clientele is more limited, so in order to cater for local customers, they also keep a few carefully selected synthetics in the selection. He was regretful that people increasingly favour synthetics over naturals, as they are simply not only more affordable, but their fragrance is also immediately felt and lasts longer. In contrast, naturals take time to evolve and have a lighter note.

Each of the three shops caters to different clientele and the views of the shopkeepers on the religious significance of attars were similarly varied.

RELIGIOUS SIGNIFICANCE OF ATTARS

All the interviewees stated the prophetic Sunna of Muslim law as the most important religious motivation behind the use of attars. They considered their profession respectable and blessed because it facilitated following one aspect of religion. However, their differing religious backgrounds reflected in the way they interpreted the significance of attars.

In Raqibuddin's luxurious shop, the association with the Sunna is established through the conspicuous display of agarwood that features prominently in hadith literature, where it is mentioned as a favorite fragrance of the Prophet. Furthermore, healing qualities are attributed to it and its fragrance is said to pervade paradise.[11] The shop is given an Arabic name *Bait al-ʿŪd* ('The House of Agarwood') and chunks of agarwood are showcased. However, it should be kept in mind that the use of attars is not instituted by religion as such. Instead, it was a common practice during the early centuries of Islam and became sanctioned by the Islamic religious tradition. It is also noteworthy that the normative scriptures do not dictate the use of attars. The two fragrances mentioned in the *Qur'ān*, camphor (A. *kāfūr*; Qur LXXVI:5) and musk (A. *misk*; Qur LXXXIII:26), have all but disappeared from Indian perfume culture.[12] Agarwood and the attar prepared from it, on the other hand, have remained status symbols that express a desirable identity. When a religious signification is added, they also make their wearer a good Muslim. Thus, the attars assume a role of a religiously sanctioned luxury. On the whole, at Raqibuddin's shop, the religious significance of the attars forms a vague background notion for their use while the olfactory sensation and the associated identity are on the foreground.

In contrast to this general religious notion, Zia Siddiqui insisted that the prophetic Sunna is the only relevant reason for wearing attars. According to him, their main function is practical: to hide body odours and contribute to the state of purity when people are praying. He singles out agarwood

11 Raqibuddin, unstructured interview, 5 March 2014. The hadiths mentioned by Raqibuddin are included in the two most important hadith collections, Ṣaḥīḥ al-Bukhārī and Ṣaḥīḥ Muslim.

12 Selling and possession of natural musk is forbidden by law. However, even the synthetic versions have not become particularly popular and camphor is not available in the attar shops at all.

as the most important attar because of its being mentioned in hadiths. However, it is too expensive for most people. This goes against the anti-extravagant spirit of the late nineteenth century founding fathers of Dār al 'Ulūm Deoband and for this reason the selling and use of synthetics is justified. Such conceptualization leaves little room for pondering about the origins of attars. It does not matter if an attar is natural or synthetic, as long as it fulfills its function in disguising bad smell. The only requirement for attar, according to Siddiqui, is that it should not be ritually polluting, that is, contain alcohol. However, Siddiqui acknowledged that even though the synthetics fulfill their designated function, they lack the *tāṣīr* (effect or specific action) of naturals.

In Unani medicine, each food and medicinal substance has its specific temperament (*mizāj*) – it is either hot or cold, or dry or moist in varying measure – and its *tāṣīr* is based on these qualities. Many Indian Muslims are on a general level aware of the basic differentiation of hot (*garam*) and cold (*sard*) items, especially when it comes to food. For example, foods considered especially hot, such as sesame seeds and peanuts, are consumed in the winter, whereas cold items such as cucumbers and yoghurt feature in the summer menus. Even though this variation is partly connected to the seasonal availability of the certain food items, its origins lie with the attempt to maintain the balance of the human constitution when environmental factors change.[13] Similarly, in the case of attars, any connoisseur knows that vetiver and sandal, for instance, are cold and should be worn in the summer. Agarwood and saffron, on the other hand, are extremely hot, whereas rose balances the disharmonies. This is the *tāṣīr* that the synthetics, according to Siddiqui, lack.

Kamal Nizami agrees with Siddiqui but adds that the *tāṣīr* can be used to boost one's religious practice. As we noted above, Unani medicine uses aromatic substances in treating the heart and keeping the spirit free of worries. Drawing from this concept, Nizami contests that in addition to being the Sunna of the Prophet, attars constitute *ghiẕā-yi rūḥ*, nourishment for the spirit that dwells in the heart. Not only do they refresh the spirit, they also strengthen it. Nizami foregrounded *shamāmat al-ʿambar* as the best attar to serve this purpose, while others like agarwood, ambergris and rose would work as well.

What is notable about this selection is that the temperament of the first three attars is very hot whereas the last, rose, balances.[14] The boosting of

13 See e.g. Roger (1995).

14 Although *shamāmat al-ʿambar* includes sandalwood, its other ingredients like ambergris and saffron are among the hottest aromatic substances used in attars.

the spirit with hot substances is in line with the descriptions of intensive practice of *ẕikr* found in Indian Sufi manuals on meditation. *Ẕikr* literally means remembrance, but as a technical Sufi term it covers a range of meditative techniques that involve repeating different religious formulas and names of God. This can assume the shape of a collective practice or solitary meditation during which the formulas are repeated either aloud or silently. One of the most influential manuals of Sufi meditation, *Kashkūl-i Kalīmī* (F. 'The Alms Bowl of Kalīm Allāh') written by the Chishti Shaikh Kalīm Allāh Shāhjahānābādī (d. 1729) repeatedly mentions feeling the heat and sweating as indications of successful practice (KK: 8, 10, 51). The use of hot attars appears to derive from a desire to boost this feeling.

Although the concept of nurturing the spirit is found in Unani medicine, Nizami explicitly associates the effect of attars with religion as well. In addition to the prophetic Sunna, he evokes their mythical origin. According to him, when Adam was banished from paradise, god bestowed on him a dress that would substitute the leaves he and his consort Eve had begun to wear after consuming fruits from the forbidden tree. However, this was no ordinary dress, but was made of paradisiacal plants, 'agarwood, sandalwood, vetiver, saffron, rose and all kinds of flowers.'[15] On earth, Adam alighted in Sri Lanka, which, according to Nizami, is the reason why the finest aromatic substances are found in India and the surrounding areas.[16] Thus, the role of attars as nourishment for the spirit also derives from their blessed origin that can lead the wearer closer to paradise and god.

PERSONAL AND RITUAL USE

In personal use, attars are simply applied on the skin or brushed on clothes. It is also common to soak a cotton wad in attar and place it in the curve of the right ear. Beggars carrying little phials of attar are a normal sight in many mosques of the Basti. They offer small helpings to the devotees and receive a few coins in remuneration. Before attending an assembly of Sufi music (*samāʿ*) or a communal *ẕikr* gathering, a Sufi master often shares

15 Nizami, unstructured interview, 1 March 2014.

16 This tradition was evoked by Āzād Bilgramī (d. 1786) when he glorified India as the best place in the world and second only to paradise. In the version quoted by him, Adam descended carrying a heavenly sapphire and a leaf. The former became the black stone in the eastern corner of the Kaaba whereas from the latter grew all the aromatic plants. See Ernst (1995).

attar with the participants, who receive it on the back of the right hand and then smear it on their faces, wrists and clothes.

Different scents pervade the air at the Nizamuddin shrine. Rose petals and rosewater sprinkled on the tombs exude a sweet fragrance while synthetic attar applied on them by the pilgrims adds an overpowering aroma. The custodians of the shrine are suspicious of the latter, because not all pilgrims are aware that their offerings should not include alcohol. Pilgrims may also light incense sticks in a holder standing in the corner of the courtyard. The majority of pilgrims belong to the lower-income classes and their offerings are also inexpensive. Rosewater and attars are synthetic and so are the incense sticks that are, fortunately, burned in the open allowing the potentially injurious smoke to evaporate immediately.

The daily rituals conducted by the custodians of the shrine do not involve the use of aromatic substances. This contrasts with the practice at several other Sufi shrines. In the most important Sufi shrine of South Asia belonging to Khwāja Muʿīn al-Dīn Chishtī (d. 1235) in Ajmer (Rajasthan), the tomb chamber is purified by burning frankincense or agarwood before closing it for the night. In the major shrines of the Deccan, the tombs are cleaned daily. Sandalwood paste mixed with attars is applied on the head side of the tomb and frankincense smoke is fanned under the cloth covering it.

At the Nizamuddin shrine, attar stars in the rituals of the saint's birthday celebrations. To my knowledge, the birthday celebrations that take place in the night of the 27th of Safar (21 December 2014) are a relatively late addition to the ritual life of the shrine. They are mentioned for the first time, together with the characteristic washing of the tomb (*ghusl*), in an early eighteenth century hagiography of the saint titled *Shawāhid-i Niẓāmī*. The text also states that the water used during the ritual washing provides a cure for all kinds of diseases.[17]

Today, these festivities attract a large crowd of pilgrims. They start to gather at the shrine around nine in the evening. Many pilgrims present the custodians with attars to be offered during the ritual washing of the tomb. At midnight, the marble lattices of the tomb chamber are covered so that the view inside is obstructed. The custodians enter and lock the door behind them. Unseen by outsiders, they uncover the cenotaph. According to Afsar Ali Nizami, the cenotaph is first washed with water and then with rosewater. These liquids are collected and distributed to the pilgrims over the following year. After the cenotaph has been dried, it is anointed with a

17 See Bulāq (1900: 5).

melange (*shamāma*) of the attars provided by pilgrims and the custodians. The attars used for this purpose are, according to Nizami, all natural, since the custodians do not want to let synthetics to get in touch with the cenotaph itself. The *shamāma* is allowed to settle into the recesses and niches of the carved marble before the tomb is covered with a white cotton cloth and a coloured velvet cloth. Over the following days, an overpowering fragrance of mixed attars covers the smell of fresh roses and incense smoke wafting from the corner of the courtyard.

CONCLUDING REMARKS

Attars are potent perfume oils that embody the essence of the plant or, more rarely, the animal substance they are manufactured from. A complex culture of scent has evolved around them in India, evoking associations with the Mughal past and royal pleasure gardens. Attars were also prescribed by physicians practicing Unani medicine as a treatment for a faint heart. In the light of my interviews in contemporary Delhi, however, the religious significance overshadows the medical reasons for using attars and lies at the centre of the culture of scent. All my interviewees quoted the example set by the Prophet Muhammad (embodied in the Sunna) as the most important reason for their use.

In addition to this fundamental premise, other meanings are attached to attars, not all of them religious. Religion contributes to sanctioning this particular luxury product, and wearing attar, especially of agarwood, endows one with a desirable identity in which being a pious Muslim plays a significant role. As luxury products, fine attars are also valued offerings in the Sufi shrines. At Nizamuddin, they have an important function during the annual washing of the saint's tomb.

The medical association of scents with the heart has given rise to a specifically Sufi interpretation of attars. As Kamal Nizami noted, attars constitute nourishment for the spirit that dwells in the heart. By strengthening the spirit, attars add vigour to the religious practice. In line with the concept of increased heat evoked in Indian Sufi manuals of meditation, hot attars are perceived to best fulfill this function. The effect is further increased by the mythical origins of aromatic plants in paradise.

The link between attars and medical theory necessarily involves the question of whether the increasingly used synthetics can substitute naturals. If attars are simply perceived to contribute to a person's cleanliness by hiding body odours, their origin is of little relevance. As Zia Siddiqui noted, it is enough if they are free of the polluting alcohol. Such an attitude also de-mystifies the attars by reducing their character to an immediately perceived olfactory sensation. However, for Sufis, who emphasize the effect of the attar, the composition is as important as the fragrance. For them, the naturals have a dimension that is not immediately perceived, but can be felt by the wearer. From this point of view, the synthetics have little value.

In the case of attars, the religious interpretation directs consumption patterns and bears immediate relevance to the future culture of scent. Will the traditional ways of producing attars and the mystical associations attached to them survive, or will the synthetics eventually take over? The latter are emerging as a viable option for those who cannot afford the naturals or simply do not care about the origins of the scents they use. However, the emerging interest of middle-class Muslims in costly natural attars may help the traditional trade and culture of scent survive in contemporary India. In conditions where international brands increasingly constitute the choice of middle-class consumers this development may prove highly significant.

ABBREVIATIONS AND REFERENCES

A. = Arabic F. = Farsi (Persian) U. = Urdu

ĀA — Abū'l-Fazl ʿAllāmī. (1977). *The Ā'īn-i Akbarī*. Vol. I. Trans. H. Blochmann, rev. and ed. D.C. Phillot. New Delhi: Oriental Books Reprint Corporation.

Alavi 2007 — Alavi, S. (2007). *Islam and Healing. Loss and Recovery of an Indo-Muslim Medical Tradition, 1600–1900*. Ranikhet: Permanent Black.

Attewell 2007 — Attewell, G. (2007). *Refiguring Unani Tibb. Plural Healing in Late Colonial India*. New Delhi: Orient Longman.

Bazin 2013 — Bazin, N. (2013). 'Fragrant Ritual Offerings in the Art of Tibetan Buddhism.' *Journal of the Royal Asiatic Society* 23(1): 31–38.

Bulāq 1900 — Bulāq, Kh.M. (1900). *Shavāhid-i Niẓāmī Mashhūr ba-Maṭlūb al-Ṭālibīn*, Muḥammad Ẓāmin ʿAlī (tr.). Delhi: Maṭbaʿ-i Jān-i Jahān.

Currim and Michell 2004 — Currim, M. and G. Michell (eds) (2004). *Dargahs. Abodes of the Saints*. Mumbai: Marg Publications.

Ernst 1995 — Ernst, C. (1995). 'India as a Sacred Islamic Land.' In Lopez, Jr., D.S. (ed.), *Religions of India in Practice*, pp. 556–63. Princeton: Princeton University Press.

Ernst and Lawrence 2002 — Ernst, C.W. and B.B. Lawrence (2002). *Sufi Martyrs of Love. The Chishti Order in South Asian and Beyond*. New York: Palgrave-Macmillan.

Fo 2013 — Fo, J.S. (2013). 'Scented Trails: Amber as Aromatic in Medieval China.' *Journal of the Royal Asiatic Society* 23(1): 85–101.

Grami 2013 — Grami, B. (2013). 'Perfumery Plant Materials as Reflected in Early Persian Poetry.' *Journal of the Royal Asiatic Society* 23(1): 39–52.

Hermansen 2001 — Hermansen, M. (2001). 'Common Themes, Uncommon Contexts: The Sufi Movements of Hazrat Inayat Khan and Khwaja Hasan Nizami.' In Khan, P.Z.I. (ed.), *A Pearl in Wine. Essays on the Life, Music and Sufism of Hazrat Inayat Khan*, pp. 322–53. New Lebanon: Omega Publications.

Husain 2012 — Husain, A.A. (2012). *Scent in the Islamic Garden. A Study of Literary Sources in Persian and Urdu*. Karachi: Oxford University Press.

IUCN — International Union for Conservation of Nature; UK Office. (2014). *IUCN Red List of Threatened Species*, http://www.iucnredlist.org/ (accessed 15 April 2015).

Jung 2013 — Jung, D. (2013). 'The Cultural Biography of Agarwood: Perfumery in Eastern Asia and the Asian Neighbourhood.' *Journal of the Royal Asiatic Society* 23(1): 103–25.

KK — Kalīm Allāh Jahānābādī (n.d.). *Kashkūl-i Kalīmī*. Delhi: Maṭbaʿ-i Mujtabā.

Kemp 2012 — Kemp, C. (2012). *Floating Gold. A Natural (& Unnatural) History of Ambergris*. Chicago: The University of Chicago Press.

Manuel 2008 — Manuel, P. (2008). 'North Indian Sufi Popular Music in the Age of Hindu and Muslim Fundamentalism.' *Ethnomusicology* 52(3): 378–400.

McHugh 2012 — McHugh, J. (2012). *Sandalwood and Carrion. Smell in Indian Religion and Culture*. New York: Oxford University Press.

McHugh 2013 — McHugh, J. (2013). 'Blattes de Byzance in India: Mollusk Opercula and the History of Perfumery,' *Journal of the Royal Asiatic Society* 23(1): 53–67.

Metcalf 1993 — Metcalf, B. (1993). 'Living Hadith in the Tablighi Jama`at.' *Journal of the Royal Asiatic Society* 52(3): 584–608.

Metcalf 2003 — Metcalf, B. (2003). 'Travelers' Tales in the Tablighi Jamaʿat.' *The Annals of the American Academy of Political and Social Science* 588(136): 136–48.

Michaels 2013 — Michaels, A. (2013). 'Foreword.' *Journal of the Royal Asiatic Society* 23(1): 3–4.

Qur — *Qur'ān*. Abdel Haleem, M.A.S. (tr.) (2008). *The Qur'an. A New Translation*. Oxford: Oxford University Press.

Roger 1995 — Roger, D. (1995). 'The Influence of the Indo-Persian Medical Tradition on Muslim Cookery in Hyderabad, India.' In Delvoye, F. (ed.), *Confluence of Cultures: French Contributions to Indi-Persian Studies*, pp. 217–36. New Delhi: Manohar.

Saniotis 2008 — Saniotis, A. (2008). 'Enchanted Landscape: Sensuous Awareness as Mystical Practice among Sufis in North India.' *The Australian Journal of Anthropology* 19(1): 17–26.

Schimmel 2005 — Schimmel, A. (2005). *The Empire of the Great Mughals. History, Art and Culture*. Oxford: Oxford University Press.

Troll 2004	Troll, C.W. (ed. 2004). *Muslim Shrines in India. Their Character, History and Significance.* New Delhi: Oxford University Press.
Turin 2006	Turin, L. (2006). *The Secret of Scent. Adventures in Perfume and the Science of Smell.* London: Faber and Faber.
Yunjun 2013	Yunjun, C. (2013). The Perfume Culture of China and Taiwan: A Personal Report.' *Journal of the Royal Asiatic Society* 23(1): 103–25.
Zohar and Lev 2013	Zohar, A. and E. Lev (2013). 'Trends in the Use of Perfumes and Incense in the Near East after the Muslim Conquests.' *Journal of the Royal Asiatic Society* 23(1): 11–30.

Chapter 5

The Bodhi Tree and Other Plants in the Pāli *Tipiṭaka*

ANTONELLA SERENA COMBA[1]

This chapter explores botanical species mentioned in the Pāli *Tipiṭaka* and investigates distinct aspects of the Buddha's view on plants. The first part of the chapter discusses ethical concerns and early medical practice. Though we learn from the *Vinayapiṭaka* that the Buddha allowed ill monks to take medicines derived from plants, in general he was averse to the destruction of plants or picking fruits from trees. Monks were also instructed to avoid eating seeds, which could generate new plants. The second part of the chapter engages with monasticism and soteriology. When the Bodhisatta left his palace, he went into the forest to achieve liberation from *saṃsāra*. The forest was reputedly the most suitable place where an ascetic could let go of any worry and worldly bondage. The Buddha awakened under a *Ficus religiosa*, which became the symbol of his realization with the name Bodhi tree. Living 'at the root of a tree' is one of the thirteen ascetic practices (*dhutaṅga*) listed for the first time in the *Parivāra* (the last book of the *Vinayapiṭaka*). These practices purify virtue and provide a firm basis for concentration and wisdom, as explained in later texts such as the *Buddhavaṃsa-Aṭṭhakathā*.

1 Antonella Serena Comba is Research Fellow (Habil. Associate Professor) in Indology and Tibetology, Faculty of Humanities, University of Turin (Italy).

THE BUDDHA'S RESPECT FOR PLANTS

In the *Brahmajālasutta* of the *Dīghanikāya*, the Buddha Gotama (Skt. Gautama) preaches three kinds of virtue (*sīla*): minor (*cūḷasīla*), middle (*majjhimasīla*) and great (*mahāsīla*). Speaking about *cūḷasīla*, he says: 'The ascetic Gotama refrains from injuring the group of seeds and the group of vegetables.'[2] Buddhaghosa (fourth to fifth centuries CE), in his *Sumaṅgalavilāsinī* (*Dīghanikāya-Aṭṭhakathā*), interprets these words thus:

> He refrains from injuring, from damaging, that is cutting, breaking, cooking, etc., the fivefold group of seeds – the roots' seed, the trunks' seed, the knots' seed, the tops' seed and the seeds' seed – and the group of vegetables – the blue-green grass, the blue-green trees, etc.[3]

Dhammapāla's sub-commentary *Līnatthappakāsanā* (*Dīghanikāya-Ṭīkā*) (sixth to ninth centuries CE) adds:

> Here 'group' (*gāma*) is a multitude (*samūha*). [Objection:] now, trees, etc., are not living beings (*jīva*), because they are deprived of mind (*cittarahita*); and it is necessary to understand that they are deprived of mind because they don't throb, because even if cut they grow, because they put forth in every direction, because they are not included in the four kinds of origin (*catuyoni*),[4] and even if [for example] sprouts, stones and salts increase, this is not a reason for them to have a condition of living beings; moreover, [their] grasp of objects is only a supposition, like the tamarind's sleep, etc., like the longing of a pregnant woman, etc. So why he is supposed to refrain from injuring the group of seeds and the group of vegetables? [Answer:] because they are fit to ascetics (*samaṇasāruppato*), and because of protection of beings connected with [them] (*sannissitasattānurakkhaṇato*). Therefore he said: 'O foolish man, the human beings indeed know that in a tree there are living beings!' (*jīvasaññino hi moghapurisa manussā rukkhasmiṃ*), etc. (*Vinaya* III.156). 'The blue-green grass, the blue-green trees, etc.': the green (*alla*) grass, the

2 *bījagāmabhūtagāmasamārambhā paṭivirato samaṇo gotamo'ti* (DN I.5). All Pāli texts, if not otherwise indicated, are from CST. All the translations from the Pāli are by the author.

3 *bījagāmabhūtagāmasamārambhāti mūlabījaṃ khandhabījaṃ phaḷubījaṃ aggabījaṃ bījabījanti pañcavidhassa bījagāmassa ceva, yassa kassaci nīlatiṇarukkhādikassa bhūtagāmassa ca samārambhā, chedanabhedanapacanādibhāvena vikopanā paṭiviratoti attho* (DN Aṭṭhakathā I.77)

4 The four *yonis* or ways of generation are *aṇḍaja* (oviparous), *jalābuja* (viviparous), *saṃsedaja* (moisture-sprung) and *opapātika* (spontaneous). See PED p. 559.

> green trees, etc. With the word 'etc.', medicinal herbs, plants, creepers, etc. should be known.[5]

The *Dīghanikāya*'s 'middle morality' (*majjhimasīla*) fully develops the ideas presented within *cūḷasīla*:

> Then, venerable ones, while some ascetics and *brāhmaṇas*, eating the food which can be given on faith, are engaged in injuring the group of seeds and the group of vegetables, that is the five [kinds of seeds], the roots' seed, the trunks' seed, the knots' seed, the tops' seed and the seeds' seed, the ascetic Gotama refrains from injuring the group of seeds and the group of vegetables. Thus the common worldling would praise the Tathāgata.[6]

Comparing these words with *Dīghanikāya-Aṭṭhakathā* above, we can see how Buddhaghosa used the very same ideas to explain DN I.4. But here, unlike the commentary, there is no example for the 'group of vegetables.' Buddhaghosa explains so this lack:

> What is the meaning of 'the group of seeds and the group of vegetables,' which ascetics and *brāhmaṇas* are engaged in injuring? Explaining that, he said 'the roots' seed,' etc. Here, 'the roots' seed' means the *haliddi*,[7] the *siṅgivera*, the *vacā*, the *vacatta*, the *ativisā*, the *kaṭukarohiṇī*, the *usīra*, the *bhaddamuttaka*, etc.; 'the trunks' seed' means the *assattha*, the *nigrodha*, the *pilakkha*, the *udumbara*, the *kacchaka*, the *kapitthana*, etc.; 'the knots' seed' means the *ucchu*, the *naḷa*, the *velū*, etc.; 'the tops' seed' means the *ajjaka*, the *phaṇijjaka*, the *hirivera*, etc.; 'the seeds' seed' means the *pubbaṇṇa*, the *aparaṇṇa*, etc. All this, when separated from the tree, capable of growth (*viruhana*), is called 'group of seeds'; when not separated from the tree, not dry (*asukkha*), is called 'group of vegetables.' Here the damage to the group of vegetables is to be considered a fault entailing confession (*pācittiya*); the damage to the group of seeds is to be considered a wrong action (*dukkaṭa*).[8]

From the above passages we learn that seeds and vegetables are equated in that they can both propagate botanical species. But while the seed is dry, the vegetable is fresh. The damage to a fresh part is a *pācittiya* offense, more serious than hurting a dry seed, which is a *dukkaṭa* offense. These passages bear witness to the Buddha's compassion for plant life, a practice differentiating him from other ascetics and *brāhmaṇas*. In general a

5 DN Ṭīkā I.157.

6 DN I.5.

7 See table 5.1 at the end of this chapter.

8 DN Aṭṭhakathā I.81.

Buddhist *bhikkhu* (monk) should not damage, cut or uproot a plant, nor eat its most vital parts, i.e. seeds. He should only eat fruits without seeds, or those fruits whose seeds have fallen down naturally. There is, however, an exception. According to Jyotir Mitra, in the Buddhist Theravāda Pāli Canon or *Tipiṭaka* and in its commentaries, 498 plants are mentioned (Mitra 1974: 73–130). The largest group of plants is included in the *Mahāvagga* of *Vinayapiṭaka*, where the Buddha authorizes the monks to use some of them as medicine (*bhesajja*). Here the plants are listed as remedies and are cataloged under headings indicating the part to be used, the plant's effect or the kind of preparation, e.g. roots (*mūla*), astringent-decoctions (*kasāva*), leaves (*paṇṇa*), fruits (*phala*), resins (*jatu*) and perfumed powders to mix with collyria (*añjana-upapisana*). The roots are from *haliddī*, *siṅgivera*, *vacā*, *vacattha*, *ativisa*, *kaṭukarohiṇī*, *usīra* and *bhaddamuttaka*. The astringent decoctions are from the *nimba*, *kuṭaja*, *pakkava* and *nattamāla*. The leaves are from the *nimba*, *kuṭaja*, *paṭola*, *sulasī* and *kappāsika*. The fruits are from *vilaṅga*, *pippala*, *marica*, *harītaka*, *vibhītaka*, *āmalaka*, *goṭha*. The resins are from *hiṅgu*, *hiṅgujatu* (*hiṅgu* resin), *hiṅgusipāṭika*, *taka* (gum), *takapatti*, *takapaṇṇi*. The powders for collyria are from *candana*, *tagara*, *kāḷānusāriya*, *tālīsa* and *bhaddamuttaka*.[9]

The rationale for regulations on harming trees distinctly emerges in debates in ancient Indian society on the presence of soul (or consciousness) in plants. In early Āyurvedic literature, we learn that, according to some, plants are like animals and human beings, having body and mind, although they can only move very slowly. Every living being can be born again as a plant and experience the typical dull mind of vegetable life. From this perspective, it is very important to be nonviolent towards plants, because they could contain the *jīva* (living principle) of a much loved relative passed away. According to others, the vegetable world is completely deprived of *jīvas*, so there is a fundamental difference between human and non-human animals, on the one hand, and plants, on the other. From this perspective, there is no karmic residue resulting from the cutting of trees and damaging plants.[10]

The Buddha adopted a middle way. For him, plants were not living beings, but were to be respected because they were 'fit for ascetics' and could be a dwelling for many other living beings.

9 ViPi I.201–03; Bhikkhu Thānissaro 2013: 56–57; Zysk (1991: 34–35). See table 5.1.

10 CaS.Sū I.48 and Cakrapāṇidatta's eleventh century commentary *Āyurvedadīpikā* thereon. Even if the text attributed to Caraka can be dated, in the extant shape, in the first century CE, its content is much more ancient.

THE RULES ABOUT CUTTING TREES IN THE *VINAYAPIṬAKA*

The Buddha's view on plants is best seen in two passages of the *Vinayapiṭaka*, the 'Book of the Discipline.' The first one is that from which Dhammapāla's *ṭīkā* extracted a quotation:

> At that time the Lord Buddha was living at Kosambī, in Ghosita's Park (Ghositārāma). At that time a householder, the personal attendant of the Venerable Channa, said to him: 'Venerable, find out a site for a dwelling (*vihāra*). I shall order a dwelling to be built for the Venerable.'
>
> Then the Venerable Channa, making clean a site for the dwelling, caused to cut a sacred tree (*cetiyarukkha*), honored (*pūjita*) by the village, honored by the market town, honored by the town, honored by the province, honored by the kingdom. Human beings (*manussa*) became annoyed, vexed and displeased, [saying:] 'How can indeed these ascetics (*samaṇa*), belonging to the Son of the Sakyas [=the Buddha], cause to cut a sacred tree honored by the village... [etc.], honored by the kingdom? The ascetics, belonging to the Son of the Sakyas, hurt (*viheṭhenti*) a living being (*jīva*) which has one faculty (*ekindriya*)!'
>
> The *bhikkhus* listened to these human beings annoyed, vexed and displeased. The *bhikkhus* desiring little, contented, conscientious, scrupulous, fond of the training, became annoyed, vexed and displeased. [They said:] 'How can indeed the Venerable Channa cause to cut a sacred tree honored by the village ... [etc.], honored by the kingdom?'
>
> Then these *bhikkhus*, having scolded in various ways the Venerable Channa, informed the Lord about that matter. And the Lord, on that ground, in that occasion, having gathered the Saṅgha of the *bhikkhus*, asked the Venerable Channa: 'Channa, is it true, as is said, that you caused to cut a sacred tree, honored by the village... [etc.], honored by the kingdom?'
>
> 'It is true, Lord,' [he said].
>
> The Lord Buddha scolded him, [saying]:
>
> 'Foolish man, this is inappropriate, unsuitable, not fit, unworthy of a recluse, improper, it should not be done! How can you, foolish man, cause to cut a sacred tree, honored by village... [etc.], honored by the kingdom? O foolish man, human beings indeed know that in a tree there are living beings (*jīvasaññino, hi, moghapurisa, manussā rukkhasmiṃ*). This does not lead, foolish man, to the faith (*saddhā*) of nonbelievers, nor increase [the faith] of believers; rather, foolish man, it leads to the absence of faith in nonbelievers and to doubt (*aññathattā*) of some believers.'
>
> Then the Lord, having scolded in various ways the Venerable Channa... [etc.],[11] said: 'So, *bhikkhus*, look to this rule (*sikkhāpada*): if a large dwelling is being built by a *bhikkhu* for his own use, having a donor, [that *bhikkhu*]

11 See ViPi III. 20–21.

should bring *bhikkhus* to point out the site. These *bhikkhus* are to point out a site without involving damage (*anārambha*) and with a space around it (*saparikkamana*). If a *bhikkhu* should build a large dwelling on a site involving damage and without a space around it, or if he should not bring *bhikkhus* to point out the site, there is an offence entailing a formal meeting of the Saṅgha (*saṅghādisesa*).'[12]

This anecdote shows that a rule against damaging plants was necessary with respect to sacred trees honored by the people. But the Buddha extended it to all plants (the word *an-ārambha* comes from the same root of *sam-ārambha* quoted above). However, it is worth mentioning that the sentence '*Jīvasaññino, hi, moghapurisa, manussā rukkhasmiṃ*' is ambiguous. The word *saññino* means 'endowed with *saññā*,' and *saññā*, usually translated as 'perception,' can be interpreted as either true cognition or misunderstanding, based on context. So, if people believed that the trees had *jīvas*, this could be interpreted matter-of-factly (that deities, animals, et cetera abide in trees), or as a conviction that every tree has its own *jīva*, a living principle or a soul, like human beings and animals.

The second passage of the *Vinaya* tells the story of a deity living in a tree. It so emerges that cutting trees could be dangerous because the beings abiding them could take revenge:

At that time the Lord Buddha was living at Āḷavī, in the Aggāḷava shrine. At that time the *bhikkhus* of Āḷavī, engaged in building work, either cut trees or caused them to cut. A certain *bhikkhu* of Āḷavī began to cut a tree. The deity (*devatā*) residing in that tree said to the *bhikkhu*: 'Venerable, if you desire to build your dwelling, don't cut my dwelling.' The *bhikkhu* did not take any heed and cut it, striking the arm of that deity's youngster. Then the deity thought: 'What now if I were to deprive this *bhikkhu* of life?' After that, the deity thought: 'It is not suitable (*patirūpa*) for me to deprive this *bhikkhu* of life. What now if I inform about this matter the Lord?' Then the deity went to the Lord and informed him about that matter. 'Very well, deity! It was good that you, deity, did not deprive that *bhikkhu* of life. If today you, deity, had deprived that *bhikkhu* of life, you would also have brought forth a great demerit (*apuñña*). Go, deity: in a certain open space there is a secluded tree where you can go.'

Human beings became annoyed, vexed and displeased, [saying:] 'How can indeed these ascetics, belonging to the Son of the Sakyas, either cut or cause to cut a tree? The ascetics, belonging to the Son of the Sakyas, will hurt (*viheṭhessanti*) a living being (*jīva*) which has one faculty (*ekindriya*)!'

12 ViPi III.155–56.

> The *bhikkhus* listened to these human beings annoyed, vexed and displeased. The *bhikkhus* desiring little... [etc.] became annoyed, vexed and displeased. [They said:] 'How can indeed the *bhikkhus* of Āḷavī either cut or cause to cut a tree?'... [etc. The Lord asked:] '*Bhikkhus*, is it true, as is said, that you either cut or cause to cut a tree?'
>
> 'It is true, Lord.'
>
> The Lord Buddha scolded them, [saying]:
>
> 'Foolish men [etc.], how can you either cut or cause to cut a tree? O foolish men, human beings indeed know that in a tree there are living beings. This does not lead, foolish man, to the faith of nonbelievers... [etc.]. So, *bhikkhus*, look to this rule: in the destruction of a group of vegetables there is an action entailing confession (*bhūtagāmapātabyatāya pācittiyaṃ*).'[13]

The *Vinaya* corpus elaborates on plants and parts of plants, and within *bhūtagāma* (the group of vegetables) it distinguishes between five kinds of 'seeds' (*pañca bījajātāni*): (1) root seed (*mūlabīja*), like the *haliddi*, etc.; (2) trunk seed (*khandhabīja*), like the *assattha*, etc.; (3) knot seed (*phaḷubīja*), like the *ucchu*, etc.; (4) top seed (*aggabīja*), like the *ajjuka*, etc.; and (5) seeds' seed (*bījabīja*), like the *pubbaṇṇa*,[14] etc. If a *bhikkhu* was to cut or cause to cut, break or cause to break, cook or cause to cook them, knowing they are 'seeds,' he would be commiting an action demanding confession.[15] According to the *Vinayapiṭaka-Aṭṭhakathā*, where for the first time there is no difference between the *bhūtagāma* and the *bījagāma* (in fact they seem to be synonymous), when the *bhikkhu* of Āḷavī lifted the hatchet, he could not control it and cut the youngster's arm 'up to its root in the chest.' The text further elaborates the reason behind the wrath of the deity:

> Once on the Himālaya, as is said, there was in the fortnight days a meeting of deities. There they asked: 'Are you steadfast or not in the tree-Dhamma (*rukkhadhamma*)?' It is called tree-Dhamma, the fact that a deity does not produce any anger in its mind when [its] tree is being cut. There [on the Himālaya] any deity not steadfast in the tree-Dhamma could not attend the deities' meeting. Therefore that deity saw the danger which is a cause for the absence of steadfastness in the tree-Dhamma, and, in front of the Lord, remembered a former life-story, when the Tathāgata was a six-tusked

13 ViPi IV.34. Cf. ViPi IV.32–33: *bhikkhus* cannot dig, because 'the human beings indeed know that in the ground there are living beings.'

14 Cf. DN-Aṭṭhakathā 1.81 above. For sake of brevity, here I mention only the first plant of each kind.

15 ViPi IV.34–35 (*pācittiya*). The text gives many other examples of seeds.

[elephant],[16] etc., in accordance with the Dhamma teaching heard earlier. So it thought: 'It is not suitable for me to deprive... [etc.].'

'What now if I inform about this matter the Lord?' Then it considered: 'This *bhikkhu* is a son with a father. Certainly the Lord, having heard that he behaved in that way, will fix a limit, declaring a religious rule.' [...] Then the Lord told the deity this stanza:

> Who controls his suddenly uprisen anger as a roaming chariot,
> he is what I call a 'driver.' Other people are [just] rein-holders.[17]

At the end of the stanza the deity was established in the fruit of 'Entering the Stream' (*sotāpattiphala*).[18] Then the Lord, teaching the Dhamma to the assembly gathered there, told this stanza:

> Who removes his suddenly uprisen anger – like the one who, by medicines, removes a snake poison which is spreading [in all his body] –,
> he is a *bhikkhu* who leaves the near and the further shore – like the snake leaves its old and worn out skin.[19]

Here the first stanza went in the Dhammapada's collection, the second in the Suttanipāta's one, the story in the Vinaya. Then the Lord, teaching the Dhamma, reflected upon a place to stay for that deity; having seen a suitable place, he said: 'Go, deity: in such and such open space there is a secluded tree. Go in it!' The tree which became the property of the deity so exhorted, as is said, was not in the realm of Āḷavī, but in the enclosure of the Jeta Wood; therefore it was called *vivitta* ('secluded'). From that time, the deity who got the care from the Perfectly and Completely Enlightened (*Sammāsambuddha*) became his protector.[20]

In this narrative we find three interesting elements: first, the tree-deity is never called '*yakkha*.'[21] Second, the condition of these tree-deities

16 See *Chaddanta-jātaka*, J v.37–57.

17 Dhp 222 (17.2).

18 *Sotāpatti* is the freedom from the first three fetters of personality – belief, skeptical doubt and attachment to mere rules and rituals (Nyanatiloka Mahathera 1984: 20–21).

19 *Suttanipāta* I.

20 ViPi *Aṭṭhakathā* IV.759–761.

21 *Yakkha* (Skt. *yakṣa*) and *yakṣinī* (Skt. *yakṣiṇī*) are non-human beings (*amanussa*) who can be helpful or harmful towards human beings. They can be invisible or assume any shape at will. In Buddhist literature they are sometimes identified with tree deities. See Malalasekera (1937–1938: vol. 2, 675–78); Coomaraswamy (1993); Sutherland (1991).

resembles that of human beings: they do not live blissfully in a heaven, but on earth; they are subject to anger, but can let go of it; they practice a tree-Dhamma of their own. Third, if they are propitiated, they can become protectors of human beings.

LIVING AT THE ROOT OF A TREE

In the *Vinayapiṭaka* the Buddha lists the four requisites (*nissaya*) of a monk's life: lumps of alms food (*piṇḍiyālopabhojana*), a robe made of rags taken from a dust heap (*paṃsukūlacīvara*), a dwelling at the root of a tree (*rukkhamūlasenāsana*) and fermented urine (usually from cows) as medicine (*pūtimuttabhesajja*). Other kinds of food, robes, dwellings and medicines are considered extra allowances (*atirekalābha*) (ViPi I.58).

Further examples of the importance of trees in ascetic life can be found in a variety of texts. Amongst these, *Buddhavaṃsa*[22] tells how Buddha Gotama, in one of his preceding lives as Sumedha, a *brāhmaṇa* by caste, firstly gave up his home and wealth and went to the Himalaya where he built up a leaf-hut. After some time he abandoned the hut and went to meditate under a tree, because he knew that it was the kind of lodging (*senāsana*) which does not produce greed and protects from hindrances to spiritual progress:

> I gave up the leaf-hut, endowed with eight defects.
> I went to the root of a tree, provided with eight qualities.[23]

In *Visuddhimagga*, Buddhaghosa listed thirteen ascetic practices (*dhutaṅga*) aiming to perfect fewness of wishes, etc., and to cleanse virtue (*sīla*). These practices are not described in details in the Pāli Canon but are enumerated in the *Parivāra*, the last book of the *Vinayapiṭaka* (V.131, 193). The ninth *dhutaṅga* is the tree-root-dweller's practice (*rukkhamūlikaṅga*), which is undertaken uttering the words 'I refuse a roof' or 'I undertake the tree-root-dweller's practice.' While explaining this practice, Buddhaghosa describes its benefits: one can put in practice the Buddha's instructions; appreciate impermanence by observing the changing of leaves; give up envy of houses; live with the deities; and realize qualities like fewness of wishes, et cetera. Then he says:

22 This text is a relatively late addiction to the Canon. It was not accepted by the reciters (*bhāṇakas*) of the *Dīghanikāya* (Norman 1983: 94).

23 BV VIII.

From where could it come, to a secluded one, an abode equal to the root of a tree, praised by the best of Buddhas and named 'support' (*nissaya*)?[24]

Removing the envy of houses, being protected by deities,
being secluded, the life at the root of a tree is indeed a good habit.

The vision of the leaves of a tree [becoming] red, blue-green, yellow and falling down dispels the perception of permanence.

Therefore a wise man should not despise the tree's root, a secluded abode for he who is applying himself to mental cultivation (*bhāvanā*), the Buddha's heritage.[25]

Buddhadatta's commentary *Madhuratthavilāsinī* on *Buddhavaṃsa* explains further the reason why a tree is better than a leaf-hut. The hut has eight defects: (1) it has to be built using a considerable amount of material; (2) it has to be always repaired with grass, leaves, clay, etc.; (3) the lodging inevitably decays, causing the ascetic to emerge from concentration at an improper time; (4) by living in a hut one gets used to being protected from the cold and the heat and so one's constitution becomes delicate (*sītuṇhassa paṭighātena kāyassa sukhumālakaraṇabhāvo*); (5) it permits concealment from blame, thus one may think: 'going into a house one can do any evil action' (*gharaṃ paviṭṭhena yaṃ kiñci pāpaṃ sakkā kātunti garahapaṭicchādanakaraṇabhāvo*); (6) having possessions and relatives, one can think: 'this is mine' (*mayhamidanti sapariggahabhāvo*); (7) having a home is like living with a companion; (8) the leaf-hut is 'shared by many [other beings]' (*bahusādhāraṇabhāvoti*): lice, fleas, house-lizards, et cetera.

Eventually, having realized these eight disadvantages, the great being (*mahāsatta*) Sumedha left the leaf-hut and decided to live at the root of a tree. This accommodation is praised for having ten qualities: (1) it requires minimum preparation (*appasamārambhatā*); (2) it is blameless; (3) seeing the continuous changes in the leaves of a tree, one learns the perception of impermanence (*aniccasaññā*); (4) there is no envy of other forms of lodging; (5) there is no feeling that a wrong act has been performed (*pāpakaraṇārahābhāva*); (6) it does not require any possession; (7) it is an abode where one can live with deities; (8) it is the opposite to any form of concealment (*channapaṭikkhepa*); (9) it is easy to use; (10) it is not necessary

24 ViPi I.58: *rukkhamūlasenāsanaṃ nissāya pabbajjā, tattha te yāvajīvaṃ ussāho karaṇīyo* ('The ascetic life has a dwelling on a root of a tree for its support. Thus this is the endeavor to be done for the length of your life.')

25 VM 74–75.

to look for it, because it is easy to obtain a lodging at the root of a tree by simply going from one place to another.

At the end of this list, Buddhadatta quotes the verses of VM as told by the *brāhmaṇa* Sumedha.[26]

THE BODHI TREE IN THE *TIPIṬAKA*

The most important tree in the Pāli Canon is the one under which the Buddha achieved enlightenment (*bodhi*). This is discussed as: (1) Bodhi tree (*bodhi-rukkha*), (2) *bodhi* or (3) a particular plant. According to the tradition, the Buddha Gotama became enlightened under an *assattha* tree, but the *Mahāpadānasutta* (DN II.1–71) speaks of seven Buddhas of whom the Buddha Gotama is the last one. Every Buddha became enlightened at the root of a different tree: the Buddha Vipassin at a *pāṭalī*'s root; the Buddha Sikhin at a *puṇḍarīka*'s root; the Buddha Vessabhū at a *sāla*'s root; the Buddha Kakusandha at a *sirīsa*'s root; the Buddha Konāgamana at an *udumbara*'s root; and the Buddha Kassapa at a *nigrodha*'s root.[27]

In the first four *nikāyas* of the *Suttapiṭaka*, fragments of the Buddha Gotama's life are scattered in various discourses. As the aim of such passages is the teaching of the Dhamma, biographical information is not given in much detail. In most of these reports, the Bodhi tree is absent (Comba 2010: 55–84). In the *Mahāpadānasutta* of DN quoted above, after listing the different features of each Buddha, the Buddha Gotama tells his disciples of the life of Buddha Vipassin, the first Buddha. Some events are common to the lives of the other Buddhas (e.g. to be a Tusita deity[28] before entering one's own mother's womb; DN II.12); others are peculiar to the Bodhisatta Vipassin. Among the latter is the ability to see without blinking which

26 *Madhuratthavilāsinī* or *Buddhavaṃsa-Aṭṭhakathā* 77–78.

27 The tradition of the seven Buddhas should be considered a later development of the doctrine although one already popular at around the third century BCE. Cf. the inscription on the Nigālī Sāgar pillar: '(A) When king Devānāṃpriya Priyadarśin [Aśoka] had been anointed fourteen years, he enlarged the Stūpa of the Buddha Konākamana to the double (of its original size). (B) And when he had been anointed [twenty] years, he came himself and worshipped (this spot) [and] caused [a stone pillar to be set up].' (AL). In later narratives, such as those reported in BV, there are listed twenty-four Buddhas, each associated to a different Bodhi tree. See Horner 2007: xli–xlvi, where a full list of Bodhi trees is given.

28 A Tusita deity is an inhabitant of the Tusita world, the fourth of the six *deva* worlds (see Malalasekera 1937–1938: vol. 1, 1033–34).

provides an explanation of his name (*vipassin*: 'he who sees clearly') (DN II.20). The text also tells us that after four sights (an old man, a sick man, a corpse at a funeral and an ascetic), Bodhisatta Vipassin goes forth into homelessness. According to the words attributed to the Buddha Gotama: 'he went to his dwelling alone, in a secluded spot' (*vipassissa bodhisattassa vāsūpagatassa rahogatassa paṭisallīnassa*, DN II.30); there he remained until 'his mind was freed from the corruptions without remainder' (*anupādāya āsavehi cittaṃ vimucci*, ibid.: 35). Once turned into a Buddha, Lord Vipassin began to think: 'Suppose now I was to teach the Dhamma?' Then 'a certain Mahābrahmā' persuaded him to do so. In this account, though reference is made to 'a secluded spot,' there is no direct reference to the Bodhi tree either before or after liberation.

It is different in later texts, such as chapter thirty-six of the *Buddhavaṃsa* from *Khuddakanikāya*, where the Buddha Gotama tells his story and mentions very briefly his own enlightenment under the Bodhi tree:

> I attained supreme enlightenment at the root of an *assattha*.[29]

The Buddha Gotama's Bodhi tree is also mentioned at the beginning of the *Vinayapiṭaka*'s *Mahāvagga*. Here the narration starts after enlightenment:

> At that time the Lord Buddha dwelt at Uruvelā, on the bank of the river Nerañjarā, at the root of the Bodhi tree, just after he had become a *sambuddha*. And the Lord Buddha sat cross-legged at the root of the Bodhi tree uninterruptedly during seven days, enjoying the bliss of emancipation. Then the Lord (at the end of these seven days) during the first watch of the night fixed his mind upon the chain of causation (*paṭiccasamuppāda*), in direct and in reverse order [...]. Then the Lord, at the end of those seven days, arose from that state of meditation, and went from the root of the Bodhi tree to the *ajapālanigrodha* tree.[30] And when he had reached it, he sat cross-legged at the root of the *ajapālanigrodha* tree uninterruptedly during seven days, enjoying the bliss of emancipation.[31]

Then a haughty *brāhmaṇa* approached the Buddha and spoke to him; after that, the Buddha went from the root of the *ajapālanigrodha* tree to a *mucalinda* tree, where he met the *nāga* king Mucalinda. After a week, the Buddha went to a *rājāyatana* tree, where he sat for another week, enjoying

29 *Ahaṃ assatthamūlamhi patto sambodhimuttamaṃ* (BV 66).

30 Goatherds' banyan, *Ficus benghalensis* L.

31 ViPi I.2.

the bliss of emancipation. There he received the offerings of two merchants named Tapussa and Bhallika. And once again, after a week, the Buddha came back to the root of the *ajapālanigrodha* tree. There he began to think about teaching the Dhamma.[32]

In this account the role of trees is greatly emphasized, a feature also found in *Buddhavaṃsa*, *Visuddhimagga* and *Buddhavaṃsa-Aṭṭhakathā*. In particular, the Buddha's moving over from one tree to another well exemplifies his freedom to wander about without attachment. He is not bound to a particular tree, not even to the *assattha* at whose root he attained *bodhi*. So, on the one hand, the development of the mind is successful only in a secluded place with a simple life; on the other, it requires freedom from attachment.

DEVOTION TO THE BODHI TREE

After the Buddha Gotama's death, or *parinibbāna* (complete awakening), the Bodhi tree became the symbol of his liberation. The feeling of devotion towards Bodhi trees – either the *assattha* or the other Buddhas' trees – is already testified in a later canonical text, the *Apadāna*, where the cult of the Bodhi tree is sometimes identified with devotion towards the seat – called 'the diamond throne,' 'the lion's seat,' et cetera – on which a Buddha awakened. A few examples will elucidate this further.

In *Apadāna* II.403, the *thera* ('elder monk') Sīhāsanabījiya paid homage to the Bodhi tree of the Buddha Tissa; then he took a fan (*bījana* or *vījana*) and fanned the lion's seat of the Buddha. In reward for this action, he did not experience low rebirth (*duggati*) in ninety-two eons. In *Apadāna* II.403 the *thera* Thiṇukkadhāriya, who brought with a pure mind three torches to the Bodhi tree of the Buddha Padumuttara, would not be born in any realm of misery for a hundred thousand eons. In *Apadāna* II.519–21, the story is about the *therī* ('elder nun') Pañcadīpikā, formerly a wandering ascetic (*cārikī*) from the town of wonder Haṃsavatī, where the Buddha Padumuttara was born. One day, during the dark fortnight, she saw the Bodhi tree (*bodhim uttamaṃ*) and her mind was purified. She sat at the root of the tree, had a respectful thought for the tree and then paid homage to it by lifting her folded hands in the gesture of *añjali*. Suddenly her mind was gladdened and she thought: 'If the Buddha has boundless qualities and is a matchless person, may I see a miracle, may this Bodhi tree shine.' As soon as she had this thought, the tree blazed with light shining in every

32 ViPi I.2–5.

direction, as if it was made of gold. Pañcadīpikā sat at the root of the tree for a week; then she offered five (or seven) lamps to it. As a result of her offering, she was reborn in the realm of the thirty-three gods, and then had many better lives, until she became a disciple of the Buddha Gotama and reached all attainments, including *bodhi*.[33]

Along with a variety of narratives, the Bodhi tree figures prominently in Buddhist art in India and outside. The *stūpas* where, according to the tradition, the Buddha's relics were buried have not all been preserved to our day, but we can still admire some of Aśoka's pillars, where the Buddha is symbolized as a lion, an elephant, a bull or a horse, and his doctrine is rendered by means of a wheel (*cakka*). The pillar has been often interpreted as symbolic of the Bodhi tree.

Devotion towards the Buddhas' trees grew especially in Sri Lanka, where, it is said, Emperor Aśoka sent his son Mahinda and his daughter Saṅghamittā to transmit the Buddhist doctrine. Saṅghamittā took with her a sapling of the Bodhi tree, and planted it at Anurādhapura, where it is still venerated. According to the Sinhalese chronicle *Mahāvaṃsa* (XVII.17), in the month of Kattika (October–November), Aśoka used to hold a festival in honor of the Bodhi tree. He loved it so much that one of his wives, Tissarakkhā, out of jealousy, tried to kill the Bodhi tree by pricking it with a poisonous thorn from the *maṇḍu* plant (*Mahāvaṃsa* XX.3–5). After the planting of the tree in Sri Lanka, the devotion towards it grew up to a point that Bodhipūjā ceremonies were instituted. This process is told in the *Mahābodhivaṃsa*, a work in prose and verse by Upatissa (end of the tenth century) translated from Sinhalese into Pāli (Norman 1983: 141) to which numerous commentaries have been added (von Hinüber 1996: 93–94).

THE BODHI TREE IN THE *NIDĀNAKATHĀ*

An analysis of the *Nidānakathā*, an introduction in prose and verse to the Jātakas and the opening of the *Jātaka-Aṭṭhakathā* attributed to Buddhaghosa, seems relevant to the present discourse. The text collects many elements

33 The story of Pañcadīpikā is repeated in Dhammapāla's commentary *Paramatthadīpanī* to *Therīgāthā*, 62–63, where she is called Selā. The stanzas 57–59 do not mention the Bodhi tree; stanza 57 is the same as the first stanza in the *Āḷavikāsutta* from *Saṃyuttanikāya* I.128; stanza 58 is the same as the third stanza in *Āḷavikāsutta*, while stanza 59 is different. So the account of Dhammapāla combines the story of *Pañcadīpikā* with the story of *Āḷavikā* (SN I.128–29), while the name Selā is from a completely different story (SN I.134).

of the Buddha Gotama's story from canonical texts, adding details which are not told anywhere else but which were probably widely known.

The *Nidānakathā* describes how, after a long abstinence from food, the Bodhisatta Gotama took his first meal: some milk-rice offered by a girl called Sujātā.

> The Bodhisatta, having spent the day on the bank of the river [Nerañjarā], in a fully blossomed wood of *sāla* trees, at evening time, when flowers are liberated from their stems, went towards the Bodhi tree, like an arousing lion, following a path a thousand and hundred-twenty cubits wide, festooned by the deities. *Nāgas, yakkhas, supaṇṇas*, etc., paid homage with perfumes, flowers, etc., chanting divine songs; it was as if the ten thousand-fold world system had one scent, one garland, one cheering (*Jātaka-Aṭṭhakathā* I.2).

In this passage the focus is on the marvelous relationship between the Bodhisatta and the world – deities and Nature – which is preparing to celebrate the Great Event of his Bodhi. When the Bodhisatta is approaching the Bodhi tree, from the opposite direction comes a grass-cutter called Sotthiya, who gives him eight bundles of grass to put on the Bodhi throne (*bodhimaṇḍa*). Then the Bodhisatta finds the right place to meditate (a notoriously difficult task in Buddhist literature). He makes a firm resolve to attain complete enlightenment and to bear all the challenges of Māra, the wicked *yakkha*.[34] Eventually he defeats Māra with the power of his perfections (*pāramī*), first of all the generosity he practiced in his preceding life as prince Vessantara.[35] The solid and great, but unconscious, Earth (*acetanāpi ghanamahāpaṭhavī*) witnesses his right to sit on the Bodhi throne but so far the Bodhi tree has played no particular role in the events described. Only when the Bodhisatta defeats the hosts of Māra does the tree pays homage to him: showering its shoots over his robe like sprouts of red corals (Jātaka I.75).

Although the *Nidānakathā* does not emphasize the role of the Bodhi tree in the Bodhisatta's awakening, it is worth noting its status in the list of the *sahajātas*, 'co-natals.' For the Bodhi tree is said to have been born on the same day of the Bodhisatta Gotama, his future wife Rāhulamātā Devī (the 'mother of Rāhula,' the only son of the Buddha), king Suddhodana's minister Channa (who would later become a *thera*), king Suddhodana's minister Kāḷudāyin (also a *thera*-to-be), the royal horse Kanthaka and four treasure-pots.[36]

34 For the *yakkha* nature of Māra, see *Suttanipāta* 78.

35 See the *Vessantarajātaka* (V.479–593).

36 *Jātaka* I.54; *Aṅguttaranikāya-Aṭṭhakathā* I.301; *Theragāthā-Aṭṭakathā* II.221; *Jinakālamālī* 26; sometimes the name of Ānanda is added to the list:

CONCLUSION

The Pāli passages discussed in this chapter are a significant example of the relationship between ascetic life and plants/trees in Buddhism, a bond of particular meaning as the forest was the home of the Bodhisatta after he left his father's palace, and was the abode of the first monks. This might explain the dialectic dualism encompassing Buddhist monasticism and the laity, the forest and the village, the nomadic existence of a homeless ascetic under a tree and the domestic, sedentary life of a layperson. Yet the forest, though the preferred setting for meditation, has two differing aspects. It is quiet, isolated and devoid of the human relationships typical of village life; but it is also terrifying – especially during the night. Indian forests were full of wild animals (e.g. tigers) and annoying insects (e.g. mosquitos). They could be humid, and they could be noisy because of the cries of birds and beasts.

Despite these difficult conditions, the Bodhisatta Gotama – according to the canonical tradition – chose the forest as his abode. During the time of his isolation, he managed to explore the depths of his mind while looking for a way to leave the suffering of *saṃsāra*. Eventually, using concentration (*samādhi*) and wisdom (*paññā*), he could reach awakening. Once liberated, the Buddha remained for some weeks in the forest.[37]

When he began to teach the Dhamma, his lay disciples offered him not only food, clothes, medicines, but also gardens, parks, caves and buildings as shelters, especially during the rainy season. All the same, the forest remained the background of the ascetic life: monks and nuns went to live in monasteries which were not built in the villages, but outside them, in the forest or near to it.

Early Buddhist texts show a respectful attitude towards seeds, plants and trees. Not only can they be used as medicine, they also serve as abodes of other beings and facilitate the life of the ascetic in the forest. Amongst the many trees, the Bodhi tree in particular became a symbol of the Buddha's awakening in *Apadānas*, commentaries and Sinhalese chronicles. But in the *Mahāparinibbānasuttānta* from the extant Pāli Canon, the Buddha tells Ānanda to put his remains in a *stūpa* without mentioning the Bodhi tree.[38] In the *Vinayapiṭaka*, he does not forbid disciples to represent him

Buddhavaṃsa-Aṭṭhakathā 131; *Dhammapada-Aṭṭhakathā* II.425; *Apadāna-Aṭṭhakathā* 58 and 358. For more on *sahajātas*, see Horner (2007: xliii–xlix).

37 See e.g. SN I.103.

38 DN II.141–43.

with a human shape, although he instructs them not to paint audacious portrayals (*paṭibhānacitta*) of women and men (*itthirūpaka, purisarūpaka*), but garlands (*māla*), creepers (*latā*) and *makaras*' (mythical aquatic creatures) teeth.[39] On extant Aśoka pillars there is no depiction of the Bodhi tree; however the pillar itself is sometimes seen to represent the tree. Conversely Bodhi trees are carved on *stūpas* like Amarāvatī and Sāñcī (second century BCE to third century CE, see Knox 1992: 13; Pieruccini 2013: 29–30) where they symbolize the awakening of the Buddha.[40]

Generally speaking, an appraisal of plants and trees in early Buddhism is possible only if one critically examines literary sources:

(1) The Pāli Canon, orally transmitted from the Buddha's time until the first century BCE, when it was written down in Śrī Laṅkā.
(2) Commentaries, orally transmitted until they were written down, and abundantly supplemented, by Buddhaghosa, Dhammapāla and others after the fourth century CE.
(3) Later Indian Sanskrit texts, like the *Mahāvastu* and the *Divyāvadāna*, composed from the first to the second centuries CE.
(4) Sinhalese chronicles like the *Dīpavaṃsa* (fourth to fifth centuries CE) and the *Mahāvaṃsa* (second half of the fifth century CE).

Although these texts are difficult to locate historically – they were gradually produced over the centuries – the commentaries are definitely later than canonical texts. Therefore if a concept is stated only in the commentaries and never expressed in the canonical texts, it is highly probable that it is a later one. With this in mind, it is worth considering some differences. The Pāli Canon looks like a collection of oral, sometimes personalized, instructions for the practice of Dhamma. The Pāli commentaries are conceived to be written down with the aim of explaining the texts and telling stories, including hagiographies of the Buddha, and of nuns and monks. Buddhist Sanskrit texts are also different in style and aim: they tell stories, but their authors have often added new characters and miracles (Comba 2014). Last but not least, the *Dīpavaṃsa* and the *Mahāvaṃsa* provide a poetical and devotional history linking Indian Buddhism with Sinhala Buddhism. This is the reason why the cult of the Bodhi tree is here outstandingly emphasized.

39 ViPi II.151.

40 Only later on did artists begin to represent the Buddha in a human shape under the Bodhi tree. See Knox (1992: 120); Bussagli (1984: 195).

Table 5.1. Chart of referenced plants from the Pāli *Tipiṭaka*.

Pāli name	**English name**	**Accepted scientific name**
āmalaka	Emblic	*Phyllanthus emblica* L.
ativisa	Monkshood	*Aconitum heterophyllum* Wall. ex Royle or *A. palmatum* D.Don
assattha	Sacred fig	*Ficus religiosa* L.
bhaddamuttaka	Nut-grass	*Cyperus rotundus* L.
candana	Sandalwood	*Santalum album* L.
goṭha	Turkey berry or Egyptian cucumber	*Solanum torvum* Sw. or *Luffa cylindrica* (L.) M.Roem.
haliddī	Turmeric	*Curcuma longa* L.
harītaka	Yellow myrobalan	*Terminalia chebula* Retz.
hiṅgu	Asafetida	*Ferula assa-foetida* L.
kāḷānusāriya	Benzoin	*Styrax benzoin* Dryand.
kappāsika	Cotton-tree	*Gossypium herbaceum* L.
kaṭukarohinī	Black hellebore	*Helleborus niger* L.
kuṭaja	Easter tree	*Holarrhena pubescens* Wall. ex G.Don
maṇḍu		(*Cycas circinalis* L.?)
marica	black pepper	*Piper nigrum* L.
mucalinda	Indian oak	*Barringtonia acutangula* (L.) Gaertn.
nattamāla	Indian beech	*Pongamia pinnata* (L.) Merr.
nigrodha	Banyan	*Ficus benghalensis* L.
nimba	Neem	*Azadirachta indica* A.Juss.
pakkava		*Ficus rumphii* Blume
pāṭalī	Trumpet-flower tree	*Stereospermum chelonoides* (L.f.) DC.
paṭola	Snake gourd	*Trichosanthes cucumerina* L.
pippala	Long pepper	*Piper longum* L.
puṇḍarīka	White-mango tree	(A variety of) *Mangifera indica* L.
rājāyatana	Buchanan's mango	*Buchanania cochinchinensis* (Lour.) M.R. Almeida
sāla	Sal tree	*Shorea robusta* C.F. Gaertn.
siṅgivera	Ginger	*Zingiber officinale* Roscoe
sirīsa	Siris	*Albizia lebbek* (L.) Benth.
tagara	Crepe jasmine	*Tabernaemontana divaricata* (L.) R.Br. ex Roem. & Schult.
tālīsa	Puneala plum	*Flacourtia jangomas* (Lour.) Raeusch.
tulasī	Holy basil	*Ocimum tenuiflorum* L.
udumbara	Cluster fig tree	*Ficus racemosa* L.
usīra	Vetiver	*Chrysopogon zizanioides* (L.) Roberty
vacā	Sweet flag	*Acorus calamus* L.
vacattha	White orris root	A kind of *Acorus*
vibhītaka	Beleric myrobalan	*Terminalia bellirica* (Gaertn.) Roxb.
vilaṅga	White-flowered embelia	*Embelia ribes* Burm. f.

ABBREVIATIONS AND REFERENCES

P. = Pali Skt. = Sanskrit

AL	Ashoka Library. (2015). 'Rumindei, Nigālī Sāgar minor pillar Edicts (Māgadhī and English)'. *Bibliotheca Polyglotta*, http://www2.hf.uio.no/polyglotta/index.php?page=fulltext&view=-fulltext&vid=378&mid=0 (accessed 10 August 2015).
Bhikkhu Ṭhānissaro 2013	Bhikkhu Ṭhānissaro (tr). (2013). *Buddhist Monastic Code II*. The Khandhaka Rules Translated & Explained. Third edition, revised, 2013, <http://www.dhammatalks.org/Archive/Writings/BMC_v140110.pdf> (accessed 7 November 2015).
Bussagli 1984	Bussagli, M. (1984). *L'arte del Gandhāra* (Storia universale dell'arte. 2. Le civiltà dell'Oriente). Torino: UTET.
BV	*Buddhavaṃsa*
CaS	*Carakasaṃhitā*. Trikamji, J. (ed.). (1981). *Carakasaṃhitā*. Fourth edition. Bombay: Munshiram Manoharlal.
Comba 2010	Comba, A.S. (2010). *La vita del Buddha dal concepimento al Risveglio*. Raleigh: Lulu.
Comba 2014	Comba, A.S. (2014). *La storia di Pūrṇa* (Pūrṇāvadāna). Raleigh: Lulu.
Coomaraswamy 1993	Coomaraswamy, A.K. (1993). *Yakṣas. Essays in the Water Cosmology*. Delhi: Indira Gandhi National Centre for the Arts and Oxford University Press.
CST	*Chaṭṭha Saṅgāyana Tipiṭaka*, Version 4.0.0.15. Copyright 1995. Dhammagiri, Igatpuri: Vipassana Research Institute, <http://search.tipitaka.org/solr/web?q=&fq=script%3Aromn&facet.field=volume> (accessed 8 November 2015).
Dhp	*Dhammapada*. Input by Kåre A. Lie, Jens Braarvig and Fredrik Liland (2010). *Thesaurus Literaturae Buddhica*. Oslo: University of Oslo, <https://www2.hf.uio.no/polyglotta/index.php?page=volume&vid=80#permlink> (accessed 8 November 2015).
DN	*Digha Nikaya*
Horner 2007	Horner, I.B. (2007). 'Introduction.' In Horner, I.B. (tr.) *The Minor Anthologies of the Pali Canon. Part III. Chronicle of Buddhas (Buddhavaṃsa) and Basket of conduct (Cariyāpiṭaka)*. Reprint of 1975 edition. Lancaster: Pali Text Society.
J	*Jātaka*
Knox 1992	Knox, R. (1992). *Amaravati. Buddhist Sculpture from the Great Stūpa*. London: British Museum Press.
Malalasekera 1937–1938	Malalasekera, G.P. (1937–1938). *Dictionary of Pāli Proper Names* (2 vols.). Reprint 1960. London: Pali Text Society.
Mitra 1974	Mitra, J. (1974). *History of Indian Medicine from Pre-Mauryan to Kuṣāṇa Period*. Varanasi: The Jyotirālok Prakashan.
Norman 1983	Norman, K.R. (1983). *Pāli Literature*. Wiesbaden: Harrassowitz.

Nyanatiloka Mahathera 1984	Nyanatiloka Mahathera. (1984). *Buddhist Dictionary. Manual of Buddhist Terms and Doctrines*. Reprint, 1952. Kandy: Buddhist Publication Society.
PED	Rhys Davids, T.W. and W. Stede. (1975). *Pali-English Dictionary*. New Delhi: Oriental Reprint.
Pieruccini 2013	Pieruccini, C. (2013). *Storia dell'arte dell'India: I. Dalle origini ai grandi templi medievali*. Torino: Einaudi.
SN	*Saṃyuttanikāya*
Sū	*Sūtrasthāna*
Sutherland 1991	Sutherland, G.H. (1991). *The Disguises of the Demon. The Development of the Yakṣa in Hinduism and Buddhism*. Albany: State University of New York Press.
SV	*Suttavibhaṅga*. Horner, I.B. (tr.). (1949). *The Book of the Discipline (Vinaya-Piṭaka). Vol. I (Suttavibhaṅga)*. Reprint of 1938 edition. London: Pali Text Society.
ViPi	*Vinayapiṭaka*. Oldenberg, H. (tr.) (1879–1883). *The Vinaya Piṭaka*. 5 vols. Melksham (Wiltshire): Pali Text Society.
VM	Buddhaghosa: *Visuddhimagga*. Comba, A.S. (tr.) (2010). *Visuddhimagga. Il sentiero della purificazione*. 3 vols. Raleigh: Lulu.
von Hinüber 1996	von Hinüber, O. (1996). *A Handbook of Pāli Literature*. Berlin-New York: Walter de Gruyter.
Zysk 1991	Zysk, K.G. (1991). *Asceticism and Healing in Ancient India. Medicine in the Buddhist Monastery*. New York and Oxford: Oxford University Press.

Chapter 6

Wood, Water and Waste: Material Aspects of Mortuary Practices in South Asia

ALBERTINA NUGTEREN[1]

What was the wood? What the tree
out of which they fashioned heaven and earth?
(RV X.81.4.1)

Now, Brahman handed over the creatures to Death.
The only creature he did not hand over to him was the student.
Death said to Brahman: 'Let me have a share of him also.'
Brahman replied: 'Only on the night that he fails to bring a piece of firewood.'
(BaudDhS I.4.4)

'Everything is "*paryavaran*" [environment] these days,'
grumbled the old woman when prohibited to collect firewood.[2]

The location: Bhaktapur, in Nepal. The setting: the maze of lanes leading to the river banks and the *ghāṭ*s, the steps descending to the river. A small funeral procession moves silently, hurriedly, almost stealthily towards the Hanumante river. It expertly winds its way through the city's labyrinth-like structure, finally passes an arched gate, moves through a jumble of shrines, and reaches the stone embankment, where the bier is put down. The corpse has reached its final destination. It rests, while,

1 Albertina Nugteren is an Indologist (classical and modern) and is Associate Professor in Religion and Ritual, Department of Culture Studies, Faculty of Humanities, Tilburg University (The Netherlands).

2 Conversation in Chengu Narayan, Kathmandu Valley, June 2011.

invisible to us, elsewhere in this traditional town a network of persons, paperwork and paraphernalia has been set into motion. Within a few hours it will produce the right stage for an open-air cremation: firewood, bundles of straw, ritual utensils, ghee, along with priests and a few more relatives. And after another couple of hours there will be nothing left but a few fragments of bone and a heap of ashes.

As always, there is an alternative story to this, a shadow story. It is the narrative of the low, dirty, almost stagnant river. It curls around Bhaktapur's southern edge, and apart from funerary ashes it houses plastic waste, rubbish collected by the sweeper class from homes, and other debris. Could it really be here that Hanumān-on-wings once rested and, on his way south from the Himalaya where he had collected the healing herbs for Rāma's brother Lakṣmaṇa, took some sips of refreshing water?

Likewise the scene tells the narrative of Nepal's deforestation. The fuel-intensive nature of Hindu funeral rites has started to evoke remarks on the irony that an average South Asian Hindu's ecological footprint may be actually larger in death than in life.[3] It poses the question: why this persistence on wood as the material for burning the corpse? And why the insistence on open-air cremation when more environmentally friendly, more cost-effective and less time-consuming technologically advanced methods are available?

In this chapter, I explore the rationale behind such culture-specific practices and the excessive drain they make on natural resources today. The staggering quantity of dry wood required for open-air cremation – preferably even mixed with rare woods such as sandalwood – especially trigger questions about the wasteful ways in which Hindus dispose of their deceased. Why not use electric, gas-fueled or even solar-powered crematories instead? Considering South Asian's forested past we can easily explain the practicalities of the use of wood in former-day funerary practices. But there seems to be a deeper reason for the continuing use of wood as the deceased's final resting place before he/she turns to ashes, even in an era full of alarm about deforestation, carbon emission rates and anthropogenic climate change.

From a contemporary perspective, Hindu culture is found to harbor an insurmountable contradiction: a traditionally transmitted reverence for

3 Scientific, environmentalist and newspaper reports often can't resist word plays such as in the title 'A Burning Question: The Climate Impact of 7 Million Funeral Pyres in India and Nepal', http://www.eenews.net/stories/1059989543/ (accessed 3 April 2015).

trees – many of which are still considered sacred, and the object of deeply felt devotion – coupled with an almost ruthless exploitation of wood in disposal rites. Is this a matter of an ancient symbolic order clashing with today's environmental realities? Why is the culture-specific use of wood in funerary practices so rarely mentioned, let alone critiqued, in reports on emission rates and deforestation?[4]

By relating contemporary practices to ancient narratives and entangled ritual traditions I explore the centrality of fire in Hindu rites of passage, cremation as a final sacrifice (*antyeṣṭi*), religious symbolism with which trees and especially firewood are invested, the ongoing insistence on open pyres, and emerging 'greener' alternatives.

Figure 6.1. Logs for cremation pyres, Bhaktapur, June 2011.

4 Exceptions are the E&E news bulletin mentioned above and the report 'Funeral Pyres in South Asia: Brown Carbon Aerosol Emissions and Climate Impacts' (2013) published by the American Chemical Society in *Environmental Letters: Science & Technology.*

LOCAL PRACTICES

In countries such as India and Nepal, most Hindus, whatever their lifestyle, at the moment of approaching death insist on traditional ways of disposal. The relation between the living and the dead is one of social obligation, requiring that the ancestors are satisfied. It is the obligation of family members to care for the deceased and perform the necessary rites. Failure to perform these may negatively affect not only one's own status, but also that of the dead relative. The practical interpretation of the term 'traditional' is however deeply dependent on the particular community.

For instance, in his new book *Vedic Voices, Intimate Narratives of Living Andhra Traditions*, David Knipe (2015) allows us a rare insight into the final rites for an *āhitāgni*, a brahmin priest who had maintained three fires during his life. Such an *āhitāgni*'s disposal rites include the complete combustion of the body, three separate hearths and all sacrificial implements in a final oblation. There may be no more than 600 of such priests left today, but both their lifestyle and death-style show us the sanctity, centrality and sacerdotal character of fire in the life of those who still 'live in the *Veda*' ('Vedamlo', as Knipe calls it). Their cremation rite – a final and complete absorption into Agni – illustrates the original meaning of the word generally used for cremation: *antyeṣṭi*, the final sacrifice in which man himself is the complete and most perfect offering.

By contrast, 'traditional' in the case of royal families may emphasize completely different aspects. This became evident after the massacre that took place within the royal family of Nepal on 1 June 2001, allegedly perpetrated by the crown prince Dipendra, who himself died of self-inflicted bullet-wounds two days later. The funeral procession on 2 June, with nine royal bodies, took several hours to travel from the Military Hospital to the ancient *ghāṭs* of Pashupatinath, by the Bagmati river,[5] finally reaching the area furthest upstream of the Ārya Ghāṭ that is normally reserved for royalty. The army had to build an additional temporary platform to accommodate all nine bodies. The various reports emphatically mention that all the royal pyres consisted of stacked sandalwood.

5 The Pashupatinath Temple compound, some 5 km northeast of Kathmandu, a UNESCO Heritage site since 1979, has been caught in controversies over the construction of a two-storey crematorium with a huge chimney. Meanwhile 'environment-friendly' electric ovens have been installed, with machinery supplied by Indomen Engineering Service in Kolkata. At the moment of writing (April 2015) this highly contested crematorium is not operating yet.

A similar detail is given in a relatively recent news report from Assam (*The Times of India*, 23 November 2011). When famous singer Bhupen Hazarika received his last rites on the banks of the Brahmaputra in Guwahati, the top layer of the pyre consisted of around 70 kg of sandalwood collected from the Guwahati University's Botanical Garden. A further note in related reports draws attention to the fact that the site was specially prepared for this cremation on the University's spacious grounds by the river bank since the usual place, Bharalumukh Sankardev Uddyan, had been considered neither spacious nor clean enough for the public occasion. It is further noted that the deceased's son later planted a couple of white and red sandalwood trees as compensation.[6]

These three accounts can be read as exceptional situations, but with gripping details. Reports on normal Hindu cremation practices, written either from a prescriptive 'traditionalist' perspective or, conversely, from a social change-environmentalist-activist angle, vary widely in their indication of the materials and time required. Open-air cremation is said to need between 250 and 800 kg of dry wood, but it is observed that the prescriptions about logs being piled five or even seven feet high are rarely followed today.[7] It should be wood without thorns, and there should be an odd number of logs. Wood brought from another pyre, or wood that had belonged to an outcaste should be rejected. In addition bundles of dried grass should be provided.[8] In some cases (as in Bhaktapur, among the Newars) funeral associations (*siguthī*) carry out the necessary preliminary work and provide all the services at the cremation ground. In other places priests prescribe a list of required materials (*sambhāra*) which the relatives arrange for. The items on this list may differ in details, but apart from firewood and hay, straw or even cow-dung patties[9] the minor ingredients may be: a bamboo

6 TimesofIndia.indiatimes.com/city/Guwahati/Bhupen-Hazarika's-last-journey-to-be-immortalized in Kalaksetra/articleshow/10835241.

7 The most demanding measures and quantities are found in Stevenson (1920: 149): 'Heavy logs (preferably of *bāvala* wood) are first laid on the ground to the height of a foot and a half, and upon this less expensive ordinary wood is laid, till the whole pyre is about seven feet long, and two and a half broad.'

8 Although this should be procured in a dry state, it is later dipped into the (sacred) river, and then spread over the pyre. Since it is wet when burning, it produces the characteristic white smoke of an open-air cremation just started. For bundles waiting for buyers along the processional route towards Hanumān Ghāṭ in Bhaktapur, see figure 6.2.

9 Some NGOs support cow-dung cremation as a slow but 'eco-friendly and pocket-friendly' alternative, requiring approximately 200 kg of cow-dung cakes. See figure 6.3.

bier or ladder without nails, ropes, splinters of sandalwood or sandal paste, milk, ghee/*ghṛta*, vegetable oil, an oil lamp, camphor, Gaṅgā water, white cotton, a clay water jug, puffed rice, a fire container (using a few twigs, charcoal and camphor) or simply a matchbox or a lighter, incense, sesame seeds, special rice balls (*piṇḍa*), sacred grasses, *tulasī* leaves, saffron, a *pañcagavya* or *pañcāmṛta* mixture of five liquids, a gold or silver coin (or simply seven tiny chips of gold and silver to place on the eyes, ears, nostrils and mouth), an animal hide or simply a mat, vermilion paste (*sindūra*), coconuts, nutmeg, cinnamon sticks, flowers and a variety of other condiments. As one can see, the symbolic universe of Hindu death requires an impressive material universe as well.

As to firewood, there are various indications that formerly all those who came to attend a cremation ceremony were supposed to bring along some firewood, under the condition, however, that sufficient wood had been collected before the actual fire was started (Elmore 2006: 31). Today such a custom could seriously delay and even jeopardize the entire procedure.[10] The socio-cultural character of presenting one's host with a bundle of firewood is not unique to funerary occasions. In mountainous areas in South Asia it is still a generous gesture to greet one's host with an armful of branches gathered on one's journey, just as we also find traces of this in ancient literature. *Āhitāgni*s who had left their sacred fires in the care of others were supposed to return with a bundle of firewood as a gesture of renewed commitment (Hillebrandt 1910: 49). Also *brahmacāri*s must have spent quite some time providing their *guru*s with firewood, from the first moment they arrived as students at their prospective teacher's door begging for entrance into the *āśrama*, to the moment they returned to their family residence, got married and started a round of hearths on their own. Woods with distinctive scents, such as sandal, aloe, mango, wood-apple, cedar and juniper, were favored for special occasions, in aesthetic and religious settings. As they are known to obscure the smell of the burning body, they are particularly sought in cremation rites. *Candana*, sandalwood, has an intricate and entangled socio-cultural history in South Asia, so much so that government regulations concerning its use go as far back as Surapāla's *Vṛkṣāyurveda*, an ancient manual on horticulture, including such modern-sounding things as government taxes on all forest produce, fines on illegal logging and encroachment, and priority rights of royal families over luxury products and art objects made from sandalwood. Today, the Indian government has placed a ban on the export of its timber, and

10 Today a backload of wood may sell for the equivalent of two days' wages.

Figure 6.2. Straw bundles used for cremation pyres, Bhaktapur, June 2011.

in some states all trees greater than a specified girth are state property, even on private land. When the infamous bandit Veerappan, notorious as a smuggler of ivory and sandalwood, was killed by police in 2004, this became world news.

THE PROCEDURES

As our reference to the *āhitāgni*'s cremation as his final and complete oblation illustrates, quite a few details of contemporary death and disposal practices are vestiges of specific Vedic worldviews. The origin and meaning of such details may have become obscure to even most priests – let alone to the confused relatives faced with a mixture of private emotions and family obligations – but proper funeral rites are serious business. They are often contrasted with the great range of local, regional, sectarian and historical variations of other rituals. Appearing to be rather static, prescribing a fixed order of actions, and using more or less fixed ritual elements and material objects, cremation rituals may look rigid and formal.

This supposed rigidity may indeed be enhanced by the universal fears and taboos surrounding death and the afterlife. However, on closer inspection it becomes evident that even death rituals show changes and variations often overlooked by scholars of domestic rituals in South Asia.

Seen from a textual perspective, we notice a wide range of religious action 'outside the book,' in the form of substituted embodied practices, artistic creativity, omissions or short-cuts, material mediation and fusion. Gregory Grieve, writing on Bhaktapur, defines scripturalism as 'a pattern of mediation that forces religious phenomena into the "Protestant" bed of the printed text' (Grieve 2006: 2). He convincingly contrasts this with what he terms 'prosaic religion,' the pragmatic field of quotidian religious practices. Other writers on Bhaktapur, such as Gutschow and Michaels (2005), likewise speak of pragmatic ritual repertoires and point at a parallel world of ritual dynamics and active oral handing-down of knowledge, even or especially in a place like Bhaktapur where tradition became intentionally commodified and 'medieval otherness' was strategically cultivated. The residents have obviously used both romantic and prosaic traditions to creatively construct an effective form of hybrid tradition.

Is something comparable happening in that other 'time-less' place, Varanasi? In an article titled 'Hindus Urged to Adopt "Green" Cremation', the *Los Angeles Times* (3 September 2007) starts its news flash on the introduction of greener alternatives with the usual atmospheric (some would say 'neo-colonialist' or 'exoticist') tone of voice:

> Cremation fires crackle all day long on the chipped concrete steps of this riverside holy city, the blazes spewing ash and flakes over the mourners who crowd its famous piers. Sweating, bare-chested men stoke the funeral pyres, squinting against the sting of smoke as they lug and stack the bundles of logs needed to burn the procession of Hindu dead.
>
> And when the bodies are incinerated and the families have taken away the ashes of their loved ones, the men sweep the residue into the Ganges River. The detritus of death, mingling with life. (Wallis 2007)

The mixed reception of books such as Jonathan Parry's widely read *Death in Banaras* (1994), Diana Eck's *Banaras, City of Light* (1982) and a film (consisting of comment-free visual imagery) such as Robert Gardner's *Forest of Bliss* (Gardner and Östör 1986) illustrates how in those decades some authors as well as their critics tried to escape from the above-mentioned 'bed of the printed text' by making ethnographies of a city in which dying, disposal and performance of ancestor rites have long been a core business. Since then the ethno-indological method (as used by, for instance, Axel Michaels and the Heidelberg research group 'Ritualdynamik'), being a combination of textual, contextual and ethnographic approaches, has resulted in a wealth of ritual studies showing that in spite of an astonishing continuity in disposal practices from Vedic times to the present, a significant change in both procedure and meaning has also taken place. The study of adaptations in death rituals among Hindu diaspora communities has made various authors more aware of the immediate material aspects of religion. Since both the transcendental complex and the pragmatic complex (Mandelbaum 1966) were subject to rapid change in such communities, the exigencies of prosaic material life away from South Asia demanded creative and improvisational agency. The use of electric crematories reflects as well as co-creates a shift in attitudes. Easily available means of refrigeration accommodate longer periods of waiting for relatives to arrive. The bureaucracy surrounding death certificates and legislation pertaining to cremation and the subsequent scattering of ashes forces expatriate Hindu families to adjust, postpone, truncate and fuse. Today, in the diaspora, we notice both attenuation and proliferation of tradition.

But what, exactly, is prescribed? Most lay people lack the knowledge as to how their particular *gotra* or patrilineal clan should handle post-mortem rites. The list of required material ingredients, issued by the family or by temple priests, may vary greatly in minor items, but in case of open-air cremation firewood is always at the top of the list and forms the major expense today. In the symbolic universe in which most such prescriptions originated, the world was seen as a system of correspondences. Although wood has never formally been seen as one of the four or five elements (as it is in China, along with fire, earth, metal and water), wood (*daru*) has always had a strong symbolic currency in South Asia, both in its own right and as connected to trees. In the multiple ways in which Vedic seers pondered about the origin of things, trees and wood formed one of the answers, as is shown in the Ṛgvedic text crowning this chapter. Many trees were the object of special veneration (and thus protection), particularly the banyan (*nigrodha*; *Ficus benghalensis* L.) and pipal (*aśvattha*; *Ficus religiosa* L.).[11] Other trees may have been sacred as well, but this did not necessarily save them from the axe; on the contrary, their wood was much sought-after for its symbolic capital. Many of the ancient textual passages in praise of a particular tree precede the process of ritually cutting it down in order to serve as material for sacrificial objects or, later, for statues of the deity

11 Cf. Nugteren (2005), especially Chapter One, 'Symbol and Sacredness: Trees in Ancient Religious Literature.'

(as is still done when the wooden images of the Jagannāth Temple in Puri have to be periodically made anew).[12] In some cases a singular tree could become historicized as the result of a particular event connected with it: Buddha's *bodhi*-tree in Bodhgaya, or trees figuring in the biographies of deities (some of the trees connected with Kr̥ṣṇa's sojourn in Mathura) or of illustrious persons such as the musician Tan Sen and the Bengali mystic Caitanya. In other cases trees have become so old and large that they are solid symbols of life, such as the huge banyan (with a crown circumference of over 330 meters) in the Botanical Garden of Kolkata; or so old and sacred that splinters of their wood are treated as relics, such as is the case with the *sthalavr̥kṣa* in the Ekambareshvara Temple in Kanchipuram, reputedly 3500 years old, and yielding four different types of mango. Yet, even more telling of ubiquitous veneration are the myriad of sacred trees scattered all over South Asia, with small shrines around them, or indicated merely by a stone daubed with red powder reverently placed between their roots.[13]

I have already pointed out that sanctity of trees other than banyan and pipal did not save them from the woodcutter's axe since such trees were used for sacred objects such as temple construction, sacrificial posts, statues of deities and other ritual objects. From ancient times onwards we find frequent mention of another use of wood, both ordinary and sacred, for fueling the sacrificial fires. One of the most crucial and significant acts over centuries must have been the act of kindling fire through friction between pipal and *śami* (*Acacia polyacantha* Willd.) wood in order to produce the sparks that would feed the embers for the sacrificial hearth. The upper 'male' wood, in the shape of a spindle, was twirled with a rope, with its point seated in the 'female' block of wood on the ground.[14] Once the fire was started, it had to be fed. On the part of a student an offering of firewood to a prospective teacher was a symbol of respect, humility and keenness to learn. Seen from the angle of material culture a contemporary person cannot help wondering about the quantity of firewood that may have been burned over the millennia, both for domestic purposes and in the sacrificial cult, including cremation. As sociologist Johan Goudsblom (1993) maintains in his work on fire and civilization, the domestication of fire has had far-reaching consequences. It deserves to be ranked as the

12 Ibid., especially Chapter Four, 'Gods of Wood, Gods of Stone: The Ritual Renewal of the Wooden Statues at Purī.'

13 For gripping photography, see Huyler (1999); Haberman (2013); Goswamy and Hawkes (2004).

14 See, for instance, Knipe (2015), figure 2.7 as well as the book cover.

Figure 6.3. Slowly burning cow-dung pyre, Chengu Narayan, June 2011.

first great ecological transformation brought about by humans. As fire was incorporated into human societies, so was the need for fuel. The effort of collecting fuel, keeping it dry and putting it on the fire, either for cooking purposes or for the sacrificial cult, involved social cooperation and division of labor. It required – and brought – a civilizing process. In South Asia fire became much more than that.[15] For ages it formed the ritual center and even today, what is a ritual without at least a tiny flame?

More than a tiny flame, however, is needed for cremation. Agni is portrayed as continuously hungry, and on the occasion of cremation as *kravyāda*, eater of corpses. He should be dutifully fed with ghee, firewood, and in the end, with the deceased individual's body, the final oblation (*antyeṣṭi*). In some discussions on Hindu cremation ritual there is a tendency to explain the ubiquity of open-air cremation as the result of a gradual democratization of the *āhitāgni*'s prerogative.[16] This would imply

15 'Nowhere has the production of fire assumed such a cultic significance, so important and dramatic at the same time, as in Vedic culture.' (Vesci 1985: 162)

16 As Vesci (1985: 45, fn. 74) notes in a side remark: 'Anyway, even nowadays cremation is not meant for all the Hindus, but is reserved, theoretically, to those entitled to have a sacrificial fire.'

that the rationale behind current practices would have fitted merely and exclusively the special case of those priests who had tended their fires faithfully throughout their life. After a life of offering substitutes, at death they themselves would become the sacrificial victim. A life dedicated to fire would thus culminate in a final (*antya*) and complete sacrifice (*iṣṭi*) with themselves as the victim (Krick 1982). The later general take-over of what once had been the privilege of a select group of priests would explain many surviving but now obscure details in the manuals. However that may be, open-air cremation has long been considered the traditional Hindu way to go.

Some aspects of this were made public in a court case in the UK. Migrant Hindus in other regions of the world, such as in parts of Eastern and Southern Africa, have more or less below the radar of the authorities found ways to cremate their dead outdoors. On a special request, Uganda-born religious leader Davinder Ghai in 2006 organized an open-air cremation for Rajpal Mehat in a field in Northumbria. When Ghai found out that this was considered illegal, based on the common interpretation of a law more than hundred years old (1902), he filed a court case in order to be allowed cremation on a pyre once his own time came. His main arguments were: the corpse on the pyre must be facing the sun directly[17] and the son who was to kindle the fire would have to circumambulate the body three times before he would set fire to it. These conditions could not possibly be fulfilled in a conventional British crematorium. Roger Ballard, functioning as a consulting anthropologist, wrote two reports in support of the claim (Ballard 2008). In February 2010 Davender Ghai won the case. Since the judge ruled that such a cremation (as long as it was performed in some partly enclosed structure and away from the public gaze) would be legal under the 1902 Act, some Hindu and Sikhs are now seriously investigating sites where they can perform their funerary ceremonies in a manner they consider essential. A photograph of the contested outdoor pyre in 2006 shows an improvised bonfire built of planks somewhere in the fields rather than the prescribed cross-tiers of piled logs topped with lighter woods and covered with wisps of straw.[18]

17 I haven't been able to trace this in contemporary prescriptions, where the emphasis is on the North-South position of the corpse. Could it be a remnant of that other R̥gvedic verse (RV x.16.3a): 'Let your eye go to the sun, your life-breath to the wind, [...]' (*sū́ryaṃ cákṣur gachatu vā́tam ātmā́ diyā́ṃ ca* [...]) (trs. Jamison and Brereton)?

18 This may be illustrative of the way Hindu practices have travelled through time and space, and changed accordingly. Hindu cremation ceremonies performed

In other places Hindus have drastically attenuated the procedures in their use of standard crematories. It appears that some of the sensitive issues may be negotiated with local authorities and commercial partners, but what is experienced as urgent or essential may differ from case to case. The situation of Hindus in the Netherlands may illustrate this. Being twice-migrants via Suriname, who had only just before migration to the Netherlands been offered the option of legal cremation after decades of established burial practices, they had to find out many things for themselves. Priests supply them with long lists of necessary ingredients. But whereas in Suriname Hindus now have the choice between the oven in a crematorium or a wood pyre outdoors, in the Netherlands they have to adapt to the conventions and regulations of Dutch crematoria. Some of the more urgent topics in their negotiations with crematorium officers have to do with their insistence that the *yajamāna*[19] himself must push the button, that all close relatives have direct eye contact with the fire and that afterwards they have legitimate ways to scatter the ashes over running water.[20] Further investigation among other diaspora groups, both through direct observation and through internet research, indicates that most of them are satisfied with attenuated practices or merely symbolic gestures when circumstances do not allow the real thing. When Hindus use the services of a standard crematorium the traditionally prescribed main ingredient, firewood, is often reduced to a single gesture, that of placing a few chips of sandalwood inside the coffin. The equally sensitive issue of lighting the fire – an action ideally performed by the eldest son – has produced precarious situations. There have been cases when just before the coffin was transported to the oven, small earthen lamps or *dīyas* inserted in the deceased's mouth and in other places within the coffin, were lighted. This caused fire alarm systems to go off and sound their ominous warnings. Since then, the *yajamāna* needs to perform this act symbolically by merely

in Bali, for instance, differ widely from those performed in India or Nepal. Since Ghai grew up in East Africa he may have partly followed the customs he was familiar with when he erected the pyre in the form of a bonfire. He may also have been advised to camouflage the actual burning of the corpse this way.

19 The word *yajamana* traditionally indicates the patron of a sacrifice. I use it here in the acceptation of Dutch Hindus, i.e. the one who performs a sacrifice. In other communities, the term *dāgīyā* (the one who gives fire) or simply *karmacārin* (the one who performs the rite) is more common.

20 Apart from Shirley Firth's work on Hindus in the UK (Firth 1991, 1997), see two more case-studies in Europe: Nugteren (2012) and Hadders (2013).

Figure 6.4. Cremation in process, Panauti, June 2011.

touching these body parts lightly with a hand-held *dīya*.[21] Most lists still mention *samidhs* or woods for the sacred fire, but it is not clear whether these are placed in the coffin or are meant for the concluding fire ceremony at home (*samādhi-gṛha-śūddhi-pūjā*), increasingly held on the same day as the cremation.[22]

GREENER ALTERNATIVES

The call for alternatives can be divided into two categories: (1) those voices which plead for simplified, shortened, accessible and more individualized

21 Some even call this practice 'waving *ārti* over the body,' causing Axel Michaels and Johanna Buss to speak of the 'pūjaization' of death (Michaels and Buss 2010).

22 The reduction of the traditional fortnight of mourning to a single day appears to be a practical solution in relation to the Western working week, limited domestic space and lack of funds. The insistence on the speed with which electric ovens and the Mokshda system (see below) incinerate the body, on the other hand, may be driven by the culture-specific emphasis on the idea that the body of the deceased should return to the five elements as soon and as quickly as possible.

procedures, and (2) those which plead for greener solutions. The first type is represented by a mixture of arguments. To many, the elaborate rituals appear alienating, as they no longer represent the worldview and lifestyle of the deceased, let alone their own. There may be a sense of cultural shame about the 'primitiveness' of exposed bodies, dirty *ghāṭs*, putrid water, mumbling priests, begging *sādhus*, shaven heads, bare chests and stench. Or a perception of meaninglessness and the suspicion of being taken advantage of by ruthless entrepreneurs and the 'wood mafia.' Some may even prefer simplified devotional services more in line with their religious sensitivities. Others may insist on warm recollections of the individual life that has now come to an end and reject the idea of *pretas* and *pitṛs* (ancestor spirits) altogether. Some of these arguments may well induce them to opt for the modern, hygienic and sanitized setting of an electric or gas-fueled crematorium. Interesting as these considerations are, they are not our main concern here.

The second call for change includes all kinds of environmental issues, be it for the standard crematorium or for upcoming, green alternatives. Environmental arguments for the standard crematorium include the scarcity and price of firewood, deforestation, emission of toxic fumes at the *ghāṭs*, as well as water pollution caused by half-burnt bodies, discarded cloth, ritual waste, bones and ashes. Some may articulate these arguments in a secular-scientific language, others may be devotionally dedicated to the sanctity of rivers, the divinity of the atmosphere, the purity of the five elements. At some point electric or gas-fueled crematoria were promoted as both clean and green. Meanwhile, many older installations have lost these advantages in the eyes of the public. Various reports indicate that their emission rate is unacceptably high for residential areas. But there are other reasons why existing crematoria are shunned. Not only because many do not appear to function well, but also because they are often associated with anonymous dead, unclaimed corpses, beggars and criminals. Even when people would tend to prefer a crematorium for environmental reasons, the technological backwardness of the facilities may seriously discourage them. Inventories of standard crematoriums indicate that many are dysfunctional, in need of repair, or are technologically outdated. To the bad reputation crematoria generally have in India have now been added increasing health hazards for the surrounding area.

At some point this unsatisfactory situation triggered the introduction of more eco-friendly devices and architecturally more attractive settings for crematories.[23] Vinod Kumar Agarwal, a mechanical engineer, on becoming aware of the deadlock between what the texts or *śāstras* are supposed to prescribe, and the inflated prices of firewood and disastrous environmental consequences of traditional burning practices, started to construct a device that would combine a traditional open fire with cost-effective, wood-saving and emission-reducing features. He founded an organization, Mokshda Green Cremation System (MGCS) and put his device on the market in 1992. In its original version it consists of an elevated brazier under a roof, with slats to maintain the heat while allowing air to circulate and feed the fire, and requires merely 150 kg of wood as against the minimum of 400 kg required for a conventional pyre. The basic design works on the principle that the amount of air in it is controlled and wastage of heat is restricted. It will burn an average body in two hours. Relatives and priests will be able to perform all the rituals and watch the process from all sides. In spite of its obvious advantages, this system got a poor response. The project was shelved for a year, during which some technical details were improved, and Agarwal reflected on the possible factors of resistance and reasons why people might not be ready for this change. Looking back he said:

> We realized that we don't know what happens after death. It remains a mystery and hence we don't want to divert from the tradition. People are following what's written in the shastras but they don't realize that wood was easily available those days and wood like kikar had more calorific value, it would burn more easily and produce more heat.[24]

This made him attempt to 'get religion on our side.' Following consultations with a diverse array of *paṇḍits*, environmental specialists, bureaucrats and the corporate sector he decided that the system needed some embellishment. The ambiance in which the device was to be placed was to have clean marble flooring and discrete places for mourners to gather. Equally importantly, a crematorium using his device was to have a statue of the god Shiva at the entrance. Also, he dropped any reference to the use of iron, as he realized that iron is often negatively associated with 'the dark force,' especially at death. He technically improved the system by

23 Although it is outside the range of this chapter, architectural efforts to improve the ambiance and general 'feel' of crematoriums have resulted in prize-winning designs worldwide. One example in India is the crematorium Ashwinkumar in Surat (http://architexturez.net/doc/az-cf-20472).

24 Vinod Kumar Agarwal, quoted in *The Hindu*, 18 March 2012.

Figure 6.5. Mokshda braziers, Delhi, 2014.

introducing a chimney that would catch the flaky residue produced by the fire. Spiritual leaders approved of the system and today their statements are used in educational programs, in marketing campaigns as well as on Mokshda's Facebook page (www.mokshda.org). Now that the movement is slowly gaining momentum, especially in its partnership with the Oil and Natural Gas Corporation (ONGC)'s initiative *Harit Moksha* (Green Heaven) and the Ministry of Environment's river-cleaning programs and afforestation efforts, it is promoted as a viable alternative yet in keeping with the traditions. As a fuel-efficient wood-based crematory it may prove itself as more culturally acceptable than electric furnaces. It is also drawing interest from Hindus outside India.

THE PREDICAMENT

In the South Asian debate reflected even in international news media, environmental news bulletins, NGO-magazines and UNDP publications, we see how knotty the problems are and how deeply opposed traditionalists and environmentalists can be. Although the Mokshda technology is not dismissed as heretical and could indeed be regarded as a viable compromise, it has so far made only tiny inroads. As *The Economist* phrased it: 'Traditionalists may be less horrified by the Mokshda chimney stack than by closed crematoriums, but they still prefer their funerals *al fresco*.'[25] People tend to be sentimental and emotional about these issues and bring up a wide variety of arguments against the proposed changes in culture-specific burning practices. In order to bring some system into understanding these widely varying voices we now list the most frequent arguments. Instead of perusing the scriptures in order to dig up the normative, we take empirically based objections as our point of departure. In doing so, we distinguish between ritual repertoire and the underlying symbolic universe.

Ritually based objections against indoor crematoria in closed ovens include: (1) the use of iron, which is considered an unclean and inauspicious material, especially in relation to death; (2) the impossibility of circumambulating the funeral pyre (*paryagnikriyā*) and lighting it at the mouth of the dead (*mukhāgni*); (3) the impossibility of performing the act of *kapāla-kriyā* (splitting of the skull); (4) the impersonal, secular nature of electric heat instead of ritually kindled fire, an action traditionally to be performed by the main mourner; (5) the risk that the ashes will get mixed up with remains of others before they are scattered over water; and (6) for the relatives, the lack of multi-sensory contact with the dead, especially through sight.

Arguments stemming from the symbolic structure behind death rituals include: (1) the element earth (*bhū, bhūmi*) is missing, since the corpse is put on a metal tray instead of directly on the ground; (2) the element water (more particularly, water from a sacred river) is missing, since the corpse has not been partially immersed in water (*antarjalī, ardhapatha*) prior to its entrance into the oven; (3) the element fire is substituted by mechanically controlled heat; (4) the element air (*vāyu*) is missing in the enclosed space of the furnace; (5) direct exposure to the sun is missing; and (6) most importantly for our topic, the body's last resting place is not on wood.

Wood is considered integral to Hindu cremations by many. It is supposed to form a symbolic connection between the body and the earth. This is why the first layer of wood is traditionally placed directly on the ground, just as the dying person should ideally be laid on the ground in his or her last moments before death. The Mokshda system indeed uses wooden logs

25 'Burning Bodies Better: How to Make India's Funeral Pyres More Energy-Efficient,' *The Economist*, 18 June 2007.

as a first layer on which the corpse is placed: it still rests on a bed of wood, but no longer directly or indirectly on the earth. Instead it rests on a raised metal grate, allowing better air circulation. Now that many people die in hospitals instead of within the family home, this ancient custom of letting the dying person rest directly on the earth is wearing thin anyway. Instead of being carried by pall-bearers on a wooden ladder or bier (a *sīḍhī*, tied together with ropes, not fixed by nails) today most of the deceased are brought to the *ghāṭ*s in ambulances and carried to the pyre on hospital stretchers, if not in coffins.[26] Coffins are hardly seen on traditional *ghāṭ*s, but in electric crematoria outside South Asia they have become quite common among Hindus. From a symbolic perspective one could argue that such a coffin resembles the ancient bed of wood that accompanies the deceased even inside the electric oven.

Then, what is the challenge for Mokshda, with what significant details could they convince Hindus of their fuel-efficient but custom-abiding technology? There may be a social issue behind people's reluctance as well. According to representatives of the new system it is hard to convince devout Hindus that using less wood does not break with orthodoxy. This is not so much a religious issue, but rather a social code. Burning a relative, especially a parent, is a matter of obligation to the ancestors: being skimpy on firewood is considered to cause an inauspicious entrance into the afterlife. Add to that the social stigma that may still be connected to the inability to provide for the full and complete combustion of the body and the not unusual sight of partly burnt bodies floating in rivers, and we can easily understand the emotional refutation of Mokshda's argument about the reduced quantities of firewood.[27] Thorough and complete destruction opens a path for release (*mokṣa*) as well as new life. In order to become totally de-linked from this Earth, fire is considered essential: it is beautiful, it is dramatic, it drastically destroys the ties. Do Hindus need this drama in full glory? Is this why they object to its tamed rationalized version in ovens, furnaces and braziers? These suggestive questions bring us back to Vedic beginnings.

26 In some cases coffins are used for transport only, and thrown into the water afterwards. Interestingly, Müller (1992) speaks of a wooden plank or board ('Holzbrett').

27 Mokshda even claims that their system can further decrease the amount of firewood from 150 kg to a mere 44.

Figure 6.6. Mourners preparing a cremation pyre, Pashupatinath, June 2011.

Figure 6.7. Priest and mourner performing rituals, Pashupatinath, June 2011.

THROUGH FIRE

It is by offering one's own body as a final gift into the open fire that one of the deepest secrets of the sacrificial cult is fulfilled.[28] Today's sacrificial complex is a many-hued fabric, an antique carpet woven with the shimmering threads of multiple myths and patterned practices. The assimilated fragmented nature of the Vedic-Hindu continuum becomes particularly dense when faced with rituals of death and disposal. Why is the cremation rite still called *antyeṣṭi*, final sacrifice? Do we detect here the democratization of a once privileged system in which man as the final oblation completed the *āhitāgni*'s perfectly logical and coherent circle of life? After a life-long offering of substitutes the giving-up of oneself on the pyre stands as the crowning act: it speaks of a life fulfilled and 'reflects the metaphysics of dense symbolic equations and correspondences, which allow for movement between planes of reality' (Shulman 1993: 16).

Mono-causal explanations always have their pitfalls.[29] For our present topic, firewood, it will suffice to return to an earlier fire, the mythic fire at the beginning of our ordered world, as it was seen by Vedic seers. It was the first sacrifice ever, and became forever the prototype of any sacrifice. It was the cosmic blaze on which that First Being, Puruṣa-Prajāpati, was sacrificed, rather, sacrificed himself in order to create all things. Through fire, through that primordial sacrifice, through that drama of total and complete destruction (*pūrṇahuti*) the whole world sprang forth, like sparks from an endlessly generous and creative fire: 'thus the world was fashioned' (RV x.90.14).

It was not self-combustion, however. Even then, the symbolic universe needed material to act as fuel. That material was wood. And that first firewood was kindled with thrice seven faggots (*samidh*, RV x.90.15.1). From that image of a primeval pyre, on which the first sacrifice gave birth to all existence, seers deduced the secret key to maintain and renew this world. Priests figured out through a system of equivalences (*saṃpad*) how they could keep the universe going: by ritually repeating that original creative act. And this is how the sacrificial complex came into being, remaining as

28 Various scholars (such as Sylvain Lévi, Madeleine Biardeau and Veena Das) use the expressions 'death is the perfect sacrifice' or 'man is the perfect sacrificial victim.'

29 In an earlier article, in order to come to an associative understanding of sacrificial ritual, I playfully and tentatively intertwined three disparate strands of Vedic narratives, see 'Through Fire: Creative Aspects of Sacrificial Rituals in the Vedic-Hindu Continuum' (forthcoming).

a faded blueprint behind many contemporary practices. Especially in matters of life and death this template shines through the threadbare Vedic carpet. And this may explain, partly at least, why the cremation ritual is as it is: a re-enactment of that first destructive-but-life-giving cosmogonic sacrifice. Whereas man must make various offerings in his lifetime, his ultimate gift is himself, at death, in order to re-create, in order to go on, in order to renew. Just like that first sacrificial victim was placed on a pile of wood, kindled by faggots, just so should man be placed on a pile of wood and be completely destroyed in an act of total giving (*tasmād-yajñāt-sarvahutaḥ*, RV x.90.8.1). Some myths are quite enduring and some images are so compelling that they re-emerge at crucial moments. The dramatic scenario of a cremation pyre may well be such a compelling image: an image not lightly, easily or frivolously erased by the logic of energy-saving, hygienic and cost-effective technological innovations.

Other dramas, however, are lurking in the shadows: deforestation, pollution and climate change.[30] It may well be that at some point soon this other scenario will take over, as Mokshda's director puts it: in a growing awareness that this adherence to religious orthopraxis carries a heavy toll for the temporal world.

ABBREVIATIONS AND REFERENCES

Ballard 2008 — Ballard, R. (2008). *The Logic of Cremation in Indic Contexts. An Anthropological Analysis, with an addendum (2008), presented to the Newcastle City Council/High Court of Justice in the court case initiated by Davender Kumar Ghai*, http://www.casas.org.uk/papers/pdfpapers/logicofcremation.pdf (accessed 17 August 2015).

BaudDhS — Baudhāyana: *Dharmasūtra*. In Olivelle, P. (tr.). (1999). *Dharmasūtras: Law Codes of Ancient India*, pp. 191–345. New York: Oxford University Press.

Eck 1982 — Eck, D.L. (1982). *Banaras. City of Light*. Westminister, Maryland: Alfred A. Knopff.

Elmore 2006 — Elmore, M. (2006). 'Contemporary Hindu Approaches to Death: Living with the Dead.' In Garces-Foley, K. (ed.). *Death and Religion in a Changing World*, pp. 23–44. Armonk, NY: M.E. Sharpe.

Firth 1991 — Firth, S. (1991). 'Changing Patterns of Hindu Death Rituals in Britain.' In Killingley, D., W. Menski and S. Firth (eds), *Hindu Ritual and Society*, pp. 52–84. Newcastle-upon-Tyne: S.Y. Killingley.

30 See my contribution (Nugteren 2014) on layers in Hindu environmental awareness and the reception of warnings about climate change.

Firth 1997	Firth, S. (1997). *Dying, Death and Bereavement in a British Hindu Community*. Leuven, Belgium: Peeters.
Gardner and Östör 1986	Gardner, R. and Á. Östör. (1986). *Forest of Bliss*. Watertown, Massachusetts: Documentary Educational Resources.
Goswamy and Hawkes 2004	Goswamy, K. and Hawkes, S. (2004). *Sacred Trees and Indian Life*. Delhi: Aryan Book International.
Goudsblom 1993	Goudsblom, J. (1993). *Fire and Civilization*. Amsterdam: Meulenhoff and Alan Lane.
Grieve 2006	Grieve, G.P. (2006). *Retheorizing Religion in Nepal*. New York: Palgrave.
Gutschow and Michaels 2005	Gutschow, N. and A. Michaels. (2005). *Handling Death. The Dynamics of Death and Ancestor Rituals Among the Newars of Bhaktapur, Nepal*. Wiesbaden: Otto Harrassowitz.
Haberman 2013	Haberman, D.L. (2013). *People Trees. Worship of Trees in Northern India*. New York: Oxford University Press.
Hadders 2013	Hadders, H. (2013). 'Cremation in Norway: Regulation, Changes and Challenges.' *Mortality* 18(2): 195–213.
Hillebrandt 1910	Hillebrandt, A. (1910). *Vedische Mythologie (Kleine Ausgabe)*. Breslau: M&H Marcus.
Huyler 1999	Huyler, S.P. (1999). *Meeting God. Elements of Hindu Devotion*. New Haven, CT: Yale University Press.
Knipe 2015	Knipe, D.M. (2015). *Vedic Voices. Intimate Narratives of Living Andhra Traditions*. New York: Oxford University Press.
Krick 1982	Krick, H. (1982). *Das Ritual der Feuergründung (Agnyadheya)*. Wien: Österreichische Akademie der Wissenschaften.
Mandelbaum 1966	Mandelbaum, D.G. (1966) 'Transcendental and Pragmatic Aspects of Religion.' *American Anthropologist (New Series)* 68(5): 1174–91.
Michaels and Buss 2010	Michaels, A. and J. Buss. (2010) 'The Dynamics of Ritual Formality: The Morphology of Newar Death Rituals.' In Michaels, A. (ed.), *Grammars and Morphologies of Ritual Practices in Asia*, pp. 99–116. Wiesbaden: Otto Harrassowitz.
Müller 1992	Müller, K.-W. (1992). *Das brahmanische Totenritual nach der Antyeṣṭipaddhati des Nārāyaṇabhaṭṭa*. Stuttgart: Fritz Steiner.
Nugteren 2005	Nugteren, A. (2005). *Belief, Bounty, and Beauty. Rituals around Sacred Trees in India*. Leiden: E.J. Brill.
Nugteren 2012	Nugteren, A. (2012). 'Vuur, as en water: Grenzen aan de hindoestaanse crematierituelen in Nederland.' *Religie & Samenleving* 7(1): 40–55.
Nugteren 2014	Nugteren, A. (2014). 'Cosmos, Commodity, and Care: Three Layers in Hindu Environmental Awareness.' In Schuler, B. (ed.), *Environmental and Climate Change in South and Southeast Asia. How are Local Cultures Coping?*, pp. 27–42. Leiden: E.J. Brill.
Nugteren (forthcoming)	Nugteren, A. (forthcoming). 'Through Fire: Creative Aspects of Sacrificial Rituals in the Vedic-Hindu Continuum.' In Korte, A.-M., J. Duyndam and M. Poortvliet. (eds.), *The Fascination of Sacrifice*. Leiden: E.J. Brill.

Parry 1994 — Parry, J.P. (1994). *Death in Banaras*. Cambridge: Cambridge University Press.

RV — *Ṛgvedasaṃhitā*. Jamison, S.W. and J.P. Brereton (tr.) (2014). *The Rigveda. The Earliest Religious Poetry of India*. 3 vols. New York: Oxford University Press.

Shulman 1993 — Shulman, D. (1993). *The Hungry God. Hindu Tales of Filicide and Devotion*. Chicago: University of Chicago Press.

Stevenson 1920 — Stevenson, S. (1920). *The Rites of the Twice-born*. London: Oxford University Press.

VĀ — Surapāla: *Vṛkṣāyurveda*. Das, R.P. (ed., tr.) (1988). *Das Wissen von der Lebensspanne der Bäume. Surapālas Vṛkṣāyurveda.* Kritisch editiert, übersetzt und kommentiert von Rahul Peter Das. Wiesbaden: Otto Harrassowitz.

Vesci 1985 — Vesci, U.M. (1985). *Heat and Sacrifice in the Vedas*. Delhi: Motilal Banarsidass.

Wallis 2007 — Wallis, B. (2007). 'Hindus Urged to Adopt "Green" Cremation.' *Los Angeles Times*, 3 September 2007, <www.latimes.com/world/la-fg-ashes3sep03-story.html#page=1> (accessed 3 April 2015).

Section Three

Ritual, Power, Myth

Chapter 7

The Herbal Arsenal and Fetid Food: The Power of Plants in Early Tantric Exorcism Rituals

MICHAEL SLOUBER[1]

The Bhūta and Bāla Tantras are the scriptural core of a medical system whose elements are still ubiquitous in South Asian folk healing. These early medieval Tantras at once inscribed ancient folk practices and prescribed new ritual systems that reverberated down the centuries. On the basis of unpublished manuscripts, this chapter describes the vital role that plants played in early medieval religion and life, as seen through the lens of exorcism rituals from the Bhūta and Bāla Tantras. Datura, red oleander, mustard seeds, rice, sesame, garlic, fig, Flame of the forest, wood-apple[2] – these

1 Michael Slouber is Assistant Professor of South Asian Studies, Department of Liberal Studies, Washington University (USA).

2 See the Introduction of the present volume for an accounting of the difficulties of matching Sanskrit plant names with their 'accepted scientific name.' After careful consideration, I have opted to avoid the use of Latin names to reference the plants in this article. Here, I briefly state my rationale: even in the cases of plants whose identity is well known, such as *hiṅgu* ↔ asafetida, there are multiple accepted scientific names, which makes choosing between these arbitrary for a non-botanist. I also object to the Euro-centric basis of authority entailed in the use of Latinized words as the only acceptable scientific way of naming plants. Use of such names also implies a certainty about the identification that is lacking in work produced by Humanities scholars who have not been trained in botany, such as myself. For these reasons I choose to use the less precise English common names. I have reached these working identifications by consulting Monier-Williams' Sanskrit-English dictionary (MWSED), which I then check against databases such as Pandanus, FoI, and Manandhar (1989).

and many more plants formed the basis of early Tantric exorcisms. Plants were used to attract, feed and repel demons. They were made into incense, oil and weapons, as well as cakes, mannequins and medicines. Auspicious, nourishing and noxious qualities of sacred plants and trees were infused into water, milk and cooling ointments, or made into sweet fragrances or foul-smelling dhoop ('incense,' from Sanskrit *dhūpa*). Even *mantras* were understood to be 'seeds' and deities were visualized and worshiped on, and with, flowers. In short, the universe of early Tantric exorcism ritual was suffused with plants and plant powers. Comparisons will be drawn with contemporary exorcism ritual on the basis of published ethnographic research from South Asia.

INTRODUCTION TO EARLY TANTRIC MEDICINE

> Colleague: What are you working on?
> Author: A study of plants in South Asian exorcism rituals.
> Colleague: What an esoteric topic!

I initially agreed with my colleague that the subject of this chapter is esoteric, in the sense of a specialized domain of knowledge not likely to be understood by a broad audience. However, this begs the question: to whom are plants and exorcism esoteric?

Most of the world's population maintains a close relationship with plant life and plant medicines by necessity, if not by choice. Belief in demons and in the efficacy of religious healing is likewise still widespread, despite the lack of currency these carry on the social registers of modernity. Religion and spirituality – and medical beliefs based on them – are pervasive in every society. We the people in the modern West are no less exempt from the desire for extra-rational cures for our modern ills than those in the villages of contemporary South Asia. Here it manifests as faith-healing, cults, New Age spiritualities, alternative medicine, drug culture or the (temporarily) liberating oblivion peddled by the advertising and entertainment industries; there, the shortcomings of modernity are also dealt with by recourse to traditional religion and medicine.

In his 2006 tome, *The Self Possessed*, Frederick Smith sought to demonstrate the prevalence of possession in South Asia. He focused on Sanskrit literature and traced the theme of possession and its diverse analogs in sources as far-ranging as the ancient *Ṛg Veda*, classical Āyurvedic compendia, Tantric digests, modern pilgrimage guidebooks and his own ethnographic fieldwork. Smith builds on a diverse body of prior research on possession and exorcism in South Asia, both classical and modern,[3] and synthesizes it into a broader theoretical framework. Since *The Self Possessed*, Fabrizio Ferrari has expanded the discussion with his excellent edited volume *Health and Religious Rituals in South Asia: Disease, Possession, and Healing* (2011).

The present chapter takes up the theme of plants in exorcism rituals from early Tantric medicine (c. 700–1000 CE). This branch of learning involves a variety of healing practices that combine religious and medical elements, and its existence has not been recognized by most prior research; historians of South Asian medicine have tended to exclude religious material, whereas the scholars of religion have downplayed the medical nature of demonic possession. In modernity, religion and medicine are generally regarded as two separate spheres based on incompatible approaches to life and knowledge. Early Tantric medical sources, by contrast, suggest little or no distinction between these two categories.

Written in Sanskrit and systematized into a corpus of scriptures spoken by the deity Śiva, early Tantric medicine is at once obscure and foundational.[4] While one might be tempted to regard it as an eruption of popular practices into Brahmanical discourse, early medieval Indian scholars judged the Bhūta and Gāruḍa Tantras as orthodox teachings in the Śaiva religion, itself the dominant religious tradition of the time (c. 400–1300 CE) (Sanderson 2009). Both deal with possession of various types, but the Bhūta Tantras are primarily concerned with exorcism, and form the basis of the present study. The Bāla Tantras are a related class dealing with childhood demonic possession. They are sometimes counted with the Bhūta Tantras and other times deemed distinct.

Despite its popularity, Āyurveda is not a synonym for classical Indian medicine. It is rather one among many systems including Siddha, Buddhist, Yogic, and those catch-alls, tribal and folk medicine. Historians of Indian medicine have not previously recognized Tantric medicine as a distinct system, but this omission is erroneous, as I have argued in several publications.[5] And yet, these medical systems are not mutually exclusive. The stamp of Āyurveda is on all of them, and Āyurveda came to incorporate elements of each as the others grew in popularity.

3 Some additional landmarks to prior research on the historical side are Filliozat (1937); Weiss (1977); and Wujastyk (1999, 2003). On the ethnographic side, important studies include Nichter (1981); Kapferer (1983) and Dwyer (2003).

4 I develop this argument in Slouber (2016).

5 See, e.g. Slouber (2016) and Slouber (forthcoming).

One hallmark of Tantric medicine is the natural combination of religious and plant-based healing. Classical Āyurveda encompassed ritual and *mantra*, but tended to defer to specialists – which is to say, brahmins steeped in the Vedas for the earlier compendia and Tantric gurus for the later. The Āyurvedic doctors deferred to no outside authorities concerning herbal remedies, which were squarely within their purview. A modern example of this fissure between religious and herbal medicine is the tradition of snakebite medicine offered by high-caste Āyurvedic doctors in Kerala. They distinguish plant-based remedies (*viṣacikitsā*) from the use of *mantras* (*mantraprayoga*) to effect cures, the latter being essentially Tantric in character and deployment. But it would be anachronistic to read this modern rupture between the Tantric and the Āyurvedic back into early sources; they freely mix plant-based remedies and *mantra* rituals.

By way of introduction to classical Tantric exorcism, I summarize the preliminary demonology (*bhūtalakṣaṇa*) chapter of the unpublished Tantra titled *Kriyākālaguṇottara*.[6] According to this pre-eleventh century Śaiva scripture, demons were created from Śiva's own body, but because of their violent nature, Brahmā asked Śiva to control them by creating doctors who specialize in curing possession. Here the text lays out the ideal traits of a Tantric exorcist:

> He knows the prescriptions for mantras and Tantric ritual. His conduct is pure. Firmly devoted to Śiva, he is heroic, truthful and mild-mannered. He always maintains faith in scripture and protects established practices. He honors the teachers, gods and brahmins of the Bhūta Tantras, and he always honors and makes offerings to the mantras. His rites always succeed; otherwise he would go to hell. These rules have been taught for the sake of the demons and for the mantra practitioner.[7]

6 KKGU, chapter VIII. All citations to this text are based on my unpublished edition. Verse and chapter numberings are subject to change. The edition is based on three Nepalese manuscripts with occasional reference to other manuscripts and testimonia. The manuscripts used were filmed by NGMPP under reel numbers B25/32, E2189/6 and B120/11, and A149/2. The MDL has posted a transcript of B25/32, but it frequently transcribes the readings of the manuscript wrong, and it makes no significant emendations.

7 KKGU VIII.111–14ab: *mantratantravidhijñas tu śaucācārasamanvitaḥ. śivabhakto dṛḍhaḥ śūraḥ satyavādī priyaṃvadaḥ. śraddadhānaḥ sadā śāstre samayācārapālakaḥ. gurudevadvijātīnāṃ bhūtatantrasya pūjakaḥ. mantrāṇāṃ ca baliṃ pūjāṃ kārayen nityam eva ca. tasya siddhiḥ sadā karma anyathā narakaṃ vrajet. ete samayā-m-ākhyātā grahāṇāṃ mantriṇasya ca.* Note that this register of Sanskrit allows non-standard forms like '*mantriṇasya*' rather than the expected '*mantriṇaḥ*.'

In a variant of this demon-creation story in the following chapter, Śiva sees the danger of the demons and imposes limits (*samaya*) on whom they could possess, under what circumstances and for how long.[8] They are not allowed to possess someone for no reason, and thus Śiva lists various dangerous locales and behaviors that make one vulnerable to demonic possession.[9]

In order to make a diagnosis, the exorcist must learn the various *lakṣaṇa*: symptoms or characteristic signs of possession by each particular type of demon. The types include non-demonic classes of beings such as gods (*devas*) and celestial musicians (*gandharvas*), but when the possession is unwelcome, an exorcism is called for. Another popular typology is based on the demon's motivation: some demons desire sexual contact (*ratikāma*), others want to harm people (*hantukāma*), and others still possess people out of hunger for the ritual food offerings (*balikāma*) that they will receive. Once the specific type has been determined, the exorcist (*bhūtatāntrika*) speaks to the demon and reminds it that it is bound by rules laid down by Śiva, that it has an obligation to tell the truth, and that it will be punished for lying.[10] The exorcist then asks the spirit who it is, why it possessed the person, what sort of veneration it wants, and anything else it wants. He reminds the spirit that Śiva laid down rules about who can be possessed and when the possession must cease. Next, the demon is honored with perfume powders, flowers, lamps, food and drinks for three days. If it does not leave, it has broken the rules and the exorcist must punish it. The ten types of punishment are beating, burning, piercing (in general), piercing the eyes, piercing the vital points, causing fever, shaking, stabbing with a nail, and possession.[11] Note that these violent punishments are inflicted on the *patient*, who is conventionally thought to be absent during this hostile takeover, to borrow a phrase from Frederick Smith.[12] Contemporary

8 See my Master's Thesis: *The Cult of Khaḍgarāvaṇa* (Slouber 2007).

9 See my forthcoming article 'Vulnerability and Protection in the Śaiva Tantras.'

10 KKGU VIII.92–102.

11 KKGU VIII.103–106: *vaidyo daśavidhaṃ tasya daṇḍaṃ vā samabhāṣata. bandhanaṃ prathamaṃ pāśaṃ dvitīyaṃ tāḍanaṃ smṛtam. tṛtīyaṃ dahanaṃ caiva caturthaṃ bhedanaṃ smṛtam. pañcamaṃ cākṣibhedaṃ ca ṣaṣṭhaṃ marmaprabhedanam. antardāhaś ca gātrāṇāṃ sadāghaḥ saptamaḥ smṛtaḥ. aṣṭamaṃ calanaṃ proktaṃ navamaṃ śūlabhedanam. daśamaṃ caiva āveśaṃ sarvagrahavimocanam. ete daṇḍā samākhyātā grahāṇāṃ nigraheṣu ca.* The meaning of *āveśa* as a form of punishment is not clear. Perhaps it indicates that the exorcist, or God himself, possesses the demon as a sort of revenge.

12 Smith used this phrase in the title of Chapter 6 of his 2006 monograph *The Self Possessed*.

accounts of exorcism in South Asia confirm that such punishments still occur, and occasionally result in the death of the patient. Thankfully, much of the exorcism ritual is nonviolent in nature.

The Bhūta Tantras describe various rites and offerings. Most of them involve highly specialized *mantras* that are understood to be the sonic form of deities in Śaiva literature. The *Kriyākālaguṇottara* focuses on five particular *mantra*-deities that specialize in punishing demons: Khaḍgarāvaṇa, Krodheśvara, Aghora, Jvareśvara and Devatrāsa. Subsequent to these Bhūta Tantra chapters are eight Bāla Tantra chapters concerning childhood possession.

Rather than summarizing the entirety of these complex ritual manuals – much of which is unrelated to plants – I focus on several themes of interest: the use of various types of dhoop, foods and flowers to attract and drive out demons, the use of rice-flour figurines and special stakes to attack and neutralize demons, and the particular plant-based terminology of the Tantric ritual universe. I explore these topics in three sections: the first concerns the exorcism rituals found in the Bhūta Tantra chapters of the *Kriyākālaguṇottara* (KKGU VIII–XVI), the second, its Bāla Tantra chapters (KKGU XVII–XXV), and the third is common to all of Tantric literature.

THE HERBAL ARSENALS OF EARLY TANTRIC GRIMOIRES

Chapters IX–XI of KKGU constitute the *Khaḍgarāvaṇakalpa*, i.e. the grimoire of the exorcism deity Khaḍgarāvaṇa. The first two chapters of this triad explain the origin of Khaḍgarāvaṇa and his cohorts, give his root *mantra* and describe how to construct various *maṇḍalas* for exorcism rituals. The third chapter, much longer than the former two, delves into the fundamentals of exorcism itself. The first rite involves a *mantra*, a hand gesture (*mudrā*), a particular recipe for incense and an effigy. Here the material for making the effigy is not specified, but elsewhere in the chapter such figurines are fashioned out of rice flour, other flour or cow-dung. The exorcist fashions spikes out of Cutch wood (*khadira*), and proceeds to disfigure the demon's effigy while reciting a *mantra* which calls on Śiva to do the same to the demon itself. Flour may be a preferred substance for constructing the effigy because it is food – food which sustains the living body can analogously sustain the temporary ritual mirror of the demon's body. Cow-dung, while it is not a food, is considered a holy substance and is used as fuel, as a disinfectant and occasionally as an internal medicine. When the Bhūta Tantra specifies the material for making such spikes, it is almost always Cutch wood. This may simply be because it is a very dense hardwood that is widely available, but it might also be due to its intimidating thorns that can be up to two inches long. In sympathetic rites worldwide, any resemblance between the implements and their purpose increases the magic's potency.

Next, the recipe for a powerful medicinal substance is given.[13] The recipe is prefaced by the label 'Nasal-elixir-ointment-incense' (*nasyapānāñjanadhūpaṃ*), presumably indicating that it can be administered by any of these common routes. Following the recipe, however, it is solely referred to as dhoop. The recipe calls for eighteen ingredients: gum arabic, datura fruit, snake slough, cat feces, grain chaff, cotton seeds, sweet flag, neem, human hair, black pepper, bamboo bark, peacock feather, fenugreek, two types of Indian nightshade, turmeric, lotus and two final plants whose identity is in question (perhaps another fenugreek and sacred fig).[14] This incense is described as 'destructive to dreadful demons.'

Several features of these ingredients are significant. Like the Cutch wood used for hewing spikes, the first two ingredients are plants that have long, threatening spines. The seed-pods of datura are not only furnished with spines (thus the common name 'thorn-apple'), they also contain a formidable hallucinogen that can be a deadly poison in uncontrolled doses. Plant biologists have long considered the *Datura* genus to be a New World plant that did not exist in the Old World in pre-Columbian times. The name datura comes from the Sanskrit word *dhattūra*, and its long-standing history in Sanskrit literature, going back perhaps 2000 years, would seem to contradict the theory of datura's recent introduction to Asia. One possibility, skeptics argue, is that the name *dhattūra* referred to different plants over the centuries and was transferred to an imported datura species in the early modern era. This point has been countered, initially in Siklós (1994) and more comprehensively in Geeta and Gharaibeh (2007). The latter scholars propose a New World origin for the *Datura* genus, but insist that it must have traveled to Asia long before the European age of colonialism. The two Indian nightshades called for in the recipe given above are also poisonous and hallucinogenic and belong to the same family of plants as datura. It is interesting to speculate on the hallucinogenic potential of

13 KKGU xi.1 (prose section following first verse).

14 KKGU xi (prose following first verse): *gośṛṅgaṃ madanaphalaṃ bhujaṃganirmocamārjāraviṣṭhaṃ tuṣāḥ karpāsāsthivacāṃ nimbaṃ svakeśā maricā vaṃśatvacā barhiṇapicchā nirmālyaṃ bṛhatī ubhe ca rajanī padmaṃ nakhaṃ kuñjaraṃ dhūpam aṣṭadaśāṅgam etad ghorarākṣasanāśanam*

burning these plants in an enclosed treatment space. Given that they are three of eighteen ingredients, the concentration of the psychoactive component of the smoke may have been too low to have any direct effect on the patient and other attendees. If the space was small, on the other hand, the dhoop might have been capable of producing hallucinations in the patient and all present.

The inclusion of several thorny, poisonous and hallucinogenic plants in this noxious dhoop should not overshadow the animal ingredients that would be highly offensive to anyone in purity-conscious South Asia: snake skin, cat feces and human hair. It is not hard to imagine how such a foul-smelling odor would have a powerful effect on patients expressing demonic possession. Recent research in sensory anthropology, and adaptations of this research to history and the humanities, have emphasized the power of scents to mark boundaries in time, space, social register and ritual type.[15] In our context, I interpret this noxious exorcism dhoop to be more akin to one of the forms of punishing demons listed above than a formal demarcation of ritual space. On the other hand, the psychological effect left on all present would be that of an intense crisis situation, which, indeed, any pathology manifesting as demonic possession represents.

The *Kriyākālaguṇottara* goes on to give an alternative recipe (in verse rather than prose like the previous one) for an all-purpose exorcism dhoop. Ten of the ingredients overlap, but this recipe innovates with asafetida, two types of pine sap, cattle bones, milk from a young cow, hellebore, mustard seeds, goat skin and grains, all of which are ground in a mortar with goat urine. Despite the sweet-smelling pine saps and the pungent aroma of popping mustard seeds, this dhoop keeps the noxious ingredients of the prior recipe and adds a few of its own. It also specifies that it is to be used indoors, in case any faint-hearted exorcist-in-training had the idea of burning it outdoors to avoid the stench. Clearly, its purpose is for the patient, and everyone else present by default, to inhale the foul dhoop for the exorcism to work. Regardless of how one rationalizes the underlying mechanisms of demonic possession behavior, it is clear that here the dhoop is functioning as a deterrent.

Not all incense in the Bhūta Tantras was intended to repel demons. The section that follows this recipe has a long *mantra*, then the instruction to burn a sweet-smelling dhoop of neem leaves and bdellium. This pleasant incense burned in conjunction with the *mantra* attracts the demon or other possessing agent into the room. The exorcist then cuts up the effigy

15 Cf. Le Guerer (1992) and Baum (2013).

of it and grinds it in a stone mortar, effectively 'grinding the bones of the demon.'[16]

Readers might be familiar with an old European belief that one can thwart a pursuing monster or vampire by throwing a handful of tiny seeds on the ground. The rationale is that the demonic pursuer is obsessive-compulsive and cannot help but stop and count the tiny seeds before continuing on. The Bhūta Tantras often enjoin a similar practice – throwing enchanted mustard seeds at demons – but with a different rationale: 'Take mustard seeds, chant this *mantra* over them twenty-one times, and cast them down with the name of bees. This causes the demon to be eaten by bees.'[17] I interpret the elliptical phrase 'with the name of bees' to mean that one says 'bees,' perhaps repeatedly, while throwing the seeds, which would imply that the countless tiny black seeds are spiritually transformed into aggressive black bees.

FETID FOODS IN EARLY TANTRIC PEDIATRICS

The Bāla Tantra section of the *Kriyākālaguṇottara* comprises eight chapters that trace all the stages of conception and parenthood and deal with infertility, threats to the pregnant woman, threats to the developing fetus in each of the ten (lunar) months of pregnancy, demons specific to each of the newborn's first ten days, demons specific to each month in the first year, and, finally, demons that attack in particular years of childhood through the seventeenth year of life. Plant-based medicines play a role in each of these chapters and phases, but not every part is relevant to exorcism, so I focus on the final four chapters (XXII–XXV).

Like the exorcism guides described in the last section, these chapters also make abundant use of plants and sometimes noxious incense to deal with demons. Nevertheless, the approach is starkly different. Rather than threatening the demon, attacking its effigy, and driving it out with poisonous and unpleasant fumes, here the idea is to *feed* the demonesses called the 'Mothers' that are responsible for the attack. Though the offerings often consist of disgusting ingredients, the Mothers actually *prefer* such flavors, in contrast to the aversion that they induced in normal demons described in previous chapters of the Bhūta Tantra.

16 KKGU XI (prose following v. 8): *grahasya asthibhaṅgo bhavati*

17 Ibid.: *anena mantreṇa sarṣapān gṛhya ekaviṃśati vārāñ japtvā bhramarāṇāṃ nāmena nikṣipet. graho bhramarair bhakṣāpayati*

These examples represent gendered exorcism rituals. Exorcists specializing in the *mantra*-deities such as Khaḍgarāvaṇa and his scary cohorts take charge and punish the unruly demons who refuse to submit to the masculine authority of Śiva and his exorcist representative. Supporting this claim is the fact that demonic possession among adults primarily, but not exclusively, affects young women, and the demons seizing the women are generally male.[18] An insider explanation is that women are more vulnerable in general, and scholars typically agree, but expand on the mechanics of how possession serves its subjects. Mark Nichter, in his article 'Idioms of Distress' (1981), has argued that in his field context in South India, possession is the last resort in a series of idioms expressing social distress, most strongly affecting young wives and unmarried daughters who are in liminal social positions. The patient is often a powerless woman acting out her intense distress in the only socially-acceptable manner available to her. But in the realm of demonic possession of infants and young children, the situation is more likely to be handled by women directly and they might be more inclined to deal with a demon by feeding it rather than threatening it. Let us examine this alternative idiom of exorcism more closely.

The format of these chapters is simple: they begin with symptoms, the name of the demoness and the day/month/year that she attacks, and how to counteract her and make her 'let go' of the possessed child. Aside from some minor variations, this format holds for each of the thirty-nine demonesses described (ten daily for newborns, twelve monthly for the first year, and seventeen yearly thereafter). The treatment for the first ten days consists of a combination of herbal ointments, fumigation treatments and food offerings to the demoness. The recipe for each demoness is unique, although possession by certain among them is incurable, so no recipe is given in those cases. Here is a translation of the section on possession of the one-day-old newborn, as an example:

> The neck is bent backward. Saliva flows from the mouth. The limbs tremble. Food doesn't help. The demoness named Wicked seizes the child who was just born (one day old). One must make a neutralizing medicine for him: Indian madder, Fire-flame bush, lodh, yellow arsenic, and sandal. Smear his body with that and the demoness will let go. The wise one would always offer a portion to the demonesses: a fragrant garland, liquor, wine, boiled

18 Cf. Smith (2006: 68–75) for a theoretical discussion of the issue of women's possession and empowerment issues, as well as references that support the claim that women more frequently undergo possession.

rice, and whatever meat one chooses. Treated to that, my child, she will let go. Have no doubt.[19]

The overall theme of these ointment ingredients is the color: red or yellow. Yellow is a shade that is akin to red in the South Asian milieu. The color red might be significant here because of its association with childbirth and fertility.[20] Indian madder (*mañjiṣṭhā*) is famous for the red dye that can be made from its roots. Fire-flame bush (*dhātakī*) has beautiful red flowers. Lodh (*rodhra*) has yellow flowers, and also has bark from which a red powder can be prepared.[21] Yellow arsenic (*haritāla*) is, of course, important for its brilliant yellow color that sometimes ranges into the orange and red spectrums. The sandalwood (*candana*) referred to here could be the red variety. Sandal is a common base for ointments of all kinds because of its lovely fragrance and cooling properties.

The ingredients of the *bali* offering (liquor, wine, meat, rice) are typical impure substances enjoyed by demons and fierce deities alike. Deities like Bhairava and Kālī, the fierce counterparts to Śiva and Pārvatī, for example, take ritual offerings of alcohol and animal sacrifice as a matter of course. Naturally the 'impurity' of these substances is a matter of convention; high-caste Hindus tend to consider alcohol and meat impure, whereas some Tantric followers of Śiva reject the very idea of impurity on theological grounds, just as some Tantric Buddhists do on ontological grounds.

While the countermeasures for this first demoness do not specify a dhoop recipe, the majority do, and it is difficult to gauge whether it should be understood even when unstated. Then again, since the dhoop recipes vary so greatly, there is no simple default to fall back on. Examples of ingredients for the fumigation treatment of possessed newborns include hair, nails, neem leaves, mustard seeds, hair from a corpse, tiger's claw, monkey fur, spikenard and lac.[22]

19 KKGU XXII.6–8: *grīvā ca pṛṣṭhato bhagnā lālā ca śravate mukhāt. udvejayati gātrāṇi āhāraṃ ca na rocate. pāpanī sā grahī nāma gṛhṇate sadyajātakam. tasya kuryāt pratīkāyaṃ bālakasya cikitsitam. mañjiṣṭhādhātakīrodhraṃ haritālaṃ sa candanam. etena sa viliptāṅgas tato muñcanti sā grahī. bhāgaṃ dadyāt kumārīṇāṃ sarvakālaṃ vicakṣaṇaḥ. gandhamālyaṃ surā madyaṃ bhaktaṃ māṃsaṃ yathepsayā. anenaiva kṛtā vatsa mucyate nātra saṃśayaḥ*

20 On the associations of red with women, childbirth and fertility, see Selby (2005: 260–61).

21 MWSED s.v. *rodhra*.

22 KKGU XXII.9–40.

The treatment for possession by the monthly demonesses, from the first through the twelfth months of a baby's life, tends to focus more on the *bali* or sacrificial food offering. Only a few of these specify a dhoop for the demoness, and several of them are deemed incurable by any means. In contrast to the newborn offerings, however, the monthly demonesses are offered items such as clothing and sesame-oil lamps. These demonesses also come with a prescription to bathe the possessed child with a mixture of herbs called 'the five broken-branches' (*pañcabhaṅga*). The text defines it as a mix consisting of the shoots of Flame of the forest, pipal, wood-apple, bel and cluster fig.[23] This group of common and useful trees have either edible fruits, a milky medicinal latex or sap, or both, and the prescription for use of this bath-additive continues nearly every year up to the possessed seventeen-year-old youth.

PLANT IMAGERY IN TANTRIC RITUAL TERMINOLOGY

A technical vocabulary based on plant imagery underlies the whole Tantric milieu. The Tantric practitioner comes in many types – chiefly: spiritual masters, exorcists, snakebite specialists, yogins and seekers after magical powers – but several items of plant imagery are shared by all. Tantra was a pan-Indian religious phenomenon, so the stock of images differed little among Hindus, Buddhists, Jains and smaller traditions that incorporated Tantric ritual into their practices. The lotus throne is perhaps the most fundamental plant image. The exorcist, indeed any Tantric practitioner, derives his power from the ability to effectively make contact with the divine. Such contact varies from worship of externally-constructed *maṇḍalas*, full-blown internal visualizations, or even outright sacralization of oneself as the deity. In any case, the deity is imagined as seated on a lotus-flower throne. The lotus is drawn or imagined in precise detail: its stem, its petals, its pericarp, and its pistils are all specified. Eight-petaled lotuses are the norm in the Bhūta Tantra material I have accessed. The central deity, such as the 'Lord of Ghosts' Khaḍgarāvaṇa, is visualized as sitting on the central pericarp of a shining white lotus. His eight female attendants – goddesses in their own right – are seated on each petal oriented toward the cardinal and intermediate directions of the compass. Each is

23 KKGU xxiii.11: *palāśāśvatthakapitthānāṃ bilvodumbarapallavam. pañcabhaṅgo bhaved eṣa bālānāṃ tu hitāya vai*

worshiped with her 'seed syllable' (*bījākṣara*), a short *mantra* that symbolizes the goddess in her embryonic form. The general pattern in this case is for the seeds to have three or four syllables including *oṃ*, one or more syllables relating to the name of the goddess and ending with a nasalized vowel (*anusvāra*) and an additional syllable ending in an aspirated vowel (*visarga*). These seeds are then worshiped in turn in order to 'grow' them into full-fledged deities capable of any rite:

> First one worships the supreme one-syllable seed of Khaḍgarāvaṇa, and then those of the goddesses in due order. The seeds are worshipped on a seat (the lotus) which was previously prepared. The rituals of one who whispers and visualizes these most secret of seeds will be successful. [The aim of] his rite will always come to pass.[24]

What is the nature of this seed? Here, the text refers to it as the seed *of* Khaḍgarāvaṇa, but elsewhere the grammar indicates that the seed is the deity itself: 'In the beginning, one worships the seed *as* the god Śiva, the master who is the lord of all swords.'[25] The *mantra* systems thus work on a horticultural analogy: one plants the *mantra*-seed, tends it by daily worship and recitation, perfects it after a lengthy period of service (*pūrvasevā/ puraścaraṇa*), and harvests the fruit (*phala*) of the ritual action once the *mantra*-deity is ready to be launched into action. An extension of the analogy involves seed syllables encasing the name of the patient as a form of protection, a sort of back-to-the-womb healing visualization in which the patient is the germ which the *mantras* protect like the shell of a seed.[26]

A related concept common to the Bhūta Tantras and other Tantric literature is the 'root *mantra*' (*mūlamantra*). In the case of Khaḍgarāvaṇa, it is quite long, consisting of numerous words of praise, a description of his appearance, and various commands for the deity to perform. Because such a long *mantra* cannot practically be enunciated for high numbers of repetition, a heart *mantra* is also given that is only slightly longer than the seed. From the seed, heart and root *mantras*, 'sprout' a vast array of auxiliary *mantras* that can serve any ritual purpose. This garden of phonemes certainly requires an attentive caretaker to perfect.

24 KKGU XI.20: *prathamaṃ khaḍgeśvarasya bījam ekākṣaraṃ param. devīnāṃ caiva ekaikam anupūrveṇa kīrtitam. yajeta devadevīnām āsane pūrvakalpite. etān guhyatamān bījāñ japate dhyāyate ca yaḥ. tasya karmāṇi sidhyanti sadā karma bhaviṣyati*

25 KKGU XI.16ab: *ādau bījaṃ śivaṃ devaṃ khaḍgakhaḍgeśvaraṃ prabhum*

26 KKGU XXV.27ab: *sādhyā nāmākṣaraṃ skanda bījenānena saṃpuṭet*

TANTRIC EXORCISM IN THE MODERN AGE

Anthropologists and other ethnographers have long held a keen interest in possession phenomena, and approaches taken to describe these have undergone a great deal of development. The focus has shifted away from attempts to explain away possession as mere superstitious social belief or mental illness; ethnographers now seek to understand the conditions that lead to it, and the social function that it plays. These developments are certainly welcome, but belie a lingering need to explain the phenomena in the first place. This focus on making sense of possession in modernity has meant that few studies attend to the basic material culture of a rite like exorcism.

Demonic possession and exorcism are not socially-acceptable reactions to distress in the modern world – yet they persist worldwide. The narrative that they are survivors of a prior age of superstition is unacceptably derogatory. People turn to possession and exorcism for a variety of reasons, and often after having failed to find relief for their condition via 'modern' medicine.

A number of recent studies on exorcism show continuity with the early Tantric rituals. Many more studies do not exhibit continuity, however I suggest that this is often a result of the focus of the ethnographer and the choice of subjects, rather than a lack of evidence.

In 1977, anthropologist Edward Henry published a study of an eclectic healer titled Baba from eastern Uttar Pradesh, India. Henry was clearly interested in explaining how this healer's treatments might be so effective, and his analysis focuses on the patient's expectations, the process of diagnosis and the power of suggestion to shape the outcome. He describes the Baba as eclectic because he combines elements of the Brahmanical healer, shaman, herbalist, and traditional *vaids* and *hakims*. In light of early Tantric medicine, this combination of purviews is hardly unusual. It is typical of the Tantric exorcist or poison specialist. Henry notes that 'practitioners like Baba are often thought of as specialists in problems related to conception.' (1977: 312) This conforms to the range of skills ascribed to the Tantric exorcist above. Henry identifies six elements of Baba's exorcisms: divination, sweeping with a wand, *mantra*, *yantra*, curative herbs and dietary restriction, and gifting sacred ash. With the exception of the last element, all of these are also common in the Bhūta Tantras. For emotional problems as well as for demonic possession, Baba uses what Henry characterizes as 'aversion therapy' – a 'noxious concoction' of garlic juice and asafetida applied beneath the eyes for seven days, reminiscent of the foul-smelling dhoops prescribed in early Tantric medicine (ibid.: 314).

Baba's explanations of the ways people become vulnerable to possession, and his practice of transferring the demon to a crossroads, also appear to be continuations of the same medical tradition we see in early Tantric sources. Crossroads are still used as sites to leave offerings to demons in contemporary practice in Nepal: at night on the summer holiday of Ghanta Karna, housewives leave fetid offerings of curdled blood, buffalo entrails, rice, flowers and a lamp at the crossroads closest to their homes, in order to placate demons and witches that are especially active on this night (Anderson 1988: 75). Evidently, this is a continuation of a very old tradition. Such *bali* offerings are also illustrated in numerous illuminated manuscripts from Nepal related to child-snatching demonesses. At least one such manuscript is splattered with drops of blood that were evidently offered as *bali* to the pictured demonesses.[27]

The third documentary in the Bedi Films trilogy called *Sādhus: India's Holy Men* is about a particular young Aghori ascetic named Ram Nath. The middle of the episode contains footage of his guru Satya Narayan performing an exorcism in the latter's Hardwar ashram during the Navratri festival (Bedi et al. 1995: 35:38–42:39). Satya Narayan attributes his healing power to the training the gods gave him during the twenty years of his youth spent living as an Aghori. The scene opens with a congregation singing rhythmic devotional hymns to the accompaniment of drumming and chimes. The patient in question is a middle-aged woman. Her husband says he had never believed in evil spirits before, but had a change of heart after their experience. His wife was having major health problems (vomiting blood, a choking sensation in the chest, itching all over, insomnia), but the modern doctors he brought her to were unable to relieve her symptoms or explain their cause. He says that she has had some relief since coming to Satya Narayan's ashram. Later in the evening, the guru asks the woman to come forward and unbind her hair. In early Tantric medicine, unbound hair is at once a cause and a symptom of possession, and also the name of one of the demonesses that possesses young children.[28] The patient removes her headscarf and unbinds her hair, then begins rocking back and forth, a movement that culminates in a violent shaking of her head euphemistically called *khel* (play) in Hindi. This is a classic sign of possession.

27 E.g. Asha Archives 877 (1.637-I) '*Bālagrahalakṣaṇa*.' The text is in a mix of Sanskrit and Newari.

28 KKGU xx.71, xxii.26, xxvi.8.

Satya Narayan proceeds to question the demon, and I insert the possessed woman's answers in parentheses:

> Do you want to be liberated? How many are you? (Three.) What kind? (Ghoul.) How did you come here? Who sent you? (Sister-in-law.) Speak the truth or you'll be sent to the deepest hell. Tell me where you want to go. (I won't come back.) If you come back you will go to hell.

He draws a small circle with a knife in a pile of ashes, circles several cloves over the patient's head and thus transfers the demons into the cloves. He places the cloves in the circle which is marked with cloves at two edges. Assumedly, these additional cloves represent guardian divinities keeping the demons contained within the circle. The guru finally sets the central cloves on fire, extinguishes the burning mass with his fingers and carries the remains outside to complete the exorcism. Later that night, Satya Narayan and Ram Nath hold a special *pūjā* session for Bhairava. Recall that Bhairava is a fierce form of Śiva akin to Khaḍgarāvaṇa in the examples discussed above. Satya Narayan has Ram Nath offer meat and alcohol into the fire to thank Bhairava for his assistance in the exorcism.

Another recent study by J.K. Tiwari et al. focuses much more on plants: 'Ethnopaediatrics in Garhwal Himalaya, Uttarakhand, India.' This study notes the widespread use of herbal medicine globally (80 percent of the world's poor depend on it), and emphasizes the prevalence of 'mantra and tantra' in their study area. One of the plants they list as an amulet for young children, sweet flag (*vacā*), is also a recurring ingredient in the Bāla Tantra passages discussed above.

One final ethnographic account is from Frederick Smith's own fieldwork described in *The Self Possessed*. He interviews two brahmin practitioners of Āyurveda, one of whom specializes in *mantravidyā*, a tradition that I have argued is a descendent of Tantric medicine. The other doctor frequently prescribes 'fumigation with foul-smelling substances,' but substitutes the impure animal ingredients with less-offensive, but still noxious plants such as garlic and chili (Smith 2006: 547).

CONCLUSION

The universe of early Tantric exorcism ritual was suffused with plants and plant powers. From pungent dhoops to herbal ointments, bath infusions to fetid food offerings, mantric seeds and flower thrones – plants formed the

Table 7.1. Chart of referenced plants from Bhūta and Bāla Tantras.

Sanskrit Name	**Common Name**	**Use**
khadira	Cutch	wooden spike
gośṛṅga	Gum arabic	fumigant
madana	Emetic nut	fumigant
karpāsa	Cotton	fumigant
vacā	Sweet flag	fumigant/ointment/amulet
nimba	Neem	fumigant
marica	Black pepper	fumigant
vaṃśa	Bamboo	fumigant
nirmālya	Fenugreek**	fumigant
bṛhatī	Indian nightshade	fumigant
rajanī	Turmeric**	fumigant
padma	Lotus	fumigant
nakha	Fenugreek**	fumigant
kuñjara	Sacred fig**	fumigant
hiṅgu	Asafetida	fumigant/ointment
devadāru	Pine	fumigant
śrīveṣṭa	Pine	fumigant
kaṭukarohiṇī	Hellebore	fumigant
sarṣapa	Indian mustard	fumigant/projectile
guggula	Bdellium	perfume
mañjiṣṭhā	Indian madder	ointment
dhātakī	Fire-flame bush	ointment
rodhra	Lodh	ointment
candana	Sandal	ointment
vyāghranakha	Tiger's claw**	fumigant
māṃsī	Spikenard	fumigant
lākṣā	Lac tree**	fumigant
tila	Sesame	lamp oil
palāśa	Flame of the forest	bath additive
aśvattha	Pipal	bath additive
kapittha	Wood-apple	bath additive
bilva	Bel	bath additive
udumbara	Cluster fig	bath additive
(*laśuna*)	Garlic	ointment
(*lavaṅga*)	Clove	vessel for demon
(*kaṭuvīra*)	Chili	fumigant

Note: This chart includes only plants referenced in the article, which make up a fraction of the plants referred to in the early Tantric primary sources. Where the identity of the Sanskrit plant is in doubt, I indicate this in the chart with a double asterisk (**). Where the plant was referenced without a Sanskrit name, I suggest one in parentheses.

basis of every level of preparation and treatment for demonic possession. They were valued for their aesthetic beauty, medicinal and hallucinogenic properties, thorns and scents. The subject is not as esoteric as it sometimes appears from the Western academic point of view; plant medicines and demonic possession are, rather, facts of life for people all over South Asia and for much of the rest of the world. The specific rituals of exorcism based on early Tantric sources described above are still practiced in diverse communities in South Asia and in the diaspora. More research that attends to the material culture of South Asian religions will continue to enhance our understanding of this ancient civilization.

ABBREVIATIONS AND REFERENCES

Anderson 1988 Anderson, M. (1988). *The Festivals of Nepal.* Calcutta: Rupa & Co.

Baum 2013 Baum, J. (2013). 'From Incense to Idolatry: The Reformation of Olfaction in Late Medieval German Ritual.' *Sixteenth Century Journal* XLIV(2): 323–44.

Bedi et al. 1995 Bedi, N., A. Malik, D. Whyte and R. Bedi (1995). *Sādhus: India's Holy Men. Vol. 3: Aghori, Living with the Dead.* Princeton, NJ: Films for the Humanities & Sciences.

Dwyer 2003 Dwyer, G. (2003). *The Divine and the Demonic.* London: Routledge Curzon.

Ferrari 2011 Ferrari, F.M. (ed.) (2011). *Health and Religious Rituals in South Asia. Disease, Possession, and Healing.* London: Routledge Curzon.

Filliozat 1937 Filliozat, J. (1937). *Etude de démonologie indienne: le Kumāratantra de Rāvaṇa et les textes paralleles Indiens Tibétains, Chinois, Cambodgien et Arabe.* Imprimerie nationale, Paris.

FoI *Flowers of India.* <http://flowersofindia.net> (accessed 10 October 2015)

Geeta and Gharaibeh 2007 Geeta, R. and W. Gharaibeh. (2007). 'Historical Evidence for a Pre-Columbian Presence of Datura in the Old World and Implications for a First Millennium Transfer from the New World.' *Journal of Bioscience* 32(7): 1227–44.

Henry 1977 Henry, E. (1977). 'A North Indian Healer and the Sources of his Power.' *Social Science and Medicine* 11: 309–17.

Kapferer 1983 Kapferer, B. (1983). *A Celebration of Demons. Exorcism and the Aesthetics of Healing in Sri Lanka.* Bloomington: University of Indiana Press.

KKGU *Kriyākālaguṇottara*

Le Guerer 1992 Le Guerer, A. (1992). *Scent. The Mysterious and Essential Powers of Smell.* New York: Random House.

Manandhar 1989 Manandhar, N. (1989). *Useful Wild Plants of Nepal*. Stuttgart: Franz Steiner Verlag Wiesbaden GMbH.

MDL *Muktabodha Digital Library*, ©2011 Muktabodha Indological Research Institute, <http://muktalib5.org/digital_library.htm> (accessed 8 January 2014).

MWSED Monier-Williams, M., Sir. (1899). *A Sanskrit-English Dictionary*. Reprinted 2002. Delhi: Motilal Banarsidass.

NGMPP *The Nepalese-German Manuscript Cataloguing Project*. <https://www.uni-hamburg.de/ngmcp/index_e.html> (accessed 10 October 2015).

Nichter 1981 Nichter, M. (1981). 'Idioms of Distress: Alternatives in the Expression of Psychological Distress: A Case Study from South India.' *Culture, Medicine, and Psychiatry* 5: 379–408.

Pandanus *Pandanus Database of Plants*. Seminar of Indian Studies, Institute of South and Central Asia, Faculty of Arts, Charles University, Prague (1998–2009): <http://iu.ff.cuni.cz/pandanus/database/> (accessed 10 October 2015).

Sanderson 2009 Sanderson, A. (2009). 'The Śaiva Age.' In Einoo, S. (ed.), *Genesis and Development of Tantrism*, pp. 41–349. Tokyo: Institute of Oriental Culture.

Selby 2005 Selby, M.A. (2005). 'Narratives of Conception, Gestation, and Labour in Sanskrit Ayurvedic Texts.' *Asian Medicine* 1(2): 254–275.

Siklós 1944 Siklós, B. (1994). 'Datura Rituals in the Vajramahābhairava-Tantra.' *Acta Orientalia Academiae Scientiarum Hungaricae*, 47(3): 409–416.

Slouber 2007 Slouber, M. (2007). *The Cult of Khaḍgarāvaṇa*. MA Thesis: University of California, Berkeley.

Slouber 2016 Slouber, M. (2016). *Early Tantric Medicine*. New York: Oxford University Press.

Slouber forthcoming Slouber, M. (forthcoming). 'Vulnerability and Protection in the Śaiva Tantras.' In Goodall, D. and P. Filliozat (eds.), *Mélanges tantriques à la mémoire d'N.R. Bhatt*. Pondicherry: Institut Français de Pondichéry.

Smith 2006 Smith, F.M. (2006). *The Self Possessed. Deity and Spirit Possession in South Asian Literature and Civilization*. New York: Columbia University Press.

Tiwari et al. (2010) Tiwari, J.K., R. Ballabha and P. Tiwari. (2010). 'Ethnopaediatrics in Garhwal Himalaya, Uttarakhand, India (Psychomedicine and Medicine).' *New York Science Journal* 3(4): 123–26.

Weiss 1977 Weiss, M.G. (1977) *Critical Study of Unmāda in the Early Sanskrit Medical Literature. An Analysis of Ayurvedic Psychiatry with Reference to Present-Day Diagnostic Concepts*. PhD Thesis: University of Pennsylvania.

Wujastyk 1999 — Wujastyk, D. (1999). 'Miscarriages of Justice: Demonic Vengeance in Classical Indian Medicine.' In Hinnells, J. and R. Porter (eds.), *Religion, Health & Suffering. A Cross-Cultural Study of Attitudes to Suffering and the Implications for Medicine in a Multi-Religious Society*, pp. 256–75. London: Routledge.

Wujastyk 2003 — Wujastyk, D. (2003). *The Roots of Ayurveda*. New York: Penguin Books.

Chapter 8

Tree-Hugger: The Sāmavedic Rite of *Audumbarī*

FINNIAN M.M. GERETY[1]

PRELUDE: 'HUG THE TREES!'

Such was the rallying cry of the *chipko andolan* ('hugging movement') in Himalayan Uttarakhand in the early 1970s (Weber 1988: 11, 40). Local villagers, in a bid to stop logging and despoliation of habitat by outsiders, clasped hands and ringed tree trunks with their arms and bodies. Over the next decade, Chipko was hailed worldwide as a paragon of grass-roots activism and its techniques were widely imitated.[2] The gesture of embracing a tree seeped into global consciousness, and along with it the term 'tree-hugger.' By the late 1980s, the term had enough currency in the U.S. to inspire a backlash, becoming the attack epithet of choice for anti-environmentalist conservatives (DeLoach, Bruner and Gossett 2002). By now, the term has been reclaimed to some extent as a badge for an environmentally conscious lifestyle.

In this chapter, 'tree-hugger' is a point of departure for the exploration of ritual in ancient South Asia. The rite I will discuss features the embrace of a tree, but the context and particulars are worlds away from Chipko. My tree-hugger is the brahmin officiant of the Vedic liturgical singing tradition called *Sāmaveda*, who embraces the trunk of a type of fig tree known in Sanskrit as *udumbara*. My analysis, which centers on this moment of

1 Finnian M.M. Gerety is Visiting Assistant Professor, Department of Religious Studies, Brown University and Research Associate, Department of South Asian Studies, Harvard University (USA).

2 For a critique of the received Chipko narrative, see Rangan (2000: 13–42).

contact between human and plant, consists of four parts. In the first part, I discuss the *udumbara*'s name and characteristics; touch on some fundamentals of Vedic texts, ritual and hermeneutics; and show how the tree has been represented in the Vedic corpus. Next, I present the praxis of the rite along with its interpretations, aiming to reconstruct the flow and the meaning of the rite according to its composers and performers. Third, I situate the rite within the broader frames of cosmology and domestic habitation, arguing for relations between the post of *udumbara*, the cosmic pillar of Vedic myth and the central post of the prototypical Vedic dwelling. Finally, I explore the prehistory of the rite, emphasizing features of its praxis that suggest an enactment of an ascent to heaven, with possible antecedents in the religious cultures of Central and North Asia.

THE UDUMBARA TREE

While many of the sacred trees in South Asian religious cultures are living, others are the trunks of felled trees erected for the purpose of ritual and worship.[3] My focus is the trunk of a tree that Vedic texts call *udumbara*, identified by modern botanists and Indologists as *Ficus racemosa* L. (syn. *f. glomerata* Roxb.), commonly known as the 'cluster fig.' The tree fruits in abundant clusters along its main branches – a mature tree, some 60 feet tall, produces thousands of figs – and its wood contains a milky, sticky sap (Minkowski 1989: 7–9).[4] The Sanskrit name *udumbára* is of uncertain etymology (Mayrhofer 1992–2001, s.v.). The derivative term *audumbara*- ('made of *udumbara* wood') is found already in early Vedic texts to describe an amulet of this material, which brings prosperity and nourishment (AVŚ xix.31). The Sāmavedic rite concerns a 'post made of *udumbara*' (*sthūṇā audumbarī*; cf. BauŚS vi.26), called in most sources simply *audumbarī*.

The *audumbarī* rite is part of the *agniṣṭoma*, the paradigmatic Soma sacrifice in the system of *śrauta* ritual.[5] The sacrifice is performed for the

3 On the significance of sacred posts in a variety of South Asian contexts, see Brighenti (2012: 105–125), Witzel (2012: 135), Biardeau (2004), Staal (1991: 90) and Kuiper (1983: 241).

4 Minkowski (1989) contains further references to the modern botanical literature on *udumbara*. Cf. Mukharji's recent critique of the scholarly convention of glossing a 'plant's cultural name with a botanical name' (2014: 65), a practice he dubs 'retro-botanizing.'

5 The *agniṣṭoma*, 'praise of Agni,' serves as the building block for more elaborate Soma sacrifices. *Śrauta* ritual is so called because it is composed from *śruti* ('that which is heard'), another name for the Vedic corpus.

yajamāna, a 'sacrificer' or patron whose participation is guided throughout by several groups of brahmin officiants. Each group is led by a specialist in a particular liturgy: the *adhvaryu* recites formulas (*yajus*) from the *Yajurveda*; the *hotṛ* recites verses (*ṛc*) from the *Ṛgveda*; the *udgātṛ* sings melodies (*sāman*) from the *Sāmaveda*.[6] The Sāmavedic officiants participate *only* in the Soma sacrifices; the non-Soma rites in the *śrauta* system do not include *Sāmaveda* at all. The *agniṣṭoma* is a five-day ritual culminating in the pressing and drinking of *soma*, the psychoactive plant that features so prominently in the ritual, interspersed with Ṛgvedic recitations (*śastra*) and Sāmavedic songs (*stotra*) praising various Vedic deities. Within a space oriented towards the east, there are fire altars made of earthen bricks and structures made of other perishable materials (wood, thatch, grass). The central structure is the 'sitting place' (*sadas*), the main venue for *soma*-drinking and chanting. The *audumbarī* stands at its center (ŚB III.6.1.1–2; Eggeling 1885: 140n3).

While it is a rite of great complexity, the goals of the *agniṣṭoma* are straightforward: to procure the sacrificer's material and spiritual well-being, including prosperity while he lives and a long stay in heaven when dies. In pursuit of these aims, the officiants guide him through rites that enact his rebirth as a sanctified participant, ascent to heaven and return to earth. The Sāmavedic officiants play a crucial role in the sacrificer's soteriology, their songs propelling him to heaven.

The Vedic texts that concern us are the Saṃhitās, collections of *mantras*; the Brāhmaṇas, interpretations of the rites; and the Śrauta Sūtras, codifications of praxis. Although these genres represent different strata of the corpus, composed over almost a thousand years, Vedic ritual was a conservative institution and the texts work as a hierarchical, synchronic system (see Minkowski 1992: 29, 34–35). For example, the relatively late codifications of the Śrauta Sūtras, where we find detailed information on how the rituals are to be performed, assume the authority of earlier texts and try to remain consistent with them. These lines of authority grew in 'branches' (*śākhās*) or schools, corresponding to the brahmin populations of a particular tribe or area (Witzel 1997b: 259). My primary focus here is the *audumbarī* rite as it was codified and interpreted by the Jaiminīya branch of the *Sāmaveda*, c. 800–500 BCE in the central region of the Vedic heartland.[7]

6 A fourth priest, the *brahman*, superintends the proceedings in silence and speaks expiatory *mantras* as necessary; in late-Vedic texts, his role is associated with the *Atharvaveda*.

7 For the dating and localization of Jaiminīya texts and traditions, see Witzel (1987: 189–92).

Nevertheless, the rite has a long history and draws on *mantras*, praxis and interpretations from earlier strata and other branches.

Any study dealing with Vedic texts must grapple with a distinctive mode of hermeneutics, which I shall refer to by the technical term *bandhu* ('bond'; more loosely, 'correlation').[8] The *bandhu* hermeneutic establishes meaning by correlating an element of ritual with some entity from the human, natural or divine realms. The discovery of such correlations is the fundamental aim of the Brāhmaṇas, the genre of texts composed 'by brahmins, for brahmins' (Witzel 1996: 2) as compendia of esoteric knowledge to be actualized in the performance of ritual. In the ubiquitous refrain of these texts, 'the one who knows' (*ya evaṃ veda*[9]) can leverage this knowledge to be a more potent ritual actor: any action he undertakes in ritual will simultaneously affect correlates in the human, natural and divine realms. For instance, the officiant who knows that 'the *udumbara* is nourishing strength' (*ūrg udumbaraḥ*; JB I.71) will gain personal nourishment and strength from his contact with the tree, while passing the same along to the gods.

In Vedic texts, the *udumbara* signifies nourishment and abundance. Christopher Minkowski has attributed this to the botanical characteristics of this 'most prolific of all trees' (Minkowksi 1989: 9), emphasizing the sappiness of its wood and its abundant clusters of figs. Minkowski has shown that the Brāhmaṇas consistently correlate *udumbara* with *ūrj*, defined as 'strengthening nourishment...of a particularly liquid, vegetal kind.' 'Sap' (*rasa*) and 'sustenance' (*annam, annādyam*) often appear in apposition (ibid.: 10–11).

Udumbara has mythical and etiological associations with the creator god Prajāpati (Minkowski 1989: 7): after Prajāpati nourished his divine offspring with *ūrj*, the leftovers became the *udumbara* tree (JB II.183). Prajāpati is the ascendant deity of the Brāhmaṇas; an anthropomorphic embodiment of sacrifice, he is conceived in continuity with the Ṛgvedic myth of the cosmic man (*puruṣa*, cf. RV X.90), whose sacrifice engenders the cosmos. Myths about Prajāpati's cosmogonic agency form the cornerstone for what Sylvain Lévi has called 'la doctrine du sacrifice' (Lévi 1898): the

8 Farmer, Henderson and Witzel (2002: 49–53) argue persuasively in favor of 'correlation' as an umbrella term for this brand of hermeneutics; they also give references to the substantial body of Indological work on Vedic hermeneutics.

9 This turn of phrase and its variants are widespread in Vedic prose, as a concluding flourish at the end of a topic (e.g. AB I.22, 2.23) or as a repeated refrain (e.g. ŚB VI.7.1.17–21).

conviction that sacrificial action, rooted in Prajāpati's primeval activity, has an efficacy that can be harnessed by authorized brahmin officiants. We will see in the next section that the qualities of the *udumbara* prized in the Vedic texts – sap, strength, nourishment – along with its mythical connection to Prajāpati, are of great moment in the Sāmavedic rite of *audumbarī*.

THE RITE OF *AUDUMBARĪ*: PRAXIS AND INTERPRETATION

I now turn to a step-by-step account of the praxis according to the codification of the *Jaiminīya Śrauta Sūtra*, presented under the heading 'rules for the erection of the *audumbarī*' (*audumbaryutthāpanavidhi*; JŚS I.6).[10] Offering my own translations of the *sūtras*,[11] I aim to reconstruct the sequence of actions and *mantras* that constitute the rite. To complement this reconstruction, I gather and translate the interpretations of the rite in the *Jaiminīya Brāhmaṇa*[12] and *Pañcaviṃśa Brāhmaṇa* of the *Sāmaveda*; and the *Śatapatha Brāhmaṇa* of the *Yajurveda*. By integrating these accounts of praxis and interpretation, I hope to arrive at an assessment of the rite close to that of its ancient performers and interpreters.

The rite takes place on day four of the *agniṣṭoma*, when the *adhvaryu* and his helpers are engaged in preparing the *sadas*, the roofed, walled enclosure at the center of which the *audumbarī* will be erected. The post of *udumbara* wood, cut to match the height of the sacrificer and with two forked branches at the top, lies east of the hole already dug for it. The *adhvaryu*, leading the sacrificer, approaches the post, sprinkles it with water

10 For the praxis according to the *Kauthuma-Rāṇāyanīya* branches of *Sāmaveda*, see the parallel section (*audumbaryucchrayana*) in LātŚS I.7.19/DŚS II.3.1–21; cf. Parpola (1969: 112–17). While their praxis differs from that of the Jaiminīyas in some respects, the fundamentals are the same. This reflection of the shared ritual culture of the Sāmavedic branches is further attested in the basic parallelism of the interpretations in each branch.

11 In preparing my translation, I benefited from the guidance of Masato Fujii, with whom I read sections of the JŚS during his visit to Harvard in spring 2011. I base my translation on an unpublished critical edition of the JŚS by Asko Parpola, who has given me permission to reproduce the Sanskrit *sūtras* in these notes. The most useful published edition remains that of Gaastra (JŚS [1906]).

12 I use the numbering of Vira and Chandra's 1954 edition of the JB, consistent with Bodewitz (1990). However, in interpreting this difficult text, I benefited from the chance to consult Gerhard Ehlers' unpublished critical edition and translation (with revised numbering). I have incorporated several of his emendations into the JB text reproduced in the notes below.

and then undertakes a series of actions and *mantras* (BauŚS vi.26; ĀpŚS xi.9.11–12; KātŚS viii.5.25–28). At this point the *udgātṛ* enters the scene:

> When [the *adhvaryu* and his helpers] are scattering down sand to make the fireplaces [in the *sadas*], having taken up a vessel for melted butter along with dipping ladle, having gone around to the north of the *āgnīdhra* and the *sadas*, having entered the *sadas* by the western door, [the *udgātṛ*] grasps the *audumbarī* from behind [the *adhvaryu*] with the formula: 'I seat you in the seat of life, in the shade of the helper, in the heart of the ocean. Homage to the ocean! Homage to the eye of the ocean! May *yonorvām* not abandon me!'[13] (JŚS i.6.1)

According to the commentator Bhavatrāta, when the *udgātṛ* 'grasps the post from behind' he does so taking hold of the *adhvaryu*, who directly handles the post.[14] The *adhvaryu*'s mediation applies throughout much of the praxis, a fact confirmed by the duplication of many steps in the Yajurvedic *sūtras* codifying his role. In other words, the *udgātṛ* does not unambiguously touch the post until his climactic embrace, which he performs alone.

The 'taking hold' in this *sūtra* is not only the beginning of the *audumbarī* rite, it is the *udgātṛ*'s first action of the entire Soma sacrifice. According to the Sāmavedic Brāhmaṇas, this action serves to elect him to his priestly office. 'One chooses the other priests, but not the *udgātṛ*. When the *udgātṛ* through his first act takes hold of the *audumbarī* from behind [the *adhvaryu*], he chooses himself for the priesthood through his own deity'[15] (JB i.70; cf. PB vi.4.1). The problem here is the *udgātṛ*'s ritual authority: while the lead officiants of the *Yajurveda* and *Ṛgveda* are chosen by the sacrificer in ceremonies that establish their authority and relation

13 *yadā dhiṣṇyān nivapanty athājyasthālīṃ sasruvām ādāyottareṇāgnīdhraṃ ca sadaś ca parītyāparayā dvārā sadaḥ prapadyaudumbarīm anvārabhata: āyoṣ ṭvā sadane sādayāmy avataś chāyāyāṃ samudrasya hṛdaye / namaḥ samudrāya, namaḥ samudrasya cakṣaṣe / mā mā yonorvāṃ hāsīr iti*

14 'He grasps from behind the *adhvaryu* who is grasping the *udumbara*-wood post of the *sadas*' (*sadasaḥ sthūṇām audumbarīm ārabhamāṇam adhvaryum anvārabhate*). Bodewitz (1990: 214n3), commenting on a parallel passage JB i.70, agrees that some sort of cooperation between *adhvaryu* and *udgātṛ* is intended. The *Āpastamba Śrautasūtra* (xi.9.13; xi.10.1) uses the expression *sahodgātrā* 'together with the *udgātṛ*' to describe the *adhvaryu*'s subsequent manipulations of the post.

15 *vṛṇate 'nyān ṛtvijo nodgātāraṃ / yad udgātā prathamena karmaṇaudumbarīm anvārabhate svayaiva tad devatayātmānam ārtvijyāya vṛṇīte*

to divine counterparts, the *udgātṛ* lacks such an 'election' (*pravara*) in Jaiminīya texts.[16] The solution is to designate this first action of the ritual as a de facto election. When he takes hold of the post, he chooses himself 'through his own deity,' namely Prajāpati.

The relation between Prajāpati and the *udumbara* tree parallels that between god and officiant: 'the *udumbara*, indeed, belongs to Prajāpati. The *udgātṛ* belongs to Prajāpati'[17] (PB vi.4.1; cf. JB i.70). The *udumbara* tree is the *bandhu* that connects the two, their common denominator: the *udgātṛ* takes hold of a post made from Prajāpati's primeval creation; in this way, 'the *udgātṛ* is Prajāpati'[18] (JB i.70, 72; cf. ŚB iv.3.2.3; PB vii.10.16). Although the liturgy of the Jaiminīyas lacks an official election, the texts take the *udgātṛ*'s first action as a substitute that asserts his independence and establishes his special relationship to Prajāpati.

The *mantras* that make up the rest of this *sūtra* allude to the imminent action of placing the post in the hole. The JB (i.70) correlates the cosmological content of the *mantras* with the ritual context: thus, the 'seat of life' is the place of sacrifice; the 'shelter' is the roofed *sadas*; and the 'heart of the ocean' bespeaks the *audumbarī*'s location in the middle of the structure. With the twin salutations to the 'ocean' and 'the eye of the ocean,' the *udgātṛ* salutes two faculties essential for the performance of his office, 'speech' and 'mind,' respectively. By imploring *yonorvām* – a hapax glossed in the Brāhmaṇas as 'the *sāman*' (JB i.70 *yonorvān*, PB VI.4.8 *yūnarvan*)[19] – he averts problems that may arise in the performance of his office.

The erection of the post continues as the *udgātṛ* (with the *adhvaryu*) raises it up and fixes it in place. When the post is raised, the forked branches at its top must align with the eastern direction; it should also be the tallest post in the *sadas* (BauŚS vi.27; ĀpŚS xi.10.1, 5).

16 By contrast, the Kauthuma branch *does* codify a separate rite of election for the Sāmavedic officiants (cf. LātŚS i.10.25–27; DŚS iii.3.1–3; Caland and Henry 1907: 166–67). This Kauthuma election rite seems modeled on the election of non-Sāmavedic officiants at another point in the ritual sequence (Caland and Henry 1907: 186–88; Caland 1931: 105n3 on PB vi.4.1). In view of the fact that the JŚS is an older text than the others, it seems likely that the Kauthuma *pravara* is a later innovation in response to the same basic problem confronted by the Jaiminīyas.

17 *prājāpatyo vā udumbaraḥ / prājāpatya udgātā*

18 *prajāpatir udgātā*

19 For discussion, see Caland and Henry (1907: 96n5); Caland (1931: 106n1) on PB vi.4.8; and Bodewitz (1990: 214n8).

> Then he raises it up with the formula: 'Prop up the sky! Fill the atmosphere! Make the earth firm with the base!'[20]
>
> Next he fixes it in place: 'May Dyutāna Māruta fix you in place with the firm *dharma* of Mitra and Varuṇa.'[21] (JŚS I.6.2–3)

The content of each *mantra* parallels the action it accompanies. For instance, in the *mantras* above, 'prop up...' corresponds to the raising of the post; 'fix in place' to the fixing of the post in the hole. This synergy between words and action suggests an underlying correlation between the erection of the post and cosmogony. The three sections of the post – top, middle, base – act on the corresponding levels of the cosmos: sky, atmosphere and earth. The *mantra* also invokes divine precedent, mentioning the primeval officiant Dyutāna Māruta, who erected the *audumbarī* of the gods.[22]

Figure 8.1. Nampūtiri brahmins in the Jaiminīya tradition perform the *audumbarī* rite as part of the Atirātra-Agnicayana in Panjal, Kerala, April 2011. The *udgātṛ* (Tōṭṭaṃ Kṛṣṇan Nampūtiri, center, holding bowl) 'stretches' an oblation of ghee along the length of the post (JŚS I.6.4) while others assist. The sacrificer's *daṇḍa* is held against the post. Photograph by Gireesan Bhattathiripad.

20 *athainām ucchrayaty: ud divaṃ stabhānāntarikṣaṃ pṛṇa pṛthivīm upareṇa dṛṃheti*
21 *athainām minoti: dyutānas tvā māruto minotu mitrāvaruṇayor dhruveṇa dharmaṇeti*
22 Cf. TS VI.2.10.3 and ŚB III.6.1.16.

Now the *udgātṛ* 'stretches' an oblation of ghee up and down the height of the post (figure 8.1):

> Then he pours an oblation over it with melted butter, having commenced from the top and stretching it out, so to speak, to the base, with the formula: 'Heaven and Earth, be satisfied with butter! Make the plants bear fine fruit, *svāhā*!'[23] (JŚS I.6.4)

The cosmological correlations continue here, with the top and base of the post related to heaven and earth, respectively. In the logic of the *bandhu* hermeneutic, an oblation of ghee that stretches from the top of the post to its bottom effectively spans the cosmos, sprinkling the earth as rain waters the plants. According to the Yajurvedic texts, the first half of the *mantra* accompanies the pouring of ghee across a piece of gold which the *adhvaryu* has placed between the forked branches at the top of the post (cf. BauŚS VI.27).

> Then three times to the right he heaps filling-sand around it with the formula: 'I heap around you who are winner of *brahman*, winner of *kṣatra*, winner of fine offspring, winner of much increase of wealth!'[24]

> Then with the staff of the consecrated [sacrificer] he strengthens it saying: 'Strengthen *brahman*, strengthen *kṣatra*, strengthen offspring, strengthen wealth, strengthen increase of wealth, strengthen the kin for the sacrificer!'[25] (JŚS I.6.5–6)

These two *sūtras* refer to stabilizing the post in the hole with earth or sand, and then beating the fill to compress it. The use of the sacrificer's staff (*daṇḍa*) as implement is significant: made of *udumbara* wood (Minkowski 1992: 141), it is well suited to the task of strengthening the *audumbarī* in its mooring. This pair of *mantras* contains wishes for the welfare of the ruling alliance of priesthood (*brahman*) and nobility (*kṣatra*), followed by wishes for prosperity and fertility. If the earlier *mantras* evoked the post's cosmological valence, these ones treat its social dimension.

23 *athainām ājyenābhijuhoty agrād upakramyā mūlāt saṃtanvann iva: ghṛtena dyāvāpṛthivī āprīṇīthāṃ, supippalā oṣadhīḥ kṛdhi svāheti*. The wish for plants to bear 'fine fruit' (*supippalā*) as a result of this oblation recalls the Sanskrit name of another member of the fig family, the *pippala* (pipal = *Ficus religiosa*).

24 *athaināṃ triḥ prasalī purīṣeṇa paryūhati: brahmavaniṃ tvā kṣatravaniṃ suprajāvaniṃ rāyaspoṣavaniṃ paryūhāmīti*

25 *athainām dīkṣitadaṇḍena dṛṃhati: brahma dṛṃha, kṣatram dṛṃha, prajām dṛṃha, rayim dṛṃha, rāyaspoṣaṃ dṛṃha, sajātān yajamānāya dṛṃheti*

The *adhvaryu* participates in all the actions and *mantras* in *sūtras* 2–6.[26] A Yajurvedic Brāhmaṇa interprets the *mantras* accompanying the planting of the post and the heaping and pressing of dirt around it quite literally (ŚB III.6.1.11–18). The same text remarks that the method of planting of the *audumbarī*, with the fill compressed level with the ground, differs from that of planting a conventional tree but resembles divine practice. Our interpretive texts rarely miss an opportunity – even in the most seemingly mundane details – to stress the *audumbarī*'s affinity with the divine realm.

The *udgātṛ* now dresses the post (figures 8.2 and 8.3). The Yajurvedic texts do not mention these steps, so it seems likely that the *adhvaryu* does not participate.

Figure 8.2. The Nampūtiri *udgātṛ* (left) dresses the post with 'grass with its tips pointing upwards.' (JŚS I.6.7) Photograph by Gireesan Bhattathiripad.

26 Some of these same *mantras* (*sūtras* 2–6) also appear in the Yajurvedic liturgies on raising the sacrificial stake (*yūpa*), and may have been borrowed from that rite; indeed, one text (ĀpŚS XI.9.11) explicitly says that at least as far as the *adhvaryu*'s role is concerned, the entire *audumbarī* rite should be performed on the model of the *yūpa* rite.

Figure 8.3. The *audumbarī* fully dressed with grass, muslin and grass string wrapped around. The rings of grass attached stand for the *stotras* that have already been sung, in accordance with Nampūtiri Jaiminīya practice. The *hotṛ* of the *R̥gveda*, Nāras Ravindran Nampūtiri, faces away from the post and does not touch it as he recites. Photograph by Finnian M.M. Gerety.

> Then he wraps it around to the right with blades of grass with tips pointing upwards.[27]
> Then he covers it all around with cloth so it will not be naked.[28]
> (JŚS I.6.7–8)

The *udgātṛ* covers the post and the grass all around with cloth. The *sūtra* anthropomorphizes this last action, explaining that it conceals the

27 *athainām ūrdhvāgrais tṛṇaiḥ pradakṣiṇaṃ pariveṣṭayati*

28 *athainām vāsasā paridadhāty anagnatvāya*

nakedness of the *audumbarī*. Beyond this rationale, however, Vedic texts are silent about the purpose of the post's preparation in this fashion.[29]

Now the *udgātṛ* embraces the post with both hands. This *sūtra* has no parallel in Yajurvedic texts, suggesting that the *udgātṛ* acts alone. Whereas before he took hold of the post with the *adhvaryu* as intermediary, he now comes into unambiguous, direct contact with the *audumbarī*.

> Next he embraces it with both hands, saying: 'Place nourishing strength and food in me!'[30] (JŚS I.6.9)

As he hugs the post, he beseeches it to place in him the qualities of the *udumbara*, namely 'nourishing strength' and 'food.' Recall that the *audumbarī* occupies the centermost point within the sacrificial geography: it is raised up in the center of the central structure. In the conception of the sacrifice as the body of Prajāpati, 'the *sadas* is Prajāpati's belly. The *udumbara* is nourishing strength. When the *audumbarī* is fixed in the middle of the *sadas*, [the *udgātṛ*] places nourishing strength, food right in the middle of his offspring'[31] (JB I.71; cf. PB VI.4.11; ŚB III.6.1.2). The freshness of this wet and sappy wood is crucial to its capacity to nourish – when the *audumbarī* wears out, hunger ensues (JB I.71; PB VI.4.11–12). In this way, the post serves as a conduit through which nourishment passes from the cosmic to the human realm. The *udgātṛ*'s embrace of the post, at the climax of the rite, is a gestural expression of this idea.

And this is a reciprocal arrangement: not only does the god feed the singer through the post – the singer feeds the god. During most of their

29 We may look for insights by comparing the modern performances of Vedic ritual by the Nampūtiris of Kerala, whose Sāmavedic priests follow the Jaiminīya praxis. The Nampūtiris press a bunch of grass with tips upward against the post (see figure 8.2) and then wrap the grass and post with white muslin. Next they wrap a string of grass around the post a number of times, corresponding to the number of *stotras* that the *udgātṛ* will sing in the *sadas*. Thus, in the *agniṣṭoma*, with eleven *stotras* in the *sadas*, the string is wrapped eleven times; in the *atirātra-agnicayana*, with twenty-eight, it is wrapped twenty-eight times (see figure 8.3). As he proceeds through each *stotra*, the *udgātṛ* transfers a ring of grass from his finger to the corresponding turn of the string, allowing him to mark his progress in what is a grueling all-night session of singing. See Staal (1983: I, 579, 582–83; 1991: 89–92).

30 *athaināṃ hastābhyāṃ parigṛhṇāti: mayy ūrjam annādyaṃ dhehīti*

31 *prajāpater vā etad udaraṃ yat sada / ūrg udumbaro / yan madhyatas sadasa audumbarī mīyate madhyata evaitat prajānām annam ūrjaṃ dadhāti /*

songs, the *udgātṛ* and two other Sāmavedic officiants sit on the ground in the center of the *sadas*. The *udgātṛ*'s position is closest to the *audumbarī*, facing the north with his back to the post, allowing him to 'lean' (*śrayate*) against the post as he sings. His 'melody' (*sāman*) becomes divine sustenance, with a potency that emanates from the *audumbarī*:

> The *sāman* is the gods' food. The *udumbara* is nourishing strength. When the *udgātṛ* leans on the *audumbarī*, he places the gods' food, nourishing strength, right in the *sāman*. And so when the priests perform their office with the *sāman*, the gods eat very well.[32] (JB I.71; cf. PB VI.4.13)

Again, this speaks to the notion of the *audumbarī* as spanning human and cosmic realms. When the *udgātṛ* comes into contact with the post, he fortifies not only his offspring but also his musical repertoire with the nourishing strength of *udumbara*, which he can then share with the gods by singing. In short, the gods feed on his *sāmans*. In this way, the *udgātṛ* re-enacts Prajāpati's primeval distribution of *ūrj* to the gods, the leftovers of which became the first *udumbara* (JB II.183; PB VI.4.1).

The *udgātṛ*'s embrace of the post is the climax of the *audumbaryutthāpana* and the key moment of contact between the singer and the post. But even after the *audumbarī* rite proper is over, the *udgātṛ* re-establishes contact every time he sings, as the final *sūtra* indicates:

> In this same way, at every *stotra* he embraces it.[33] (JŚS I.6.10)

These repeated embraces occur with the singing of every *stotra* but one in the *agniṣṭoma*, for a total of eleven more times.[34]

For the Jaiminīyas, contact with the *audumbarī* is not without its risks. Their Brāhmaṇa worries that if the *udgātṛ* touches the *audumbarī*, showing a desire for its sustaining potency, the food inside it may be driven away; on the other hand, if he does not touch it, he will deprive himself. '"To touch or not to touch?" – so they deliberate'[35] (JB I.71). According to

32 *sāma devānām annam / ūrg udumbaro / yad udgātaudumbarīṃ śrayate samann evaitad devānām anna ūrjaṃ dadhāti / tasmād yatra sāmnārtvijyaṃ kurvanti tad eva devā bhūyiṣṭham ivādanti /*

33 *evam eva stotre stotre parigṛhṇāti*

34 The exception is the very first *stotra* (*bahiṣpavamāna*), which is sung outside of the *mahāvedi* and which 'has no close connection with the *audumbarī*' according to Bhavatrāta.

35 *upaspṛśyā3ṃ nopaspṛśyā3m iti mīmāṃsante*

Bodewitz, 'the problem is how to touch and at the same time not to touch too much' (Bodewitz 1990: 215n23).[36]

The solution proposed by Brāhmaṇa authors is doubly ambiguous: it involves a combination of touching and not touching, and it is expressed in language that has remained obscure to modern interpreters of the relevant passages.[37] In addition to physical contact with the post, this tension between touching and not touching may also refer to the musical contact between the melody (*sāman*) and verse (*ṛc*) of the *udgātṛ*'s song, itself 'a very loose form of touching' (Bodewitz 1990: 215n23). In this 'cryptic' (*parokṣam*, JB I.139) mode of singing, also known as 'unexpressed song' (*aniruktagāna*),[38] the lexical verse is obscured by the interpolation of non-lexical syllables (*stobha*). *Aniruktagāna* is a specialty of the Jaiminīyas, who make it the basis of their little-known Upaniṣad, the *Jaiminīya Upaniṣad Brāhmaṇa*.[39]

And it is precisely Prajāpati, the deity authorizing the *udgātṛ*'s election, who is associated with the quality of 'unexpressedness' (*aniruktatvam*) throughout the Brāhmaṇas: every ritual action not directed to a specific (*nirukta*) deity goes by default to Prajāpati, the 'unexpressed' (*anirukta*) god who pervades the entire proceedings.[40] Thus there is a nexus of correlations between Prajāpati, the *audumbarī*, the *udgātṛ* and *aniruktagāna*. When the singer simultaneously touches and does not touch the post, the

36 See Parpola (2012: 376–78) for a Mīmāṃsā controversy on the topic of touching or not touching the *audumbarī*.

37 See Caland (1931: 106n2 on PB VI.4.13), Bodewitz (1990: 215n23) and Ehlers (n.d. on JB I.67) for possible emendations and interpretations.

38 '[The diction *narcam upaspṛśed* in JB I.139] refers to a particular way of singing the *sāman*, which is also denoted as *parokṣam*. The *sāman* can be made obscure or esoteric by avoiding every 'contact' with the underlying *ṛc*, i.e. by singing in such a way that the *ṛc* is hardly recognizable...' (Bodewitz 1977: 154). This description fits *aniruktagāna* exactly. Moreover, JB I.139 explicitly observes that the song under discussion, the second *pṛṣṭhastotra* sung on the *vāmadevya* melody, is performed *anirukta* (cf. PB VII.8.3). For these reasons, I understand the expression *parokṣaṃ gāyati* as synonymous with the technique of *aniruktagāna*, although Caland (1919: 42n16) and Bodewitz (1977: 154) stop short of asserting such a connection.

39 A central theme of the *Jaiminīya (or Talavakāra) Upaniṣad Brāhmaṇa* is the *anirukta-gāyatra-sāman*, the proper singing of which brings immortality (cf. Fujii 1984). On the JUB, which has been called 'the earliest Upaniṣad' (Fujii 2004: 1), see Fujii (1984, 1997, 2004).

40 See Renou and Silburn (1954: 70–74). The correlation between *anirukta* and Prajāpati is reinforced by the god's frequent epithet, the indefinite pronoun *ka* ('Who'; Renou and Silburn 1954: 72); cf. Caland (1931: 153nn1, 2 on PB 7.8.3).

ambiguity of the praxis evokes the 'unexpressedness' of his deity as well as his signature style of singing.

In sum, the Sāmavedic Brāhmaṇas understand the rite almost exclusively in terms of the efficacy and authority of Sāmavedic ritual performance. The significant moments are marked by the singer's contact – indirect or direct – with the post. When he 'takes hold' with the *adhvaryu* as his first act of the rite, the *udgātṛ* elects himself to his office with the authority of Prajāpati, thereby making up for the lack of an official election in the Jaiminīya liturgy. And when he 'embraces it with both hands,' the *audumbarī* serves as source of 'nourishing strength' and 'food': erected in the *sadas*, the belly of Prajāpati, it nourishes the singer, his offspring, his repertoire of *sāmans* and even the god himself. Beyond this, the post also serves as an emblem of the relationship between Prajāpati and the Sāmavedic officiants; by establishing it, they honor the god and receive his honor in turn.[41]

Since the *adhvaryu* participates with the *udgātṛ* throughout much of the rite, the Yajurvedic Brāhmaṇas also weigh in on its significance. The ŚB, for example, correlates the post with 'nourishing strength' and 'food'; and agrees that raising the post puts food in the 'belly' of the sacrifice (ŚB III.6.1.2). Beyond this, the ŚB also attends to the significance of the *adhvaryu*'s manipulations that are not shared by the *udgātṛ*. Thus, his digging the hole, sprinkling water with barleycorns into it and raising the post are interpreted as bestowing the characteristic qualities of the *udumbara* (strength, food, sap) and rendering the implements ritually pure (III.6.1.7–15). Once the post is raised, his pouring of water heals any injury done to the earth by his digging; while his pouring of ghee from the top of the post provides further strength and sustenance (III.6.1.19, 21). It is striking that one of the *adhvaryu*'s actions is to make the sacrificer touch the post while speaking a *mantra* (VS V.28) invoking firmness and the gratification of his wishes (ŚB III.6.1.20). In this way, the sacrificer's contact with the post – just like that of the *udgātṛ* – gains him a share of its potency.

This concludes my reconstruction of the rite's praxis and interpretation according to the JŚS and various Brāhmaṇas. Still, there is much to be explored about the *audumbaryutthāpana* beyond the purview of these texts. Let us now consider the rite from several disparate but ultimately

41 A minor Sāmavedic Brāhmaṇa (ṢaḍB IV.3.6) articulates this idea quite explicitly, presenting the *audumbarī* as a monument to the 'honor' (*apaciti*, glossed by Sāyaṇa with *pujā*) shared by Prajāpati and the singers.

intertwined perspectives: Vedic cosmology, Vedic habitation and the prehistory of the *śrauta* ritual.

COSMIC, DOMESTIC AND SACRIFICIAL POSTS

The widely attested cosmogony in Vedic religion of the 'world axis,' 'cosmic pillar' or 'tree of life' that props up heaven and earth (*skambha/stambha*; Kuiper 1983: 12–13, 23) has parallels in religions worldwide (Witzel 2012: 135; Eliade 1971 [1949]: 12–18; 1991 [1952]: 41–48). It has been argued that the *audumbarī*, like the *yūpa* and other Indian posts or poles (cf. Brighenti 2012: 105–10), should be understood in these terms (Bodewitz 1977–78: 65; 1990: 214n4; 216nn35, 36; Staal 1983: 95, 1991: 89) and indeed, *mantras* accompanying the raising of the post strongly suggest some such cycle of myths: 'Prop up the sky! Fill the atmosphere! Make the earth firm with the base!' These exemplify the ritual construction of the cosmos, whereby formulas and actions in the sacred space govern correlates in the cosmic and natural realms (see Smith 1989: 50–81).

The cosmological significance of Vedic posts is not limited to *śrauta* ritual, but extends also to domestic habitation. 'All kinds of pillars and posts have to be connected with the *axis mundi*, the cosmic pillar, along which heaven was raised at the creation of the universe... The central pillar of the house symbolizes the centre or navel of the earth...' (Bodewitz 1977–78: 65). To better understand the relations between the cosmic pillar of Vedic cosmology, the *audumbarī* of Vedic ritual and the central post of a Vedic dwelling, let us consider what we know about domestic structures in Vedic times.

Although there are no archeological remains of such dwellings, the textual corpus provides some details as to their form and construction. The manuals of domestic ritual (Gr̥hyasūtras) refer to the supporting post, often made of *udumbara*, as *sthūṇā* (Renou 1939: 484–85). While there were several such posts in any dwelling, the 'middle post' (*madhyamā sthūṇā*) or 'king-post' (*sthūṇā-rāja*) is singled out (485). Rafters (*vaṃśa*) supporting the roof (*chadis*, lit. 'covering'; 487) were attached transversely near the top of the posts (Renou 1939: 486; Bodewitz 1977–78: 64). From the highest point in the center, the roof would slope down sharply to the low encircling walls (Bodewitz 1977–78: 63).

The *Atharvaveda* alludes to a ritual accompanying the construction of the house (Renou 1939: 499). One *mantra* addresses the rafter itself: 'ascend the post, o rafter! (*sthūṇām adhi roha vaṃśa*, AVŚ III.12.6). The Gr̥hyasūtras provide further information on the ritual of house construction (Renou 1939: 482–88; cf. ĀśGS II.8–10; ŚāṅGS III.2–3; PGS III.4.). The post-hole, filled with water at sunset, becomes the receptacle for the central post when it is erected at sunrise. According to Bodewitz (1977–78: 65–66), the hole with water represents the subterranean ocean in which the cosmic tree is rooted, where the sun disappears in the evening and whence it rises in the morning. The raising is accompanied by a *mantra* that spells out this correlation: 'I raise up this navel of the earth'[42] (PGS III.4.4; cf. Bodewitz 1977–78: 65). From this perspective, the Vedic dwelling is the universe in microcosm: the raising of the post corresponds to the cosmogonic propping up of heaven and earth. In solar terms, the cosmos-spanning post corresponds to the sun's daily ascent (Coomaraswamy 1997 [1939]: 10–11; Bodewitz 1990: 214nn4–7), while its rafters (*vaṃśa*), raised up, are the sun's rays on the rise (Bodewitz 1977–78: 66). According to the Jaiminīyas: 'the sun, they say, is the post (*sthūṇā*) supporting the sky'[43] (JUB I.10.9).

Equipped with this sketch of Vedic dwellings and cosmology, let us revisit the *audumbarī*. The *audumbarī* serves as the central *sthūṇā* for the *sadas*, whose construction closely resembles that of the domestic dwelling, including a number of additional posts (*sthūṇā*), rafters (*vaṃśa*) and a thatched roof (*chadis*) sloping down to low walls (ŚB III.6.1.2; Renou 1939: 495). The *mantras* accompanying the raising and fixing of the *audumbarī* in the earth, like those of the domestic post, suggest a cosmological interpretation. The location of the *audumbarī* at the center of the *sadas*, which itself is the central structure of the sacrificial space, supports the same idea. Whether domestic, sacrificial or cosmic, these posts participate in mutual relations: they share technical terminology, ritual praxis and mythology. In terms of Vedic hermeneutics, we can think of the *audumbarī* as a physical *bandhu* ('bond') linking the domestic dwelling, the sacrificial structure and the cosmos. The raising of the post in the sacrifice echoes both the roof-raising of a human dwelling and the propping up of the sky. All three actions mark the establishment of larger structures organized around a common center; in all three cases, the posts link the three cosmic realms of earth, atmosphere and heaven.

42 *ucchrayāmi bhuvanasya nābhiṃ*

43 *sthūṇāṃ divastambhanīṃ sūryam āhur*

REINTERPRETING THE RITE OF *AUDUMBARĪ*: FROM 'TREE-HUGGER' TO TREE-CLIMBER

Insofar as they are conceived as spanning the cosmos, posts in Vedic ritual can serve as a means of ascension, as ladders leading to heaven. In the *vājapeya* ritual, for example, the sacrificer climbs the sacrificial stake (*yūpa*). Reaching the top, he spreads his wings like a bird and announces that he has ascended to heaven (ŚB v.2.1.9–20; Witzel 2012: 135; Staal 1991: 89; cf. Brighenti 2012: 105–10 for a critical discussion of this rite and its interpretations). Although the cosmological significance of the *audumbarī* has been acknowledged (Staal 1983: i, 95; 1991: 89), no one has ever suggested that ascension is part of the *audumbarī* rite; unlike the case of the *yūpa*, there is no ritual sequence in which the *audumbarī* is explicitly climbed. In spite of this, I shall now explore the idea that the *audumbarī* was historically a rite of ascension and that the praxis preserves traces of this prehistory.

Ascension is a central feature of the Sāmavedic liturgy as a whole. As Masato Fujii has shown, the *udgātṛ* and his assistants are charged with a key responsibility in the sacrificer's soteriology: guiding him on his ascent to heaven (Fujii 1986 on JŚS i.10–11). Some passages conceive this journey as a ship bound for heaven (ŚB iv.2.5.10); some as a tree to be climbed by singing special syllables (JUB i.3.1); others as the sun's track across the sky, which is a cosmic post to be ascended (cf. JUB i.10.9 above). The officiants enact the ascent by leading the sacrificer eastwards to the main altar. Proceeding to the north, they sit on the periphery of the sacrificial geography near a pit regarded as the door to the sun (ŚB iv.2.5.5; JUB i.5.5; Fujii 1986: 13, 20; cf. Coomaraswamy 1997 [1939]: 10–15). Here they sing 'unexpressed' songs intended to ensure the sacrificer's immortality. For the rest of their songs, they gather in the *sadas*, feasting and drinking *soma* with the gods in heaven; the *udgātṛ* – whose name literally means 'up-' or 'north-singer' – sits facing the northern direction, with his back against the *audumbarī*. Also evoking a flight to heaven are the 'ascent verses' muttered by the sacrificer as he holds on to the *udgātṛ*: 'You are a falcon with *gāyatrī* as your meter. From behind I take hold of you, carry me safely across!'[44] (JŚS i.11.13–15; ŚB xii.3.4.3–5; cf. Fujii 1986: 17–18; Caland and Henry 1907: 180).

All in all, the evidence of the Sāmavedic liturgy portrays the *udgātṛ* as a specialist in cosmic ascents, a singer entrusted to sing the sacrificer to heaven. If such is the nature of his role, then we might reconsider his contact with the *audumbarī*, the ritual correlate of the cosmic pillar. As we

44 *śyeno 'si gāyatracchandā, anu tvārabhe, svasti mā saṃpārayā mā*

have seen, his contact with the post is important: it elects him to his office, connects him to the supreme god Prajāpati, and assures the success of his singing. This contact between human and tree-trunk is expressed most directly in a gesture of embrace, which brings nourishment and prosperity to the entire proceedings. This gesture's importance is further reflected in the fact that it is repeated throughout the liturgy: he embraces the post at the performance of every *stotra*. Throughout this study, I have referred to this gesture as 'hugging' or 'embracing' the post, a reading justified by the diction (*pari* + √*gr̥h-*, lit. 'to grasp around'): according to the *sūtra*, the *udgātr̥* 'embraces it with both hands' (*athaināṃ hastābhyāṃ parigr̥hṇāti*). But if we think in terms of ascension, this diction suggests other possibilities: when the *udgātr̥* 'grasps around' the *audumbarī*, perhaps he is not hugging but *climbing* the post; perhaps he is not a tree-hugger, but a tree-*climber*. Interpreted this way, the gesture may preserve traces of a rite of ascension, which was no longer understood as such by the Vedic interpreters of the rite.

Another aspect of the praxis points to the 'grasping around' as a ritualized gesture of climbing. One detail, never explained in the texts, is suggestive: the dressing of the *audumbarī* with 'thatch' (*tr̥ṇa*) and 'cloth' (*vāsas*) around its midsection 'so that it won't be naked' (JŚS I.6.8). Why is the post of *udumbara* clothed in thatch? And why is a tree-trunk anthropomorphized in this fashion?

We have seen that the *sthūṇā audumbarī* has strong affinities with the central post (*madhyamā sthūṇā*) of the prototypical Vedic house: both are made of *udumbara* wood; stand in the center of their respective sacred and domestic spaces; support a rafter (*vaṃśa*) and a thatched roof (*tr̥ṇa*) extending down to low walls; and serve as the focal point of rites of construction. In the *Atharvaveda* hymn cited above, which uses the same technical terms (*sthūṇā*, *vaṃśa* and *tr̥ṇa*), a dwelling is anthropomorphized as a woman 'wearing thatch' (*tr̥ṇaṃ vasānā*, AVŚ III.12.5; cf. *tr̥ṇair āvr̥tā*, AVŚ IX.3.17). The roof may be considered to be the dress of the 'lady of the house,' as the house has 'a form of a hut with a high roof...and very low walls' (Bodewitz 1977–78: 63). With this imagery in mind, I suggest that the grass and cloth around the *audumbarī* represent the thatched roof of a domestic house around its central post; the (feminine!) *audumbarī* is the central trunk of the 'lady of the house...wearing thatch.' One might conceive the ensemble as a miniaturized dwelling with its roofline about waist-high and the central post rising up to the actual roof of the *sadas*. A standing man of average stature would grasp the post near the height of his shoulders, well above the roofline represented by the post's thatch-and-cloth dressing. Viewed in this light, the mise-en-scène presents the *udgātṛ* grasping around the post as a house-climber at the apex of his ascent.

Such an interpretation of the *audumbarī* rite and the *udgātṛ*'s gesture makes sense in terms of the correlations already noted between domestic, sacrificial and cosmic posts. While the gesture of 'grasping around' the *audumbarī* post has a range of attested meanings pertinent to ritual performance, it may also evoke the climbing of the central post of a dwelling and the ascent of the cosmic pillar. Cosmic ascent is well attested in the Sāmavedic liturgy and Vedic ritual generally; however, as far as I know, the ascent of a dwelling is not mentioned in the Vedic corpus. While it is easy to justify an interpretation of cosmic ascent, it is more difficult to explain why the *udgātṛ* should be conceived as climbing the post of a house.

The answer, I think, lies deep in the prehistory of Vedic ritual. A number of scholars have stressed the parallels between Vedic rites and those of North and Central Asian shamanism.[45] The strongest parallel is what Eliade has called the 'underlying theory' (1989 [1964]: 411) of both Vedic ritual and Asian shamanic rites: ascent to heaven. As described in several accounts of North Asian shamanism (Coomaraswamy 1997 [1939]: 17–20; Eliade 1989 [1964]: 190–96), the shaman climbs a tree-trunk erected through the central chimney-hole of a dwelling and perches at the top, a sequence interpreted as his ascent of the cosmic pillar. The oft-cited Vedic parallel, already noted above, is when the sacrificer ascends the stake during the *vājapeya*.

Interpreted as a rite of ascension, the *audumbarī* rite likewise has striking affinities with the tree-climbing rites of North Asian shamanism. Let me briefly sketch the initiation of Altaic shamans according to Mikhailovksii's compression (Mikhailovskii and Wardrop 1895: 74–78) of the traveler Radloff's nineteenth century account (Radloff 1893: II, 20–50), on which Eliade based his own version.[46] A birch tree is erected in the center of the dwelling so that its upper branches poke out through the chimney-hole. The trunk is hewn with a number of notches corresponding

45 Coomaraswamy (1997 [1939]: 17–20); Eliade (1989 [1964]: 126, 199, 403–05, 411); Staal (1983: I, 95; 1991: 89); Witzel (2012: 135); and Brighenti (2012: 105–10). On shamanism in the *Ṛgveda*, see Thompson (2003b); Oguibénine (1968).

46 Eliade, in composing his now classic account of an Altaic initiation and horse sacrifice which includes the rite of tree-climbing (1989 [1964]: 190–98), seems to have closely paraphrased Mikhailovskii's faithful summary of Radloff's travelogue. While valuable testimony on their own terms, these nineteenth century sources do not rise to the standard of modern ethnographic practice. Thus, Kehoe's criticism of Eliade's 'armchair' engagement with shamanism (Kehoe 2000: 40) – and, by extension, her critique of the broad academic and

to the levels of heaven through which the shaman will pass on his ascent. Before his ascent, he mimes a cosmic flight sitting on a straw effigy of a goose; chants a series of non-lexical syllables in imitation of the goose's call; and mimes the feasting of unseen spirits and deities. Then he ascends, pausing at each notch to narrate his progress to those assembled. When he passes the roofline, he praises his supreme deity.

Like the Altaic rite, the Sāmavedic rite of the *audumbarī* 'initiates' the *udgātṛ*, establishing his authority. Other common elements include the preparation of the post from a tree with portions of the upper branches intact; the conception of the tree-trunk as cosmic pillar; grasping around the trunk; the evocation of a bird in cosmic flight; chanting of non-lexical syllables; enactment of feasts for the gods; and praise of the supreme god. My suggestion is that the traces of ascension in the praxis of the *audumbarī* rite stem from North and Central Asian antecedents. Elements of the same prehistoric religious cultures that later emerged in the 'shamanism' of Radloff's account could have influenced the formation of the Sāmavedic liturgy and especially the *udgātṛ*'s role.

On the basis of linguistic and ritual data, some Indologists have recently attempted to locate antecedents of Vedic religious culture in Central and North Asia (Witzel 2004; Thompson 2003b; Brighenti 2012: 110). In particular, Frits Staal has argued that much of the Sāmavedic liturgy is a Central Asian contribution to *śrauta* ritual (2004: 548).[47] For Staal, this history is encoded in certain features of the *agniṣṭoma* praxis, for instance, in the seating arrangement of the *sadas*, where the Sāmavedins sit facing away from the other officiants. (Their exclusion from the rite of election, for which the *audumbarī* serves as a substitute, supports such an idea.) Staal argues that, as outsiders, the Sāmavedins were 'inferior' and accorded lesser status (2004: 46; cf. Hillebrandt 1897: 100–01), a state of affairs rooted in the prehistory of *śrauta*, when the specialists of Sāmaveda were integrated into the prevailing Vedic ritual scheme.[48] Inferior as they may have

popular use of the term 'shamanism' which Eliade's work has inspired – seems justified to some extent. On the other hand, Witzel (2012: 382) contends that modern scholarship has vindicated Eliade's work on North Asian shamanism.

47 Staal has in mind an unspecified population of 'indigenous' specialists, perhaps speaking a non-Indo-European language, whose contributions may be substantiated by the non-Indo-European names of a number of *sāmans* in the Sāmavedic corpus (2004: 546n12).

48 This integration would have occurred sometime between the *Ṛgveda* and the Mantra period under the authority of the increasingly influential Yajurvedins (Staal 2004: 548; cf. Witzel 1997a: 266–68).

been in the eyes of the others, the singers were nevertheless considered indispensable, for they were integrated into the *śrauta* system at the highest level, that is, in the Soma sacrifices, rites of paramount importance for the sacrificer's soteriology.

My analysis of the *audumbarī* rite adds another piece to this puzzle of prehistory. The traces of ascension in the *audumbarī* rite support the idea that the historical *udgātṛ* was integrated into the *śrauta* system as a specialist in rites that we might today label 'shamanistic', with elements including the climbing of a tree-trunk, cosmic flight, songs with non-lexical syllables and trance induced by psychoactive flora (cf. Thompson 2003a). His expertise in these areas may have proven attractive to a priesthood keen on conveying their patron on a cosmic flight of his own, all the way up to the door of the sun. When the *udgātṛ* 'grasps around' the trunk of the *udumbara* tree, it is a multivalent gesture, both tree-hugging *and* tree-climbing. His contact with the tree simultaneously asserts his authority and potency in the fulfillment of his *śrauta* duties; and encodes his prehistoric background as a specialist in ascending to heaven.

ABBREVIATIONS AND REFERENCES

AB — *Aitareyabrāhmaṇa.* Aufrecht, T. (ed.) (1879). *Das Aitareya Brāhmaṇa.* Bonn: Adolph Marcus.

ABORI — *Annals of the Bhandarkar Oriental Research Institute*

ĀpŚS — Āpastamba: *Śrautasūtra.* Garbe, R. (ed.) (1882, 1885, 1892). *The Śrauta Sūtra of Āpastamba.* Bibliotheca Indica. Calcutta: Asiatic Society of Bengal.

ĀśGS — Āśvalāyana: *Gṛhyasūtra.* Stenzler, A.F. (ed., tr.). (1864). *Gṛhyasūtrāṇi.* Vol. I: *Āśvalāyana.* Leipzig: Abhandlungen der Deutschen Morgenländischen Gesellschaft 3.4.

AVŚ — *Atharvavedasaṃhitā, Śaunaka* recension. Roth, R. and W.D. Whitney (eds.) (1856). *Atharvaveda Saṃhitā (School of the Śaunakas).* Berlin: F. Dümmler.

BauŚS — Baudhāyana: *Śrautasūtra.* Caland, W. (ed.) (1904–1924). *The Baudhāyana Śrauta Sūtra Belonging to the Taittirīya Saṃhitā.* Bibliotheca Indica 163. Calcutta: Asiatic Society of Bengal.

Biardeau 2004 — Biardeau, M. (2004). *Stories About Posts. Vedic Variations around the Hindu Goddess,* translated by A. Hiltebeitel, M.-L. Reiniche and J. Walker. Chicago: University of Chicago Press.

Bodewitz 1977 — Bodewitz, H.W. (1977). 'Notes on the Jaiminīya Brāhmaṇa.' JRAS. GBI 109: 150–57.

Bodewitz 1977–1978 — Bodewitz, H.W. (1977–1978). 'Atharvaveda Saṃhitā 3,12: The Building of a House.' ABORI, 58–59: 59–68.

Bodewitz 1990 Bodewitz, H.W. (1990). *The Jyotiṣṭoma Ritual: Jaiminīya Brāhmaṇa* I, 66–364. Leiden: E.J. Brill.

Brighenti 2012 Brighenti, Francesco. (2012). 'Hindu Devotional Ordeals and Their Shamanic Parallels.' *Electronic Journal of Vedic Studies* 19(4): 103–75. http://dx.doi.org/10.11588/ejvs.2012.4.307 (accessed 4 March 2016).

Caland and Henry 1907 Caland, W. and V. Henry (1907). *L'agniṣṭoma: description complète de la forme normale du sacrifice de soma dans le culte védique*, I and II. Paris: Leroux.

Caland 1919 Caland, W. (1919). *Das Jaiminīya Brāhmaṇa in Auswahl*. Amsterdam: J. Müller.

Caland 1931 Caland, W. (tr.). (1931). *Pañcaviṃśa-Brāhmaṇa: the Brāhmaṇa of Twenty Five Chapters*. Bibliotheca Indica 255. Calcutta: Asiatic Society of Bengal.

Coomaraswamy 1997 Coomaraswamy, A.K. (1997 [1939]). '*Svayamātṛṇṇā*: Janua Coelis.' In *The Door in the Sky: Coomaraswamy on Myth and Meaning*, 6–61. Princeton, NJ: Princeton University Press.

DeLoach, Bruner and Gossett 2002 DeLoach, M., M.S. Bruner, and Gossett, J.S. (2002). 'An Analysis of the "Tree-Hugger" Label.' In Meister, M. and P.M. Japp (eds.), *Enviropop: Studies in Environmental Rhetoric and Popular Culture*, pp. 95–110. Westport, CT: Praeger.

DŚS Drāhyāyaṇa: *Śrautasūtra*. Reuter, J.N. (ed.) (1904). *Drāhyāyaṇa-Śrautasūtra with the Commentary of Dhanvin*. Acta Societas Scientiarum Fennicae XXV(2). London.

Eggeling 1885 Eggeling, J. (tr.). (1885). *The Śatapatha-Brāhmaṇa According to the Text of the Mādhyandina School*, II. Sacred Books of the East 26. Oxford: Clarendon Press.

Eliade 1971 Eliade, M. (1971 [1949]). *The Myth of the Eternal Return*, tr. Willard R. Trask. Princeton, NJ: Princeton University Press.

Eliade 1989 Eliade, M. (1989 [1964]). *Shamanism: Archaic Techniques of Ecstasy*, tr. Willard R. Trask. New York, London: Arkana.

Eliade 1991 Eliade, M. (1991 [1952]). *Images and Symbols: Studies in Religious Symbolism*, tr. Philip Mairet. Princeton, NJ: Princeton University Press.

Farmer, Henderson and Witzel 2002 Farmer, S., J.B. Henderson and M. Witzel. (2002). 'Neurobiology, Layered Texts, and Correlative Cosmologies: A Cross-Cultural Framework for Premodern History.' *Bulletin of the Museum of Far Eastern Antiquities* 72: 48–90.

Fujii 1984 Fujii, M. (1984). 'On the Unexpressed *Gāyatra-Sāman* in the Jaiminīya-Upaniṣad-Brāhmaṇa.' *Journal of Indian and Buddhist Studies* 32(2): 1123–21 (1–3).

Fujii 1986 Fujii, M. (1986). 'The Bahiṣpavamāna Ritual of the Jaiminīyas.' *Machikaneyama Ronso (Philosophy, Osaka University)* 20: 3–25.

Fujii 1997 Fujii, M. (1997). 'On the Formation and Transmission of the Jaiminīya-Upaniṣad-Brāhmaṇa.' In Witzel (1997a: 89–102).

Fujii 2004 Fujii, M. (2004). *The Jaiminīya-Upaniṣad-Brāhmaṇa: A Study of the Earliest Upaniṣad, Belonging to the Jaiminīya Sāmaveda*. Publications of the Institute for Asian and African Studies 4. Helsinki: Valopaino Oy.

Griffiths and Houben 2004 Griffiths, A. and J.E.M. Houben (eds.) (2004). *The Vedas: Texts, Language and Ritual*. Groningen: Forsten.

Hillebrandt 1897 Hillebrandt, A. (1897). *Ritual-Litteratur, Vedische Opfer und Zauber*. Strassburg: K.J. Trübner.

JAOS *Journal of the American Oriental Society*

JB *Jaiminīyabrāhmaṇa*. (1) Vira, R. and L. Chandra (eds.) (1954). *Jaiminīya Brāhmaṇa of the Sāmaveda*. Sarasvati-vihara Series, 31. Nagpur: International Academy of Indian Culture. (2) Ehlers, G. (ed.). Unpublished critical edition, translation and notes.

JRAS.GBI *Journal of the Royal Asiatic Society of Great Britain and Ireland*

JŚS Jaimini: *Śrautasūtra*. (1) Parpola, A. (ed.) (n.d.) *Jaiminīya Śrauta Sūtra*. Photocopy of unpublished typewritten manuscript. (2) Gaastra, D. (ed.) (1906). *Bijdrage tot de kennis van het vedische ritueel. Jaiminīya Śrautasūtra*. Leiden: E.J. Brill.

JUB *Jaiminīyopaniṣadbrāhmaṇa*. Oertel, H. (ed., tr.) (1896). *The Jaiminīya- or Talavakāra-Upaniṣad-Brāhmaṇa*. JAOS 16: 79–260.

KātŚS Kātyāyana: *Śrautasūtra*. Weber, A. (ed.) (1859). *The Śrauta Sūtra of Kātyāyana, with Extracts from the Commentaries of Karka and Yajnikadeva*. Berlin: Ferd. Dümmler's Buchhandlung.

Kehoe 2000 Kehoe, A.B. (2000). *Shamans and Religion. An Anthropological Exploration in Critical Thinking*. Prospect Heights, Ill.: Waveland Press.

Kuiper 1983 Kuiper, F.B.J. (1983). *Ancient Indian Cosmogony*. New Delhi: Vikas.

LātŚS Lāṭyāyana: *Śrautasūtra*. Ranade, H.G. (ed., tr.) (1998). *Lāṭyāyana-Śrauta-Sūtra*. Kalāmūlaśāstra Series 27–29. Delhi: Motilal Banarsidass.

Lévi 1898 Lévi, S. (1898). *La Doctrine du Sacrifice dans Les Brāhmaṇas*. Bibliothèque de l'école des hautes études, Sciences religieuses, vol. 11. Paris: Ernst Laroux.

Mayrhofer 1992–2001 Mayrhofer, M. (1992–2001). *Etymologisches Wörterbuch des Altindoarischen*, 3 vols. Heidelberg: Carl Winter Universitätsverlag.

Mikhailovskii and Wardrop 1895 Mikhailovskii, V.M. and O. Wardrop. (1895). 'Shamanism in Siberia and European Russia, Being the Second Part of "Shamantsvo".' *Journal of the Anthropological Institute of Great Britain and Ireland* 24: 62–100.

Minkowski 1989 Minkowski, C. (1989). 'The Udumbara and its Ritual Significance.' *Wiener Zeitschrift für die Kunde Südasiens*, 33: 5–24.

Minkowski 1992 Minkowski, C. (1992). *Priesthood in Ancient India. A Study of the Maitrāvaruṇa Priest*. Vienna: Sammlung de Nobili, Institut für Indologie der Universität Wien.

Mukharji 2014 Mukharji, P.B. (2014). 'Vishalyakarani as *Eupatorium ayapana*: Retro-botanizing, Embedded Traditions, and Multiple

Historicities of Plants in Colonial Bengal, 1890–1940.' *Journal of Asian Studies* 73(1): 65–87.

Oguibénine 1968 — Oguibénine, B. (1968). 'Sur le symbolisme du type chamanique dans le R̥gveda.' *Uchenyie Zapiski Tartuskogo Gosudarstvennogo universiteta* 201: 140–50.

Parpola 1969 — Parpola, A. (1969). 'The Śrautasūtras of Lāṭyāyana and Drāhyāyaṇa and their Commentaries.' *Commentationes Humanarum Litterarum: Societas Scientiarum Fennica* 43(2): 1–273.

Parpola 2012 — Parpola, A. (2012). 'The Anupadasūtra of Sāmaveda and Jaimini: Prolegomena to a Forthcoming Edition and Translation.' In Voegeli et al. (eds.), *Devadattīyam. Johannes Bronkhorst Felicitation Volume*, pp. 363–404. Bern: Peter Lang.

PB — *Pañcaviṃśabrāhmaṇa.* Vedāntavāgīśa, Ā. (ed.) (1870–1874). *Tāṇḍya-Mahā-Brāhmaṇa.* Bibliotheca Indica 62. Calcutta: Asiatic Society of Bengal.

PGS — Pāraskara: *Gr̥hyasūtra.* Stenzler, A.F. (ed.) (1878). *Indische Hausregeln = Gr̥hyasūtrāṇi: Sanskrit und Deutsch / II, Pâraskara.* Leipzig: Brockhaus.

Radloff 1893 — Radloff, W. (1893). *Aus Siberien. Lose Blätter Aus Meinem Tagebuche,* II. Leipzig: T.O. Weigel.

Rangan 2000 — Rangan, H. (2000). *Of Myths and Movements.* London: Verso.

Renou 1939 — Renou, L. (1939). 'La maison védique.' *Journal Asiatique* 231: 481–504.

Renou and Silburn 1954 — Renou, L. and L. Silburn. (1954). '*Nírukta* and *ánirukta* in Vedic.' In Agrawal, J.N. and B.D. Shastri (eds.), *Sarūpa-Bhāratī, or, The Homage of Indology being the Dr. Lakshman Sarup Memorial Volume,* pp. 68–79. Hoshiarpur: Vishveshvaranand Institute Publications.

RV — *R̥gvedasaṃhitā.* Van Nooten, B. and G. Holland (eds) (1994). *Rigveda. A Metrically Restored Text.* Cambridge, Mass.: Department of Sanskrit and Indian Studies, Harvard University.

ṢaḍB — *Ṣaḍviṃśabrāhmaṇa.* Eelsingh, H.F. (ed.) (1908). *Ṣaḍviṃśabrāhmaṇam Vijñāpanabhāṣyasahitam. Het Ṣaḍviṃśabrāhmaṇa van de Sāmaveda, uitgegeven met een Inleiding, de op naam van Sāyaṇa staande Commentaar en Aantekeningen.* Leiden: E.J. Brill.

ŚāṅGS — Śāṅkhāyana: *Gr̥hyasūtra.* Oldenberg, H. (ed., tr.) (1878). *Das Śāṅkhāyanagr̥hyam.* From *Indische Studien* XXV: 1–166. Leipzig: F.A. Brockhaus.

ŚB — *Śatapathabrāhmaṇa,* Mādhyaṃdina recension. Weber, A. (ed.) (1855). *The Śatapatha Brāhmaṇa in the Mādhyaṃdina-Śākhā.* Berlin: F. Dümmler.

Smith 1989 — Smith, B.K. (1989). *Reflections on Resemblance, Ritual, and Religion.* New York: Oxford University Press.

Staal 1983 — Staal, F. (1983). *Agni. The Vedic Ritual of the Fire Altar,* I and II. Berkeley: Asian Humanities Press.

Staal 1991 — Staal, F. (1991). 'The Centre of Space: Construction and Discovery.' In Vatsyayan, K. (ed.), *Concepts of Space, Ancient and Modern,* pp. 83–100. Delhi: Indira Gandhi National Centre for the Arts.

Staal 2004	Staal, F. (2004). 'From *Prāṅmukham* to *Sarvatomukham*: A Thread Through the Śrauta Maze.' In Griffiths and Houben (eds.), *The Vedas*, pp. 521–55.
SV	*Sāmaveda*
Thompson 2003a	Thompson, G. (2003). 'Soma and Ecstasy.' *Electronic Journal of Vedic Studies*, 9, <http://www.ejvs.laurasianacademy.com/ejvs0901/ejvs0901e.txt> (accessed 15 April 2015).
Thompson 2003b	Thompson, G. (2003). 'Shamanism in the Ṛgveda and its Central Asian Antecedents.' Presentation at the 5th Harvard Round Table on the Ethnogenesis of South and Central Asia, 9–12 May 2003, <http://www.people.fas.harvard.edu/~witzel/Thompson.pdf> (accessed 3 September 2015).
TS	*Taittirīyasaṃhitā*. Weber, A. (ed.) (1871–1872). *Die Taittirīya Saṃhitā. Indische Studien* XI and XII. Leipzig: F.A. Brockhaus.
VS	*Vājasaneyisaṃhitā*. Weber, A. (ed.) (1852–1859). *The Vājasaneyi-Saṃhitā in the Mādhyaṃdina-Śākhā*. Berlin: F. Dümmler.
Weber 1988	Weber, T. (1988). *Hugging the Trees. The Story of the Chipko Movement*. Delhi; New York: Viking.
Witzel 1979	Witzel, M. (1979). 'On Magical thought in the Veda.' Leiden: Universitaire Pers. <http://archiv.ub.uni-heidelberg.de/savifadok/90/1/Magical_Thought_1979.pdf> (accessed 3 September 2015).
Witzel 1987	Witzel, M. (1987). 'On the Localisation of Vedic Texts and Schools (Materials on Vedic Śākhās, 7).' In Pollett, G. (ed.), *India and the Ancient World. History, Trade and Culture before* A.D. *650. P.H.L. Eggermont Jubilee Volume*, pp. 173–213. Orientalia Lovaniensia Analecta 25. Leuven: Departement Oriëntalistiek.
Witzel 1996	Witzel, M. (1996). 'How to Enter the Vedic Mind? Strategies in Translating a Brāhmaṇa Text.' In Garzilli, E. (ed.), *Translating, Translations, Translators. From India to the West*, pp. 163–76. Harvard Oriental Series, Opera Minora 1. Cambridge, Mass.: Department of Sanskrit and Indian Studies, Harvard University.
Witzel 1997a	Witzel, M. (ed.). (1997). *Inside the Texts, Beyond the Texts. New Approaches to the Study of the Vedas*. Harvard Oriental Series, Opera Minora 2. Cambridge, Mass.: Department of Sanskrit and Indian Studies, Harvard University.
Witzel 1997b	Witzel, M. (1997). 'The Development of the Vedic Canon and its Schools: The Social and Political Milieu (Materials on Vedic Śākhās 8).' In Witzel (1997a: 257–345).
Witzel 2004	Witzel, M. (2004). 'The Ṛgvedic Religious System and its Central Asian and Hindukush Antecedents.' In Griffiths and Houben (2004: 581–636).
Witzel 2012	Witzel, M. (2012). *The Origins of the World's Mythologies*. Oxford; New York: Oxford University Press.
YV	*Yajurveda*

Section Four

Myth, Food, Nature

Chapter 9

Caryota urens: From Vegetable Manifestation of God to Sacred Tree of the Shamans of Odisha

STEFANO BEGGIORA[1]

Under British rule, most of India's forest land was considered a colonial asset and was administrated by the State Forest Department. Colonial policies on matters of forestry tended to look at forest dwellers as illegal intruders on land belonging to the Crown. This resulted in a series of protests and rebellions in many parts of the country. Independent India has continued with this line of forest management and so far the basic human rights of *ādivāsīs*, the 'indigenous peoples' of India known today as 'Scheduled Tribes,' have been denied, even though their livelihood continues to depend to a large extent on a balanced use of environmental resources (e.g. hunting, collecting of forest produce and shifting cultivation). Notwithstanding this situation, a new trend has emerged in the last decades. Given the high rate of deforestation and the resulting soil erosion in many protected areas, indigenous culture is increasingly looked at as a resource that can contribute towards the safeguarding of forest areas.[2] The sustainability of the forest ecosystem amongst *ādivāsī* groups is one built on the knowledge of a set of social rules, often of a religious nature, whose dynamics ultimately regulate the relations between human beings and the ecosystem.[3]

1 Stefano Beggiora is Research Fellow (Habil. Associate Professor) in Indian History, Department of Asian and Mediterranean African Studies, Ca' Foscari University of Venice (Italy).

2 See the website of the Ministry of Environment, Forest and Climate Change: http://envfor.nic.in. Also see Guha et al. (2012: 1–12).

3 Besides the major celebrations dedicated to the *bana devatā* or *dongor devatā*, gods/spirits of the forests and mountains respectively, that have different

In this chapter I propose a study of the relation between some *ādivāsī* communities of Odisha[4] and the vegetal landscape in which their culture is inscribed. In particular, I discuss the place of the sacred jaggery palm, or *Caryota urens* L.,[5] among the Lanjia Saoras.[6] From this particular type of palm, a liquor is obtained which is thought to facilitate the communication of human beings with the subtle world surrounding them. The jaggery palm – as a living being central to Saora cosmology and a revered mother who feeds her children – fits the discourse on multinaturalism presented by Descola (2005) as well as the ideas proposed by Latour (2014: 306) on the necessity to negotiate 'how forests think' about their inhabitants, a crucial question for any form of forest management in the future (Padel et al. 2013).

In animist/indigenous societies nature is deeply entangled with culture (Jena et al. 2006: 189; Descola 2011: 20). In the case of Indian *ādivāsīs*, the trees and plants of the forest (Skt. *vana*; O. *bana*; So. *kānreṇ*) are perceived as living creatures akin to human and non-human animals (Seeland 1997: 101–12). Living beings are all simultaneously architects and artisans, constantly working on changing the profile of this immense green cathedral that is the forest.

FROM JUICE TO LIQUOR: PROPRIETIES AND PROCESSING TECHNIQUES

Among the Saoras, but also other *ādivāsīs* of Odisha (e.g. the Kondhs), there exists the concept that each species of plant has a gendered connotation.

regional features, indigenous communities across India observe festivities with similar names and forms, e.g. the ritual celebration of the first harvest of mango, the processing of *mahul* flowers for the preparation of liquor, the spring festival, et cetera (Gowtham Shankar 2007: 111–14).

4 The data discussed here stem from extensive fieldwork conducted discontinuously from 1997 to 2012 in Odisha, mainly among the Kuttia Kondhs (Kandhmal district) and Lanjia Saoras (Rayagada district), two communities presently classified as PVTGs (Particularly Vulnerable Tribal Groups).

5 From the Greek κάρῦον (= nut) and Latin *urens* (= burning; stinging).

6 The Saoras are an indigenous people of Odisha mainly settled in the districts of Rayagada and Gajapati. According to the last Census of India the total population count was 534,751 people (cf. Chaudhuri 2013: 144). The subgroup of Lanjia Saoras inhabit the area of the highlands of Pottasing over the *taluka* (subdivision) of Gunupur.

Plants mature (germination and flowering) and have sexual relationships (pollination). They also enjoy social life, family and community connections. Such bonds are developed in parallel to those of human and non-human animals, and are consecrated by means of the various beverages that ooze from symbolically charged trees (Beggiora 2013: 37–54).

As I had the chance to observe among the Saoras and other *ādivāsīs* of Odisha as well as in the sub-Himalayan region and the Northeastern Frontier,[7] alcohol – which is an essential ritual item in most ceremonies – is not just used to induce the Saora *kuran* (shaman-like ritual specialist and healer) into a trance. The custom of drinking fermented products is a characteristic feature of *ādivāsī* culture. It creates sociality, enshrines communal relations among the clans and consecrates rites of passage such as weddings, births and funerals. Furthermore, the consumption of alcohol produced from the plants of the forest, where survival is always a challenge, contributes to reduce the levels of anxiety among community members (Dash 2009: 92–98). In the last few years, I have documented the traditional techniques of production of fermented beverages from rice, wheat, potato, milk and various plants of the forest.

Fermentation is a process of great interest for historians of food and, more generally, scholars within cultural studies. A naturally occurring metabolic process responsible for the conversion of sugars to alcohol, fermentation has been employed for the storage and processing of food, to increase the nutritional value of various edibles and, in some cases, for the development of drugs and medicinal concoctions. In some geographically remote areas of India, there survive traditional techniques of fermentation which suggest a profound knowledge of the environment and particularly of its flora. The various communities of *ādivāsīs* inhabiting Indian forests demonstrate awareness of and familiarity with a number of microbiological starter cultures. Some of these are used to produce alcoholic beverages such as various qualities of palm wine (Steinkraus 1996: 398).

Palm wine is consumed all over India. The fermented palm sap is generally known as toddy, or *kallu*. This is prepared from the coconut palm (*Cocos nucifera* L.) or from the palmyra palm (*Borassus flabellifer* L.) and represents the most widespread type of palm wine in the subcontinent. Yule and Burnell inform us that toddy is 'a corruption of Hind. *tāṛī*, i.e. the fermented sap of the *tāṛ* or *palmyra*, Skt. *tāla*, and also of other palms,

7 In particular I refer to the Monpas, Mijis, Apatanis, Nishis, Hill Miris, Adis and Mishmis of Arunachal Pradesh (fieldwork conducted between 2001 and 2002).

such as the date, the coco-palm, and the *Caryota urens*; palm-wine. Toddy is generally the substance used in India as yeast, to leaven bread.' (HJ 927)

Tribal areas of Odisha are known for the production of local palm wine, such as *salap* or *salpo*, which is produced by brewing the juice of the *salap* tree (*Caryota urens*).[8] Generally speaking, palm wine is a popular beverage among lower-income groups and is prepared wherever palm trees are cultivated or grow wild, either on the hillsides or in the jungle tracts.

Palm wine (So. *ālin*)[9] is a handmade product that is also appreciated by non-tribal people who venture onto the hills in search of this cheap liquor. Besides the *Caryota urens*, alternatively known as fishtail wine palm for the characteristic shape of its leaves, I noted the frequent use of other species of palm trees with similar properties, such as the silver date palm (*Phoenix sylvestris* [L.] Roxb.) and the palmyra palm (*Borassus flabellifer* L.). The names of these plants may have regional variations, but they all belong to the same family (Arecaceae) and the same order (Arecales) as *Caryota urens* and concurrently as the coconut palm. In some hill areas, along with palm wine, there exists a variety of liquor produced from the dried corollas of the *mahul* flower (*Madhuca longifolia* var. *latifolia* [Roxb.] A.Chev.) and known as *mahua*, or *mahuli* (O.). The plant, which belongs to the Sapotaceae family and the Ericales order, requires a more complex preparation, similar to distillation, in order to obtain the final product which is then used for the same social and ritual uses as *salap* by indigenous communities.

A palm tree requires a long time before reaching maturity, beginning to produce after at least ten years of growth. The techniques for the extraction of juice, and its fermentation for the production of wine, are roughly the same. The liquid can be obtained from the fruits of the tree or from the latex that oozes from an incision made at the top of the trunk or on the branches in proximity to the inflorescence (figure 9.1). In general, the tree owner oversees the collection, but often it is the young men or boys of a village who have the task of climbing the trees. In exchange for a certain amount of product to take home as a reward, they collect the full pots strategically positioned below the incisions.

8 The term in Odia is *salapa* (pron. salpɒ); variant: *saḍapa*. It specifically designates the tree *Caryota urens* L., whereas the alcoholic beverage made from it is called *salapa-rās* (*salap* juice). The word is probably a loan from local Munda languages of the word for 'tree' (cf. Anderson and Zide 2002: 56–58; Donegan 1993: 18).

9 The Saora language, or Sora, is classified as Austro-Asiatic, Munda (Ethnologue ISO 639-3 srb).

Figure 9.1. The collection of sap from the jaggery palm, Pottasing area, 2005.

Fresh palm sap is generally dirty brown, but it becomes pale and eventually opalescent if the yeasts multiply. The latex produced from *Caryota urens* is generally of a milky whitish color. Although palm wines are generally sweetish, the *salap* variety can have a sour aftertaste. The consistency is strong, milky, sometimes lumpy. It is, however, a vigorously effervescent alcoholic beverage, the alcohol content of which is not very high, and is consumed as a mildly alcoholic beverage similar to beer: from a standard content of 1.5–2.1 percent for the so-called toddy, it can reach 3.5–4 percent and more for the products of Odisha and the Northeastern areas (Steinkraus 1996: 385). Besides its ritual and social use, this wine is traditionally believed to be good for health, particularly for eyesight. It also serves as a sedative, and it is used as a mild laxative relieving constipation. In general, it is prescribed as a tonic for those recovering from various diseases (Sekar and Mariappan 2007: 111–20).

Across *ādivāsī* settlements of Odisha, alcohol produced from plants is considered a resource and its consumption is based on sharing. Even though trees are owned by families or individuals, the salap obtained from its fruits is usually offered to the rest of the community. Among the Desia Kondhs[10] of Khandamal district there exists the custom of adopting trees

10 The Kondhs are one of the most important *ādivāsī* groups of Odisha. They live mainly in the districts of Khandmal, Kalahandi, Ganjam and Koraput, but a few

as members of the community, as if to emphasize the versatility of an empathetic relationship between different degrees of existence (human/non-human). So emerges a sense of collective responsibility for plant life, as trees become part of the clan. The stepfather of the palm invites friends and relatives to gather at the foot of the tree. The collection site thus becomes a place for meeting, discussion and tasting of the product. Among the Didayis[11] of the Koraput district, the householders are owners of trees and the property is inherited by the sons after the death of the father; in case one does not have children, the property is transferred to a nephew. The Lanjia Saoras of Rayagada district usually gather to consume liquor just before sunset at precise locations outside the villages. It is customary for farmers to stop along the paths leading back from their work in the terraced fields, where they sit and drink large quantities of palm wine while discussing the most disparate topics.

Some groups are organized for the sale of the product, the owners of the trees positioning themselves at the side of the road with the palm wine in large aluminum jugs, waiting for customers. In this context, the possession of one or more trees of *Caryota urens* is an asset for the family. A glass of *salap* or *mahua* is sold for 3 or 4 rupees, but a pot can be sold for around ₹150. In a year, this amounts to a fair supplementary income for the seller (Mahapatra 2011: 78–80).

Production techniques may differ. In some areas of the Khandmal district, I observed that the *salap* is left to ferment inside the pots hanging from the trees. The wine is thus naturally prepared; when it is believed to be ready for consumption, it is collected and sold or distributed. However the most common way to prepare *salap* requires the liquid to be preliminarily boiled and then fermented after adding a mixture of spices and roots.[12]

---

sub-tribes dwell in neighboring states. Divided into several sub-groups, e.g. Dongaria, Desia, Kutia, Sitha, Muli, et cetera, their main languages, Kui and Kuvi, are from Dravidian stock (Ethnologue ISO 639-3 kxu and kxv). The Desias are an Odiya-speaking subgroup that lives in the plains.

11 The Didayis are an indigenous community of southern Odisha, located in the district of Koraput. With a total population of slightly more than 8000 people, they speak Odiya, Telugu and a tribal language called Gata (Ethnologue ISO 639-3 gaq) or Didayi (Chaudhuri 2013: 158).

12 These may vary from area to area. Commonly chips of the bark of *Bahuinia malabarica* Roxb. are tied in small bundles and are added to *salap* to increase its intoxicating action. In some areas, the dried pith of the *Caryota* is pounded and boiled in water; this makes a thick drink that is a variation of *salap* (Banik 2012: 35, 37).

The process for the production of *mahua* is different. *Ādivāsīs* collect *mahul* flowers in March and April in the plains or in some remote forest areas. The flowers are dried and stored in bamboo baskets or in cups made of *siali* leaves[13] so that they can be consumed throughout the year. Many inhabitants of the hills buy the flowers at weekly markets, due to the scarcity of *mahul* trees in the highlands. The liquor is prepared by means of a simple distillation process. The flowers are left soaking in a clay pot for few days. This is then warmed with fire and then covered with a second pot, identical in shape, which serves as a lid and, at the same time, permits internal condensation. Over these two pots, a smaller jar may be placed, which only contains cold water to encourage condensation. The distillate trickles out from a side opening in the upper jug to which is attached a piece of cane that guides the droplets into another suitably placed container.

In lowland areas, the traditional production techniques of the *ādivāsīs* of Central India (Madhya Pradesh, Bihar, Jharkhand, Chhattisgarh, Odisha) include other varieties of beers such as *paise*, made from fermented finger millet or *rāgi* (*Eleusine coracana* [L.] Gaertn.) and the popular *handia*, obtained from the fermentation of rice.

A mixture of elements (dried and powdered bark, leaves, tuberous roots, flowers and seeds of different plants) is often used to accelerate the fermentation process, and to make the beverages more alcoholic. Powders are then thoroughly mixed with flour in the ratio of 1:2 and rolled into small *ranu* (cakes or tablets). Even though today chemical agents are used to simplify the preparation of palm wine, the complex alchemy of traditional techniques, still in use in indigenous villages, remains prevalent. This includes the use of toxic and psychotropic substances.[14]

13 *Bauhinia vahlii* Wight and Arn., also known as *mahul patta*, is a giant creeper of the Indian jungle. The leaves of *siali* are collected and stitched together into plates and cups which are then sold in local markets. Alternatively they can be used as compost.

14 The following species are often used: *Argyreia bella* (C.B.Clarke) Raizada (unresolved name); *Bombax ceiba* L; *Buchanania cochinchinensis* (Lour.) M.R.Almeida; *Casearia graveolens* Dalzell; *Cassine glauca* (Rottb.) Kuntze; *Catunaregam spinosa* (Thunb.) Tirveng; *Cissampelos pareira* L.; *Crotalaria albida* B. Heyne ex. Roth; *Cryptolepis dubia* (Burm.f.) M.R.Almeida; *Datura metel* L.; *Elephantopus scaber* L.; *Euphorbia meloformis* Aiton; *Hemidesmus indicus* (L.) R.Br.; *Holarrhena pubescens* Wall. ex G.Don; *Knoxia sumatrensis* (Retz.) DC.; *Pueraria tuberosa* (Roxb. ex Willd.) DC.; *Scoparia dulcis* L.; *Senecio nudicaulis* Buch.-Ham. ex D.Don; *Symplocos racemosa* Roxb.; *Tylophora rotundifolia* Buch.-Ham.ex Wt.; *Wattakaka volubilis* (L.f.) Stapf. (cf. Ekka 2012: 353–59).

RITUAL USE OF *CARYOTA URENS* AMONG THE LANJIA SAORAS

An understanding of the diverse forms of existence in the forest and their symbiotic relationship is essential to appreciate *ādivāsī* ritual culture and social life. Since the forest is considered the abode of ancestral deities, it follows that individual trees are seen to be their manifestation and their products are believed to have associated properties. For this reason, the use of palm wine tends to be associated with a range of solemn and domestic functions. Even when toddy is not explicitly used in ritual contexts, it is enshrined in forms of collective social communication that contribute to the inclusive character of the rules governing the clan and the tribe. Alcoholism, however, is not infrequent. The abuse of liquor and the state of intoxication resulting from it are seen as ominous and potentially dangerous. The disorderly state of being drunk puts the individual at risk of unconsciously breaking a series of taboos, such as entering restricted holy places, inadvertently upsetting bowls or plates of offerings, et cetera. Further, being vulnerable, one is likely to fall prey to evil spirits. The unaware drunk is more susceptible to being possessed, or followed, by malign entities who will then enter the village. This explains why recreational over-consumption of palm wine is seen as a social problem. Conversely, within the framework of social rules and ritual actions (under the guidance of a shaman), the fermented juice of the jaggery palm figures prominently in all ceremonies, from rites of passage to major offerings to the nature spirits (*sonum*) and to the ancestral deities of the forests and the hills.

Such is true, for example, in the case of marriage negotiations. When two youths intend to get married, the boy is supposed to go to the girl's house and leave outside the front door a small pot of *ālin* as a gift. If this is accepted by the parents of the girl, additional gifts will be presented in the following weeks and the quantity of wine provided will gradually increase. The receiving family pretends to be unaware of the identity of the mysterious donor. By accepting the series of gifts, it gives the signal that the marriage can be considered and that it is ready to negotiate a dowry.[15] In a similar fashion, when a child is born to a couple, the name-giving

15 Marriage by capture is a remnant of the past but, I was informed, sometimes a performance is enacted to speed up the gift of wine. The girl is abducted by her lover in the absence of her parents. She pretends despair even though the event has been pre-planned and is known to all. Her brother intervenes to defend her and points to the offense caused by the suitor who will then have to pay compensation in the form of wine to the family of the bride-to-be.

ceremony, a ritual that connects the newborn to the ancestors, is celebrated by means of animal sacrifice and wine offerings.

Alcohol, along with the blood of selected ritual victims, is the core offering in most *ādivāsī* communities of Odisha as well as in Śākta contexts. Among the Saoras, alcoholic beverages are essential to major sacrifices in which the cosmogonic event is recreated. Even more than water, alcohol has dissolving and germinal properties which are symbolically evoked in the ritual. Liquor is also used in collective rituals of the domestic type, where the first sip is not swallowed but spat into the fire as an offering to the guardian spirits of the house.

Caryota urens and other varieties of the palm tree figure prominently in the *anitals*, wall paintings that decorate Saoras' huts (figure 9.2). The preparation of such drawings requires the artist, or the shaman, to spend a night sleeping at the foot of the wall, waiting for precognitive dreams which should indicate the subject of the *anital* as well as the mode of execution. A preliminary offering of *salap* is presented to the ancestors of the clan; then the artist should observe a strict fast. Only palm wine can be drunk, an observance aiming to favor inspiration. The main frame of the *anital* is usually the sketch of a house. This is filled with various characters; some appear busy preparing the wine while others – the so-called "dancers" – hold jugs over their head in an act that supposedly evokes the

Figure 9.2. *Anital*, Odaser village, 2012.

advancing of the spirits with their offerings of *salap/ālin*. The palm tree seems to hold together the structure in the painting and, it may be argued, functions as a symbolic *axis mundi*. At the end of the performance, jugs with fermented wine are hung in front of the *anital*. Since the painting is considered the new abode of guardian and tutelary spirits, these are supposed to be offerings to them.[16]

This brings us back to the cosmogonic myth of the Lanjia Saoras. According to the narrative I recorded in Pottasing area (20 km from Gunupur, Rayagada district), in the beginning there were no shamans, and the hungry nature spirits (*sonums*) and deities roamed the world afflicting men. They caused illnesses and calamities of all types. So Kittung (a primordial divinity and the hero/demigod of this oral epic), moved by pity for the human situation, decided to designate someone among mortals who could protect and heal the people. He hunted high and low for a suitable candidate. Eventually, while wandering through the forest, he met a poor man who lived there alone as he had neither wife nor children. Kittung chose this man to become the healer. The man asked Kittung how a poor, inexperienced and ignorant man could possibly accomplish such a difficult task. Kittung then gave him new rice (So. *ruṇku*) in a new winnowing fan (So. *ojeren* or *tedungan*) and new *ālin* in a new pot, and finally provided for him a large group of animals, such as goats, owls and pigs. Then he consecrated the man as a *kuran* and sent him to the nearest village where many people were sick. By shaking the winnowing fan, the man called the spirits; by means of animal sacrifices, he fed them; and with the wine he made a covenant with them. Finally, he healed the sick villagers and from that day he became the protector and healer of his people.[17]

In the myth of the first Saora shaman[18] one can easily detect the centrality of the palm tree as well as of *salap/ālin*. In some rare cases, the jar filled with wine – shaken rhythmically so as to create a lapping sound to accompany the singing of the invocation – is considered a means to induce a trance, just like the sound produced by the winnowing fan.[19] The

16 Many of the existing *anitals* are quite old. From the interviews collected during my fieldwork, I found that the ritual drawing of such auspicious sketches is becoming rare due to its censure by Christian missionaries. This notwithstanding, shamans in many villages continue to draw *anitals*.

17 Elwin is the only other writer to report a similar legend (cf. Elwin 1955: 131).

18 There exist similar narratives where the protagonist is a female shaman, or *kuramboi*.

19 The winnowing fan is an agricultural tool used to separate rice and other cereals from chaff and other impurities. Among the shamans of Odisha, the

widespread use of agricultural tools as accessories to ritual is here complementary to the use of alcohol for the successful completion of a core ritual performance.

Toddy and spirits in general are used on a number of ritual occasions. One such case is during funeral ceremonies (Guār Pūjā), when various edibles are presented to the dead. The Lanjia Saoras prepare little bundles of food (the equivalent of the *piṇḍas* in the Hindu *śrāddha*) which are supposed to sustain the departed one in the afterlife. This is preceded by an oblation with alcohol. Three droplets of blood and three droplets of *ālin* are deposited on the rice bundles before being wrapped in *siali* leaves and sealed with bronze rings. Meanwhile the *kuran* tries to achieve a trance-like state (So. *meʔer*).[20] Once this is accomplished, he accepts offerings of alcohol in great quantities. The thirsty spirits then emerge from the underworld (*kinorai*) and possess the *kuran* to drink directly from his mouth.[21] The ritual may last for several hours; typically the shaman will physically collapse at its conclusion. While the shaman, his assistants and the relatives of the dead participate in the Guār Pūjā, at the center of the village the same offerings are presented on a larger scale. All bystanders are presented with the meat of a buffalo that has been sacrificed, and pots full of palm wine are passed around. It appears that the *ālin*, along with the blood/meat of a sacrificial victim, permits the renewal of the pact between the living and the dead, between the village and its ancestors.

THE THIRST OF THE SPIRITS

In Indian traditions, spirits – particularly the souls of the deceased – are considered to be in a condition of pain. The concept of endless suffering and torment is mirrored in the idea that a spirit (O. *bhūto*) is an entity tormented by thirst. Among the Saoras, the underworld is dark and arid and *ālin* is unavailable there, as are vegetation and water.[22] The offering of alcohol is therefore intended as a way to alleviate the sufferings of the dead, to

---

rhythmical shaking of the tool, and the sound produced by the grain in it, is used to induce a state of trance.

20 This is different from the state of alcoholic intoxication (So. *tadai*).

21 Some shamans report that in their state of possession during the trance, the *salap* has no taste and they can drink it in large quantities without suffering the effects.

22 This is evocative of the hell of the Christian tradition in which fire and flames are evocative of torment.

provide relief and to transform their status from thirsty angry spirits into ancestors and tutelary entities.

Within this network of beliefs, the plant which yields alcohol is a looked upon as a 'vegetable' manifestation of the divine. In particular, the trees exuding the precious latex are symbols of divine maternity.[23] Palms such as *Caryota urens* are considered sacred and for this reason they are sought after by spirits and the souls in pain who try to come back to life. Offerings and libations of *ālin* are essential in the performance of *karja*, a major ritual celebration in February–March in memory of the ancestors of the clans, as well as on the occasion of minor observances such as *limma*, *sikunda* and *lajap*.[24]

23 'It is said among the Gond that the palm that is tapped for beer and wine, which they call *salphi*, comes from Tallur Muttai, the Mother Earth. It is said that seven *salphi* maidens were born to the Earth Mother, but there was but one placenta among them. After Tallur Muttai cut the cord and was burying the placenta, the seven maidens ran away and hid where they could never be found. When she discovered her loss, Tallur Muttai went to where she had buried the placenta and, in sorrow, let the milk from her breast fall upon the Earth. Soon a wonderful tree grew from the placenta, the sago palm, the tree born from milk that always gives milk, the milk of Earth Mother.' (Harrod Buhner 1998: 129)

24 Such rituals make up the funerary ceremonies of the Lanjia Saora. They are crucial offerings in that the quality of the afterlife of the dead as well as the relations they will maintain with the living, depend upon their outcome, i.e. whether or not they will be accepted by the gods/spirits. The *limma* is celebrated one day after cremation, when ashes and bones are collected. These are gathered and inhumed. On this occasion, a miniature hut is built and filled with the deceased's goods. This will act as the temporary abode of the deceased until the *guār* ceremony, i.e. the actual funeral, when it will be dismantled. Relatives bring a large jug of wine which is sprinkled on the hut and then drunk – the first sip is offered to the deceased by means of an ablution or spitting in the direction of the hut. The *sikunda* is a minor celebration which is performed between Guār Pūjā and *karja* (see below), when the clan (So. *birindan*) gather to remember the recently departed along with those who have preceded him/her. On such occasions, too, the rite is ended by a libation of wine. Unlike *sikunda*, the *karja* is a sumptuous collective commemoration which requires the opening of the gates between this life and the world of the dead. In some villages, the *karja* is celebrated once a year, or even once every three years. This is regulated by a variety of rules. Since time stops and the dead are summoned by the living, among whom they are supposed to live for a while, all works are interdicted. Just like during the Guār Pūjā, wine is heavily consumed and many buffaloes are sacrificed. Finally, the *lajap* – held at the end of the rainy season – is the natural continuation, and conclusion, of the *karja*. The ritual

The liturgy of a Guār Pūjā recited by the *kuramboi* (female shaman) Bhambro Gajino and recorded in the village of Regintal on 6 February 1999, provides an example for a better understanding of the place of palms, palm wine and the spirits of the dead.[25] Accompanied by her assistants, the *kuramboi* emphasizes the act of presenting the soul of the deceased to the community of the ancestors by repeatedly offering wine:

[...] Oh ancestors you are here,
please accept your son,
we put the [memorial] stone in your place,
please accept it.
Tatago Gomango, Moroja Gomango,
you are my ancestors,
Isparu Gomango, Gobanno Gomango,
you were in our family,
Pujano Gomango, you're my nephew,
you are like my son,
I'm offering you wine
I beg you all, accept it.

Sitting with her legs stretched next to the *ganuar*, the place of erection of memorial stones, where the ashes of the dead are buried, the shaman addresses them singing this long chant. After repeating the names of the founding fathers of the community, she summons the village chieftains (*gomango*) of previous generations by offering them food and *ālin*. She then continues:

[...] Kusulu Buyan, Kulu Buyan,
Benu Buyan, Sinu Buyan,
Ratu Buyan, Ranu Buyan,
Moroja Buyan, Morai Buyan,[26]
I call you!
I'm offering you food,
I'm offering you liquor, please come!

---

is celebrated within the domestic abode or in the open, usually in the family fields. A cockerel is sacrificed and its blood is mixed in palm wine and offered to the dead to favour abundance of crops during the following season.

25 See Beggiora (2010: 129–48) for a lengthier and slightly different version of this liturgy and the ones below.

26 The *buyan* or *buyya* is a ritualist alternative to the shaman, but inferior in rank. He often acts as advisor of the tribal chief. In this liturgy, the *kuramboi* invokes the *buyyas* of past generations.

After invoking other ritual specialists and village councilors and leaders (*buyan*, or *buyya*), the shaman calls the gods:

> [...] My golden gods and goddesses of gold,
> I offer you food and wine, please come!
> [...] If I commit a mistake
> or if I show uncertainty,
> please come and help me!
> If I made a mistake or
> I failed in anything,
> since I'm offering you wine
> Come and forget it!

The alcoholic offering here serves to mitigate the risk of disaster in case something goes wrong in the performance of the rite and the spirits get angry. Finally, the *kuramboi* calls upon all her predecessors in the initiatory line, reeling off all the names, generation after generation, and asking for their protection:

> [...] Likumboi, Jaipailikumboi,
> you remember me, I will tell you what I mean;
> Iderekumboi, Jemakumboi,
> I remember you, you are my mothers and I tell you everything;
> Subonikumboi, Durginikumboi,
> Surgikumboi, Morikumboi, Jaurikumboi [...]
> I remember you, I invoke you, I call you, I tell you,
> My sisters, my aunts,
> I remember you, I invoke you, I call you, I tell you;
> I appeal to you and I offer you this spirit.
> [While saying this, she sprinkles with alcohol the memorial stone and other offerings.]

The act of sprinkling palm wine requires the use of a particular hollow carved gourd (So. *kūn*) (figure 9.3). The use of such particular items is generally intended to ensure that the offerings will be accepted by the spirits and the gods.

Figure 9.3. *Kuramboi* with gourd under her arm, Regingtal village, 1999.

CONCLUSION

The production, social exchange and ritual consumption of *ālin* prove significant markers of tribal identity among the Lanjia Saoras. Many things, however, are changing in Odisha. Indigenous traditions are fast disappearing as a result of various factors such as urbanization, globalization and industrialization. Further to that, Christian missions, in the name of evangelization, are significantly contributing to the homogenization of most *ādivāsī* communities. It is not by chance that among converted *ādivāsīs*, drinking *salap* and other spirits is considered a major sin, not so much because it is seen as a vice leading to antisocial behavior, but because the act of drinking palm wine is part of a cultural (tribal) identity that is to be deleted.

Another threat to indigenous cultures comes from the alcohol business and the capillary distribution of cheap liquor even in the most remote jungle areas, which has resulted in growing alcoholism to the extent that it is now a major social plague.[27] This, however, is not the only problem.

27 On this issue, see Jena (2008), Agrawal (2013), Nayak (2014) and Nanda et al. (2006).

Market requirements in contemporary India demand intensive farming techniques. Indigenous communities are increasingly integrated in a working pattern that privileges monocultures against local crop varieties and ancestral agricultural techniques. This market economics is erasing indigenous forest culture and the knowledge base of sustainability that, it so appears, lasted for millennia as long as the delicate equilibrium between nature and tribal communities was left in isolation, undisturbed. Today Saoras, Kondhs and other local tribes are learning at their own expense that demographic growth (both internal and external) followed by rampant deforestation are jeopardizing archaic techniques of subsistence which are no longer sufficient to sustain the population of their villages in the long term (Mohanty and Paikaray 2009: 52–75; SCSTRTI 2009). In other words, the indigeneity paradigm raises questions of a global order, including that of human cultural roots, here symbolized by the jaggery palm and palm wine.

ABBREVIATIONS AND REFERENCES

O. = Odia So. = Sora Skt. = Sanskrit

Agrawal 2013 Agrawal, S. (2013). 'Health and Nutritional Disadvantage among Tribal Women and Children of Orissa: An Enquiry from a Large Scale.' *Survey Journal of Community Nutrition & Health* 2: 1–12.

Anderson and Zide 2002 Anderson, G.D.S. and N. Zide. (2002). 'Issues in Proto-Munda and Proto-Austroasiatic Nominal Derivation: The Bimoraic Constraint.' In Macken, M.A. (ed.), *Papers from the 10th Annual Meeting of the Southeast Asian Linguistics Society*, pp. 55–74. Tempe: Arizona State University.

Banik 2012 Banik, A. (2012). 'Identification and Utilization of Wild Edible Plants Used by the Tribals of Bastar Region (Chhattisgarh).' *Life Sciences Leaflets* 12: 29–76.

Beggiora 2010 Beggiora, S. (2010). 'The Whisper of the Spirits. Shamanic Kinship and the Cult of the Ancestors among the Lanjia Saoras of Orissa.' In Ferrari, F.M. (ed.), *Health and Religious Rituals in South Asia*, pp. 129–48. London: Routledge.

Beggiora 2013 Beggiora, S. (2013). 'Ecologia, sviluppo e sostenibilità: problematiche sociali e ambientali della Forest Policy nell'India contemporanea.' *Ethnorêma* 9: 37–54.

Chaudhuri 2013 Chaudhuri, S. (ed.) (2013). *Statistical Profile of Scheduled Tribes in India 2013*. Ministry of Tribal Affairs, Government of India, Noida.

Dash 2009 Dash, K. (2009). 'Drinking – A Socio-Cultural Practice among the Tribals Odisha.' *Adivasi* 49(1): 92–97.

Descola 2005	Descola, P. (2005). *Par-delà nature et culture par Philippe Descola*. Paris: Gallimard.
Descola 2011	Descola, P. (2011). 'Human Natures.' *Quaderns* 27: 11–25.
Donegan 1993	Donegan, P. (1993). 'Rhythm and Vocalic Drift in Munda and Mon-Khmer.' *Linguistics of the Tibeto-Burman Area* 16(1): 1–43.
Ekka 2012	Ekka, A. (2012). 'Some Interesting Alcoholic Beverages among the Tribal Communities in Chhattisgarh, India.' *International Journal of Pharmaceuticals and Bio-Sciences* 1(4): 353–59.
Elwin 1955	Elwin, V. (1955). *The Religion of an Indian Tribe*. Bombay: Oxford University Press.
Ethnologue	Lewis, M.P., G.F. Simons, and C.D. Fennig (eds.). (2015). *Ethnologue: Languages of the World*, 18th edition. Dallas, Texas: SIL International. Online version, <http://www.ethnologue.com> (accessed 10 August 2015).
Gowtham Shankar 2007	Gowtham Shankar, K.J.N. (2007). 'Tribal Indigenous Knowledge – Its Relevance for Endogenous Development (With Reference to Primitive Tribal Group).' *Adivasi* 47(1–2): 111–14.
Guha et al. 2012	Guha, R., N. Sundar, A. Baviskar, A. Kothari, N. Pathak, N.C. Saxena, S. Lélé, D.G. Roberts, S. Das, K.D. Singh and A. Khar. (2012). *Deeper Roots of Historical Injustice. Trends and Challenges in the Forests of India*. Washington, DC: Rights and Resources Initiatives.
Harrod Buhner 1998	Harrod Buhner, S. (1998). *Sacred and Herbal Healing Beers. The Secrets of Ancient Fermentation*. Boulder, CO: Siris Books.
HJ	Yule, H. and A.C. Burnell (1903). *Hobson-Jobson. A Glossary of Colloquial Anglo-Indian Words and Phrases, and of Kindred Terms, Etymological, Historical, Geographical and Discursive*. New edition, William Crooke (ed.). London: J. Murray.
Jena 2008	Jena, M. (2008) 'Food Insecurity among Tribal Communities of Orissa.' *Economic and Political Weekly* 43(6): 18–21.
Jena, K.M. et al. 2006	Jena, K.M., K.S. Murty, K.K. Patnaik, K. Seeland and P. Pathi. (2006). *Forest Tribes of Orissa. Vol. 2: The Kuttia Kondh*. New Delhi: DK Printworld.
Latour 2014	Latour, B. (2014). 'Another Way to Compose the World (Executive Session of the AAA Annual Meeting, Chicago, November 23, 2013).' *Journal of Ethnographic Theory* 4(1): 301–07.
Mahapatra 2011	Mahapatra, B. (2011). *Development of a Primitive Tribe. A Study of Didayis*. New Delhi: Concept Publishing Company.
Mohanty and Paikaray 2009	Mohanty, S.C. and B.K. Paikaray. (2009). 'Impact of Deforestation in Tribal Life and Livelihood: A Case Study of the Lanjia Saora of Puttasing.' *Adivasi* 49(1): 52–75.
Nanda et al. 2006	Nanda, S., K. Mishra and B. Mahapatra (2006). 'Substance Abuse amongst Adolescent Girls of Donghria Kondhs, a Primitive Tribe in Orissa.' *Indian Journal of Preventive and Social Medicine* 37(1–2): 49–54.

Nayak 2014	Nayak, J.K. (2014). 'A Case Study on Factors of Influencing Protective Health Ecology for Alcoholism among the Hill Bonda Tribal Group of Odisha.' *Man in India* 94(4): 555–71.
Padel et al. 2013	Padel, F., A. Dandekar and J. Unni. (2013). *Ecology, Economy. Quest for a Socially Informed Connection*. Delhi: Orient BlackSwan.
SCSTRTI	Scheduled Castes & Scheduled Tribes Research and Training Institute, Bhubaneswar (2009). 'Quick Impact of Assessment on Implementation of ST and Other Forest Dwellers (Recognition of Forest Rights).' *Adivasi* 49(2).
Seeland 1997	Seeland, K. (1997). 'Indigenous Knowledge on Forests in a Cross-Cultural Perspective'. In Seeland, K. (ed.), *Nature is Culture. Indigenous Knowledge and Socio-Cultural Aspects of Trees and Forests in Non-European Cultures*, pp. 101–12. London: Intermediate Technology Publications.
Sekar and Mariappan 2007	Sekar, S. and S. Mariappan. (2007). 'Usage of Traditional Fermented Products by Indian Rural Folks and IPR.' *Indian Journal of Traditional Knowledge* 6(1): 111–20.
Steinkraus 1996	Steinkraus, K.H. (1996). *Handbook of Indigenous Fermented Foods*. New York: Marcel Dekker.

Chapter 10

Rice and Rice Culture: Cultivation and Worship of a Divine Plant in Western Odisha

UWE SKODA[1]

British anthropologist Edward E. Evans-Pritchard noted: 'As every experienced fieldworker knows, the most difficult task in social anthropological fieldwork is to determine the meanings of a few key words, upon an understanding of which the success of the whole investigation depends' (cited in Needham 1963: viii–ix). This dictum certainly holds for categories across different societal domains, but food – being 'a basic need and a basic pleasure' (Harriss-White 1994: 2) – ranks often if not always among the most significant key categories (see Berger 2007).[2]

As in other parts of Asia (Hill 1977; Mintz 1994; Ohnuki-Tierney 1993) rice is not just the staple food of millions of farmers, but, I argue in this chapter, is one such 'key category,' arguably the most important one, that provides access to what I call a Western Odishan 'rice culture.' Accordingly, one aim of this chapter is to make the multiple distinctions in relation to land, paddy and most importantly rice more visible. Its various subcategories, as distinguished by the people of Odisha, are as complex as the practices and methods of cultivation I only learned to differentiate in the course of my research among farmers of Western Odisha, primarily belonging to the Aghriā caste.[3]

1 Uwe Skoda is Associate Professor of India and South Asia Studies, Department of Global Studies, Aarhus University (Denmark).

2 Berger (2007) provides a comprehensive overview of anthropological research on the links between food and society broadly, as well as of debates on food in India in particular.

3 The classifications of rice and data regarding rice cultivation, as well as the rice rituals presented here, are based on eighteen months of field research carried

However, to cultivate and eat rice is far more than simply a necessity to live, i.e. the social dimension of food cannot be underestimated (Douglas 1997). Rather, rice – standing in a synecdochic relationship with food as such – might in fact be best understood as a 'total social fact' (Mauss 1990 [1925]). Food and practices around it are often gendered and intrinsically tied to status, hierarchies or dependency. Preparation or consumption may be in- or exclusive (e.g. through commensality) while food has a ubiquitous, almost democratic dimension (Mintz 1994: 108), i.e. everybody is somehow involved in forms of production or at least consumption and may be able to relate to or is affected by the 'backbreaking symbolic load' food is burdened with (ibid.: 103) and which this chapter tries to trace in the case of Aghriā farmers.

To begin with, rice is not only the most important plant in the agricultural cycle, but also a crucial element in life-cycle rituals. In fact, rice is actually tied to the making of a person. As Parry (1985: 613) noted: 'One who eats not only absorbs the qualities of the cook, but also the intrinsic properties of the food itself. In Hindu culture, a man is what he eats. Not only is his bodily substance created out of food, but so is his moral disposition.' In the Aghriā context this is expressed during the feeding of the first rice as a crucial step in the life-cycle believed to be the moment of acquiring a soul. Without rice and its transformative qualities there is no soul and no full social persona formed together with life energy and shadow.

Moreover, as recent research in central eastern India has documented (Gregory and Vaishnav 2003; Otten 2014), rice is a pivotal offering to the gods and is associated with – and in fact considered to be – Lakṣmī (or Mahālakkhī). Extensive epics performed in honor of the goddess celebrate the value of fecundity and fertility broadly. But they may also be understood as allegorical elaborations of the introduction of intensive rice cultivation or of a shift from millet to rice, and thus refer to the

out among Aghriā peasants between 2000 and 2003. This peasant caste gradually migrated into areas and former princely states in northwestern Odisha mainly populated by *ādivāsīs*. They took possession of land, in many cases taking over the roles of village chiefs and tax collectors for the local kings, and initiated intensive plough cultivation, especially of wet rice. Until today, a relatively dominant caste in the region, the Aghriā and other peasant castes have contributed to a transformation of the landscape by clearing jungles and creating new rice fields, as well as playing a central role in the transformation of society by expanding the state and broadening its revenue base, not least from the intensive rice cultivation they introduced.

agrarian history of Middle India located between the rice-growing east and millet-producing west of India (Gregory 2004).

Rice appears to be a medium not only of social but ritual communication and at the same time an embodiment of the divine. Specifically among Aghriās, rice and Lakṣmī together link and synchronize (Iteanu 1999) three important cycles that farmers are concerned with, namely the life-cycle, the annual cycle and the ritual cycle – the last culminating in the month-long celebration of Lakṣmī Pūjā coinciding with the harvest season. The elaborate worship of Lakṣmī Devī clearly identifies her with rice, while the story of Lakṣmī, circulating in Middle India and read out on this occasion, sends out a strong message aptly summarized by Marglin (1985: 180): 'Without Lakṣmī there is no food, no life-sustenance.'

DECODING 'RICE': CATEGORIES

LAND

'Food is a carefully chosen and classified means of social communication and the object of a richly expressive and varied aesthetic.' (Harriss-White 1994: 2; also Mintz 1994: 104) Before we turn to the communicative dimension and the elaborate ritual arrangements involving rice, we need to understand its different categories. Aghriās recognize an impressive number of different types of paddy and rice in various stages of processing. Not only does this confirm the enormous importance of rice in this regional culture, it also bears witness to ways in which language, culture and environment are intertwined. In order to fully comprehend classifications of rice, one first needs to turn to the soil, land and fields.

Aghriā farmers differentiate between three types of soil (*māet*) as seen in table 10.1.

Table 10.1. Types of soil, land and fields.

Balyā māet	***Māet***	***Khalya māet***
• sandy (*balyā*)	• mixed soil	• sticking (*khalya*)
• no cracks when dry	• *māl* and *bernā* land	• cracks when dried up
• *guḍā* land (below)		• capacity to retain rainwater
• *dihi* land (houses)		• *bāhāl* land
worst quality <--> best quality		

In addition, farmers distinguish between four basic categories of land:[4]

(1) *guḍā*: lowest quality land consisting of dry fields and the land at high altitude. Following rain, it is usually dry after a day. *Guḍā* is the cheapest land, used for early varieties of paddy.
(2) *māl*: medium quality land (*māl* is also used as super-category for all kinds of land), i.e. it remains wet after rain for three to four days. It commands a medium price.
(3) *bernā*: also medium quality land, but more valuable than *māl*, it usually stays wet until October if there are occasional showers in the monsoon months. The price is medium.
(4) *bāhāl*: highest quality land of low-lying plains, it usually stays wet until April (the hot season). This type of land has standing water for the longest period after the monsoon and is the most suitable for late varieties of paddy. It is also the most expensive category of land, yielding the highest profit.

Even though this classification produces a hierarchy of fields, the quality is to some extent relative. If there are exceedingly heavy rains, it may be an advantage to have some *guḍā* land too. Nonetheless, while one can expect a yield of around twenty bags weighing 75 kg each of paddy per acre on *māl* land, one can get between thirty and thirty-five bags on *bāhāl* land.

PADDY/RAW RICE: DHĀN

Paddy as a central category is further differentiated into white *dhān*,[5] i.e. paddy that is light brown in color rather than being completely white, and *bagrā dhān* (*bagrā*: red-layered, with red stripes), darker paddy or paddy with dark spots. In ritual contexts, white *dhān* is always preferred. Even more importantly perhaps, *dhān* as a central category is subdivided into *atimotā* ('over-fat'), *motā* ('fat'), *saru* ('small') and *atisaru* ('over-small', sometimes also called *aruā*). The most common varieties in the region are *motā* and *saru* (table 10.2).

4 There is another category known as *khāri* (fertile) land, which refers to one to two acres of land on each side of the village road, which is naturally irrigated via the road at the time of the monsoon. Monsoon water mixed with cow-dung is regarded as especially fertile. Furthermore, the land known as *panku māti* near the hills and mountains is considered to be particularly rich because the water from the hills carries humus and naturally fertilizes the field.

5 White: O. *saphā*, or *dhob*. Often, however, farmers and various classes of agricultural laborers use the English word *white*.

Table 10.2. *Dhān*: category, size and price.

Dhān	**Size**	**Price (in 2002) and quality**
atimotā	biggest	lowest (₹310/€4.15 per bag of 75kg)
motā		
saru	smallest	highest (₹330/€4.42 per bag of 75kg)
atisaru		

There is a correlation between the quality of land, the ripening of rice and the sub-categories of *dhān*, which in turn are linked to value and price (table 10.3). Laborers are usually paid in *motā dhān*, or in *saru* if there is a good harvest. Though agricultural workers might prefer a wage in *atisaru*, landlords would consider it too expensive.

Table 10.3. Relationship between quality of land and cultivation of paddy.

Quality of land	**Category of paddy (*dhān*)**	**Varieties of paddy**
guḍā	only *motā*	early varieties (60–90 days)
māl	*motā / saru*	middle varieties (125 days)
bernā	*motā / saru*	middle varieties (125–35 days)
bāhāl	*atimotā, motā, saru, atisaru*	late varieties (150–60 days)

The types of rice used are either older, or *deśi* (indigenous), varieties (e.g. *kalmā, bhujni, geel-singh*) or modern high-yielding varieties (*sābitri, utkāl prabhā, svarnā*) produced outside the village (table 10.4). Generally speaking, for well-to-do farmers cultivation has more or less completely shifted from *deśi* to modern varieties in recent years.

Table 10.4. Categories of *dhān* and related varieties (early, late etc.).

Category of *dhān*	**Varieties**
atimotā	1009 / *sābitri; sariā dhān* (earliest variety)
motā	*annapūrṇa*
saru	1030 / *utkāl prabhā; kalmā dhān*
atisaru	*bādhsā bhog; gagan ahuiel*

The different varieties of paddy or rice have different ripening periods, the longer ripening period producing the better quality (table 10.5). Nevertheless there are risks associated with paddy requiring longer periods for ripening. For example, late varieties are more difficult to thresh when compared to early varieties, the separation of paddy and chaff being more time-consuming.

Table 10.5. Varieties of paddy and their ripening periods.

Variety	**Name**	**Harvested after**
early varieties	*sariā*	60 days
	hirā	60 days
	annapūrnā	90 days
late varieties	*sābitri*	160 days

SEEDS

The seeds available in the market are classified by the Seed Corporation, a government company. High-yielding seeds are specially protected against fungus and insects. Accordingly, 'nuclear' seeds are the best protected, thus offering maximum harvest, while 'certified' seeds are less protected and consequentially produce less. Seeds are sold in different 'modern' varieties, such as *sābitri*, in four categories. 'Foundation' and 'certified' seeds are the most common, as the higher quality varieties are often considered too expensive. Poorer villagers may not even be able to afford 'certified' varieties and may simply use the older *deśi* seeds that they have produced themselves.

Table 10.6. Seeds: category, age and price.

Seeds	**Age**	**Price (in 2002) per 30 kg**
nuclear	directly from the laboratory	₹3000/€40
breeder	after 1 year	₹900/€12
foundation	after 2 years	₹600–700/€8-9.38
certified	after 3 years	₹300/€4 (formerly ₹400–500/€5.36–6.70)

HUSKED PADDY: CHĀUL

In the neighboring state of Chhattisgarh, or in Madhya Pradesh, certain varieties of paddy are grown principally to be eaten by farmers and their families whereas higher-yielding varieties are usually produced to be sold. Such distinctions are less common in Odisha. Varieties of paddy, such as the *utkāl prabhā*, are valued because of their taste, while others, like *sarnā*, are considered to be higher-yielding, but less palatable in terms of taste. The main categories are as follows:

(1) *aluā* (S)/*aruā* (O): relatively pure variety of *chāul*, principally because it is not parboiled. Two sub-categories can be distinguished:
   (a) a smaller variety traditionally used for rituals to feed the ancestors, such in the case of the preparation of *khiri* (sweet rice) and fried rice;
   (b) a larger one employed to prepare cakes such as *dosā*, *chakel* (S) and *babrā* (S).

   Aruā is traditionally produced with the auxilium of a *ḍhenki* (husking pedal) but nowadays modern mills are used. *Aruā* breaks easily without parboiling and becomes sticky while boiling and thus is relatively more indigestible.
(2) *uṣnā* (S)/*uṣunā* (O): the name is derived from *uṣuneibā* (to bake). This variety is also called *khāibā chāul* in landlord families, as it is eaten daily (*khāibā*). *Uṣnā* is produced by parboiling the paddy with a little water, or by steaming it and drying it in the shade before it is husked like *aluā*. The traditional preparation of *uṣnā* takes up to six or seven days, depending on the outside temperature. As a result of the parboiling, *uṣnā* does not break easily while being husked.
(3) *balkā*: the lowest variety of *chāul*. Its name is derived from *balkeibā* (to boil), indicating that it is produced by parboiling paddy with more water than *uṣnā*. It is dried in direct sunlight for eight to ten hours before husking – and therefore is more yellowish or even brownish. It can be produced within one day and is considered the daily rice for the poor who may not have verandas to dry paddy in the shade.

While the colors of *chāul* indicate a hierarchy – the whiter *chāul* as in case of *dhān* being preferred and considered superior – the value of different kinds of *dhān* is also expressed in their transformation into *chāul*. The higher the quality of *dhān*, the more likely it is to be used in the production of *aruā* and vice versa.

Table 10.7. Relationship between categories of *dhān* and their utilization as *chāul*.

Chāul* \ *Dhān	***balkā***	***uṣnā***	***aruā***
atimotā	yes	no	rarely, if at all
motā	yes (rarely)	yes	yes (only white *dhān*)
saru	no	yes (very common)	yes (only white *dhān*)
atisaru	no	yes	yes (for rituals)

FURTHER TRANSFORMATIONS

Once husked, rice is turned into further derivative products, such as:

(1) *kudha*: the smallest remains of *aruā* after paring, offered to the ancestors as cakes but also used to prepare *papad*.
(2) *bhāt*: rice boiled for the first time as *aluā* or for the second time as *uṣnā* or *balkā*.
(3) *pakhāḷa*: *bhāt* with water (and spices) as a main dish.
(4) *phaklo-liā* (S)/*khai* (O): rice produced by heating paddy (usually *motā dhān*) in a pot already half filled with sand, the rice subsequently being separated with a special sieve-basket (*ghari*).
(5) *murhi* (S), *liā* (S), *muḍhi* (O): *balkā-chāul* instead of paddy heated on sand as above.
(6) *chunā*: rice-powder produced from *aruā-chāul*.
(7) *chuḍā*: boiled rice flattened by *ḍhenki*.

Here too, the quality of *dhān* has an impact on the production of *khai*, *chunā*, et cetera.

Table 10.8. Secondary products of rice and categories of *dhān* or *chāul* used.

Secondary products	**Categories of *dhān/chāul* used**
khai	*motā/aṭimotā-dhān* and often *bagrā-dhān* (big grains are necessary)
murhi	*saru – white dhān*
chunā	*aruā*
chuḍā	all categories of *dhān* except *atisaru* (too expensive)
kusnā (rice beer)	*balkā chāul*
tarpan (rice beer for ancestors)	preferably *aruā chāul*

To sum up this part on the classification of rice including land and paddy, there are several categories of grain that indicate and are imbued with status and wealth. 'Food represents us; it sends our distinctive messages,' as Mintz (1994: 103) stated, and one finds this principle expressed in manifold ways in the case of rice. A few examples may suffice to illustrate this close tie between rice and social stratification. The *aluā/aruā* rice offered to the gods in rituals by Aghriā landlords is explicitly not parboiled, any cooking process would pollute it. Similarly, only landlords and wealthier families have the facilities to produce *uṣnā/uṣunā* at home and tend to avoid the darker *balkā*. Additionally, in Aghriā village interactions it often depends on one's caste background, but also on marital status, whether one is allowed to accept *dhān*, *chāul* or even *bhāt* – rice in its raw, parboiled or boiled form – from another community (Skoda 2005: 551ff), while a in different religious context such as the eating of *mahāpraśād* at the temple of Lord Jagannāth these rules may temporarily be suspended.

RICE IN THE AGRICULTURAL CYCLE: CULTIVATION

While most Aghriā farmers agree that the Hindu calendar begins in the month of Caitra according to the *pāñjji (horoscope)*, they also concur that the agricultural cycle begins with the month of Baiśākh. A third relevant starting point is the month of Pouṣ, when yearly contracts with laborers (*guti*) et cetera are drawn up or renewed. Below is a brief overview of the agricultural cycle with particular reference to rice and its cultivation. Most of these activities scheduled on a monthly basis refer to largely unirrigated fields with one harvest per year, though in some areas two harvests are not unusual. Along with rice, other plants are usually cultivated, such as chilly, mustard, groundnuts, et cetera. These activities keep the farmers busy after the paddy harvest.

Figure 10.1. Harvesting paddy, Sambalpur district, northwestern Odisha, 2001.

Baiśākh (mid-April to mid-May – the marriage season)

1. Collecting cow-dung and taking it to the field as fertilizer
2. Beginning to plough (depending upon the rain)
3. Dry sowing (before the rains but always after ploughing); first sowing on Akṣaya Trutīyā (see below)

Jyeṣṭha (mid-May to mid-June)

1. Collecting cow-dung and taking it to the field as fertilizer
2. Drying of seeds before sowing
3. Ploughing (with the beginning of rain)

Āṣāḍh (mid-June to mid-July – usually the monsoon period)

1. Collecting cow-dung and taking it to the field as fertilizer
2. Ploughing and paddling
3. Wet sowing (after the beginning of the monsoon rain)
4. Growing of small rice plants for transplanting
5. Cleaning sidewalls of rice fields and repairing gaps
6. *Bihuḍā* work (ploughing after sowing)

Śrābaṇ (mid-July to mid-August)

1. Fertilizing the land after paddling and before transplanting
2. Transplanting small rice plants (after paddling and Bihuḍā Pūjā – see below)
3. Pulling up grass in the fields
4. *Bihuḍā* work
5. Arranging rice plants after *bihuḍā*

Bhādraba (mid-August to mid-September – Nuā Khāi or time of eating the first rice)

1. Transplanting if late
2. Checking the water level
3. Checking the rice for fungus and insects
4. Pulling out grass
5. Fertilizing the fields
6. Harvesting the first paddy

Āśbina (mid-September to mid-October)

1. Checking the water level
2. Checking the rice for fungus and insects, and applying fungicides and pesticides
3. Fertilizing the fields
4. End of ploughing and paddling
5. Harvesting paddy (early varieties)

Kārttika (mid-October to mid-November – month for religious merit)
1. Harvesting and cutting paddy
2. Checking the water level (late varieties)

Mārgaśīra (= Mr̥gaśira) (mid-November to mid-December)
1. Harvesting paddy
2. Threshing paddy
3. Watering paddy fields (if necessary)

Pouṣ (mid-December to mid-January – month without religious merit)
1. Harvesting paddy (last month)
2. Threshing paddy
3. Parboiling paddy (*chāul*)

Māgha (mid-January to mid-February)
1. Parboiling paddy (*chāul*)

Phālgun (mid-February to mid-March)
1. Ploughing (if there is rain)

Caitra (mid-March to mid-April)
1. Ploughing (if there is rain)

PLOUGHING

Ploughing is known as *hala dharibā* (*hala*: plough; *dharibā*: to catch) but several kinds are distinguished. When rice is sown, at least three rounds of ploughing are necessary. The first time, after the early rain in Phālgun, Caitra or Baiśākh (rarely up to Jyeṣṭha), is called *uār*. Its date is often decided by an astrologer. The second time, in the months of Jyeṣṭha and Āṣāḍh (after *uār*) is to loosen the fields before sowing and to destroy the grass, is known as *dun*. Finally, the field is ploughed once more after sowing in the months of Jyeṣṭha, Āṣāḍh or Śrāban, when it is called *bun* or *tinpuriā*. Occasionally, the field is ploughed a fourth time, this being called *batar* (or *charpuriā*). This is done for the early varieties (up to 100 days) on *guḍā* and *māl* land, two to three days after the wet sowing (*batri bunā*). The same is true for loosening the soil, a kind of ploughing known as *bihuḍā* that is necessary for the late varieties of paddy, though optional for the early varieties. Until the *bihuḍā* ritual for the village goddess has been performed, no loosening (*bihuḍā*), ploughing or transplanting is allowed. The Bihuḍā Pūjā performed during day-time in the wet season is part of larger cycle of rituals for the village goddess, complemented by the Grām Śrī Pūjā in the hot season (before sowing) and the Niśā Pūjā in the cold season (after the cutting of the paddy) – all of them indicate the aspect of the village goddess as an earth goddess.

Ploughing too is an indicator of income level. Formerly, the number of ploughs and pairs of bullocks used for ploughing was an indicator of the wealth of a family, in the same way that owning a tractor is today. Moreover, there are different types of ploughs, corresponding to the aim of and the animals used for the ploughing. The normal plough (*naṅgala*) varies in size, a larger one being used for the tallest bullocks and a smaller one for ordinary bullocks. A third type of plough is that known as a *bihuḍā naṅgala* or *khuni naṅgala* (*khuni*: murderer). It is the smallest type and is used to loosen (*bihuḍā*) the soil.

All the items necessary for ploughing, namely the plough, the yoke (*jueḍ*), the ploughshare (*luhā*), et cetera, as well as the instruments for levelling the ground before paddling and after ploughing (*kural* and *kapar*), are regarded as male. Women are prohibited from using them. It is tempting to interpret the male instruments as a symbolic counterpart to the female earth.

Another firm restriction regulates the use of a wooden stick or *bhār*, the traditional mode of carrying goods on the shoulder, which is forbidden to women.[6] However, in contrast to other communities, there is no restriction on Aghriā women touching the plough (*naṅgala*). On the contrary, during the ritual of Harli Uāns, women worship the plough and have to touch it. Significantly, the plough is worshiped among the Aghriās, which other communities do not do, neither on Harli Uāns nor on Akṣaya Trutīyā. While touching of the plough is possible for Aghriā women in a ritual context, it is forbidden for them to tie the bullocks or connect the plough to the yoke.[7]

Apart from gender restrictions, ploughing is limited to certain times of the year. It is taboo on Raja Saṅkrānti (13 and 14 June), as the menstruation (*raja*) of Mother Earth (Dharati Mātā) is believed to happen on these days. While the earth is menstruating (*bhuin raja*), ploughing is is considered a crime and is punished by the villagers collectively. This indicates again that the soil is conceived of as female, which is further substantiated by the association of the village land with the village goddess. Another period

6 Though the hoe is also seen as male, women are allowed to use it, e.g. to gather sand from the river or to build or repair the irrigation system in the fields.

7 There are no such restrictions for a tractor, but I never saw a woman driving one.

in which ploughing is prohibited is the fortnight of the ancestors (*pitru pakṣa*), particularly on the ninth and tenth days, on which all female and male ancestors are remembered, on *uāns* (days of the new moon) and on the days of the deaths of recently departed ancestors.

SOWING AND BIHUḌĀ

Sowing is generally regarded as 'throwing' or *bunbār*, and in the case of paddy it is also known as *dhān bunā*. Paddy can be sown before the rain; this is called 'dry throwing' or *kharli bunā*. On the other hand, it can also be done after the beginning of the monsoon, and this is called 'wet throwing' or *batri bunā*. Dry sowing can be done on every type of land, though wet sowing is preferred for land at higher elevations. However, dry sowing is a more risky procedure, as seasonal rains could be delayed. In any case, the first sowing or *muiṭh nebār* (S.) / *muthi nebā* (O.) has to be done on an auspicious day, a Wednesday, after the performance of Grām Śrī Pūjā during which paddy offered by the village headman to the village goddess is subsequently distributed amongst the villagers by the ritual specialist (*kālo*) in order to start a new agricultural cycle.

After sowing, when the water still covers the fields (i.e. the soil is not visible), an additional ploughing, or loosening of the soil, is required, known as *bihuḍā*. Such procedure is intended to reduce the density of rice plants. If the water level is still high enough after the *bihuḍā*, a *kapar* can be used to uproot and break up some varieties of grass, which subsequently decompose in the water and act as a natural fertilizer.

After the *bihuḍā* work, when the soil is loose, another important step takes place. This is known as *baṭiā khelā* (*baṭiā*: big clay clods; *khelā*: to play, to scatter). Clods with rice plants already germinated are taken from the middle of the field, where the majority of plants tend to grow, and replanted along the perimeter. In practice, the farmers, standing ankle-deep in water, use their hands to scoop up loose clods with rice plants from below – they are never pulled out – and throw them into the corners of the field – a rather playful activity. *Baṭiā khela* is performed only when rice is sown in *māl*, *bernā* or *bāhāl* fields and it is sometimes combined with cleansing the field of grass, a procedure known as *laṭā ghichā* ('to pull out grass').

TRANSPLANTING

Transplanting rice, or *jagābār*, is generally done in the case of larger production. It is an expensive technique as more labor is required. While in the case of sowing a field must be ploughed three times, this increases to six or seven times in the case of transplanting. Transplanting should be finished as early as possible, that is by the beginning of August, but this is not always feasible. Farmers know that the later the transplanting, the less the harvest is likely to be, due to insects or fungi. However, transplanting is supposed to be done only after Bihuḍā Pūjā. Until then, the small paddy seedlings (*palhā*) have to remain in the nursery field known as the *palhā ghāri*. It takes fifteen to twenty-one days for the *palhā* to grow sufficiently in order to be transplanted. The seedlings, also regarded as Lakṣmī, can then be picked – a process considered to be the same as killing them (*palhā marā*) – and subsequently transplanted. For enough seedlings to transplant into a field of approximately ten acres, one needs at least 0.2 acre of *palhā ghāri* sown with roughly 3.5 bags (75 kg each) of seeds.

Guḍā land is generally preferred for a *palhā ghāri*, because of its sandy soil from which the seedlings can be removed easily. After removing the seedlings from the *palhā ghāri* and packing them in bundles of roughly sixty seedlings each, they are transported to the pond for a process known as seedling washing (*palhā duā*) or cleaning (*palhā saphā*). Often laborers are paid on the basis of how many bundles they have managed to pack (on average around eighty per person). In some villages, however, they are paid a daily wage.

Early transplantation also entails a risk: grass. If the grass grows too quickly compared to the rice, it has to be pulled out by hand. This results in additional labor, which eventually has an impact on the profit. Cleansing the field of grass before transplanting is called *laṭā bachhā*. A big rake known as *kaḍṭā kapar* is pulled by a tractor, or by bullocks. This is used against the grass, as well as to break up the remaining clods of soil, thus levelling the field.

Before transplanting the seedlings, the soil also has to be paddled to produce the necessary mud. Various instruments, such as a scraper connected to a tractor, or a tractor to which *kej* (metal) wheels have been attached, can be used. Between ploughing and paddling on one hand, and transplanting on the other, there should be one or two days in which the grass destroyed by the plough starts to decompose below the surface and fertilizes the field in a natural way. After two days in the field, this 'fallen' mud (*bāsi kādo*) – which is preferred to the 'fresh' mud (*rukā kādo*) stirred up immediately after paddling – is used to host rice plants. These are placed together in groups of two or three, arranged in rows where each bunch is followed at a short distance (about a span) by another.[8] At the end of the transplanting, laborers usually mark each other's foreheads with a *ṭikā* of mud as a kind of joke. Then a feast is offered to the laborers – particularly seasonal laborers – known as the *kādo chheḍ* ('end of mud'), which traditionally includes non-vegetarian food and even wine.

CUTTING AND TRANSPORTING THE PADDY

Before cutting, the *guras dhāre* ritual, a milk (*guras*) oblation (*dhār*: flowing) followed by an offering of incense and a Lakṣmī Pūjā, is performed. The ritual is performed on a Friday, an auspicious day for new beginnings. A family member, preferably a daughter-in-law, but never a laborer, cuts the first rice stalks. Before the actual cutting, plants may be pressed (*marā*) to one side with a big bamboo-stick (*lāeṭh*). This is necessary if the paddy has fallen to different sides naturally. Cutting is done with a sickle (*dā*), and it is known as *dhān duā*. After this procedure, the stalks of paddy are bound (*bandhibā*) with rope made of straw (*beṇṭiā*) and the bundles of paddy (*dhān*

Figure 10.2. Collecting paddy spikes after the harvest, Sambalpur district, north-western Odisha, 2001.

muṭhiā) are transported to the threshing floor. The transport (*dhān kaḍhā*) may be done by simply carrying (*buhā*) on the shoulder two bundles at the ends of a wooden stick (*suil* – similar to a *bhār*) or by putting them on a bullock cart or trailer.

The remains of the paddy, that is, the spikes left on the ground, are collected by hand – a process known as *dhān kuljā*. This may either be done for the landlord by hired laborers (*butiyā*), or the laborers may do it themselves, if the landlord allows them to take away the spikes. For some landlords it is important to collect the fallen spikes as well because they regard it as disrespectful to leave paddy, i.e. the goddess Lakṣmī, in the field instead of bringing her home – even if this means paying laborers and collecting it may cost more than the actual value of the collected paddy. Thus, the landlords do not view the cultivation of rice from a purely economic perspective.[9] Children and old people may often be deputed to collect the remaining spikes. The spikes that have fallen down while transporting the paddy also have to be collected. When the bundles of paddy reach the threshing place, they are placed in different stacks (*khari karibā*) according to the variety of the rice.

On the last day of cutting (*chheḍ*, 'end'), usually a Tuesday, the laborers receive a bonus payment known as a *chuḍā chitkā*, which consists of flattened rice (*chuḍā*), *khai* and molasses. Some people consider this to be *praśād*, that has been offered to god, even though it does not follow any ritual performance. However, the last cutting of paddy is usually done in a particularly joyful atmosphere, with laborers calling out the names of gods, such as Jagannāth, while transporting the paddy.

THRESHING AND WINNOWING

The paddy is spread on the threshing floor (*khalā*) in the morning. The quantity of paddy to be threshed in one go is known as *paer*, while the threshing procedure is known as *dhān maḍā* or *madāibā*. Before the threshing commences, some water mixed with *tulasī* (*Ocimum tenuiflorum* L.), often with a little piece of gold placed in it, is sprinkled (*paer jhiṭā*) over

8 Often seasonal laborers are hired, and occasionally landlords complain that they are trying to cheat by increasing the distance between the rice plants.

9 Ohnuki-Tierney (1993: 28) also mentions cases of urban Japanese arguing against the import of rice, which actually works 'against their own economic interests,' indicating that the value of rice cannot be measured in purely economic terms.

the paddy to purify the threshing floor. A young girl is expected to perform this task. The rationale of the ritual is not just purification but an attempt to get rid of the evil eye and the *motiā* (supernatural beings who are believed to steal paddy). This is done by drawing a line with coal powder around the *paer.*

The paddy is then loosened (*tali dharā*) before the tractor rolls over it, or before bullocks thresh it by circling continuously around a wooden post (*merkhuṇṭ*) at the center of the threshing floor. Occasionally, a wooden roller (*ghuḍ ghuḍi*) pulled by bullocks is also used. In between, the rice is loosened again and turned around (*dhān jhāribā*) either by hand or using an instrument called a *karālī*, a small blunt sickle with a long stick. The paddy is threshed again and again, and subsequently the straw (*puāl*) is separated from it and bundled up, a process known as *puāl biḍā*.

To separate the remaining straw from the grain, the paddy is swept with special brooms (*bāḍhun*). In any other context the sweeping would be an insult to the Goddess Lakṣmī, but on the threshing floor (*khalā*) this is allowed. In some cases laborers walk barefoot through the grain on the floor to turn it around for extra drying, if necessary. The remaining blades of straw are separated by pressing the paddy through a bed (*khaṭ* – a wooden structure with ropes functioning as a sieve), a procedure (*dhān galābār*) that permits the filtering of grain and chaff.

Figure 10.3. Threshing paddy, Sambalpur district, northwestern Odisha, 2001.

The winnowing stage (*dhān dhukā*) – a process aiming at separating the chaff from the grain – commences in the afternoon. Traditionally, winnowing baskets (*kulā*) are used, but in recent years fans have replaced these. The paddy is often winnowed twice to get rid of all impurities. There are two types of chaff: (a) *cherpeṭiā* is a mixture of chaff with a little remaining paddy, which is usually fed to cattle; (b) *pol* is the chaff proper, used in constructing mud houses, or simply thrown on the compost heap. *Cherpeṭiā* has a little more value than *pol*, which is completely deprived of grains. While winnowed, paddy grain or *dhān* falls directly to the ground, whereas *cherpeṭiā* – not as heavy as paddy – falls at a slight distance, and *pol*, lighter than both *dhān* and *cherpeṭiā*, is blown even further away.

MEASURING AND STORING PADDY/RICE

The smallest unit used to measure paddy, or *chāul*, is known as *pā*, a little less than ¼ of a kilogram. Two *pā* fit into one *mān* (c. 425 g), and two *mān* form a *tāmi* (c. 850 g). However, sometimes different standards are used for measuring rice and for ritual purposes, the unit measure in the latter

Figure 10.4. *Mān* measuring container made of bell metal, decorated with elephant – also considered Lakṣmī's *bāhan* or divine carrier, Sambalpur district, northwestern Odisha, 2001.

case being slightly smaller than a *mān*. A *tāmi*, also called a *ser*, is usually produced of brass or bell metal, while a *kaṭhā* is made of tin. Twenty *tāmi* form a *khandi* (12.5 kg).

Paddy is also measured and weighed using special baskets called *dasmaniā*. One *dasmaniā* contains ten *mān*. On the threshing floor, *dhān* is measured using a basket known as a *tupā*. The *tupā* is a rectangular basket that has four leather applications on the lower side. These are produced by a *camār*, a member of a class of leather-workers, who receives some paddy for his service.

The next unit is known as *purug*. The smaller *purug* measures 8 *khandi* and can hold one quintal of rice, whereas a larger one corresponds to 24 *khandi* (8 small *tupā*), and the largest is equal to 34–35 *khandi*. Such a big *purug* is therefore equivalent to eight big *tupā* and can hold over four quintals of rice. The *purug* is used not only to measure rice, but to store it. It is usually a round container made of straw ropes (stabilized by clay) and stands on a wooden platform as a protection against rats and other animals. The *purug* is also used in the ritual of "selling" or "throwing away" children, as elaborated elsewhere (Skoda 2007).

Another way to measure and store paddy is by using bags, each one containing around 75 kg (in the case of a small *tupā*, two *tupā* = one bag). Roughly six bags would fill the biggest *purug*. Apart from the *purug*, paddy is kept in the house in a *kuṭhi* (Odia: *koṭhi*). Often a *dhān ghar* – a room used to store paddy in the house – is subdivided into smaller chambers (*kuṭhi*), each holding a different variety of rice. In the past, due to the fear of drought and fewer opportunities to sell the grain, paddy would be sold only after the following year's harvest. Nowadays it tends to be sold soon after the harvest.

Table 10.9. Measuring units and their approximate weight.

Unit	**Weight in g/kg**
pā	~ 220 g
mān	~ 425 g
tāmi, kaṭhā, ser	~ 850 g
khandi	~ 12.5 kg
tupā	~ 37.5 kg (= 3 *khandi*); ~ 60 kg (= 4.8 *khandi*)
bag	~ 75 kg
purug	~ 100 kg (= 8 *khandi*); ~ 300 kg (=24 *khandi*); ~ 425 kg (= 34 *khandi*)

APOTHEOSIS: LAKṢMĪ AND RICE RITUALS

Conversations among Aghriā farmers in the summer months often revolve around agriculture. Before the transplanting of rice in July, their attention tends to focus specifically on the rain, while in August and September their main concern is the possible loss that insects and fungi can cause at this time. A little later in the annual cycle, for example in October, the small talk revolves around harvesting with men asking each other: How much rice has been harvested? Is the threshing already over? What is the price for paddy being paid by different middlemen? At the same time, women are usually busy preparing for ritual worship of the goddess Lakṣmī, who embodies rice and good fortune.

January onwards, the Aghriās are less concerned with agriculture. The marriage season has just begun. Friends and relatives exchange the latest news regarding arranged marriages, newly established relationships or remarkable wedding feasts. Once again Lakṣmī plays a central role, since every bride is considered to be the goddess. This brief sketch already indicates ways in which the annual agricultural cycle, the ritual cycle and the life-cycle are closely intertwined through rice and the goddess Lakṣmī.

Figure 10.5. Worshiping Goddess Lakṣmī accompanied by elephants in front of a heap of paddy, Sambalpur district, northwestern Odisha, 2001.

Though ancestors are also associated with the fields and their blessings are sought for a good harvest, the connection between rice and the Goddess Lakṣmī is even more important. This culminates during Mārgaśīra, when Lakṣmī is worshiped every Thursday (*gurubār*). In addition, the goddess is specially worshiped by Aghriā women on every Thursday that falls on the tenth day of the lunar cycle (this combination is known as Sudasa Brata, the auspicious tenth), on Akṣaya Trutīyā or Nuā Khāi.

According to the annual cycle, Lakṣmī Pūjā commences with the auspicious Akṣaya Trutīyā, a ritual celebrated on the third day (*trutīyā*) of the bright half of the month of Baiśākh. *Akṣaya* means 'never ending,' a reference to the permanent nature of the ritual and its role in the agricultural cycle in general. The first sowing of the year is performed on the auspicious day of Akṣaya Trutīyā. In a special ritual performed before sunrise, the landlord first offers the seeds to the village goddess for her blessing - an act that ideally nobody should witness. In addition, an astrologer is consulted to establish the precise timing of the sowing and the auspicious direction in which the seeds should be sown. Following astrological charts (*pāñjji*), he determines which family member should perform the ritual. The ritual of 'throwing the seeds' or *dhān bunā* is also called *dhān muthi*, with reference to the seven handfuls (*muthi*) of rice that are 'thrown' during the first sowing.

Figure 10.6. Aghriā house shrine decorated for Lakṣmī Pūjā, Sambalpur district, northwestern Odisha, 2001.

Figure 10.7. Detail of house shrine showing *Lakṣmī khatli*, with a bunch of paddy draped in red cloth representing Lakṣmī, Sambalpur district, northwestern Odisha, 2001.

The evening before Akṣaya Trutīyā, a ritual takes place in farmers' houses, usually in a courtyard or in the kitchen, and always facing towards the eastern direction. During this ritual a plough with an iron ploughshare (*luhā*), a yoke (*jueḍ*), a hoe (*koeḍ*), a *tāmi* measuring vessel and a new sowing basket (*burni*) are worshiped. *Mān* or *tāmi* are filled with rice and regarded as Lakṣmī. They are decorated with flowers and painted with a mixture of rice flour and water. In addition, seven handprints are put on the kitchen's eastern wall. Only then can the sowing begin.

Another major step in the ritual cycle is the eating of the new rice, called Nabānna or Nuā Khāi. Nabānna, the Sambalpuri name of the ritual, literally means 'new rice,' or in the extension of *anna* to mean rice as well as food, actually 'new food' – a meaning closer to the Odia name Nuā Khāi, which means 'new eating' (that is, new rice). The equation rice = food is not unique to Odisha, but rather shared with other rice cultures such as in Malaysia (Hill 1977: xv). If possible, the house is painted for the occasion, or at least cleaned, and all family members wear new clothes, all of which symbolizes renewal. Nabānna is celebrated on the fifth day of the bright half of the month Bhādraba, one day after Gaṇeś Pūjā, and can only be performed after Bihuḍā Pūjā. Invitations are sent to all family members, even if the day is already fixed and well known. This is indicative of renewal or reinvigoration of social relationships.

Nabānna coincides with the beginning of the harvest; the first and earliest rice is harvested two to three days before. The earliest variety that is eaten on this occasion is called *sariā dhan*. However, it is not necessary for every family to grow its own *sariā*. The rice should not be ground in an electric mill, but in a traditional mill worked by foot husking-pedals (*ḍhenki*) that have been purified with cow-dung. The *sariā* is only husked and not parboiled. Thus, preferably one eats *aruā-chaul* (not *uṣnā* or *balkā*) together with a particular mixture of rice and curd, sugar, honey, ghee and milk, also called *sariā*.

Women perform a ritual to honor Lakṣmī and also worship Brahmā, Viṣṇu, Śiva, Samlei as a former tutelary deity of the Sambalpur Rajas and and an important regional goddess, a banyan tree, a pipal tree, the rice fields, the *tulasī chaur* (the shrine of the holy basil plant or the Goddess Tulsī) and the cattle barn (*guhāl*). In the village, the temple priest performs a special ritual in the local Śiva Mandir, while the ritual specialist (*kālo*) of the village goddess performs one at her shrine. The whole family is expected to gather on that day, including servants (especially *gutis*). A portion of uncooked rice (*kharchchā*) is offered to the *barttaniā* (barbers, washermen, et cetera, who provide specific services to their patrons). If someone from the family is not able to participate, the ritual eating of the first rice may be delayed until Daśarā. At the beginning of the meal, each person gives him/herself a *ṭikā* (mark) on the forehead. After eating the new rice, younger people pay respect (*namaskār*) to the elders of the village and ask for their blessing.

At least a day or a night before Nuā Khāi, the *kālo* should bring *śiśā* for the doors of the houses. *Śiśā* consists of an ear of rice (*kheḍ/keḍḍā dhān*) wrapped in a *bheluān* (*Semecarpus anacardium* L.f.) leaf which is fixed on a corner of the door. This rice is first offered to the village goddess and then distributed among villagers. Some Aghriā see it as a sign that the goddess has accepted the new rice and received her share. In return, the *kālo* receives sweets or *khai* from the villagers on Nuā Khāi.

The ceremony, along with the rituals associated with the Rāth Jātrā, is considered a very auspicious day to feed a newborn the first rice (*bhāt khuā*, 'eating rice'). A child should eat the first rice circa six months after his/her birth. The role of the mother's brother (*māmu*) during *bhāt khuā* is of the utmost importance: he should be the first to feed the child. At the same time, the *māmu* is expected to offer his nephew (*bhanjā*) gifts such as sweets, money and, if he is financially well off, some gold jewelry. He will also hand over a plate made of a special bronze (*kansā*), or in rare cases of silver or gold. Some Aghriā call these gifts *māula bhār*, thus associating them with the gifts a mother's brother presents on the occasion of his sister's child's wedding. This reflects the important relationship between *māmu and bhanjā* in the Aghriā life-cycle. When feeding the child, the *māmu* should say something like: 'Every day you should receive as much nectar (*amṛta*) as possible. Every day, five fingers should go to your mouth (i.e. you should always have enough to eat). My nephew (*bhanjā*) / my niece (*bhanji*) should get sweet rice like this every day.' Other relatives may then repeat the feeding and also offer some money or jewelry. The importance of eating the first rice is also demonstrated by the fact that children are not brought before gods till this ceremony is performed. In particular, they should not be brought before Lord Jagannāth. Perhaps even more importantly, some Aghriā believe that a child receives his soul (*ātman*) while eating the first rice offered by the *māmu*.

While the eating of the first rice represents an important point in the life-cycle, and more generally eating the new rice is important in the annual cycle, it is the Lakṣmī Pūjā performed every Thursday in the month of Mārgaśīra that represents the climax of the rice worship. Women begin to set the arrangements for the ritual every Wednesday. These preparations include the binding of flower garlands and the procuring of water lilies (*kain*), which replace the lotus flowers normally associated with Lakṣmī but more difficult to obtain in the area. On top of each door frame, and in particular at the entrance of the house, ten mango leaves are hung on a thread.[10] Moreover, the throne (*khatli*) of Lakṣmī is carefully cleansed, just like the *tulasī chaur* and the rest of the house. If possible, the house is also painted, and all places for the rituals, including the entrance to the house (*khoel*) and the threshing floor, are purified with cow-dung.

Auspicious images and symbols called *jhoti* are drawn on the threshing floor (*khalā*), at the entrance of the house and in the *pūjā ghar* (room). The favorite symbols are the lotus, the conch, fishes, and footprints of cattle and of the goddess herself. The latter always lead into the house. On the inside, geometric and circular sketches are more common. These are drawn by women using a mixture of rice flour and water. Sometimes more articulate *jhoti* can be appreciated, some with sixteen footprints of the goddess (*solā kathi*). Lakṣmī should be worshiped with the *chāul* (*aruā*) of the current crop, which has been ground the day before the ritual. A

10 The number ten is considered Lakṣmī's number, while mango leaves are generally seen as pure and auspicious.

meṇṭa or bunch of bright ears of rice (*saru* or *atisaru*) tied together, occasionally wrapped in a red cloth, is placed on Lakṣmī's altar, often on top of a *mān* filled with paddy. Though this *meṇṭa* resembles a broom, it is a ritual implement used by the daughters-in-law of the house, an indicator of the bond between Lakṣmī and brides. This altar arrangement, but also the subsequent worship of the paddy stacks next to the threshing floor, echo ideas of another rice culture further east of India: 'rice among the Japanese is more than an offering to the gods for consecration; every grain of rice *is* a god' (Ohnuki-Tierney 1993: 61–62), or rather goddess in this context.

Special provisions must be observed before and during the ritual. On the Wednesday preceding the *pūjā*, ghee should be used instead of oil. In addition, only the consumption of *aruā chāul* is allowed. Non-vegetarian food is strictly prohibited. On Thursday nothing should be cooked directly in the fire (for example, sweet corn or *khai*), and *murhi* must not be eaten. It is however permitted to boil food in water. The rules for brides and newly married women are particularly strict on this day, and they are always expected to eat after their families and husbands. Women should not use combs and may tie their hair only loosely in a knot[11] and, some say, cotton

Figure 10.8. Women drawing *jhoti* on the threshing floor, Sambalpur district, northwestern Odisha, 2001.

11 In most cases, women wash their hair on Wednesday because there is not enough time for a full hair wash early the next morning.

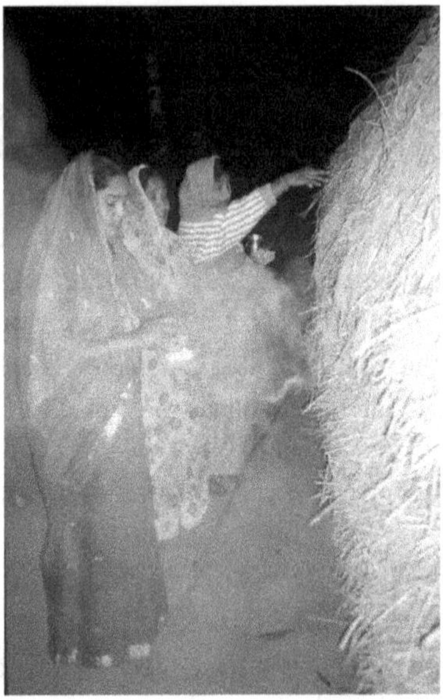

Figure 10.9. Lakṣmī Pūjā: women worshiping Lakṣmī in the form of paddy on the threshing floor, Sambalpur district, northwestern Odisha, 2001.

should not be cut. Aghriā also stress that parents should not beat their children and that there should be no arguments in the house, which is supposed to be filled with harmony.

On the day of Lakṣmī Pūjā, women take an early bath before sunrise, usually around three in the morning. They wear predominantly white clothes[12] and perform a first ritual at the entrance (*khoel*) of the household to invite in Lakṣmī, who is believed to wander around at night. The goddess is welcomed as an auspicious guest who brings wealth. At the entrance, *dhūpa* (incense), *dīpa* (light), a ritual seat (*kalas*) and flowers are offered to the goddess on the *jhoti*. The auspicious sounds of a gong and conch-blasts accompany the ritual, and often women produce the characteristic *hulhuli* sound while the goddess's painted footprints are decorated with *ṭikā*, raw rice and flowers.

After the goddess has been invited in this way, a first ritual takes place in the *pūjā* room. In many families, one of the daughters-in-law reads throughout the rituals passages from a text entitled *Mārgaśīra Māsa Mātā*

12 The clothing is never completely white like the saris of widows, but has light patterns such as small blue flowers.

Mahālakṣmī-nka Gurubār Brata, in which the goddess is first called by using her various names: Lokmātā (Mother of the People), Ṭhākurāṇī (a name often used for village and earth goddesses), Mahāmāyā (the Great Mother, a title associated with Durgā) or Mahālakṣmī. Often handwritten copies of the text circulate on this occasion. These are linked to or are considered part of the *Lakṣmī Purāṇa*, a work ascribed to the poet Balarām Dās (sixteenth century). The story describes Goddess Lakṣmī as roaming around to observe rituals in her honor. In fact, she finds that many people neglect her worship while in the house of a *caṇḍāla* (low/impure caste) a dedicated woman is regularly doing her service, thus obtaining the goddess's blessing. Upon returning home to her husband, Lord Jagannāth, and her elder brother, Balabhadra, Lakṣmī is confronted for visiting the house of a so-called untouchable lady. At the behest of Lord Balabhadra she is thrown out of the temple by her husband. Subsequently, however, Lakṣmī takes revenge by reducing Lord Jagannāth and Lord Balabhadra to the status of starving beggars since without Lakṣmī's presence there is no food. Eventually the brothers realize their mistake and Lakṣmī returns, on condition that she can be worshiped in every household.[13]

The story clearly links Goddess Lakṣmī to cooking and harvest and expresses that the 'power of women is the power of life and it is non-hierarchical' (Marglin 1985: 181). Lakṣmī is presented as 'the feeder and sustainer of life' (ibid.: 175), while Lakṣmī's revenge might bring out a tinge of resistance against male dominance or discrimination on the basis of social hierarchies of purity. Access to the goddess is therefore generally open to everybody and she can bless devotees from all social strata. Lakṣmī's story and its reading run parallel to the wider performance of Lakṣmī Pūjā – each enforcing and lending credibility to the other.

The *Mārgaśīra Māsa Mātā Mahālakṣmī-nka Gurubār Brata* text not only tells devotees about Lakṣmī's immense power but serves as a manual for worship describing what should and should not be done to please the goddess. Accordingly, after a seat (*āsana*) and a bath (*śuddha jalasnāna*) are offered, followed by *pañchāmṛt* (a mixture of curd, milk, ghee, honey and molasses), symbolic clothes (*bastra upabastra*), garlands of flowers (*puśpamālā*), ornamental lotus flowers (*alankāra padmaphul*) and fragrant sandalwood (*candan*). Ten lights on small chandeliers are lit, incense is burnt and, once again, the sound of the gong and the conch resonate along with women's *hulhuli*. As prescribed in the text, two radishes and two sugarcane plants are also presented. In front of the domestic shrine ten kinds of fruits are

13 For a larger version of the text see also Marglin (1985: 175ff).

offered – indicating abundance – and later eaten as *praśād*.[14] The food, i.e. boiled rice (a crucial gift) but also vegetables that have been prepared in the meantime, is offered at the shrine ten times (ten being the number associated to the goddess).[15] Animal sacrifices are absent. The arrival (*āgamana*) of the goddess is then praised with a cascade of flowers (*puṣpāñjalī*). Lakṣmī is respectfully saluted (*praṇām*) and a prayer for forgiveness (*kṣamā prārthanā*) is uttered, along with the reading of *Mārgaśīra Māsa Mātā Mahālakṣmī-nka Gurubār Brata* (*Lakṣmī Purāṇa*).

After this ritual, sweets and other dishes are prepared in the kitchen for the goddess. Sweets such as *manda* or dumplings filled with coconut and fried with ghee are very popular on this occasion. Ten sweets or other food offerings (*neibedya*) are presented to the goddess in another ritual which includes *dhūpa*, *dīpa* and *hulhuli*. Tulsī is venerated using the same ritual objects, and another short ritual takes place directly on the threshing floor on the *jhoti*. Water is sprinkled before flowers while *duba* grass (Skt. *dūrvā*; *Cynodon dactylon* [L.] Pers.), *buro* leaves (Skt. *badara*; *Ziziphus Mauritiana* Lam.), *anla/aonla* leaves (Skt. *āmalaka*; *Phyllanthus emblica* L.) and *dhān* are placed there. Lamps (*dīpa*) and incense (*dhūpa*) are circled over rice stacks, around the threshing floor, and are subsequently worshiped with flowers, milk, *chāul and pañchāmr̥t*. Since rice is Lakṣmī, the stacks are marked with *ṭikā* and *chanda bindu* (the shape of a new moon with a dot) using vermilion (*sindhur*). Additional *ṭikā* placed on the footprints of the goddess are meant to lead her back into the house.

CONCLUSION

Rice (*anna*) in Odisha is not just a plant turned into secondary products. It is food par excellence. Festivals such as Nabānna/Nuā Khāi do not just celebrate the eating of new rice after the harvest, but 'new food' as such. The child's first eating of solid food, called *annaprasana*, is synonymous with eating the first rice, and rulers were, and occasionally still are, respectfully addressed as *annadata*, that is nurturers or 'breadgivers.'

14 Though fruits can vary (e.g. pomegranate, banana, guava, papaya, apples, oranges, sugarcane or coconut), they are expected to be of ten different varieties.

15 This does not necessarily mean that ten different types of food are required. Usually one notices ten offerings of the same dish, which may be *khiri*, *dāl*, spinach (*bhāji sāg*), tomatoes, curry, *aruā-chāul* (*atisaru*) or 'cakes'/*piṭha* (each prepared with ghee).

The different rice categories and semantic distinctions, as well as the agricultural practices discussed here, show the extensive knowledge of Aghriā and other farmers in Odisha, and emphasize the centrality of rice in the local culture. But the importance of rice goes far beyond mere nutrition. Rice as a *total social fact* combines a variety of transcendent societal dimensions in domains such as agriculture, economy, religion and kinship. Rice unites and synchronizes different cycles. The Aghriās believe that children receive their soul with the eating of the first rice. A particularly auspicious time for the feeding of the first rice is Nabānna, that is the ritually marked eating of the new rice that is celebrated every year.

In the rice culture of Odisha, the production and consumption of rice is intrinsically linked to the divine sphere. The village goddess (or Grām Śrī) associated with earth and territory is clearly involved. Every season relevant for farmers cultivating rice also has a ritual for Grām Śrī; e.g. the Grām Śrī Pūjā itself in the hot season performed before sowing, the *bihuḍā* ritual in the wet season before loosening the soil and transplanting rice, and the *nisa* ritual in the cold season after cutting the paddy. Each major agricultural stage associated with rice cultivation is thus performed with the blessing of the village goddess. However, Grām Śrī is not the only goddess worshiped during the production. Lakṣmī is primarily tied to the cultivation of paddy/rice and its subsequent agricultural processes.

Religious, agricultural and life-cycles are first and foremost synchronized through Goddess Lakṣmī as the central symbol. Lakṣmī is identified with rice as staple food, but also with the bride – marriage being the most crucial rite in a life-cycle. Such phases are intertwined through activities and restrictions on Thursdays, i.e. Lakṣmī's day. It is not only that the worship of the goddess is regularly scheduled on 'her' day, but – as stated by informants – paddy should never be sold on Thursdays and a bride should never be sent to her in-laws on a Thursday either. Rice, or broadly food, tells us 'not only how people live but also how they think of themselves in relation to others' (Ohnuki-Tierney 1993: 3) – humans as well as deities.

REFERENCES AND ABBREVIATIONS

O. = Odia S. = Sambalpuri Skt. = Sanskrit

Berger 2007 — Berger, P. (2007). *Füttern, Speisen und Verschlingen. Rituale und Gesellschaft im Hochland von Orissa, Indien*. Berlin: Lit.

Douglas 1997 — Douglas, M. (1997). 'Deciphering a Meal.' In Counihan, C. and P. Van Esterik (eds.), *Food and Culture. A Reader*, pp. 36–54. London: Routledge.

Gregory 2004 — Gregory, C.A. (2004). 'The Oral Epics of the Women of the Dandakaranya Plateau: A Preliminary Mapping.' *Journal of Social Sciences* 8(2): 93–103.

Gregory and Vaishnav 2003 — Gregory, C.A. and H. Vaishnav. (2003). *Lachmi Jagar. Gurumai Sukdai's Story of the Bastar Rice Goddess*. Kondagaon: Kaksad Publications.

Harriss-White 1994 — Harriss-White, B. (1994). 'Introduction.' In Harriss-White and Hoffenberg (1994: 1–26).

Harriss-White and Hoffenberg 1994 — Harriss-White, B. and R. Hoffenberg (eds.) *Food. Multidisciplinary Perspectives*. Oxford: Blackwell.

Hill 1977 — Hill, R.D. (1977). *Rice in Malaya. A Study in Historical Geography*. Kuala Lumpur: Oxford University Press.

Iteanu 1999 — Iteanu, A. (1999). 'Synchronisations among the Orokaiva.' *Social Anthropology* 7(3): 265–78.

Marglin 1985 — Marglin, F.A. (1985). *Wives of the God-King. Rituals of the Devadasis of Puri*. Delhi: Oxford University Press.

Mauss 1990 — Mauss, M. (1990 [1925]). *Die Gabe. Form und Funktion des Austauschs in Archaischen Gesellschaften*. Frankfurt/M.: Suhrkamp.

Mintz 1994 — Mintz, S. (1994). 'Eating and Being: What Food Means.' In Harriss-White and Hoffenberg (1994: 102–15).

Needham 1963 — Needham, R. (1963). 'Introduction.' In *Emile Durkheim and Marcel Mauss's Primitive Classification*. Chicago: University of Chicago Press.

Ohnuki-Tierney 1993 — Ohnuki-Tierney, E. (1993). *Rice as Self. Japanese Identities through Time*. Princeton: Princeton University Press.

Otten 2014 — Otten, T. (2014). 'The Pat Gurumai and the Communication with Gods and Gardeners: The Epic Bali Yatra – a Preliminary Sketch.' In Otten, T. and U. Skoda (eds.), *Dialogues with Gods. Possession in Middle India Rituals*, pp. 247–76. Berlin: Weissensee Verlag.

Parry 1985 — Parry, J. (1985). 'Death and Digestion: The Symbolism of Food and Eating in North Indian Mortuary Rites.' *Man (NS)* 20(4): 612–30.

Skoda 2005 — Skoda, U. (2005). *The Aghria. A Peasant Caste on a Tribal Frontier*. Delhi: Manohar.

Skoda 2007 — Skoda, U. (2007). 'Children Sold and Thrown Away: Temporary Identifications in a Converging Tribal and Caste Society.' In Malinar, A. (ed.), *Identities in Time. Concepts and Practices*, pp. 157–84. Delhi: Manohar.

Chapter 11

Agriculture, Floriculture and Botanical Knowledge in a Middle Bengali Text

FABRIZIO M. FERRARI[1]

This chapter offers an overview of botanical lore in *Śūnyapurāṇ*, a heterogeneous Bengali liturgical work attributed to Rāmāi Paṇḍit.[2] The text celebrates the god Dharmarāj, or Dharma Ṭhākur, through a lengthy cosmogonic narrative and various ritual tracts that define the practice of Dharmapūjā. After a brief introduction about the text, its authorship and date, I will discuss the use of flowers and rice in the worship of Dharmarāj in three of its sections: the plucking of flowers (*puṣpatolān*); the birth of paddy (*dhānyer janma*), which includes the popular tale of the farming (*kṛṣak*) Śiva, and the auspicious song of the husking pedal (*ḍheṅkīmaṅgal*).

1 Fabrizio M. Ferrari is Professor of Indology and South Asian Religions, Department of Theology and Religious Studies, University of Chester (UK).

2 When citing from Bengali sources I use a modified version of the International Alphabet of Sanskrit Transliteration (IAST) based on the principles formulated by Rahul Peter Das (1984: 66–67). Further to that: (1) toponyms, personal names as well as terms used to indicate religious traditions are given according to the most used acceptance (e.g. Bengal and not Baṅga/Vaṅga; Śiva and not Śib; Vaiṣṇava and not Boiṣṇab); (2) spelling oddities will be noticed by those familiar with Bengali. Passages from the *Śūnyapurāṇ* are cited as they appear in MS material and in the three printed versions. Where there is a discrepancy, this has been noted.

THE *ŚŪNYAPURĀṆ*: AN INTRODUCTION

Since the end of the nineteenth century, with the publication of Haraprasad Śāstrī's *Discovery of Living Buddhism in India* (1897), the *Śūnyapurāṇ* has attracted the attention of a number of scholars, primarily because of its alleged crypto-Buddhist origin. More generally, ŚP has been unanimously presented as the most ancient ritual text of the 'Dharma cult.'[3]

Dharmarāj, or Dharma Ṭhākur, is a solar god indigenous of the Rāṛh region of West Bengal where he is worshiped under a variety of titles. The all-white Dharma is invoked as Nirañjan (Spotless), Nirākār (Formless) and Ādyapati (Primordial Lord). He is Sūrya (the Sun) and Yama (the Lord of the Dead). His aspect overlaps with various forms of the Bengali Śiva, such as Nīleśbar (Blue Lord), Bāṇeśbar (Lord of Arrows), Kṣetrapāl (Lord of the Fields) and the farming (*kr̥ṣak*) Śiva, or Lāṅgaleśbar (Lord of the Plough).

The *Śūnyapurāṇ*, which is written in Middle Bengali using mainly the *paẏār* and *tripadī* meters (but also presenting portions in half-prose), is a combination of mythological, ritual and eulogistic elements reflecting pre-modern Bengali Śaivaism, Tantrism, vernacular religions and, to a lesser degree, Vaiṣṇavism and even Islamicate culture.[4] The Buddhist component evoked by the title (*śūnya* = void) is wanting (cf. Śāstrī 1897, Pāl 1976: 155–65), the only reference to *śūnya* being in the first chapter (*sr̥ṣṭipattan*)[5] where the Lord Nirañjan/Nirākār creates the world ex nihilo on the back of his mount, the owl Ullūk. Further to that, occasional references to Śūnya Yuga (e.g. $ŚP_1$ 74–75, *sandhyapāban*, 14),[6] the age that follows Kali Yuga, are found in the spatial diagram visually rendered during

3 A list of studies on Dharmarāj from the nineteenth century to the first decade of the twenty-first century is given in Ferrari (2010: 24–27).

4 The arrival of Muslims in lower Bengal is vividly reported as a great calamity (*baṛa biṣam gaṇḍagal*) in *Śrīnirañjaner Uṣmā* ('The wrath of Lord Nirañjan,' $ŚP_1$ 140–42), a twelve-verse composition in *tripadī* meter interpolated at the end of ŚP.

5 *Sr̥ṣṭipattan* is the longest chapter of $ŚP_1$ (1–22); it consists of 225 verses in *paẏār* meter.

6 When citing from Bengali sources, I indicate page numbers followed by name of chapter/section (if available) and verses (if numbered).

Table 11.1. The *maṇḍala* of *Śūnyapurāṇ*.

Ages	Satya Yuga	Tretā Yuga	Dbāpar Yuga	Kali Yuga	Śūnya Yuga
Priests	Setāi Paṇḍit	Nīlāi Paṇḍit	Kaṁsāi Paṇḍit	Rāmāi Paṇḍit	Gosāi Paṇḍit
Directions	West	South	East	North	–
Door-keepers (*koṭāl*)	Candra	Hanumān	Sūrya	Garuḍa	Ullūka
Female attendants (*āminī*)	Basuẏā	Caritrā	Gaṅgā	Durgā	Abhaẏā
Followers (*gati*)	400	800	1200	1600	Innumerable
Colors	white	blue	yellow	red	green
Materials	gold	silver	copper	bell-metal	diamond
Doors	Paścim Dbār	Laṅkā Dbār	Udaẏ Dbār	Gājan Dbār	Śūnya Dbār

Note: The word used for female attendant (*āminī*) is a *tadbhava* loanword from Skt. *āmnāyikā*: female ritualist with expertise in a (Tantric) tradition (*āmnāya*).

the Gājan festival[7] as a *mel'ghar* (assembly hall) and, in fact, a *maṇḍala* (see table 11.1).

ŚP exists in three, almost identical, published versions. None is a critical edition. The first was published by Nagendranāth Basu in 1314 BS (1907/08 CE) for Baṅgīẏa Sāhitya Pariṣat. This is primarily excerpted from MS G5424 of the Asiatic Society of Calcutta.[8] Received in 1902 by an anonymous donor, the manuscript – which is reported to be complete – is held under the classification '*Dharma-maṅgal*' and is ascribed to Rāmāi Paṇḍit.

7 The Gājan (possibly from Skt. √*garj*: to roar; to thunder; to produce a loud sound) is the annual celebration of Dharmarāj in the month of Caitra, during the vernal equinox. Currently, the Gājan is mostly known as Śiber Gājan (Śiva's Gājan). It is unclear whether the original Gājan was the apotheosis of Dharmarāj or it did belong to Bengali Śaivism. It is significant that as early as the end of the sixteenth century, in the *Śib'pujā pracār* chapter of Mukundarām's *Caṇḍīmaṅgal*, we find a description of the Gājan, inclusive of its distinctive devotional services (e.g. piercing of the tongue, hook-swinging, loud drumming, etc.), as a ceremony for the worship of Śiva (CM 102).

8 See Basu's notes on the making of the text (*granthakārer paricaẏ*, in $ŚP_1$ 1–17). Basu admits using other (unspecified) material (cf. Śāstrī 1897: 18). Dasgupta notes that: '[...] the original manuscript of Mr. Vasu [= Basu] is not [...] available to the public.' (1946: 461n1)

It is described as: '[...] country made paper (Shreerampur),[9] 13½ x 14¼ inches. Folio 46, lines 13 on a page. Character: Bengali in a modern hand. Appearance, fresh.' The MS (containing 'six lines of Nirañjaner uṣmā') is said to have been 'printed and published by N.N. Base [sic] for Bangiya Sahitya Parishad' (DCBM).

The second version ($ŚP_2$) was published in 1336 BS (1929/30 CE). The core material is substantially the same of $ŚP_1$ although it becomes apparent that the Genesis chapter is regarded as the actual *Śūnyapurāṇ*. The text is preceded by two introductory articles by Muhāmad Śahīdullāh and Basanta Kumār Caṭṭopādhyāẏ, and a preface by Cārucandra Bandyopādhyāẏ, the editor of the volume.

Nearly fifty years later, in 1977, Bhaktimādhab Caṭṭopādhyāẏ republished the text. In his *sūcīpatra* ($ŚP_3$ *ca-ja*), he explains how he has arranged the same textual material used by Basu in four separate sections: '(a) *sr̥ṣṭi pattan* (called *Śūnyapurāṇ*); (b) *saṁjāt paddhati* 1 (*dharmapūjā bidhi o rājā haricandrer dharmapūjā*); (c) *saṁjāt paddhati* 2 (*bāramatipūjā paddhati*);[10] and (d) *dharmapurāṇ*.' To this, he adds an appendix (*pariśiṣṭha*) titled *Śūnyapurāṇ*, also ascribed to Rāmāi Paṇḍit. This is taken from MS G5438 (Asiatic Society, Kolkata), written down in 1117 BS (1710/1 CE) by Arjun Paṇḍit, son of Daẏārām Paṇḍit ($ŚP_3$ 181–82).

AUTHORSHIP AND DATE

Dating ŚP has proved a difficult exercise, and so far an inconclusive one. The text printed in all published versions is a collation of at least three MSS (G5424, G5449, G5438) from different epochs and whose assemblage awaits justification. The title '*Śūnya Purāṇ*' – though appearing in the first line of MS G5424 (*śrīśrīdharmāẏa namaḥ | śūnya purāṇa likhyate |*) – is neither found in any of the colophons of the manuscript nor anywhere else in the text or, to the best of my knowledge, in any other Bengali or Sanskrit source.

9 This is likely to be the Shrirampur village (23.35°N 88.12°E) under the jurisdiction of Purbasthali *thān* (police station) in the Kalna subdivision of the Bardhaman (Burdwan) district.

10 Some material of these two sections is excerpted from MS 5449 of the Asiatic Society (*Saṅgajāt Paddhati*). The text, partly in Sanskrit (in Bengali script) is divided into four parts: (1) sacrifice of the goat (folios 1–5): (2) *mantras* for the worship of Dharma (folios 6–9); (3) four leaves marked 1 to 4 beginning: *atha dharmapūjāvidhi likhyate* (folios 10–13) and (4) ritual directions on Dharmapūjā (folios 14–88).

Jogeś'candra Rāẏ (1338 BS: 72) noted this and argued that Basu crafted the title himself to back up his theory of Dharmapūjā as a relic of Northeastern Buddhism.[11] In fact, Rāmāi Paṇḍit calls his work *Dharmapurāṇ*[12] and *Āgampurāṇ*.[13] The former title is evocative of Maẏūr'bhaṭṭa's *Maṅgal'kābya* (c. twelfth century),[14] often presented as *Dharmapurāṇ* but popularly known as *Hākandapurāṇ*[15] and in all probability the earliest text on Dharmarāj. In view of that, Basu was probably led to conclude that ŚP was just an alternative title for *Hākandapurāṇ* (see *granthabicār* section in Basu's introduction to $ŚP_1$). This conclusion however may be inaccurate. First, none of the works ascribed to Rāmāi make reference to the Lāusen saga, which is core to the Dharmamaṅgal tradition of which Maẏūr'bhaṭṭa is unanimously considered the *ādikabi*, or initiator (hence Ādi Maẏūr'bhaṭṭa).[16]

11 See also Rāẏ's earlier article (1316 BS). Cf. Basu's reply (1316 BS) and Vasu (=Basu) (1911: 109ff).

12 *ḍāk diā bale har jata deb'gane | suniba anādda kathā dharmmar purāne* || $ŚP_1$ 97, *debsthān*, 1.
In the library of Visvabharati University there are two MSS (n. 129 [94 folios] and n. 130 [58 folios]) called *Dharmapurāṇ* and attributed to Rāmāi Paṇḍit (see *bhanitā* in MS 130: *śrīdharmapurāṇ'gā̃thā apūrbba jāhā kathā biracila rāmāñi paṇḍit* ||). MS 129 is dated between 1744 and 1753 and three scribes are recorded: Kuṛārām Paṇḍit (from Gabpur [?]), Kr̥parām Paṇḍit and Gaṇeś Paṇḍit.

13 *rāmāi paṇḍit kahae āgam purāne* || ($ŚP_1$ 107, *muktisnān*, 22b; also ibid. 9b)

14 Bhaṭṭācārya (1998: 730), Sen (1911: 47–48, 55) and Śahīdullāh (1360 BS) agree in tentatively locating Maẏūr'bhaṭṭa in the twelfth century. The printed version of *Dharmapurāṇ* edited by Basantakumār Caṭṭopādyāẏ (1337 BS) is not the original work invoked by most *maṅgal* poets (see below n. 16) (Rāẏ 1338 BS: 66–69 and Dasgupta 1946: 470n.1). Unless new MS material is found, Maẏūr'bhaṭṭa's original *maṅgal'kābya* should be considered lost.

15 See, for instance, Ghan'rām Cakrabartī:
sabe bala hari hari *saṅgīt ārambha kari*
śrabaṇe pātakī tare yāẏ |
hākanda purāṇ māte *maẏūr'bhaṭṭa pathe*
jñāngamya śrīdharma sabhāẏ || DhM^{Gh} 14, I.84.
The name Hākaṇḍa appears to be a toponym designating the place where two legendary events related to Lāusen, the hero of the Dharmamaṅgal sagas, took place, namely his miraculous conception and his resuscitation after self-sacrifice, both at the hand of Dharmarāj.

16 Bhaṭṭācārya (1998: 726–28) has demonstrated that Ādi Maẏūr'bhaṭṭa is mentioned in most Maṅgal'kābyas, including the works of Rūp'rām Cakrabartī (1662–1663), Rām'dās Ādak (1662–1663, or slightly later), Khel'rām Cakrabartī (1692 CE), Ghan'rām Cakrabartī (1711), Sītārām Dās (mid-eighteenth century), Māṇik'rām Gāṅguli (second half of eighteenth century) and Gobindarām Bandyopādhyāẏ (end of eighteenth century).

Conversely, we know that in all Maṅgal'kābyas, where the focus is entirely on Lāusen's *gotra* (clan) and his heroic exploits, Rāmāi Paṇḍit is seldom mentioned (Bhaṭṭācārya 1998: 722–23).[17] Secondly, in the sections making up ŚP (including Arjun Paṇḍit's version) and in *Dharmapūjābidhān*[18] – also ascribed to Rāmāi – there is no mention of Maẏūr'bhaṭṭa,[19] and the texts are never referred to as *Hākandapurāṇ*.

In the absence of the original work of Maẏūr'bhaṭṭa, any attempt to date ŚP should be suspended, although it can be reasonably argued that Rāmāi Paṇḍit lived earlier than the earliest Dharmamaṅgal'kābyas, i.e. the works of Rūp'rām Cakrabartī and Rām'dās Ādak, both composed in 1584 Śaka (1662–1663 CE) (Mukhopādhyāẏ 1960: 235–38), and presumably of the original work of Maẏūr'bhaṭṭa (twelfth century?). I thus tend to concur with Dasgupta when he argues that:

> [...] among the poets of the later times there was the tradition of some liturgical text containing all the details of Dharma-worship and the text of the *Śūnya-purāṇa* in its modern form may represent some confusedly collected portions of the aforesaid text. (Dasgupta 1946: 468)

17 In the *Śāle bhar pālā* of the *maṅgal'kābyas* of Ghan'rām Cakrabartī and Narasiṁha Basu, a priest called Rāmāi – no doubt named after the initiator (*prabartak*) of Dharmapūjā – acts as the ritual advisor of Queen Rañjābatī, the mother-to-be of Lāusen (DhM^{Gh} 33, V.21; DhM^{NB} 53, VI.153). This Rāmāi, who works along with low/impure (*antyaj*) castes like *hāḍi* and *ḍom* assistants and the *ḍom āminī* Sāmulyā, instructs the queen to sacrifice herself to Dharmarāj in order to be blessed with a son. Whether with or without the guidance of Rāmāi, all *maṅgal* poets describe in their *Śāle Bhar Pālā* Queen Rañjābatī performing a series of austerities culminating with *śāl'kā̃ṭā* (or *bā̃ś'kā̃ṭā*): She throws herself on a plank (*pāṭ*) of *śal* wood (*Shorea robusta* C.F.Gaertn.) studded with bamboo (*bā̃ś*) spikes or iron pegs. Impressed by her devotion, Dharmarāj brings her back to life and grants her the boon of a son, Prince Lāusen, Dharma's champion and the rightful heir to the throne of Gauṛ (Mitra 1957: 247).

18 Published by Nanīgopāl Bandyopādhyāẏ (1323 BS), *Dharmapūjābidhān* is excerpted from MS 5438 (Asiatic Society, Kolkata). It is written in Middle Bengali and Sanskrit, and is made of 21 folios divided in three sections: (1) a summary of the various arrangements for *pūjā*, attributed to a devotee called Raghunandan; (2) a detailed *pūjāpaddhati* by Rāmāi Paṇḍit; and (3) an appendix on ritual also authored by Rāmāi Paṇḍit.

19 Cf. MSS 129 (*Dharmapurāṇ*) and 131 (*Dharmamaṅgal*, 52 folios, dated mid eighteenth century) in the library of Visvabharati University. MSS are inclusive of: (1) a section on creation called *Nirañjan'purāṇ* which shows similarities with *sṛṣṭipattan* of ŚP, and (2) ritual tracts ascribed to Maẏūr'bhaṭṭa. In both MSS the *bhaṇitās* confirm Rāmāi as the main author.

Moving to authorship, we know that the name Rāmāi Paṇḍit[20] is appended at the end of almost every section of ŚP and DhPB. Neither work however provides sufficient information to trace an accurate historical profile. Conversely Rāmāi Paṇḍit is highly regarded in a portion of *Yātrāsiddharāẏer Paddhati* (nineteenth century)[21] and before that in the published version of the *Dharmapurāṇ*, a work ascribed to Ādi Maẏūr'bhaṭṭa but in fact a seventeenth century text. In *Rāmāi Paṇḍiter Janma* (DhP 13–21) we learn that Rāmāi was miraculously born under an auspicious asterism in the proximity of Rām'śilātīrtha (hence his name), the son of Paṇḍit Biśbanāth, a devotee of Viṣṇu, and his wife Kam'lā.[22] Rāmāi is predicted a glorious destiny: he will become the first priest of Dharmarāj.[23] After a series of unfavorable events following the death of Biśbanāth, a man ostracized by the rest of the Brahmanical community, Rāmāi is rescued by Dharma Ṭhākur who inflicts leprosy (*kuṣṭha*) or vitiligo (*dhabalakuṣṭha*) on his opponents headed by the authoritative and charismatic sage Mārkaṇḍeya. Following the curse, Rāmāi is acknowledged as Dharma's protégé, and his rivals are miraculously healed.[24]

This event is followed by Rāmāi's initiation by means of which he becomes the first Dharma-priest of the present age. The ritual, still current in Bengal and undertaken by *deẏāsīs* and *pūjākas* as well as consecrated

20 Alt. spelling: Rāmāñi/Rāmāñī Paṇḍit; Rām'dās; Rām'paṇḍit; Dbij Rāmāi; Paṇḍit dbij; Rām Paṇḍit; Paṇḍit Rām.

21 Yātrāsiddhā (or Yātrasiddhi) Rāẏ is the name of Dharmarāj in Maynāpur, where the local tradition looks as Rāmāi as the beginner of a lineage of *ḍom pūjāris*. The section on Rāmāi is found in Bhaktibinode (1313 BS: 84–92) as well as in Basu's introduction to $ŚP_1$ (*granthakārer paricaẏ*).

22 *daś mās daś din pūrṇa yabe haẏ | prasabe kam'lā ek sundar tanaẏ ||*
boiśākhī sit'pañcamī nakṣatra bharaṇī | rabibār śubha yoge prasabe brāhmaṇī ||
(DhP 13)
Cf. Śahīdullāh ($ŚP_2$ 35), who notes that it is impossible to find a Sunday (*rabibār*) on the fifth day (*pañcamī*) of the light (*sita*) fortnight of the month of Vaiśākha under the Bharaṇi asterism (*nakṣatra*).

23 *sarbbaśāstre e bālak supaṇḍit habe | ei śiśu dharmakīrtti jagate charābe ||*
kali ebe haibe yuger adhipati | kalaṅkit tāhāte haibe basumatī ||
bināśiẏā dharaṇīr kaluṣ kālimā | pūrbasam pṛtibī karibe manoramā ||
rāmśilā tīrthe jāt jagat rāmāi | bicār kariẏā nām thuinu rāmāñi ||
yāthā hate dharmapūjā pracār haibe | dharmer icchāẏ śiśu ekhāne udbhave ||
(DhP 15–16)

24 Dharmarāj continues to be worshiped as a protector from eye- and skin-diseases as well as infertility. This appears in few verses of Rāmāi's work ($ŚP_1$ 107, *muktisnān*, 20–22).

sannyāsīs before the beginning of the Gājan, is called *tāmra saṁskār*. It consists of: purification (*adhibās*); wearing the sacred thread (*poitā neoẏā*); applying the sacred mark (*ṭīkā pāban*); and putting on a copper ring and a copper bracelet (*tāmra dhāraṇ*).[25] Interestingly for this chapter, among the various ritual paraphernalia, we learn from ŚP that the branches of selected trees are required, namely: *śimul* (*Bombax ceiba* L., the Silk-cotton tree) and *sāl* (*Shorea robusta* C.F.Gaertn., the Sal tree) (ŚP$_1$ 136; *tāmra dhāraṇ*, 7). The ritual concludes with a *stotra* in (Bengalized) Sanskrit where Dharmarāj, who is also invoked as Nirañjan, is praised as a remover of sins (*pāpa*), pains (*duḥkha*) and obstacles (*vighna*).[26]

Further details of the status of Rāmāi can be extrapolated from ŚP and DhPB. There he acts as the ritualist who directs the complex sacrificial offerings presented by King Hariścandra and his wife Madanā in order to conceive a son (ŚP$_1$ 32–34, *haricandrer dharmapūjā*; 36–38, *dān'patir ghar dekhā*). It has been argued that King Hariścandra may be the only historical character in ŚP, thus permitting a tentative reconstruction of the life of Rāmāi. On this basis, Sen (1924: 358) places Rāmāi between 900 and 980[27] (see also Śahīdullāh in ŚP$_2$ 30–35 and Sen 1975: 29–30), whereas Śāstrī (1897: 10–11) and Vasu (1911: 100) locate him during the reign of Dharmapāla II (eleventh century). Regardless of the actual epoch in which Rāmāi lived, ŚP 'in its present form [...] contains nothing that on linguistic evidence can be considered earlier than the sixteen century' (Ghosh 1948: 77; see also Dasgupta 1946: 400).

Coming back to the hagiographic account of the new Maẏūr'bhaṭṭa, Rāmāi – now an influential member of his community – marries Keśabatī, a girl born from Dharmarāj's feet (DhP 64), who will beget him a son, Dharmadās. In due time, Dharmadās is initiated like his father and marries

25 The rite is evoked in ŚP$_1$ 135–36 (*tāmradhāraṇa*).

26 *pāduke pāduke namaste*
gaganāgaganāpāraṃ paraṃ parameśvaraṃ īśvaraṃ ūrddhamukhaṃ |
taṃ praṇamāmi nirañjan pāpaharaṃ ||
sarvapāpavināśāy sarvaduḥkhaharār ca |
mama vighnavināśāy dharmarāj namohasta te ||
dharma īśasta devānāṃ devatāhitakārakaḥ |
mama vighnavināśāy dharmarāj namohasta te || (ŚP$_1$ 137–38)

27 Sen (1924) has argued that the Hariścandra of ŚP might be: (a) King Hariścandra of Sābhār (in Dhaka district), who reigned in the eleventh century (cf. Laskar 1920 and Bhattasali 1920); (b) a Buddhist chief of the Candra dynasty (tenth century); or (c) the father-in-law of King Gopicandra (Govindacandra) (reigned eleventh century).

Satyabatī, the daughter of Brahmadatta, a local *paṇḍit* (DhP 83).[28] In the years to follow, Dharmadās will have four sons: Mādhab, Madhusūdhan, Satya and Sanātan (DhP 150). Rāmāi's four grandsons will continue the *gotra* of *dharmapaṇḍits* and will disseminate the instructions for Dharmapūjā across Rāṛh.

OFFERING FLOWERS DURING DHARMAPŪJĀ

Rituals such as *puṣpapani*, *puṣpajal* (presentations of flowers and water) or *puṣpāñjali* (showering flowers on the god's image or *mūrti*) abound in works like ŚP and DhPB, and mirror an established ritual pattern.[29] The *puṣpa tolan* ('plucking flowers') section of $ŚP_1$ (28–32), a unit of forty-four verses in the *paẏār* meter,[30] does not limit itself to illustrating ritual procedure but shows remarkable knowledge of floral species (cf. DhPB 126–34; Śib 311–15).

In this section, a *baṛu* (Skt. *baṭu*: young [brahmin] boy) is described while picking flowers from a variety of trees, shrubs and branches for the worship of Nirañjan.[31] The first offering to the Eternal Lord (Anādi Debnāth)

28 In the tradition associated to Maynāpur, Dharmadās marries the daughter of a *ḍom*, a member of a scheduled caste of Bengal popularly perceived as *acchut* (impure, 'untouchable'). This is reflected in the various Dharmamaṅgal'kābyas where the *ḍoms* are portrayed as a warrior community (cf. n. 17 above) assisting Lāusen. The sons of Dharmadās are thus regarded by Bengali *ḍoms* as the beginners of a lineage of *ḍom paṇḍits* that goes back to Rāmāi (Bhaktibinode 1313 BS: 92). According to numerous oral narratives, Rāmāi Paṇḍit himself was a *ḍom*.

29 See RgV III.31. Flowers are mentioned in III.31.164b.

30 The *paẏār*, which is the most common meter in Middle Bengali literature, consists of two rhyming verse-units (*pāda*) separated by a caesura. The first unit contains eight beats and the second six. One should be aware that poets tended to switch from *miśrabṛtta* (when closed syllables are counted as two beats) to *dal'bṛtta* (which reflects actual pronunciation) very often. Also, poems were written to be sung, and discrepancies in prosody were usually corrected during performance.

31 *hāt pātiā nirañjan sṛjilen chiṣṭi* | *pādukā sthāpit karila kūrumar piṣṭi* || $ŚP_1$ 29, *puṣpa tolan*, 10.
The garden described here is reminiscent of Śiva's luxurious flower garden (*puṣpaban*) found in Bengali and Assamese myths and guarded by either the god's sons (Gaṇeśa and Kārttikeya) or his *gaṇas* (Smith 1999: 216, 219). The narrative is also evocative of an episode in Mukundarām Cakrabartti's *Caṇḍīmaṅgal* (aka *Abhaẏamaṅgal*) in which Nīlāmbar, Indra's son, is picking flowers with a

is the heavenly flower (*sbargar puṣpa*), or *pārijāta*.[32] Then the boy enters in the four sectors of the garden (*mālañca*), each pointing at a cardinal direction and each requiring a wicker-tray (*sāji*) and a picker (*ākuṛi*)[33] made of a different material.

Table 11.2. Varieties of flowers listed in ŚP, *puṣpa tolan*.

Bengali name	Sanskrit name	English name	Botanical name
(a) Western sector (*pādas*: 3–11): golden wicker-tray and golden picker.			
padma	*padma* (=*kamala*)	Sacred Lotus	*Nelumbo nucifera* Gaertn.
tulsī	*tulasī*	Holy Basil	*Ocimum tenuiflorum* L.
bak (=*bakphul*)	*āgastya*	Agastya	*Sesbania grandiflora* (L.) Pers.
nāpāli	*naipālī*	Arabian Jasmine	*Jasminum sambac* (L.) Aiton.
siali (=*seālī, śiuli, śephalī, śephālikā*)	*śephālikā*	Night-flowering Jasmine	*Nyctanthes arbor-tristis* L.
kālā kāsānd (=*kāl'kāsandā, kāl'kāsundā*)	*kāsamarda*	Senna	*Senna sophera* (L.) Roxb.
indībar phul (=*indibar*)	*indīvara*	Blue Lotus	*Nymphaea nouchali var. caerulea* (Savigny) Verdc.
aśok	*aśoka*	Ashoka	*Saraca asoca* (Roxb.) J.J. de Wilde
kiṁśuk	*kiṃśuka*	Flame of the Forest	*Butea monosperma* (Lam.) Kuntze
jātī	*jātī*	Jasmine	*Jasminum grandiflorum* L.
dubaṭī (=*dopāṭi*)	*duṣparijatī*	Garden Balsam	*Impatiens balsamina* L.

hook in the Nandan forest, Indra's heavenly garden. After gathering a hundred beautiful and fragrant flowers in his basket, Nīlāmbar begins to prepare for the worship of Śiva. Indra showers the flowers gathered by his son on Śiva's head when a few thorns cut the god's scalp. Śiva initially lets it go but when he is bitten by some ants, he becomes furious (alt. version: goddess Caṇḍī transforms herself in a poisonous stingy ant). Nīlāmbar is summoned by Śiva who curses him to be born on earth as Kāl'ketu, the son of the hunter Dharmaketu. This fulfills the plan of the goddess who wished to turn Nīlāmbar into her first worshiper among mortals (CM 107–19). Mukundarām's *Caṇḍīmaṅgal* is of great importance as one of the few pre-Caitanya *maṅgal* poems and a work of great impact on the later poets of the same tradition.

32 See in this volume, Chapter 1, pp. 5–10.

33 The noun *ākuṛi* is a regional variant of *ā̃kaśī* (Skt. *aṅkuśa*) and indicates a pole with a hook fixed to one of its ends and used for plucking fruits and flowers (and in a different context as an elephant goad).

Bengali name	Sanskrit name	English name	Botanical name
kurubak	*kurabaka*	Porcupine Flower	*Barleria prionitis* L.
karabī	*kāravī*	Black Caraway	*Carum carvi* L.
labaṅg	*lavaṅga*	Cloves	*Syzygium aromaticum* (L.) Merr. & L.M.Perry
kadamba	*kadamba*	Kadamba	*Neolamarckia cadamba* (Roxb.) Bosser
kanak	*kanaka*	Maple-Leaved Bayur Tree	*Pterospermum acerifolium* (L.) Willd.
(b) Southern sector (*pādas*: 12–17): silver wicker-tray and silver picker.			
kaṅgal	*kamala*	Sacred Lotus	*Nelumbo nucifera* Gaertn.
kusum	*kusumbha*	Safflower	*Carthamus tinctorius* L.
raṅgan (=raṅgaṇ)	*raṅgaṇa*	Jungle Geranium	*Ixora pavetta* Andr. or *Ixora coccinea* L.
jhāṭi[34] *(=jhiṇṭī, jhāṭī, jhā̃ṭī)*	*jhiṇṭī(kā)*	Philippine Violet	*Barleria cristata* L.
cāmalī (=cāmeli, cāmelī)	*mālatī*	Jasmine	*Jasminum grandiflorum* L.
gandhali[35] *(=gā̃dā)*	*genduka*	A type of Marigold	*Tagetes erecta* L. or *Tagetes tenuifolia* Cav.
śrīphal	*śrīphala (=bilva)*	Bengal Quince	*Aegle marmelos* (L.) Corrêa
duibaṭī (=dopāṭī)	*duṣparijatī*	Garden Balsam	*Impatiens balsamina* L.
belāl (=bilba)	*bilva*	Bengal Quince	*Aegle marmelos* (L.) Corrêa
toāl (=tamāl, tamālī)	*tamāla*	Egg Tree	*Garcinia xanthochymus* Hook.f. ex T.Anderson
piāl (=piẏāl)	*priyāla*	Buchanan's Mango	*Buchanania cochinchinensis* (Lour.) M.R.Almeida
sāila (=śāl)	*śāla*	Sal	*Shorea robusta* C.F.Gaertn.
ākaṛ (=ā̃kaṛā, ā̃koṛ)	*aṅkoṭa*	Sage-leaved Alangium	*Alangium salviifolium* (L.f.) Wangerin
jāi (=jāti)	*jāti/jātī*	Jasmine	*Jasminum grandiflorum* L.
jui (=yūthī, yūthi, yūi, jūi)	*yūthikā*	Juhi	*Jasminum Auriculatum* Vahl
mārūā (=māṛuẏā, māṛoẏā)	*madhulikā*	Finger Millet	*Eleusine coracana* (L.) Gaertn.

34 BBA cites ŚP$_1$ *puṣpa tolan* 14[a] and identifies *jhāṭi* as either the flower of *kurubak* (see above) or of *jhā̃ṭi* (alt. spell. *jhiṇṭi*), cf. MIB: 249.

35 Cf. BBA (666) where *gandhali* is a local variant of *gandāl* or *gandabhādāl/gandabhāduli*, i.e. the skunkvine, *Paederia foetida* (L.).

Bengali name	Sanskrit name	English name	Botanical name
(c) Eastern sector (*pādas* 18–26): copper wicker-tray and copper picker.			
śrīphal	*śrīphala (=bilva)*	Bengal Quince	*Aegle marmelos* (L.) Corrêa
kunda	*kunda*[36]	Indian Jasmine	*Jasminum multiflorum* (Burm.f.) Andrews
kuṛaci (=kuṭaj)	*kuṭaja*	Easter Tree	*Holarrhena pubescens* Wall. ex G.Don
ṭagar	*ṭagara*	East India Rosebay or Crepe Jasmine	*Tabernaemontana divaricata* (L.) R.Br. ex Roem. & Schult.
seati (=seuti, sẽoti, sẽuti)	*sevatī*	White Rose	*Rosa moschata* Herrm.
māl (=mālatī)	*mālatī*	Jasmine	*Jasminum grandiflorum* L.
jātī	*jātī*	Jasmine	*Jasminum grandiflorum* L.
campā (=campak, cā̃pā)	*campaka*	Champak	*Magnolia champaca* (L.) Baill. ex Pierre
nāgeśbar	*nāgakesara*	Indian Rose Chestnut	*Mesua ferrea* L.
belyā (=beliphul)	*mallikā, madayanti(kā), śītabhīru, vārṣikī* etc.	Arabian Jasmine	*Jasminum sambac* (L.) Aiton.
gõṅgci (=guñjā)	*guñjā*	Indian Licorice	*Abrus precatorius* L.
bhocā	?	?	?
ākaṛā[37] *(=ā̃kaṛā/ ā̃koṛ)*	*aṅkoṭa*	Sage-leaved Alangium	*Alangium salviifolium* (L.f.) Wangerin
niali (=neālī)	*naipālī*	Arabian Jasmine	*Jasminum sambac* (L.) Aiton.
dhuturā	*dhattūra*	Thorn-apple	*Datura metel* L.
jhiṭi (=jhiṇṭī, jhāṭī, jhā̃ṭī)	*jhiṇṭi(kā)*	Philippine Violet	*Barleria cristata* L.
mārūā (=māṛuẏā, māṛoẏā)	*madhulikā*	Finger Millet	*Eleusine coracana* (L.) Gaertn.
kācali	?	?	?
jabā	*javā/japā*	China Rose	*Hibiscus rosa-sinensis* L.
tulsī	*tulasī*	Holy Basil	*Ocimum tenuiflorum* L.

36 Cf. MWSED 291: a kind of jasmine (*Jasminum multiflorum* or *pubescens*); fragrant oleander (*Nerium odorum* L. [ASN: *Nerium oleander* L.]).

37 Basu ($ŚP_1$ 144) interprets *ākaṛā* as *okaṛā phul* which, according to DBSE (554, s.v.), may be 'The name of three plants, viz. Xyris Indica, Verbena nodiflora [ASN: *Phyla nodiflora* (L.) Greene], and Hibiscus esculentus [ASN: *Abelmoschus esculentus* (L.) Moench].'

Bengali name	Sanskrit name	English name	Botanical name
uṛuk (=ūrubak, kurubak)	*kurabaka*	Porcupine Flower	*Barleria prionitis* L.
karañc (=karañj)	*karañja(ka)*	Indian Beech	*Pongamia pinnata* (L.) Merr.
belāl (=bel)	*bilva*	Bengal Quince	*Aegle marmelos* (L.) Corrêa
mālatī	*mālatī*	Jasmine	*Jasminum grandiflorum* L.
kiālā (=keẏā, ketakī)	*ketaka; ketakī*	Screw Pine	*Pandanus odorifer* (Forssk.) Kuntze
ketakī	*ketaka; ketakī*	Screw Pine	*Pandanus odorifer* (Forssk.) Kuntze
mati[38]	?	?	?
palās (=palāś)	*palāśa*	Flame of the Forest	*Butea monosperma* (Lam.) Kuntze
kāñcan	*kāñcana*	Mountain Ebony	*Bauhinia variegata* L.
ām	*āmra*	Mango	*Mangifera indica* L.
jām	*jambū*	Jambul	*Syzygium cumini* (L.) Skeels
(d) Northern sector (*pādas* 27–34): bamboo wicker-tray and bamboo picker.			
karabī	*kāravī*	Black Caraway	*Carum carvi* L.
maratar phul[39] *(=moraṭā)*	*moraṭā*	Indian Bowstring-hemp	*Sansevieria roxburghiana* Schult. & Schult.f.
mādhabīlatā	*mādhavīlatā*	Bengal Hiptage	*Hiptage benghalensis* (L.) Kurz
āmalā (=āmalakī, āmalak)	*āmalaka*	Emblic	*Phyllanthus emblica* L.
kusum	*kusumbha*	Safflower	*Carthamus tinctorius* L.
bakul	*bakula*	Indian Medlar	*Mimusops elengi* L.
śāluk (=śālūk)	*śāluka*	Water Lily stalk	Stalk or root of various plants of the *Nymphaea* genus
rakta kambal	*rakta kamala*	Indian Red Waterlily	*Nymphaea rubra* Roxb. ex Andrews

Note: Names of plants are given as they appear in the original text. Although no evident taxonomy seems to be applied, the flowers of the plants listed seems to loosely follow the *maṇḍala* of ŚP according to which each cardinal direction is associated with a color (W = white; S = blue; E = yellow; N = red). There are however various exceptions. This may be justified by the presence of local variants of a listed plant and/or differences of cognitive color perception cross-linguistically.

38 BBA (1713–14): 'a kind of flower' (*puṣpabiśeṣ*); BSK (1715): 'a kind of creeper' (*śāk'biśeṣ*).

39 Cf. BSK (1834): *moraṭ* = *aṅkoṭhpuṣpa*.

In the concluding *pādas* (35–44), the *baṛu* offers Dharmarāj the flowers gathered and obtains *darśan* of the lord. The *dān'pati* (the sponsor of the ceremony, but also the officiating ritualist) is then assisted by the *āminīs* Basuẏa, Caritrā and Durgā in the preparation of garlands. Fire, flowers and water are offered to Gaṇeśa; and finally – after worshiping the *āminīs* – the *dān'pati* invokes and worships Dharmarāj with camphor (*karpūr*; *Cinnamomum camphora* [L.] J.Presl) and betel leaves (*tāmbūl*; *Piper betle* L.) (ŚP$_1$ 32, *puṣpa tolan*, 43).

The only other section of ŚP dealing with flowers is the *puṣpāñjali* (showering of flowers) chapter (pp. 94–97).[40] Names of flowers are not explicitly mentioned, but the text shows the great pomp associated with a ritual which continues to be performed on occasion of the Gājan festival in West Bengal.

The male and female head-ritualists (*mūl sannyāsī* and *mūl mahilā bhaktya*) enact the Dharmapūjā originally performed by King Hariścandra and his wife Madanā. Attended by a multitude of devotees, in a way that is reminiscent of the *maṇḍala* given in ŚP (see table 11.1), they throw water and flowers towards the four cardinal points, each marked with a flag (*patākā*) on a bamboo stick. In so doing, they 'open the doors' and permit the awakening of Dharmarāj.[41] Then, the chief ritualists engage in circumambulations (*pradakṣiṇa*) around the seat of the god (*dharmasiṁhāsan*), usually hosted in a temple (*deula*) in the form of *śil* (slab stone) or *pādukā* (footprints). Mild austerities, such as *daṇḍabat*, or *daṇḍīkāṭā* ('lying as a stick'),[42] are usually performed while male devotees loudly shout *'jaẏ! jaẏ!'* and women produce auspicious ululations (*uludhvani*).

40 Cf. DhPB 250 *et passim* where the offering of flowers is associated to the ritual service of the *āminīs*.

41 *paccim duāre rājā jal puppa lae | cāri saa gati pūjae jaa jaa die* || 7 [...]
sat sat padakhina karenta rājā rānī | añjali kariā pāe dila puppapāni || 12 [...]
dekhila duāre rājā jal puppa loiā | āṭ saa gati pūjae jaa jaa diā || 16 [...]
sat daṇḍabat kare rājā rānī | añjali kariā pāe dilā phul pāni || 21 [...]
purab duāre rānī jalpuppa loiā | bāra saa gati pūjae jaa jaa diā || 25 [...]
sat sat daṇḍabat karae rājā rānī | añjali kariā pāe dilā puppa pāni || 30 [...]
gājan duāre rājā jalpuppa laā | sola saa gati pūjae jaa jaa diā || 33 [...]
sat sat daṇḍabat karae rājā rānī | añjali kariā pāe dee puppapāni || 38
(ŚP$_1$, 94–97, *puṣpāñjali*).
See also the *dbār'mocan* section in ŚP$_1$ *rājā haricandrer dharmmapūjā*, 32–34.

42 This is associated with *hatyā deoẏā*, which involves rolling on the ground to obtain Dharma's favor. Both practices are also referred to as *aṣṭāṅga praṇām*.

THE CREATION OF PADDY

The chapter on agriculture (*cāṣ*) in ŚP is called *dhānyer janma* (DhJ; $ŚP_1$ 107–15).[43] It is the longest section after *sr̥ṣṭipattan* and consists of eighty verses in the *paẏār* meter. The text is evocative of the Śibāẏan literature, which began to spread in written form from the end of the seventeenth century.[44] The best preserved texts are the *Śibāẏan* of Rām'kr̥ṣṇa Kabicandra (1618–1684) and Rāmeśbar Bhaṭṭācārya's *Śib'saṁkīrtan* (c. 1711–1750).[45] Another noteworthy work is the *Matsyadharā Pālā* in Śaṅkar Kabicandra's *Śib'maṅgal* (c. 1680) (Bhaṭṭācārya 1998: 222).

The Śiva of these texts is described as a *kr̥ṣak deb* (a peasant god) performing the humblest tasks (weeding; seeding; ploughing; cutting grass; building ridges) in very harsh conditions along with other poor farmers. The story reflects the practical concerns of a predominantly farming population. The culture that emerges from these narratives and the beliefs behind them have little in common with technical manuals on agriculture or ancient ritual texts, where rice is primarily an oblation. If anything, they remind us of the domestic offerings to various gods for the promotion of agriculture as well as other material gains.[46]

In DhJ, Śiva – who is addressed as *gosāī* and *prabhu* – is a beggar who lives on alms of *harītakī* and *beheṛā*.[47] He is exhorted to take on agriculture because 'sometimes there is food, [but] sometimes you have to fast.'[48]

43 An alternative version is found in $ŚP_3$ 234–41. It is excerpted from the MS G5438 written down by Arjun Paṇḍit. The section is discussed in Smith (1999: 224–26).

44 On Śibāẏan literature, see Das Gupta (1929), Chaudhuri (1939), Clark (1955). See also Bhaṭṭācārya (1998: 199–200).

45 Rāmeśbar's lengthier text does not describe advanced agricultural techniques, possibly to emphasize the hardships of the peasants' lives (e.g. ŚS 215–39). Description of crops is also limited, as Bengal is known as a predominantly rice-producing land.

46 In Vedic times Indra, Agni, Sarasvatī, the farming god Puṣān and a generic Kṣetrapati ('Lord of the Fields') were particularly worshiped (Gonda 1987: 167–68).

47 *jakhan āchen gosāñi haā digambar | ghare ghare bhikhā māgiā bulen īsar ||* 3
rajanī parabhāte bhikkhār lāgi jāi | kuthāe pāi kuthāe na pāi || 4
hattukī baeṛā tāhe kari din'pāt | kata haras gosāñi bhikkhāe bhāt || 5 ($ŚP_1$ 108, DhJ)
Hattukī is the fruit of *harītakī*, or chebulic myrobalan (*Terminalia chebula* Retz.; also known as *śivā*); *baeṛā* or *beheṛā* (Skt. *vibhītaka*) is the beleric myrobalan; *Terminalia bellirica* (Gaertn.) Roxb.

48 *āmhar bacane gosāñi tumhi cas cās | kakhan anna hae gosāñi kakhan upabās ||* 6 ($ŚP_1$ 108, DhJ). In DhPB (*dhānya janma*, pp. 227–37), the goddess Durgā invites

Hara accepts the advice and is happy with his new occupation. Cultivating crops, we are then informed, is of the greatest importance as not only it provides food, fibers and other necessary items but because it makes it possible to offer suitable gifts to Dharmarāj (cf. DhPB 229).[49]

> O Lord, if there is food (*anna*)[50] in the house, we will eat it with pleasure. But without rice, how miserably shall we suffer! [9] O Lord, cultivate cotton, so that we will put on clothes. How long do you think you could wear a tiger-skin? [10] Please Lord; do cultivate sesame (*til*)[51] and mustard seeds (*sarisā*).[52] How long do you think you could cover your body with ashes? [11] Cultivate green gram (*mug*),[53] chickpeas (*bāṭalā*)[54] and sugar cane (*ikhu*).[55] Then we will have the pleasure to offer *pañcāmṛta* to propitiate God [=Dharma]. [12] Cultivate all kinds of crops, O Lord, and grow plantains.[56] We need all possible items (*drabya*) to worship Dharma. [13] (ŚP$_1$ 108–109, DhJ, 9–13)

Hara appreciates the many advantages of this plan. So he creates Man (Mind) and Paban (Wind), the two ploughing bullocks (*hele*), along with a golden plough (*lāṅgal*) and a silver coulter (*phāl*). Śiva pierces holes through each side of the yoke (*joyal*) and equips it with couples of staves (*sali*). Then he fastens the harness (*joti* = Skt. *yotra*) with great care to the handle of the plough (*āṅgad*). More tools are needed: he builds a harrow (*mai*: lit. ladder)[57] with ten parallel sticks (*das kuā*). Each side of it is attached with two

---

Śiva to give up mendicancy and start the cultivation of paddy. This will ensure food and clothes, and a more respectable position. Śiva is then sent to Indra to request suitable land. When this is obtained, the god is helped by Viśvakarmā, who fashions a plough out of his *triśūl* and attaches it to Hara's bull and Paravatī's tiger (DhPB 229–30). In ŚS (215–18, *cāṣer bibaraṇ*), Gaurī, Śiva's young wife, invites her husband to abandon begging and find proper employment. Śiva replies that he has no wealth (*sampatti*) to start a business (*bāṇijya*), and certainly cannot work for mortals. Agriculture seems thus a good choice, and Śiva begins working as a farmer with the help of other gods (ibid. vv. 2108–26).

49 The text seems to suggest that Śiva was regarded as subordinate to Dharma. See also the birth of Śiva in: ŚP$_1$ 18–22, *sṛṣṭipattan*, 184 *et passim*.

50 The word *anna* is used to indicate both food in general and rice.

51 Skt. *tila*; *Sesamum indicum* L.

52 Skt. *sarṣapa*; *Brassica rapa* L.

53 Skt. *mudga*; *Vigna radiata* (L.) R.Wilczek.

54 Skt. *caṇaka*; *Cicer arietinum* L.

55 Skt. *ikṣu*; *Saccharum officinarum* L.

56 Skt. *kadalī*; *Musa × paradisiaca* L.

57 Cf. *mayikā* in KP 118, 181–82: a tool in the form of ladder used to level rice fields.

ropes made of straw (*sali daṛi*) to the yoke and the bullocks are governed with a golden driving stick (*pācan bāṛi*) (DhJ 14–18).

In a style evoking the short aphorisms of Ḍāk and Khanā,[58] the author of DhJ succinctly summarizes the main operations for the cultivation of what I assume is *āman*, autumn rice. During Māgha, Hara is busy preparing the land for receiving the seedlings (DhJ 19–20). Meanwhile Pārvatī feels lonely and asks her husband to return to Mount Kailaśa. Immersed in erotic dalliances, Śiva's sexual desire arises. From his emission of semen the *kāmad* paddy is created, and from it all other species.[59] These are promptly planted and ripen during the rainy season, between the months of Śrāvaṇa and Bhādra (27–28). Paddy grows stronger in Āśvina and Kārtika, (28–29a) and finally in Agrahāyana stalks (*śiṣ*) are ready to be harvested (29b–30) (cf. ŚS *śasyotpatti*: 2302–33; Khanā's advice on sowing in Gopal 2008: 866).

For this last operation, specific tools need to be provided. Śiva summons Viśvakarmā (cf. DhPB 229–31), who fashions a hundred golden sickles (*kāste*) (DhJ 35). Nandi, Śiva's bull and attendant, offers his strength (36–38), Bhīma acts as chief workman (*moṛal'giri*) (39–42) and Hānuman offers his services as guardian (42b).[60] Notwithstanding his exceptional energy, Bhīma's harvest is believed insufficient by Śiva who, furious with anger, commands the crop to be destroyed in a great fire.[61] Bhīma calls Varuṇa as witness (*sākhī* = Skt. *sākṣīn*) and the latter brings with him Hiṅgula Devī. Meanwhile Pārvatī and all the gods are alerted by the heat (48). Only then does Śiva realize the misery he has caused to human beings. He summons Indra, who readily showers nectar-rain ('*amarta barisan*' = *amṛta barṣaṇ*) on

58 There is no complete translation, or edited version, of the sayings (B. *bacan*; Skt. *vacana*) of Ḍāk and Khanā (Wojtilla 2006: 45–47 and 51–53). On Khanā and rice culture in Bengal, see Chaudhuri 2008: 540–43.

59 *koutuk karite sibe upajil kām | kāme upajil dhān kāmad bali nām* || 23
ek dhāne hoibāk sahasrek nām | ihāte āsiā lakkhī kariba birām || 24 ($ŚP_1$ 110, DhJ).

60 Hanumān is the protector of agriculture in AgP CXXI: 51–52. *Mantras* celebrating Hanumān are found in KP 195 for the protection of paddy, and in SuVĀ XV.162 to keep rats, insects and pests away from plants. This might explain the presence of Hanumān in the Bengali *cāṣ* narratives. Further to that, in ŚP Hanumān is the *koṭāl* of Tretayuga and the keeper of the southern direction (see above) (see also: $ŚP_1$ 25, *jal pāban* 20; $ŚP_1$ 33, *rājā haricandrer dharmmapūjā* (*dbār'mocan*) 4; $ŚP_1$ 41, *canā pāban* 8; $ŚP_1$ 46, *ṭīkā pratiṣṭhā* 4; $ŚP_1$ 53, *yamrājsaṅgbād* 11; $ŚP_1$ 122, *hom yajña* 12) whereas in Maṅgal'kābyas he is the emissary of Dharmarāj and the protector of Lāusen.

61 *suniā krodhita haila har mahāsae | sunu bhīm khetti se dhāne āguni bhejāe* || 45 ($ŚP_1$ 112, DhJ). Cf. $ŚP_3$ 239, *dhānyajanma.*

the burning fields (53).[62] In the following verses, the Lord himself cleanses the land of impurities and debris, and restores all the paddy.[63] DhJ 56–78 is a list of over a hundred varieties of rice created by Śiva (see table 11.3).

The narration concludes with a rendition of Śiva's activities once the land has been prepared. Pre-germinated seedlings are transplanted in the wet field and covered in silt (*pali*).[64] This permits the production of *jalidhān*, or floating rice, a kind of cultivation which takes into account regular flooding: to survive plants grow fast up to five meters. Then, at the time of harvest, paddy is reaped and put together in bundles (*biṛā*).[65] These operations anticipate the post-harvesting drying, of which we have no evidence in ŚP, and the successive husking (see below). In the colophon, Rāmāi Paṇḍit says that Dharma will reward his chief devotee.[66]

62 Cf. $ŚP_3$ 139 (*dhānyajanam*), where Bhīma utters a *mantra* to shower rain on the fields:
japiyā barānamantra jal dila bhīm | arddhek bā̃cila dhānya sehat asim ||

63 *gosāñi dilen tabe biunir bāa | jata chila chār pā̃s uṛiāt jāa* || 54
punarapi gosāñi chihattha bulāila | jemati dhān chila pūrbba temati haila || 55
($ŚP_1$ 112–13, DhJ).
The creation of paddy after fire is not without significance. Smith (1999: 225) has noted that the mythical account of the *kṛṣak* Śiva is evocative of a slash-and-burn cultivating technique known as *jhum*. The term is reported as 'a word used on the eastern frontiers of Bengal for that kind of cultivation which is practiced in the hill forests of India and Indo-China, under which a tract is cleared by fire, cultivated for a year or two, and then abandoned for another tract, where a like process is pursued.' (HJ 460). Capt. Lewin's report vividly evokes the destruction of fire rendered in ŚP: 'The firing of the jooms is sometimes a source of danger, as at that season of the year the whole of the surrounding jungle is as dry as tinder, and easily catches fire. In this way sometimes whole villages are destroyed, and people have lost their lives. I have myself seen a whole mountain-side on fire for four days and four nights, having been ignited by joom-firing. It was a magnificent sight, but such a fire must cause incalculable injury to the forest.' (Lewin 1869: 11)

64 Cf. $ŚP_1$ 108, DhJ, 7, where Śiva takes the wet land (silt?) from the shore of the pond, fertilizes the fields and irrigate them, and $ŚP_1$ 110, DhJ, 27 when provision is made during Bhādra for both the wet lowland (*ḍaha*) and the dry upland (*ḍāṅga*).

65 *jalār dhān bā̃kui bune loṭāiā jaa | āthal palie dāa biṛā baa lāa* || 79 ($ŚP_1$ 115, DhJ).
Cf. Das Gupta (1929: 203) who interprets corrupted lexemes as varieties of paddy. The same problem is found in Niyogi (2008: 694), who has reported Das Gupta's findings almost verbatim in her appendixes (ibid.: 693–99).

66 *kahen rāmāi paṇḍit dhānar janam sāa | bhakta nāeke dhamma haba baradāa* || 80 ($ŚP_1$ 115, DhJ).

Table 11.3. Varieties of paddy in ŚP.

pād	Name of paddy	*pād*	Name of paddy
		23b	*kāmad*
		56b	*muktāhār*
57a	*jeṭh dhān; chicharā; āmla*	57b	*ālācit*; phepheri*
58a	*sanā khaṛaki*; duggābhog; āsaāṅga; kala*	58b	*muktāhār*
59a	*kālā mugaṛ*	59b	*nāgar juān**
60a	*tulā sāli*[67]	60b	*āsati*
61a	*bak kaṛi*	61b	*gotam palāl; pātal*
62a	*pāṅgusiā; bhāddamukhi; khemrāa**	62b	*tulān dhān; dudurāa*
63a	*gujurā; boāli; ḍār; hāti pāñjar*	63b	*buṛā māttā*
64a	*til sāgari*		
65a	*latāmou; moukalas; khejur chaṛi*	65b	*pabbat jirā; gandhatulsī; dalā guṛi*
66a	*bandhi; bā̃s'gajā; sītāsālī*	66b	*hukuli; harikāli*; kusum māli*[68]
67a	*raktasāl; candan sāl*	67b	*rāj dal; moukalas*
68a	*uṛāsālī; bindhasali; lāuśālī*	68b	*bhādolī*
69a	*rājdal; moukalas; ājān siali (=śāli)*	69b	*kālā kāttik; megi*
70a	*khīr kambā; ranaja^{n}a*	70b	*kāmad*
71a	*(khudda) dudurāa; bhajanā; bā̃kai*	71b	*mūlāmuktahār*
72a	*pipiṛā; bā̃s'gajā; kakaci**	72b	*mādhabalatā; bāgan bici*
73a	*koṭā; rāagaṛ; tojanā*; bora*	73b	*koṅgar bhog; jalā rāṅgi*; kanakcur*
74a	*lāl'kāminī; solpanā*; pārcchā bhog*	74b	*āndhārkuli; gopāl'bhog*
75a	*bukhi; ājān lakkhī; bā̃s'matī*	75b	*sāl chāṭī; kāṅgad; gandhamālatī*
76a	*ām pāban*; gaā bāli; pātharā*	76b	*masi loṭ; jhiṅgā sāl; tasarā**
77a	*sam dhunā; suā sān; ṭāṅgan*	77b	*hari; mahīpāl; bā̃k'sāl*
78a	*bā̃k'cur; puān; biṛi; gõṛi; gopāl**	78b	*huṛā; bā̃s'kāṭā; maric; maipāl (=mahīpāl, 77b)*

Note: Without a physical description of each type of paddy any effort toward an accurate identification would be inaccurate (see Introduction, pp. xxix–xxx). The large part of the varieties of paddy recorded in ŚP is listed in an anglicized form in sources such as RRI, CRRI or the list of notified and denotified varieties of paddy in DRD. Entries marked with * have not been identified.

67 *Śāli* (etymology unclear; cf. Witzel 2009: 17, fn. 121) is the autumnal paddy, which exists in many varieties. It is mentioned in early medical compendia (c. first–fourth centuries CE) as healthy food (cf. CaS.Sū. v.12). Bhāvamiśra (sixteenth century) enumerates some varieties of *śāli dhānya* in BhPr.Pū. VI.9.3–16. Other kinds of rice are: *vrīhi* (17–21), *ṣaṣṭika* (22–26) and *śūka* (27).

68 All editions of ŚP report *kusum mālī*. I believe this should be *kusum'śāli* (cf. RRI 331; Das Gupta 1929: 202, paddy variety no. 40). My reasoning is based on the

THE AUSPICIOUS SONG OF THE HUSKING PEDAL

The use of rice as an offering is well attested in ŚP.[69] Amongst the various occurrences, Rāmāi sings the ceremony for the husking of rice in the *ḍheṅkīmaṅgal*, a short section of just nine verses in the *laghu tripadī* meter ($ŚP_1$ 77–79).[70]

The *ḍheṅkī* is a traditional agricultural tool largely used across South Asia to remove the hulls and coats of cereals.[71] It is primarily associated with women's labor. It consists of a two-meter-long wooden lever, usually made from the wood of a mango or jackfruit tree, suspended by a pivot between two vertical posts and balanced at one end with pressure from the foot. At the other end of the lever, mounted at right angles, is a short cylindrical piece of wood (c. 60 cm long and of 20 cm diameter) with its base covered with an iron plaque which works as a pestle. When the lever is raised, the woman operating it removes the pressure so that the beam is released and the pestle drops on the cereals stored in a circular hovel topped with a thick wooden board. A rope usually hangs from the roof to enable a woman to keep steady while rhythmically pressing down the lever. At the other end, another woman alternately removes the smashed grains and adds new ones.[72]

The word *ḍheṅkī* is of obscure etymology (cf. CDIAL 317). It may be an onomatopoeic term derived from the sound (*ḍhak ḍhak*) produced by the pestle hitting the mortar (BŚK 1008). Pre-modern works such as Purāṇas and Śāstras are of little help, since the word *ḍheṅkī* is a local lexeme (*deśī*). We also know that in ancient India the husking process was carried out by means of mortar and pestle. Alternately, as recommended by Kāśyapa,

---

fact that the word *śāli* (unhusked rice) in ŚP is often spelt with an initial dantya sa (স) rather than with tālabya śa (শ) (the sound of the two consonants is the same) and the Bengali consonants স (/sa/) and ম (/ma/) are easily confounded in MSS.

69 $ŚP_1$ 36, *dān'patir ghar dekhā*, 2; 59 *rājā haricandrer dharmmapūjā*, 2); 62–66, *beḍāmanui*, 3, 10, 17, 24); 76, *manui*, 5; 77–78, *ḍhẽkī maṅgalā*, 2, 8; 100, *muktā maṅgalā*, 10; 120, *ṭikā pratiṣṭhā*, 3, 6, 9, 12; 124, *barāri rāg*, 8; 133, *yajña*, 2.

70 The *laghu* (light) *tripadī* consists of three verse units (*pāda*) of various lengths (here 6-6-8 *mātrās*) with two caesurae and an internal rhyme.

71 See in this volume, Chapter 10, pp. 216–17 and 233.

72 This operation is usually followed by further cleansing by means of a winnowing tray or basket (*śūrpa*). Women put the cereal on their winnowers and then move them so that the grains are repeatedly thrown in the air so that lighter elements (chaff, dirt, etc.) get blown away by the wind.

the threshing of ears was accomplished with sticks (*daṇḍa*) (KKS 563) and, successively, by letting cattle (bulls and buffaloes) trample the grains on the threshing floor (KKS 487).[73] The only Sanskrit Kr̥ṣiśāstra that mentions a tool resembling the *ḍheṅkī* is Daśaratha's *Kr̥ṣiśāsana* (x.79), which was composed in 1909. The author refers to the *ḍhauka* as a machine for pounding cereals. The *ḍheṅkī*, however, must be a quite old, and versatile, implement.[74] A pressing tool operated by a lever and called *ḍheṅku* is mentioned in a copper-plate inscription referred to as the Charter of Viṣṇusena (sixth–seventh centuries CE). On the first plate (line 8) this is described as a 'contrivance (based on the principle of lever) for drawing water from a well' (Sircar 1953–1954: 172; for a similar use see also *ḍheṁkā* in DNM IV.17).[75]

The husking pestle, generically called *muṣal*, is not just an important agricultural tool. It is also symbolic of wellbeing and good luck.[76] In rural West Bengal, where Ḍheṅkīpūjā is regularly performed, the *ḍheṅkī* is worshiped solo, or surrounded by a variety of agricultural utensils (spades, ploughs, et cetera) or small terracotta figurines representing animals associated with fertility and auspiciousness (e.g. horses, elephants, frogs and tortoises).[77] This is then decorated, besmeared with sandal paste and presented various offerings on occasions such as marriages (*bibāh*), the first giving of rice to a child (*anna prāśan*),[78] harvest festivals such as Nabānna Utsab (mid-November) or on Pouṣ Saṁkrānti (corresponding to the Winter Solstice; Skt. Makar Saṁkrānti).

73 The use of the *śūrpa* (winnowing tray/basket) is also mentioned:
puṁjīkuryāc ca rakṣec ca kāryajñas tu kr̥ṣīvalaḥ |
kṣudragrāmakaṭugrevavihīnān tu kr̥ṣīvalaḥ || 568
śūrpādivinyāsayogāt vātavījanatopi vā |
pecanāc cāmanād vāpi nirmalīkr̥tarūpakān || 569 (KKS)

74 Grierson describes various uses of the *ḍheṅkī* (alt. spell. *ḍheṅkā*, *ḍheṅkul*, *ḍheṅkulā*): (1) a crusher by which bricks are ground (1885: 90, 431); (2) a crushing-lever used by tobacco-sellers (ibid.: 95, 464); (3) a pedal for husking grain (ibid.: 118, 608); (4) a lever used in raising water (ibid.: 206, §928); (5) 'a perpendicular bar sliding down from a recess in the top of the door frame' (ibid.: 336, 1250; cf. Gopal 2008: 859).

75 I am thankful to Professor Gyula Wojtilla for his insightful notes on the *ḍheṅkī* and for drawing my attention on the above-mentioned sources.

76 See Ḍāk's *bacan* in Das Gupta (1929: 181n4).

77 I have reported elsewhere on the semantically charged place of the *ḍheṅkī* in ritual contexts, such as for instance ceremonies inviting wellbeing and fertility (see Ferrari 2015: 56).

78 Cf. Macdonald, who mentions *upanayana* too (in MacPhail 1905: 257).

The *ḍheṅkīmaṅgal* of ŚP evokes this tradition vividly. The husking pedal is praised as an agricultural implement and as the vehicle (*bahān*) of the sage (*muni*) Nārada,[79] who – accompanied by the croaks of frogs (*bhẽkar saṅgit*) – flies towards the abode of the gods.[80] There, the *ḍheṅkī* is worshiped by all the gods. Garlands of flowers are laid on it, drummers rhythmically beat their *mṛdaṅgas* and *kāṛās*, imitating the pounding sound of the *ḍheṅkī*, while women produce characteristic ululations.[81] The centrality of rice in the celebration of the *ḍheṅkī* and associated rituals is emphatically mentioned in the first, second and last *pādas*, where the assembly of the gods prepares for the narration of the creation of paddy.[82] Upon concluding the

79 *koṭāl cāri jane* *ādesi deb'gane*
nārade ānāha tarāgati |
calila tataḥpar *muni barābar*
kahila debar bhāratī || (ŚP$_1$ 77–78, *ḍheṅkī maṅgalā*, 3).
Cf. ŚS 240-141, *nārader koilās gaman-udyog* vv. 2334–55.

80 *suniā munirāj* *bāhan karila sāj*
ḍheṅkī piṭhe kari ārohan |
bhābi jugesar *calila munibar*
suniā bāramati bharan || 4
teṭhaṅgā haiā jāa *bhekar saṅgit gāa*
uṛila deb biddamāne |
dekhiā debgan *ādare tatakhan*
basāila ratnasiṁhāsane || 5 (ŚP$_1$ 78, *ḍheṅkī maṅgalā*).
The flight of sage Nārada is also told (in *paẏār* meter) in ŚS (pp. 240–41, vv. 2334–55). See also the third act of *Matsyadharā Nāṭak* (22–38), a short play of Kālidās Mukhopādhyāẏ published in 1873/74, where the *ḍheṅkī* and *debarṣi* Nārada converse about Śiva's decision to take agriculture.

81 *tideb mahārājā* *ḍheṅkīr karilā pūjā*
sugandhi puppar mālā diā |
deb'kannā meli *diā hulāhuli*
ānandeta ḍheṅkī maṅgaliā || 6
bājae jaeḍhāk *meghar sam ḍāk*
sunite sudhani bājanā |
mṛdaṅga kāṛā bāje *phular mālā sāje*
ānandeta dharmmar pūjanā || 7
paṇḍite bed'gān *nichiā pelen pān*
hului paṛae ghane ghan |
sumadhur bājanā suni *mukutā hār āmani*
ḍheṅkī e kara ārambhan || 8 (ŚP$_1$ 78, *ḍheṅkī maṅgalā*).

82 *koutuket deb'gaṇ* *karite maṅgalan*
basilā bambhā biṣṭu har |
tettis koṭī deb *basilen sab*
gandharbba kinnar || 1

celebration of the *ḍheṅkī*, presumably a women's rite, ŚP continues with a series of short ritual tracts, each providing guidance on a particular aspect of Dharmapūjā.[83]

CONCLUSION

The lyrical realism of ŚP reveals the deep familiarity with the territory of Bengali ritual and devotional culture. Although texts like *Śūnyapurāṇ*, *Dharmapūjābidhān*, *Dharmapurāṇ*, the Śibāẏan poems and the various Dharmamaṅgal'kābyas do not provide much information about agricultural and botanical technology nor do they seem to follow any taxonomy, they agree with the Kr̥ṣiśāstras in celebrating agriculture as a noble occupation. A major difference however emerges. While Sanskrit texts stress on various occasions the technicalities of agriculture and its soteriological

---

paṇḍit cāri jane ānandita pūra mane
dbādaś bhakata āmani |
muktahār dhānna āni mukutā prabāla māni
durlabh jagatet bākhāni || 2 ($ŚP_1$ 77, *ḍheṅkī maṅgalā*).
[...]
sõuri kara tār dakhin pade pār
mukutā karila nirmān |
ānandeta padatal madhukar kokanad
paṇḍit rāmāi gāan |
ehi mor manaskām tumhi nā haio bām
dānpatir cintah kallān || 9 ($ŚP_1$ 79, *ḍheṅkī maṅgalā*).

83 In $ŚP_1$ 79–81, *gāmbhārī maṅgal*, an eleven-verse section in *laghu tripadī* following *ḍhẽkimaṅgal*, Rāmāi tells of the arrangements for Gāmbhārīpūjā (a northern version of the Gājan). The short *maṅgal'gān* evokes the custom of leaving a polished trunk, usually of *gāmbhāri/gāmāri* (*Gmelina arborea* Roxb. ex Sm.; cf. Pālit 1319 BS), a tree believed to be the seat of Dharma Ṭhākur by virtue of its pale white wood (see above p. 242), in a pond for a whole year until this is brought back to life in advance of the spring equinox. ŚP describes the male *sannyāsis* while looking for the pole in the forest. When this is found, they engage in circumambulations (*pradakṣiṇa*) and then lie rolling on the earth (*daṇḍabat aṣṭāṅga*) in a devotional attitude. The *gāmbhāri gāch* is then transported to the house of the village blacksmith (*kāmar*) for its embellishment while *noibedya* (a simple presentation of raw fruits and vegetables mixed with uncooked rice, milk and curd) is offered. A further use of the *gāmbhāri* pole emerges from observation of the Gājan festival, when *sannyāsīs* use its branches to flog themselves as part of a series on self-mortifications (see n. 7 above).

component,[84] ŚP and cognate literature are more practical. The vicissitudes of Śiva – a god unusually presented as an irresponsible mendicant turned peasant – provide a more realistic background for the farmers of Bengal.[85] The god is described while taking part in the humblest tasks along with his divine helpers. He often fails, and swears! But eventually he gets the fruits of his hard work, which are promptly shared with his family and human fellow farmers.

In these narratives, agriculture and knowledge of the earth provide a different type of redemption, one that brings independence, inclusion and solidarity. The Śiva and the Dharmarāj celebrated by Rāmāi Paṇḍit are gods who protect the rural populace of Rāṛh. Their presence ensures wealth, health and offspring – all of these depending upon abundant crops. The celebration of Dharma Ṭhākur and Śiva and their association with the vegetable landscape of Rāṛh bear witness to the way in which vernacular (*āñcalik*) literary and ritual culture has been shaped by the landscape of Bengal. A variety of so far little-explored texts reveals a science of devotion which took advantage of an era of growth in commerce and communication, and built on an existing corpus of texts and technologies to enhance the celebration of a vast array on local gods and goddesses in pan-Hindu terms. The study of specific technologies of devotion, in this case with a focus on the use of plants and trees, as an aspect of material religion is no doubt an arena important for a full appreciation of the transformation of Indian vernacular traditions.

ABBREVIATIONS AND REFERENCES

B. = Bengali Skt. = Sanskrit

MANUSCRIPTS CONSULTED

Dharmamaṅgal	MS 131, Visvabharati University
Dharma-maṅgal	MS G5424, Asiatic Society (Kolkata)
Dharmapurāṇ	MS 129, Visvabharati University
Dharmapurāṇ	MS 130, Visvabharati University
Saṁjāt paddhati	MS 5449, Asiatic Society (Kolkata)
Śūnyapurāṇ	MS G5438, Asiatic Society (Kolkata)

84 See Introduction, p. xxi.
85 Chatterji (1945: 78). Cf. Ganguly's analysis of the agricultural rites in *Kṛṣiparāśara* (2008: 522–23).

AgP — *Agnipurāṇa*. Mitra, R.L. (ed.) (1873–1879). *Agnipurāṇa*. Bibliotheca Indica LXV. Calcutta: Asiatic Society of Bengal.

Basu 1316 BS — Basu, N.N. (1316 BS). 'Śūnyapurān sambondhe mantobya.' *Sāhitya Pariṣat Patrikā* 16(4): 221–24.

BBA — Dās, J. (1937). *Bāṅglā Bhāṣār Abhidhān*. 2 vols. Kalikāta: Iṇḍiẏān Pābliśiṅg Hāus.

Bhaktibinode 1313 BS — Bhaktibinode, B.K. (1313 BS). 'Rāmāi Paṇḍit o Maynāpurer Yātrāsiddhi.' *Sāhitya Pariṣat Patrikā* 13(2): 81–96.

Bhaṭṭācārya 1998 — Bhaṭṭācārya, Ā. (1998). *Bāṅglā Maṅgal Kābyer Itihās*. Eighth edition. Kalikātā: A. Mukhārjī.

Bhattacharyya 1951 — Bhattacharyya, A. (1951). *The Early Saiva Bengali Poetry*. Reprint, 1944 edition. Calcutta: Calcutta Book House.

Bhattasali 1920 — Bhattasali, N.K. (1920). 'The Math Inscription of Mahendra, Son of Harish Chandra of Sabhar.' *Dacca Review* 10(6–7): 111–15.

BhPr — Bhāvamiśra: *Bhāvaprakāśa*. Srikantha Murthy, K.R. (tr.) (1998–2000). *Bhāvaprakāśa of Bhāvamiśra (Text, English Translation, Notes, Appendeces [sic], and Index)*. 2 vols. Varanasi: Krishnadas Academy.

BŚK — Bandyapādhyāẏ, H. (2001). *Baṅgīẏa Śabdakoṣ*. Fifth printing. Natun Dillī: Sāhitya Akādemi.

CaS — *Carakasaṃhitā*. Sharma, P. (ed., tr.) (2003). *Carakasaṃhitā, Agniveśa's treatise refined and annotated by Caraka and redacted by Dṛḍhabala*. Text with English translation, 4 vols. Eighth edition. Varanasi: Chaukhamba Orientalia.

CDIAL — Turner, R.L. (1962–1966). *A Comparative Dictionary of Indo-Aryan Languages*. London: Oxford University Press.

Chatterji 1945 — Chatterji, S.K. (1945). 'Buddhist Survivals in India.' In: Bhandarkar, D.R. (ed.), *B.C. Law Volume*, Calcutta: Indian Research Institute, pp. 75–87.

Chaudhuri 1939 — Chaudhuri, N. (1939). 'Rudra-Śiva as an Agricultural Deity.' *Indian Historical Quarterly* 15: 183–96.

Chaudhuri 2008 — Chaudhuri, R. (2008). 'Agriculture as Known from *Khanā's Vacanas*.' HAI: 527–49.

Clark 1955 — Clark, T.W. (1955). 'Evolution of Hinduism in Medieval Bengali Literature: Siva, Candi, Manasa.' *Bulletin of the School of Oriental and African Studies* 17(3): 503–18.

CM — *Caṇḍīmaṅgal* of Mukundarām Cakrabarttī. Sen, D.C., C.C. Bandyopādhyāẏ, H. Basu (eds) (1924). *Kabikaṅkaṇ'caṇḍī*. Kalikātā: Kalikātā Biśbabidyālaẏ.

CRRI — Indian Agricultural Research Institute, New Delhi. (2012). *Kṛṣikoś, An Institutional Repository of Indian National Agricultural Research System. Central Rice Research Institute*, http://krishikosh.egranth.ac.in/handle/1/36850 (accessed 10 April 2015).

Das 1984 — Das, R.P. (1984). 'Review of: Dušan Zbavitel, *Bengali Literature*. Volume 9, Fascicule 3 (p. 119–307) of: *A History of Indian Literature* edited by Jan Gonda. Wiesbaden: Otto Harrassowitz 1976.' *Indo-Iranian Journal* 27(1): 51–73.

Das Gupta 1929 — Das Gupta, T.C. (1929). 'Aspects of Bengali Society (Agriculture).' *Journal of the Department of Letters* 18: 181–216.

Dasgupta 1946 — Dasgupta, S.B. (1946). *Obscure Religious Cults*. Reprint, 1946. Calcutta: Firma KLM.

DBSE — Haughton, G.C. Sir (1987). *A Dictionary Bengali-Sanskrit-English*. 2 vols. Reprint, 1883. Delhi: Caxton Publications.

DCBM — *A Descriptive Catalogue of Bengali Manuscripts*. 3 vols. [Vol. 1: Basanta Ranjan Ray Vidvadvallabha, 1926; Vol. 2: Basanta Ranjan Ray Vidvadvallabha, 1928; Vol. 3: Manindra Mohan Bose, 1930] (1926–30). Calcutta: University of Calcutta.

DhJ — *Dhānyer janma*

DhM^{Gh} — Ghan'rām Cakrabartī: *Dharmamaṅgal'kābya*. Basu, Y.C. (ed.) (1290 BS). *Śrīdharmamaṅgal. Mahākabi Ghan'rām Cakrabarttī Kabiratna Praṇīt*. Kalikātā: Baṅgabāsī-Ṣṭīm-Mesin-Pres.

DhM^{NB} — Narasiṁha Basu: *Dharmamaṅgal'kābya*. Māiti, S. (saṁpādit) (2001). *Narasiṁha Basur Dharmamaṅgal*. Kolkātā: Phārma Ke. El. Em.

DhP — Maẏūr'bhaṭṭa: *Dharmapurāṇ*. Caṭṭopādhyāẏ, B.K. (ed.) (1337 BS). *Śrīdharmapurāṇ. Maẏūr Bhaṭṭa-biracit*. Kalikātā: Baṅgīẏa Sāhitya Parisad.

DhPB — Rāmāi Paṇḍit: *Dharmapūjābidhān*. Bandyopādhyāẏ, N.G. (ed.) (1323 BS). *Dharmapūjābidhān. Śrīrāmāi Paṇḍit-biracit*. Kalikātā: Baṅgīẏa Sāhitya Pariṣat.

DNM — Hemacandra: *Deśīnāmamālā*. Pischel R. (ed.) (1938). *The Deśīnāmamālā of Hemacandra*. Second edition with introduction, critical notes, and glossary by P.V. Ramanujaswami. (1938). Bombay: Department of Public Instruction.

DRD — DACNET Project, Dept. of Agriculture and Cooperation, Patna. (2013). *Directorate of Rice Development*, http://drd.dacnet.nic.in/ (accessed 10 April 2015).

EDB — Sen, S. (1971). *An Etymological Dictionary of Bengali: c. 1000–1800 A.D.* 2 vols. Calcutta: Eastern Publishers.

EI — *Epigraphia Indica*

Ferrari 2010 — Ferrari, F.M. (2010). *Guilty Males and Proud Females. Negotiating Genders in a Bengali Festival*. Calcutta: Seagull Books.

Ferrari 2015 — Ferrari, F.M. (2015). '"Illness Is Nothing But Injustice": The Revolutionary Element in Bengali Folk Healing.' *Journal of American Folklore*, 128(507): 46–64.

Ganguly 2008 — Ganguly, D.K. (2008). 'Agricultural Technology as known in the *Kṛṣi-Parāśara*.' HAI: 637–701.

Ghosh 1948 — Ghosh, J.C. (1948). *Bengali Literature*. London: Oxford University Press.

Gonda 1987 — Gonda, J. (1987). *Rice and Barley Offerings in the Veda*. Leiden: Brill.

Gopal 2008 — Gopal, L. (2008). 'Technique and Process of Agriculture in Early Medieval (c. AD 700–1200) India.' HAI: 856–79.

Grierson 1885 — Grierson, G.A. (1885). *Bihār Peasant Life*. Calcutta: The Bengal Secretariat Press.

HAI	Gopal, L. and V.C. Srivastava. (eds). (2008). *History of Agriculture in India (up to c. 1200 AD)*. New Delhi: Concept Publishing Company.
HJ	Yule, Sir H. (1903). *Hobson-Jobson: A Glossary of Colloquial Anglo-Indian Words and Phrases, and of Kindred Terms, Etymological, Historical, Geographical and Discursive*. New edition, edited by W. Crooke. London: J. Murray.
IMP[KB]	Kirtikar, K.K. and B.D. Basu. (1918). *Indian Medicinal Plants*. 4 vols. Allahabad: Lalit Mohan Basu.
IMP[Kh]	Khare, C.P. (2007). *Indian Medicinal Plants. An Illustrated Dictionary*. New York: Springer.
Kew	Board of Trustees of the Royal Botanic Gardens, Kew. *Medicinal Plant Names Services*, http://mpns.kew.org/mpns-portal/ (accessed 10 April 2015).
KKS	Kāśyapa: *Kṛṣisūkti* Wojtilla, G. (ed.) (2010). *Kāśyapīyakṛṣisūkti. A Sanskrit Work on Agriculture*. Wiesbaden: Otto Harrassowitz.
KP	Parāśara: *Kṛṣiparāśara*. Śāstrī, D.P. (ed.) (2003). *Parāśaramuniviracitaḥ Kṛṣiparāśaraḥ*. With Hindī translation. Vārāṇasī: Caukhambā Saṃskṛt Sīrīj Ākhis.
Laskar 1920	Laskar, G.M. (1920). 'Notes on Harish Chandra of Sabhar.' *Dacca Review* 10(6–7): 107–10.
Lewin 1869	Lewin, T.H. (1869). *The Hill Tracts of Chittagong and the Dwellers Therein; with Comparative Vocabularies of the Hill Dialects*. Calcutta: Bengal Printing Company.
MacPhail 1905	MacPhail, J.M. (ed.) (1905). *Kenneth S. MacDonald, M.A., D.D. Missionary of the Free Church of Scotland, Calcutta*. Edinburgh and London: Oliphant, Anderson & Ferrier.
Meulenbeld 1974	Meulenbeld, G.J. (ed. and tr.) (1974). *The Mādhavanidāna and Its Chief Commentary. Chapters 1–10*. Leiden: Brill.
MIB	Bose, G.C. (1920). *A Manual of Indian Botany*. Bombay: Blackie and Son Limited.
Mitra 1957	Mitra, A. (1957). *Rāṛher Saṃskṛti o Dharma Ṭhākur*. Kalikātā: Phārmā K.L. Mukhopādhyāẏ.
Mukhopādhyāẏ, K. 1280 BS	Mukhopādhyāẏ, K. (1280 BS). *Matsyadharā Nāṭak*. Kalikātā: Īśvar'candra Basu Company.
Mukhopādhyāẏ 1960	Mukhopādhyāẏ, S. (1960). *Madhyaẏuger Bāṅglā Sāhityer Tathya o Kāl'kram*. Kalikātā: J. Bhardvāj & Co.
MWSED	Monier-Williams, M. Sir (1995). *A Sanskrit-English Dictionary: Etymologically and Philologically Arranged with Special Reference to Cognate Indo-European Languages*. Reprint of 1899 edition. Delhi: Motilal Banarsidass.
Niyogi 2008	Niyogi, P. (2008). 'Expansion of Agriculture in Ancient Bengal.' HAI: 637–701.
Pāl 1976	Pāl, R. (1976). *Darśanik śūnyabād o Bāṅglā Sāhitya*. Kālikātā: Phārmā Ke.El.Em. Limiṭeḍ.
Pālit 1319 BS	Pālit, H. (1319 BS). *Ādyer Gambhir. Bāṅglār Dharma o Sāmājik Itihāser Ek Adhyāẏ*. Māldaha: Māldaha Jātīya Śikṣā Samiti.

Pandanus	Pandanus (1998–2009). *Pandanus Database of Plants*, http://iu.ff.cuni.cz/pandanus/database/ (accessed 20 April 2015).
Pū	*Pūrvakhaṇḍa*
Rāẏ 1316 BS	Rāẏ, J.C. (1316 BS). 'Śūnyapurān', *Sāhitya Pariṣat Patrikā*, 16(4): 203–20.
Rāẏ 1338 BS	Rāẏ, J.C. (1338 BS). 'Śūnyapurān.' *Sāhitya Pariṣat Patrikā*. 38(2): 65–91.
RgV	Śaunaka: *Ṛgvidhāna*. Bhat, M.S. (ed.) (1987). *Vedic Tantrism. A Study of Ṛgvidhāna of Śaunaka with Text and Translation*. Delhi: Motilal Banarsidass.
RRI	The Reporter on Economic Products to the Government of India (ed.) (1980). *Races of Rice in India*. Reprint of 1911 edition. Original title: *The Agricultural Ledger. 1910*. New Delhi: Agricole Publishing Academy.
Śāstrī 1897	Śāstrī, H. (1897). *Discovery of Living Buddhism in Bengal*. Calcutta: Sanskrit Press Depository.
SBA	Biśbās, Ś. (2004). *Saṁsād Bāṅglā Abhidhān*. Seventh edition. Kolkāta: Sāhitya Saṁsad.
SBE	Biswas, S. (2003). *Samsad Bengali-English Dictionary*. Revised and Enlarged Third Edition. Kolkata: Sahitya Samsad.
Sen 1911	Sen, D.C. (1911). *History Of Bengali Language and Literature*. Calcutta: The University of Calcutta.
Sen 1924	Sen, B.K. (1924). 'Rāmāi Paṇḍit.' *Calcutta Review*, 12(2): 353–61.
Sen 1975	Sen, S. (1975). *Bāṅglā Sāhityer Itihās*, 3 vols. Reprint of 1963 edition. Barddhamān: Sāhitya Sabhā.
Śahīdullāh 1360 BS	Śahīdullāh, M. (1360 BS). 'Maẏūr Bhaṭṭa.' *Sāhitya Pariṣat Patrikā* 60(1): 13–15.
Śib	Rām'kṛṣṇa Kabicandra: *Śibāẏan*. Bhaṭṭācārya, D.C. and Ā. Bhaṭṭācārya (eds.) (1383 BS). *Śibāyan. Rām'kṛṣṇa Kabicandra Racit*. Kalikātā: Baṅgiẏā Sāhitya Pariṣat.
Sircar 1953–1954	Sircar, D.C. (1953–1954). 'Charter of Vishnushena, Samvat 649.' EI XXX: 163–81. Reprinted 1987. New Delhi: Archaeological Survey of India.
Smith 1999	Smith, W.L. (1999). 'Śiva, Lord of the Plough.' In R.P. Das (ed.), *Essays on Middle Bengali Literature*, pp. 208–28. Calcutta: Firma KLM.
ŚP	Rāmāi Paṇḍit: *Śūnya Purāṇ*. (1) Basu, N.N. (sampādit) (1314 BS). *Śūnyapurāṇ. Rāmāipaṇḍit praṇīt*. Kalikātā: Baṅgīẏa Sāhitya Pariṣat. (2) Bandyopādhyāẏ, C.C. (sampādit) (1336 BS). *Śūnyapurāṇ*. Muhāmad Śahīdullāh o Basanta Kumār Caṭṭopādhyāẏ likhite bhūmikā. Kalikātā: Basumatī Ophis. (3) Caṭṭopādhyāẏ, B.M. (sampādit) (1977). *Rāmāipaṇḍit biracit Śūnyapurāṇ (Śūnyapurāṇ, Saṅgajāt-paddhati, Dharmapurāṇ)*. Kalikātā: Phermā KLM.
ŚS	Rāmeśbar Bhaṭṭācārya: *Śib'saṁkīrttan*. Hāldār, Y. (ed.) (1957). *Rāmeśbarer Śib-saṁkīrttan bā Śibāẏan*. Kalikātā: Kalikātā Biśbabidyālaẏ.

Sū — *Sūtrasthāna*

SuVĀ — Surapāla: *Vṛkṣāyurveda*. (1) Das, R.P. (1988). *Das Wissen von der Lebensspanne der Bäume. Surapālas Vṛkṣāyurveda kritisch ediert, übers und kommentiert von Rahul Peter Das; mit einem Nachtrag von G. Jan Meulenbeld zu seinem Verzeichnis 'Sanskrit names of plants and their botanical equivalents.'* Stuttgart: Steiner-Verlag-Wiesbaden-GmbH. (2) Śrīkṛṣṇa 'Jugnū' (ed.). *Vaidhyavidhyāvareṇyasurapālamuniviracitaḥ Vṛkṣāyurveda (upavana-dakārgalavijñāna-taruropaṇa va cikitsā vidhi).* Sanskrit text with Hindī translations. Vārāṇasī: Caukhambā Saṃskṛt Sīrīj Āphis.

Tropicos — Missouri Botanical Garden. (2015). *Tropicos*, http://www.tropicos.org (accessed 10 April 2015).

uBio — The Marine Biological Laboratory, Woods Hole Oceanographic Institution (2015). *uBio Project*, <http://www.ubio.org/ (accessed 10 April 2015).

Vasu 1911 — Vasu, N.N. (1911). *The Modern Buddhism and Its Followers in Orissa.* Calcutta: Hare Press.

WDMPP — Quattrocchi, U. (2012). *CRC World Dictionary of Medicinal and Poisonous Plants. Common Names, Scientific Names, Eponyms, Synonyms, and Etymologies*. London: CRC Press.

Witzel 2009 — Witzel, M. (2009). 'The Linguistic History of Some Indian Domestic Plants.' *Journal of BioSciences* 34(6): 829–33, http://dash.harvard.edu/handle/1/8954814 (accessed 16 April 2015).

Wojtilla 1991 — Wojtilla, G. (1991). 'The Kṛṣiśāsana. The Manual of Agricultural Implements in Sanskrit: A Description of the Ploughs Types.' *Tools and Tillage* 6(4): 202–09.

Wojtilla 2006 — Wojtilla, G. (2006). *History of Kṛṣiśāstra*. Wiesbaden: Harrassowitz.

General Index

Index of Botanical Species*

agarwood, *Aquilaria sinensis* (Lour.) Spreng. (and other *Aquilaria* species): 80, 84–86, 88, 90–94
agastya, *Sesbania grandiflora* (L.) Pers.: *āgastya*, 250
Alexandrian laurel, *Calophyllum inophyllum* L.: *punnāga*, 69
aloe: 123
āmalaka, emblic: 101, 115, 238, 253
āmra, mango: 70, 123, 127, 194 fn. 3, 234, 253, 260
aṅkoṭa, sage-leaved alangium: 251, 252
anla/aonla leaves: see *āmalaka*
anna, rice (generic): 232, 238, 255 fn. 48, 256 fn. 50, 261
Arabian jasmine, *Jasminum sambac* (L.) Aiton: *mallikā*, 70, 252; *naipālī*, 250, 252
arka, purple calotropis: 70
asafetida, *Ferula assa-foetida* L.: *hiṅgu*, 101, 115, 152, 159, 161
āsana, Indian kino tree: 70
aśoka, ashoka, *Saraca asoca* (Roxb.) J.J. de Wilde: 69, 250
assattha (P.), sacred fig: 100, 104, 108–10, 115
aśvattha (Skt.), sacred fig: xiii, 19, 19 fn. 53, 21 fn. 59, 69, 126, 161
ativiṣā (P. *ativisa*), monkshood: 100, 101, 115
badara, cottony jujube: 46–47, 47 figure 2.17, 238
bakula, Indian medlar: 70, 253
bamboo, *Bambusa bambos* (L.) Voss: *vaṃśa*, xxi, 122, 151, 161, 180–81, 183, 199, 225, 246 fn. 17, 253–54
banyan, *Ficus benghalensis* L.: 3, 7, 7 fn. 14, 18–20, 20 fn. 54, 20 fn. 57, 53, 109 fn. 30, 115, 126–27, 233; *nyāgrodha*, xii–xiii, xv, 18, 20 fn. 55, 69; *vaṭa*, xxvii, 4, 18 fn. 46, 20–21, 23
barley, *Hordeum vulgare* L.: *yava*, xii, xv
bdellium,** *Commiphora wightii* (Arn.) Bhandari: *guggula*, 152, 161
bel: see Bengal quince
beleric myrobalan, *Terminalia bellirica* (Gaertn.) Roxb.: *vibhītaka*, 101, 115, 255 fn. 47
Bengal hiptage, *Hiptage benghalensis* (L.) Kurz: *mādhavīlatā*, 253
Bengal quince, *Aegle marmelos* (L.) Corrêa: *bilva*, xxv fn. 54, 48, 48 figure 2.18, 70, 156, 161, 251, 253; *śrīphala*, 251, 252
ber tree: see cottony jujube
bergamot, *Citrus × limon* (L.) Osbeck: 87
Bermuda grass, *Cynodon dactylon* (L.) Pers.: *dūrvā*, xiii, 238
betel, *Piper betle* L.: *tāmbūla*, 254
bhaddamuttaka (P.), nut-grass: 100, 101, 115

* Abbreviations: A. = Arabic; O. Odia; P. = Pali; Skt. = Sanskrit; U. = Urdu. Entries followed by ** indicate tentative/disputed identification.

spikenard, *Nardostachys jatamansi* (D.Don) DC.: 155, 161
śrīphala, Bengal quince: 251, 252
śrīveṣṭa, chir pine: 161
sugarcane, *Saccharum officinarum* L.: *ikṣu*, 238 fn. 14, 256, fn. 55
Sumatra benzoin tree, *Styrax benzoin* Dryand: *kāḷānusāriya* (P.), *kālānusāryaka* (Skt.), 101, 115
sweet flag, *Acorus calamus* L.: *vacā*, 100, 101, 115, 151, 160, 161

tagara/ṭagara, crepe jasmine: 115, 252
Tahitian screwpine, *Pandanus tectorius* Parkinson ex Du Roi: 84
tāla, palmyra palm: 195, 196
tālīśa (Skt.), *tālīsa* (P.), puneala plum: 101, 115
tamāla, egg tree: 251
tamarind, *Tamarindus indica* L.: *tintiḍīka*, xxvii, 10, 11, 11 fn. 24, 13, 14, 14 fn. 38, 15, 15 fn. 39, 15 fn. 40, 23
tāmbūla, betel: 254
tezpatta (U.), Indian bay leaf: 87
thorn-apple, *Datura metel* L.: *dhattūra*, 151, 199 fn. 14, 252
tiger's claw, *vyāghranakha*: 161
tila, sesame: xii, xiv fn. 10, xv–xvi, xviii, 91, 123, 145, 156, 161, 256, 256 fn. 51
tintiḍīka, tamarind: xxvii, 10, 11, 11 fn. 24, 13, 14, 14 fn. 38, 15, 15 fn. 39, 15 fn. 40, 23
toddy palm: see jaggery palm
trumpet-flower tree, *Stereospermum chelonoides* (L.F.) DC.: *pāṭalī*, 115
tulasī, holy basil: xxv fn. 54, 33, 62, 65, 69, 72, 73, 115, 123, 226, 233, 234, 250, 252
turkey berry (or Egyptian cucumber), *Solanum torvum* SW. (or *Luffa cylindrica* (L.) M.Roem.): *goṭha* (P.), 101, 115
turmeric, *Curcuma longa* L.: 151, *haliddī* (P.), *haridrā* (Skt.), 100, 101, 104, 115; *rajanī*, 161
tvac, cinnamon: 123

'ūd (U.), agarwood: 84
udumbara, cluster fig: xiii, xxviii, 100, 115 table 51.1, 156, 161 table 7.1, 165, 166–69, 166 fn. 4, 170 fn. 14, 171, 173, 176, 177, 179–80, 183, 186
usīra, vetiver: 84, 87, 88, 89, 91, 92, 100, 101, 115

vacā, sweet flag: 100, 101, 115, 151, 160, 161
vacattha (P.), white Orris root: table 5.1
vaṃśa, bamboo: xxi, 122, 151, 161, 180–81, 183, 199, 225, 246 fn. 17, 253–54
vaṭa, banyan: xxvii, 3, 4, 7, 7 fn. 14, 18, 18 fn. 46, 19, 20, 20 fn. 54, 20 fn. 57, 21, 23, 53, 109 fn. 30, 115, 126–27, 233
vetiver, *Chrysopogon zizanioides* (L.) Roberty: 84, 87, 88, 89, 91, 92, 100, 101, 115; *usīra* (Skt.), 100, 101, 115; *khas* (U.), 84
vibhītaka, beleric myrobalan: 101, 115, 255 fn. 47
vilaṅga, white-flowered embelia: 101, 115
vrīhi (a variety of) rice: xii, 259 fn. 67
vyāghranakha, tiger's claw: 161

white cutch tree, *Acacia polyacantha* Willd.: *śamī*, 127
white fig, *Ficus lacor* Buch.-Ham.: *plakṣa*, xiii, 69
white mango, (variety of) *Mangifera indica* L.: *puṇḍarīka*, 115
white rose, *Rosa moschata* Herrm.: *sevatī*, 252
white-flowered embelia, *Embelia ribes* Burm. F.: *vilaṅga*, 101, 115
wood-apple, *Limonia acidissima* L.: *kapittha*, 70, 123, 156, 161

yava, barley: xii, xv
yūthikā, juhi: 70, 251

za'farān (A.), saffron: 9, 9 fn. 18, 84, 87, 91, 91 fn. 14, 92, 123

www.ingramcontent.com/pod-product-compliance
Lightning Source LLC
Chambersburg PA
CBHW061001280326
41935CB00009B/795